The Faber Book of French Cinema

The Faber Book of French Cinema

CHARLES DRAZIN

faber and faber

First published in 2011
by Faber and Faber Ltd
Bloomsbury House
74–77 Great Russell Street
London WC1B 3DA

Typeset by Ian Bahrami
Printed in England by CPI Mackays, Chatham

A CIP record for this book
is available from the British Library

ISBN 978–0–571–21849–3

2 4 6 8 10 9 7 5 3 1

For Elena

Contents

Acknowledgements ix
Preface xi

1 Light and Magic 1
2 Birth of the Movie Moguls 20
3 The Changing of the Guard 30
4 The Avant Garde 45
5 Sound 60
6 A Personal Voice 80
7 The Professional 101
8 The Art House 128
9 The Golden Age 142
10 The Spirit of '36 160
11 Breaking the Rules 170
12 The Occupation 190
13 Irreconcilable Differences 220
14 Accursed Films 251
15 A Changing Culture 271
16 Exporting the Revolution 302
17 The Children of Tri-X 327
18 From Bresson to Besson 359
19 Up Till Now 370

Bibliography 397
Notes 409
Index 433

Acknowledgements

While this is a page on which to stress that one's mistakes are one's own, I would like to thank the following people who have helped me along the way: Clare Alexander, Monique and Bernard Brosse, Kevin Brownlow, Xavier de France, Walter Donohue, Michael Downes, Dinah Drazin, Elizabeth Esra, Peter Evans, Sue Harris, Geneviève Le Baut, Jim Morrissey, Christine Leteux, Philippe Quinconneau, Paul Ryan, Libby Saxton, David Sherwin, Elena Von Kassel Siambani, Kate Ward; the staff of the Bibliothèque nationale de France, the Bibliothèque du film, the British Film Institute Library and the British Library.

Preface

This story begins in the early 1980s at the Maison Française, Oxford, an institution established after the Second World War to encourage cultural exchange between Britain and France. Just a short walk from the college where I was a student, the Maison used to put on free film shows, which included some well-known titles of recent French cinema but also several obscure ones from its past. So I can recall one evening seeing the super-cool *Diva* of Jean-Jacques Beineix; and on another, a stiff but rather charming colour production of *La Princesse de Clèves*, directed by Jean Delannoy in 1960. I knew neither of the directors' names, since the French cinema in an English-speaking country was then – as now – an acquired taste beyond the ken of most twenty-year-olds. But the great value of the Maison was to put in place some basis for future appreciation.

In January 2010 the death of the film director Eric Rohmer – whose work afforded perhaps the most permanent backdrop to my love of French films – reminded me that it was the Maison that had first introduced me to him. Indeed, such is the sense I have now of having come full circle that it seems rather timely to describe that first encounter of nearly thirty years ago, which, in crystallising a certain attitude and atmosphere, offers a good insight into what this book is about.

So back to that evening at the Maison Française, in 1981 or '82, when I first saw *Le Signe du lion*. The free admission, the 16mm projector, the portable screen fixed to a tripod, even the scraping of our chairs on the parquet floor, all contributed to the sense of an occasion for devotees and enthusiasts, which with hindsight suited the strange film that followed, with its minimal plot but gripping account of one man's fall. Black and white, and filmed on the streets of late-1950s Paris, it was bracingly austere compared to the mainstream British or American films I had previously been used to.

A penniless American musician, Pierre, who lives in Paris, discovers that his aunt has left him a fortune. He is delighted by the news and, full of New World openness, throws a party for his sophisticated Parisian friends. Weeks go by. It turns out that his aunt has left her fortune to his cousin and cut him off completely. Heavily in debt, he is forced to give up his apartment. While his well-heeled friends leave the city for the month of August, he slides into destitution. With the softness of his over-privileged upbringing, he is poorly equipped to grapple with his desperate situation and continues to look for handouts rather than make any serious effort to earn his own way. When someone suggests that he use his talents and busk for some money, he answers, 'I've never made a penny from my music and it's not going to change now.' Some innate sense of failure seems to drive him on down. A *deus ex machina* ending, in which Pierre's cousin is killed in a motor accident and the inheritance reverts to him, serves only to sharpen this portrait of a failure.

As he tramps the streets, he vents his anger on the pitiless stone of the city's buildings and bridges. '*Salteté de pierre, salteté de pierre*,' he mutters, words that are also a curse against himself.*

So different from anything I had seen before, this spectacle of a man entirely at the mercy of fortune kept me under its spell long after I left the Maison. I hadn't heard of the director before and it was twenty years too early to Google the name. So when I got back to college, I looked him up in the only book on the cinema I then possessed, Halliwell's *Filmgoer's Companion*.

---

* The English subtitles, 'Bloody stone, bloody stone!', offer an example of how much can be lost in translation.

The entry was admirably succinct: 'Rohmer, Eric (1920–) (Jean Maurice Scherer). French director of rarefied conversation pieces.'

But what I had seen was elemental rather than rarefied, and, as Pierre wandered the streets of Paris mostly on his own, the opportunities for conversation were very limited.

So the next day, I made a visit to the library in an effort to solve the mystery behind this peculiar film. In *Cinema: A Critical Dictionary* Molly Haskell described 'a technically accomplished, uningratiating picture which had a small *succès d'estime* but no commercial career'. In the *Biographical Dictionary of the Cinema*, David Thomson offered more information, but also what seemed an important insight. '*Le Signe du lion*', he wrote, 'speaks much more directly of Rohmer the Parisian scraping money together to buy filmstock.' *Le Signe du lion* was startling for being so personal. When Rohmer made the film in 1959, he was about the same age as his hapless hero, at a turning point in his life, hoping to make a success out of a creative pursuit in a way that Pierre had failed to do.

From the snippets of information in these dictionaries a fascinating picture was beginning to emerge of individual willpower. 'No commercial career' was another way of saying that Rohmer's first feature film had been a flop. But he did not give up. Quoting the director himself, the *Biographical Dictionary* described Rohmer's decision to announce a series of six films, *The Moral Tales*:

I thought audiences and producers would be more likely to accept my idea in this form than in another. Instead of asking myself what subjects were most likely to appeal to audiences, I persuaded myself that the best thing would be to treat the same subject six times over. In the hope that by the sixth time the audience would come to me!

It seemed an impressive example of faith and tenacity of purpose that made up for all Pierre's self-doubt and defeatism, but also provided an example of a cinema that operated in a very different way from that of Hollywood. It suggested that '*ars gratia artis*' might be more than just a company slogan.

Many years later I learned just how great the effort of will must have been to make those six films. There was no MGM to support Rohmer. So he founded a small company, Films de Losange, to produce them. Barely longer than twenty minutes, the first, *La Boulangère de Monceau* (1963), was shot on 16mm. There was no money to spare for a professional actor, so the leading player was his partner in the company, Barbet Schroeder, a young man in his early twenties who had written articles for the magazine that Rohmer then edited, *Cahiers du Cinéma*.

The need for economy meant rarely shooting more than one take and relying on post-synchronisation rather than direct sound. The result was little more than an amateur film, which must have felt like something of a backward step after the professional production of *Le Signe du lion*, but the conviction and style with which it was made gave weight to its slight story. A shy student falls in love with a woman he encounters in the street. Just as he begins to get to know her a little, she disappears. While he looks for her in the days that follow, he begins a flirtation with a shop girl in a bakery, which serves only to confirm his commitment to the first woman when she finally reappears. It may have been only a 'short', which very few people would have had a chance to see, but with its blueprint of the romantic triangle that underpinned all the six tales that Rohmer wanted to film it provided a platform for an increase in ambition. And the next effort, *La Carrière de Suzanne* (1963) – still 16mm and black and white, but nearly a whole hour now – was a stepping-stone to the feature-length *La Collectioneuse* (1967).

This third tale should have been, according to Rohmer's original scheme, the fourth in the series after *Ma nuit chez Maud* (1969), but yet again the practicalities of no-budget film-making intervened: Rohmer shot it first because the single location at a villa near St-Tropez made it possible to eke out the meagre resources of a production that was made, in the words of one of its actors, American film critic Eugene Archer, 'on credit and little else'.[1]

If *Ma nuit chez Maud* marked Rohmer's emergence at last as a major international film-maker, the availability of a significant budget and the presence of a box-office star in Jean-Louis Trintignant were clearly significant factors in the recognition that the film received. But what seemed much more interesting to me was the attitude that had got Rohmer to this point, after so many years of struggle, as well as the cultural network that was able to support him when the commercial film industry would not. It is this different operating system – which throws into such sharp relief our Hollywood-dominated, English-language cinema – that I would like to explore in this book. It matters, I think, because perhaps no other country, from the earliest years of the cinema's existence to the present day, has done so much to defend the intrinsic worth of an extraordinary medium.

1

Light and Magic

Sortie de l'usine Lumière à Lyon (1895)

It is the evening of 28 December 1895. In the Grand Café on the Boulevard des Capucines an audience has gathered for the first public showing of the Lumière Brothers' Cinématographe. On the programme are ten short films, each less than a minute long. The very first of these, called *Sortie de l'usine Lumière à Lyon*, shows the Lumières' staff leaving work at the end of the day. The heavy wooden doors swinging back suggest the lid of a Pandora's box. This is the moment it released all the marvels and ills of the moving image. With more than a whole century between then and now, it is difficult to appreciate the original power of the contrast between that first static image of the closed doors and the spontaneous, random motion that then pours forth.

The Lumière brothers for the first time capture the poetry of everyday life on the screen. They filmed the sequence more than once. In one of the retakes – or remakes – you can see Auguste Lumière emerge from the factory just before the gates close at

the very end of the film. Having spent so much of his time thinking about the device, perhaps it should not be a surprise that
he is aware of the camera in a way that none of the workers is,
looking at it a couple of times with a quizzical stare before moving on out of the frame, looking too at his brother, Louis, who is
standing behind the camera, turning the handle.

For people who love the cinema, this spot must be a special
place. Today, the old factory is home to the Institut Lumière,
which is devoted to celebrating what the Lumières started. You
can walk through the wooden shed that you see in the film – or
rather the salvaged remains, suspended in a modern framework
of concrete, steel and glass – to a cinema. Each of the 269 seats
inside carries the name of one of the world's great cineastes, and
it is an irresistible guessing game to anticipate who has been
included. But right away, just taking in a few chance names –
D. W. Griffith, Charlie Chaplin, Akira Kurosawa, Satyajit Ray
– you can grasp the international nature of the commemoration.
The world's cinema matters to France, just as French cinema
ought to matter to the world.

It's perhaps some measure of French cultural arrogance that
the road outside the old Lumière factory was renamed the rue
du Premier-Film. It requires only the most cursory acquaintance with early film history to know this to be literally untrue.
The first 'film' – as opposed to photographic plate – was introduced by George Eastman in 1889 for his Kodak camera. Many
attempts were then made by various inventors both in Europe
and America to use that film to record moving images, but it
was the Edison Kinetograph camera that in 1891 first employed
perforated celluloid film for the accurate registration of images
and transport through a camera. It was the commercial appearance of Edison's Kinetoscope in Europe in 1894 that then caused
Auguste and Louis Lumière – who both worked for the family
business of manufacturing photographic materials – to conduct
their own experiments in moving images.[1] Even if the American
cinema would eventually come to achieve overwhelming

dominance, it is important to note a persisting pattern that could be detected from the very outset: the cinema was – and still is – a symbiotic relationship of rivalry and occasional cooperation between competing powers.

There are two versions contemporary to the time of how the Lumières came to perfect their invention. Charles Moisson, the chief mechanic of the Lumière factory, wrote in 1930 that the Lumières' father, Antoine, who founded the family photographic business, came into his office one day in the summer of 1894. Antoine took a piece of the Kinetoscope film, *Barbershop Scene*, out of his pocket, saying to Louis, 'This is what you have to make, because Edison sells this at insane prices and the agents are trying to make films here in France so they can get them cheaper.'[2] However, Auguste Lumière wrote a memoir in 1953 in which he gave this rather different account:

It was the beginning of 1895, if I remember correctly. As I passed by the rue de la République in Lyon, I noticed a shop in which a crowd had gathered to admire the Edison Kinetoscope. I joined the queue and, charmed by the tiny animated images that these machines produced, I thought to myself that if one could project such images on a screen, so that they could be seen by an entire gathering, the impact would be stunning, and so I decided to study the problem.[3]

Whether the original impulse came from Antoine or Auguste, beyond dispute is the fact that the Lumière Cinématographe was a response to the Edison Kinetoscope. Auguste suggests that the critical improvement of the Cinématographe was to provide an image that could be projected on a screen rather than viewed through a peephole. This certainly dictated the future pattern for cinema-going, yet was only one of a number of technical features that made the Cinématographe a far superior machine.

Edison's Kinetograph – the machine that recorded the images the Kinetoscope showed – was a heavy, immobile, battery-powered contraption that required a horse-drawn wagon to move it out of the 'Black Maria', the crude studio in which Edison's early films were shot. By contrast, the Cinématographe

was light enough to be carried about outdoors by a single operator. It did not require electricity to use and was extremely flexible.

As Terry Ramsaye observed in his history of the early cinema,
A Million and One Nights, critical to its huge success was the
fact that the same machine was able to carry out all three operations of motion-picture making:

It was at once a camera, printer and a projector. The Cinématographe
plus two water buckets for developing tanks and a ruby light was in
fact a portable motion picture plant complete. With it the itinerant
showman could expose films by day, project films in the evening,
and spend the dark hours of night developing and printing the day's
exposures.[4]

While Edison had produced a gimmick that would struggle to
escape the amusement arcades, the Lumières had produced a
practical machine with which to develop a new art-form. It is in
this sense of pioneering the art of cinema that the name 'rue du
Premier-Film' seems fully justified.

The early Edison films were crude novelties. The heavy camera
and the peephole method of exhibition meant that nothing more
ambitious was possible. From the very outset, the American cinema seemed to involve not capturing life, but showmanship and
contrivance. Dancers, acrobats and contortionists were booked to
come to the Black Maria to perform before the immovable God.

A short description of those early films gives us some idea of
their scope. On 17 October 1894, for example, Professor Ivan
Tschernoff and his performing dogs made two films for the
Kinetoscope called *Skirt Dog Dance* and *Summersault Dog*. The
day afterwards, it was the turn of 'the Marvellous and Artistic
Japanese Twirler and Juggler' Toyou Kichi. Other films made in
the Black Maria at about this time featured a dance by Sioux
Indians from Buffalo Bill's Wild West show and Annie Oakley
demonstrating her amazing feats of shooting.[5]

While Edison's Kinetoscope seemed intent on getting away
from normal reality – showing off the special, the exceptional,
the extraordinary – the Lumière films, by contrast, would seek

– with some important exceptions – to reflect the real and to capture everyday life. But if the versatility and portability of the Cinématographe meant that it was particularly suited to the task of recording reality as it occurred, the two approaches seem at the same time to have been rooted in more fundamental ways to their respective cultures.

While the psychology of the frontier showman, exhibiting to frontier audiences, involved a sense of creating something out of nothing, the work of the Lumières was necessarily informed by continuity with France's past, culture and traditions. No need to create crude diversions to distract from the wilderness; it was enough – and natural – to reflect, and draw upon, the consider-able civilisation that already existed.

In 1968, in a documentary film, *Louis Lumière*,[6] that was itself an epitome of French cultural continuity, the director Eric Rohmer had the founder of the Cinémathèque française, Henri Langlois, and Jean Renoir provide a commentary on the Lumière films. A notable aspect was the ease with which they were able to place these films in a broader French cultural tradition.

Not only were the whole atmosphere and ambience of late-nineteenth-century France captured in the Lumière films, observed Langlois, but all the great art of that epoch seemed to culminate in them. Comparing Monet's painting *La Gare St-Lazare* with the famous Lumière film of the train arriving at La Ciotat station, Langlois made the point that the painting and film shared the same goal: to give an impression of the impon-derable, incidental nature of life. If the Lumière films represented some kind of an apotheosis, it was because for the first time this impression was not second-hand but direct, capturing what was actually there.

Summing up the Lumière films as a great 'canvas of history', Jean Renoir recognised a quality that is equally apparent in his own films: 'They afford a complete freedom of interpretation.' Such comments convey a sense that somehow French culture – a ready home – was waiting for the cinema to come along.

The Lumières did not sell their cameras, but trained a team of cameramen who were sent around the world, both to give exhibitions of the Cinématographe and to film what they saw on their travels. This enterprise amounted to the first coherent documentation of the world – the first opportunity for a film audience to see gondolas floating down the Grand Canal, omnibuses crossing Westminster Bridge, camels strolling past the pyramids and Sphinx in Egypt. China, Russia, South America, the Middle East, Africa – operators were sent to every possible corner. While the early Edison films have value only as curiosities to a present-day audience, the Lumière films, in their systematic reflection of reality, amount to a priceless historical record. The Lumières would also make comedies and a few *films à trucs* – 'trick' films that exploited the ability of the cinema to distort reality as well as represent it – but these were somehow half-hearted in comparison to the factual films, which set the foundation for a powerful realist tradition in the French cinema.

The Lumières' efforts to please an audience were a natural extension of the properties of the Cinématographe machine. Its portability and versatility – the fact that the same device could record, process and project – made their promotional agenda of showing the world to the world logical and organic. There was a beautiful simplicity about a procedure that could have a Lumière operator arrive in a town in the morning, photograph its sights during the day, and project them back to the townsfolk in the evening. The Cinématographe was less a clever new invention than an example of cultural continuity. Its aesthetic and commercial success was, to a considerable degree, the fruit of a métier in which the Lumières had long been expert. While Antoine Lumière established the foundation for the business with a successful career as a portrait photographer, the technical ability of his two sons built the enterprise into Europe's leading manufacturer of photographic products.

Although the Cinématographe would assure the Lumières' worldwide fame, it was merely one application of a much deeper photographic expertise, which they had acquired many years before and would continue to develop many years afterwards. Equally impressive, although much less remarked upon, was Louis Lumière's invention of Autochromes, the first system of colour photography, patented in 1903 and marketed in 1907. He took out other patents for a large-screen process, a moving picture stereoscope and a device for panoramic photography called the Photorama.

The true project of the Lumières was the photographic representation of the external world, whether static or moving. But perhaps the most lasting impression one has from a visit to the Lumière museum in Lyon, where all these various devices are gathered, is the extraordinary aesthetic sense that accompanied the flair for invention. It made possible the belated celebration of Louis Lumière as not just an inventor but a film artist too. In January 1966 Henri Langlois had new prints struck from the original negatives and staged the first ever retrospective of the Lumière films at the Cinémathèque in Paris. An organic part of the society out of which they emerged, these films have a charm and beauty that defy the museum. The essence of life, whether captured in 1895 or 2005, remains the same.

The best art does not age because it provides an insight into that essence. So the films of Georges Méliès continue to live too, in their capture of an irresistible personality. Look at *L'Homme d'orchestre*, a sixty-second film that he made in 1900. He strides on to the stage with his jovial showman's panache. He counts the number of empty chairs before him on his fingers and, raising both hands up high, gestures the number to the audience: seven. He sits down on the first chair on the left-hand side of the stage, then immediately gets up again, leaving a double of himself behind. As Méliès 2 sits down in the next chair, flourishing a pair of cymbals, Méliès 1 engages him in conversation. As they chat away, Méliès 3 steps out of the skin of Méliès 2 and sits down in the third chair, cradling a large drum between his knees. So he continues to reproduce himself, bringing extra instruments to the orchestra, until all the chairs are taken.

The film was a tour de force of trickery, but at the same time true, accurately representing the extraordinary versatility of Méliès behind the camera as well as in front of it. He built and repaired his own equipment, he processed the film, he designed and painted the stage decor, wrote the scenarios, devised the trick photographic effects, directed the day's work in the studio that he had himself built in the grounds of his house in the Paris sub- urb of Montreuil and, not least, performed before the camera. With his suave, affable presence, he was surely the world's first movie star. Even back then it must have challenged possibility to do all these things. But the magic of Méliès lay not so much in this extraordinary juggling act or the visual tricks that the films featured, but in the perfect integration of charm, personal- ity and style, in the beauty and coherence of the cinematic world he created, in his eye for human detail. In *L'Homme d'orchestre* there is the wonder of the transformation, but after this obvi- ous, immediate pleasure there is a deeper, longer-lasting satisfac- tion in Méliès' gentle observation of the way the members of the orchestra behave. He captures the camaraderie of the band members chatting away amiably with one another, the delight of being in a team, in spite of the underlying conceit that they are actually the seven selves of one man.

Méliès was among those who attended the first public show- ing of the Cinématographe in December 1895. He was then the owner, manager and star attraction of the Théâtre Robert- Houdin. The core of his theatrical show was illusion. The very name of that predecessor to the cinema, the 'magic lantern', sug- gests how the path from magic show to cinema was a natural, spontaneous one for Méliès to take. Indeed, long before he had heard of the Cinématographe, the custom was for Méliès to end a conjuring show with coloured magic-lantern views.[7]

Méliès' first encounter with the moving image had occurred many years previously at the Paris Universal Exhibition of 1878. The young Méliès, still a teenager, used to attend the exhibition regularly, where his father's shoemakers' firm possessed a stall. Wandering through the displays one day, he came upon Emile Reynaud's Praxinoscope. A band of coloured images (*une bande dessinée*) was attached to the inner rim of a broad cylinder. At the cylinder's centre was a mirror drum. When the cylinder was revolved, the images reflected in the drum merged to create a moving image.[8]

Over the next decade Reynaud would go on to refine and build on his invention considerably.[9] In December 1888 he patented his Théâtre Optique, a large-scale Praxinoscope that projected a moving image on to a screen through the use of spools that carried an extended band of pictures. Each picture in turn would be held in place by a pin on the rotating mirror drum, reflecting its image to a projector system and passing on. The moving image was freed from the continuous repetition of the set number of images previously fixed to the drum. In its own way – in terms of the nature of the spectacle – this development was as revolutionary as the switch from Edison's peepshow to the Lumières' screen. It was the breakthrough that made it possible to turn a gimmick into an art.

A hugely significant date in cinema history, although it was destined to be overshadowed by the advent of the Cinématographe three years later, was the premiere on 28 October 1892 of Reynaud's Théâtre Optique at the Musée Grévin in Paris, which Méliès also attended. Here Reynaud presented the first moving images to be shown publicly on a screen. With special music by Gaston Paulin, the fifteen-minute show, 'Pantomimes Lumineuses', consisted of three 'bandes dessinées' – *Le Clown et ses chiens, Un Bon Bock* and *Pauvre Pierrot*.[10]

A review in the *Gaulois* – a newspaper run by the founder of the Musée Grévin, Arthur Meyer – captured the excitement of the occasion:

On a screen, Monsieur Reynaud projected figures who, through an ingenious device, appeared gifted with life, who changed their expressions, took up poses and made gestures like real, flesh-and-blood people. The audience witnessed a true imitation of life all the more exciting for being no more than an optical illusion.[11]

Opening as a waxworks museum in 1882 to exhibit the famous figures of the day, the Musée considerably broadened its role under the direction of Gabriel Thomas, acquiring a theatre which put on mime and illusionist shows. Méliès himself had performed there, and kept in touch with Thomas, sharing his interest in the latest spectacles and novelties.

After the show, Méliès asked Thomas to introduce him to Reynaud and congratulated the inventor, who then explained how the Théâtre Optique worked. In her biography of her grandfather, Madeleine Malthête-Méliès recreated the conversation:

'It's a lot of work, Monsieur Méliès,' he said. 'Consider that a band like *Un Bon Bock*, which lasts twelve minutes, consists of 7,000 coloured pictures, all of which I draw myself!'

'Haven't you thought of some mechanical process of reproduction?' asked Georges.

'Yes, but I haven't yet found a method that works.'[12]

Whether or not this conversation was genuine, it neatly captures why Emile Reynaud's invention was doomed to failure. Three years had passed between the date of patenting his Théâtre Optique and presenting his first show at the Musée Grévin, so labour-intensive was the process of making the *bandes dessinées*. Méliès, who was a keen amateur photographer, appreciated that the mechanical reproduction of the image would be vital to the moving image's future.

In May 1894 he was introduced to the photographer Clément Maurice and the photographic materials manufacturer Antoine Lumière.[13] The great talking point for the three men was Edison's new invention, the Kinetoscope. With this shared interest, they quickly became firm friends, and a year and a half later Méliès would be an invited guest at the first public showing of the Cinématographe on 28 December 1895.

Attending the Lumière show as invited guests were not only

Méliès but also Gabriel Thomas, director of the Musée Grévin, and M. Allemand, proprietor of the Folies Bergère music hall. These were showmen who, through their roots in Paris theatre, could see at once how to exploit the new invention. It is significant too that all these people knew each other: the development of early French cinema owed much to a well-established network of friendships and alliances.

Méliès was so impressed by the Cinématographe that he immediately asked Antoine Lumière if he could buy or hire the camera to use in his theatre. Gabriel Thomas and Allemand made similar proposals.[14]

When Antoine refused, Méliès turned to the film pioneer Robert Paul in England, who had just devised a film projector to screen Edison Kinetoscope films. Méliès bought one of these machines as well as some of the Edison films, which – with the instinct of a showman – he began to project in the Théâtre Robert-Houdin. By studying Paul's film projector, Méliès built his own film camera in the theatre workshop. Most of the components, from cogwheels to the lens itself, had to be specially made, as no market yet existed for such parts. In February 1896, just two months after the Lumière showing, Méliès had his own working camera. Unable to find any suitable raw film stock in France, he bought a case of Eastman film in London, but when he finally opened the sealed cans in Paris he discovered that the rolls were unperforated. Only the Edison company in West Orange possessed the perforation machine needed to punch the sprocket holes. Méliès therefore commissioned his own, a primitive, hand-operated machine that could punch only two holes at a time. 'Even with me changing hands alternately, my arms and shoulders were shattered after a quarter of an hour of this exercise,' he recalled in his memoirs.[15] Once he had loaded his newly sprocketed film into his homemade camera and exposed his first images, he faced another problem: how to process these images.

The first Méliès film, which was shot in the garden of his family home at Montreuil in June 1896, showed Méliès and his friends playing a game of cards. It was a repeat of a subject that the Lumières themselves had already filmed, the kind of snapshot of daily life that the Lumières were now sending around the world. Perhaps the most striking thing about it was to see the professional conjuror Georges Méliès sitting at a card table, something which, as the film historian Georges Sadoul observed, he tended to avoid, 'for the very good reason that if a conjuror wins at cards, he is bound to hear people say, "Where did you get that King of Clubs? From up your sleeve?"'[16]

The subsequent steps that Méliès took from this point would be the intuitive and spontaneous steps of an artist, but they stemmed from a considerable training or *formation* – to use the much better French word – at various points in his life: as a sculptor, a conjuror, a talented caricaturist and draughtsman, a set designer, a scenarist, a keen photographer and accomplished mechanic. It was the kind of *formation* that late nineteenth-century Paris was peculiarly equipped to provide.

Having filmed the card game, Méliès then got into his conjuror's clothes and had his assistant Lucien Reulos film him performing some magic tricks. Then he filmed his nephew Paul riding the bicycle. After that, there remained one last fifty-foot reel of unexposed film. So they went down to the bottom of the garden and filmed the gardener burning a pile of weeds. In the days that followed, in Lumière fashion, Méliès began to film daily life in and around Paris – the arrival of a train at the Gare de Vincennes, the *bateaux-mouches* cruising up the Seine, Sunday picnics in the Bois de Boulogne.

These films were then projected to audiences in the Théâtre Robert-Houdin. They were so popular that within weeks of the first showing they became an established part of the repertoire of the theatre. They would be shown between two and six daily, and then as a part of the evening conjuring show.

As audiences tired of the everyday scenes with which the cinema made its debut, Méliès quickly graduated to filming, as an early publicity brochure put it, 'fantasy and art scenes that reproduce theatre sketches and form a kind of film completely different from the Cinématographe's scenes of ordinary life'.

At first this amounted to what a later generation would disparingly dismiss as 'filmed theatre'. For in the beginning what excited Méliès – who was as much impresario as artist – was the possibility of being able to replace the flesh-and-blood performers on stage with celluloid substitutes that could find an audience of not just two hundred people in his own theatre, but tens of thousands, wherever a screen and a projector were available. But through practice he discovered possibilities in the new medium that he hadn't originally anticipated, in this way making the step from using the new invention simply as a means of recording reality to developing a genuine new art-form, *sui generis*, with its own laws.

Méliès attributed this vital switch to chance:

How did I first have the idea to use the cinema for trick effects? It was very simple. The first camera I used was a crude machine in which the film often tore or got stuck and refused to advance. One day this produced an unexpected effect when I was filming an ordinary scene in the place de l'Opéra. I needed a minute to free the film and get the camera working again. During this time, the passers-by, buses and cars had moved on of course. When I projected the film, mended at the point where it had jammed, suddenly I saw the omnibus change into a hearse and some men change into women. The trick of substitution, known as the 'stop trick', had been discovered.[17]

As Sadoul put it, this was the 'Newton's Apple' discovery. What is remarkable is the speed with which Méliès then built on its implications. It was as if his whole life had been waiting for that moment.

In his reminiscences Méliès gave no precise date for the Opéra incident, but it must have occurred at some point over the summer of 1896 when he was still filming everyday Lumière-style scenes. In October 1896 he attempted for the first time to achieve by calculation the effect he had discovered by accident. The experiment was typical of his one-man-orchestra approach.

While the Lumières were happy to train a team of cameramen to film the world on their behalf, Méliès did everything himself. In his garden at Montreuil, he stretched a sheet between two posts and painted a backdrop of a drawing room. With the sun providing the only reliable source of light, he had to film an indoor scene outdoors – a step which itself must have required a leap of imagination, in those early pioneer days. Getting his assistant to stop the camera at the appropriate point, and making the required substitutions, he then devised the following trick film. Jehanne d'Alcy, the leading lady at the Théâtre Robert-Houdin (and Méliès' mistress), sits down on a chair and begins to read a newspaper. Then Méliès himself, in his magician persona, covers her with a sheet and whisks the sheet away. The lady has disappeared. With a flourish, he proceeds to conjure a skeleton out of thin air to sit in the lady's place. Drawing the sheet over the skeleton, he takes it away to reveal the lady with the newspaper once again. Having successfully completed the trick, he takes his leading lady's hand and the pair bow. Called *L'Escamotage d'une dame chez Robert-Houdin*, it was the world's first 'special effects' film.

At the time, people would have been too impressed with the visual trick itself to have noticed, but looking at the film today, what's perhaps most striking is the poise and polish of Méliès' own performance before the camera, and the way he creates a convincing world – *his* world, of the Robert-Houdin theatre. His conviction, wit and artistry resulted in films that would have an enduring appeal beyond his own generation of first pioneers.

One by one, Méliès set about attacking the limitations that the crude early technology imposed. The size of the early film reels – when the principles of editing had yet to be developed – had imposed an arbitrary length of fifty seconds (seventeen metres). In late October 1896, with his man of the theatre's instinct for telling a story, he made a film that was three minutes long (sixty metres).

In *Le Manoir du diable* two young princesses are at prayer. Suddenly, two devils appear and snatch away their prayer-books.

By making the sign of the Cross, the princesses drive the devils away. A young prince appears. When one of the princesses gives him her hand, he turns into a devil and carries her off. Quite apart from length, the significant advance on *L'Escamotage d'une dame chez Robert-Houdin*, made only a few weeks earlier, was that the tricks in *Le Manoir du diable* were not there for their own sake, but integrated into a larger story. While others might have lingered over the novelty of the trick shot, Méliès was always eager to get on to the next thing, to push discoveries to their full potential. This was surely, to some extent, a reflection of the sophisticated milieu in which he worked. The artistic atmosphere of *fin-de-siècle* Paris encouraged such invention.

As the autumn of 1896 wore on and the weather got colder, Méliès decided to build what he called a 'studio for taking pictures' in his kitchen garden. Seventeen metres long and seven metres wide, it looked like an oversized greenhouse. At one end was a stage five metres deep, with a dressing room for performers behind it. Through a system of pulleys it was possible to move blinds across the glass panels in the roof to block out unwanted sunlight. While Edison's Black Maria had been little more than a giant booth, fit only for the crude novelty routines of the early Kinetoscope films, Méliès' building made it possible to realise scripts with actors and scenery. As such, it was the true forerunner of all the film studios that have followed since.

Opened in March 1897, it made it possible for Méliès to make an almost total switch to the cinema. From 5 September 1897, every evening at the Théâtre Robert-Houdin consisted of forty-five-minute programmes of the films that he had made in his new studio. Live performances were relegated to Thursday and Saturday afternoons. The films played to packed audiences, but far larger receipts would come from the fairground owners who bought copies of the films to exhibit.

Méliès's camera operator Maurice Astaix captures the one-man-band nature of the enterprise:

He was a man who liked to do everything himself, a hugely talented artist and a superb handyman. He was born for the cinema. He thought up the stories. We never knew what we were going to film. It was all in his head. There wasn't a synopsis. He just got together his team and we filmed. He had the idea for the story himself, he made the props and scenery himself. He would set to expertly with a hammer and pliers without us having any idea what he was going to do. When he needed a cast, he invited staff, friends, relations, neighbours. In the course of the day, he made the models, drew and painted the scenery with the help of a talented lad called Claudel. But he was very hard to fathom, because he kept everything in his head.[18]

At no point did Méliès seem ready to step aside. He took pride in his workhorse nature, even boasting about his role as projectionist:

Often I projected the films myself. Imagine having to spool and unspool by hand a thousand metres of film six times a day and sometimes more! So from the first stroke of the pencil on the first set to the last turn of the projector handle, I did everything myself.[19]

Everything about the Méliès enterprise was family-scale and *artisanal*. In the small studio at the bottom of the garden he would summon actors, actresses and assistants to sit down to lunch after the morning's work: 'A *table, tout le monde!*' Involving himself in everything, he was the antithesis of the industrial and collaborative model of the cinema that would soon be developed by the first businessmen of the cinema, Charles Pathé and Léon Gaumont. But he offered a powerful early archetype for what the French cinema would come to suggest. If the idea of a film being the work of one man took particular hold in France, never was it more true than for Méliès.

One of the people to be impressed by the enormous success of Méliès's first film shows was the French industrialist Claude Grivolas. Convinced of the huge commercial potential of the new art-form, he offered to back Méliès with capital. When Méliès turned him down, Grivolas turned instead to the Pathé brothers. A few years later when Pathé had become the largest

film company in France, Grivolas made a second offer but again
Méliès refused.

Set resolutely in his own direction, Méliès was commercially
naive and oblivious to the industrial direction in which the cinema was heading. His most celebrated film, *Le Voyage dans
la lune* (1902), was an artistic triumph, but also a mark of his
failure to understand the commercial opportunities and threats
of the medium. With no organisation in America, he relied on
agents there to exploit it. A print of the film soon fell into the
hands of his competitors, who had it copied many times over. It
may have been by far the biggest box-office success of its day,
but the fortune it made was for the American counterfeiters, not
Méliès himself.

The debacle made it amply clear that the United States was
going to be the major market for films, but Méliès' response was
totally inadequate to the scale of the challenge. Clinging as usual
to the familiar, he asked his older brother Gaston to open up an
office for him in New York. Now in retirement after two business failures, Gaston was hardly the wisest choice – what Méliès
needed was a professional organisation. While his rivals – Pathé
and Gaumont in France, the Edison Company in America – were
industrial concerns that employed thousands of people, Méliès'
company, Starfilm, amounted to just a handful.

Méliès' inflexibility also manifested itself in his inability to
adapt to a swiftly changing market. He took little interest in
the films that were being made at Pathé or Gaumont, but stuck
rigidly to his own unchanging programme. Compared to their
varied menu of crime thrillers, chase comedies and love stories,
he was beginning to seem old-fashioned.

In 1908, his old friend Clément Maurice, the photographer
who had introduced him to Antoine Lumière, invited him to go
into partnership with the new film company he had founded,
Eclair. Predictably, Méliès, who did not know how to be anything other than the *patron*, refused. Meanwhile, his brother
Gaston was lecturing him on the tastes of the huge immigrant

audience in the United States who were now flocking to the Nickelodeons. They found Méliès' films too slow; they wanted adventure stories, films that moved. Méliès agreed to the estab- lishment in September 1908 of an American production arm at Fort Lee near New York, where Gaston hired an American, Lincoln Carter, to direct Westerns. Gradually Georges Méliès himself switched away from making films to staging live per- formances again at the Théâtre Robert-Houdin.

The fact that Méliès agreed to make a film for Pathé in 1909 was a sign of how much his pride had been dented. 'My plan', wrote Charles Pathé in his memoirs, 'was to incorporate him into our weekly programmes. I would have been overjoyed to have been able to pay homage to such a talented man, who was full of ideas but seemed forgotten.' The film Méliès made, how- ever, was deemed too uncommercial to show. In Pathé's words:

Was this production of less quality than the films he had made in his early days? All things considered, I don't think so. But Monsieur Méliès had gradually lost touch with the public, while my staff and I had held on to it. We were much more up to date with the latest taste.'[20]

In 1911, the director Victorin-Hippolyte Jasset, with whom Méliès might have worked had he joined Eclair, was one of the very first people to take a considered look back at the cinema's then very short history. Over a number of weeks in the peri- odical *Ciné-Journal* he published a 'Study on Direction in the Cinema'. Méliès, he concluded,

held on to the audience he deserved for a long time, but his school of cinema perished through its refusal to evolve. He nearly always needed an elaborate setting for his stories, when the cinema was starting to prefer the bare minimum and to make as much use of the outdoors as possible. He didn't do anything to change his style. So he went out of fashion.

There is an irony to this story of Méliès stubbornly resist- ing change, refusing to keep up with the times. If he seemed clearly dated at that point, then his films are timeless today, their spontaneity and innocence retaining their power to amuse. In choosing to remain true to what he was, rather than attempt to capture some passing wave, Méliès may have brought his film-making career to a premature close, but it is the reason why today his films still live, while those of his more commercially minded contemporaries belong in a museum.

2

Birth of the Movie Moguls

Histoire d'un crime (1901)

The film that set the pace at the beginning of the twentieth century for what the cinema could become was *Histoire d'un crime*. It was a whole five minutes long. In place of Méliès' retreat into a twee fantasy world, it was urban, contemporary, re-enacting the kind of real-life drama you could read about every day in the newspapers but could not yet see on the cinema screen. It was directed by Ferdinand Zecca, the head of production at Pathé, the fastest-growing film company in the world at the turn of the century, with its finger firmly on the pulse of the public. The very title of Zecca's film suggests the thirst of this new century for narrative. The novelty of disappearances and substitutions was no longer enough. A man commits a murder, he is arrested, imprisoned and executed. There was a simple, visceral appeal to the subject that commanded the attention then and provided the basis for a kind of film-making that remains just as popular today. Here was the start of the road to Hitchcock, Hawks and Tarantino.

In spite of its extreme age, Zecca's film enjoys new life today as a post on YouTube, although you can't help remark upon its primitive nature. In his prison, the criminal lies on his bed, recalling in his dreams the events that led up to his crime and subsequent arrest. The recollected past is displayed like a thought bubble above his head. While we may admire the inventiveness, it is impossible to ignore its crudity. The film was an example of a still primitive cinema borrowing from the theatre. To see it is to appreciate the cinema's need to develop a language for flashbacks.

Méliès possessed a personal style that made up for any want of technique. He had an intuitive sense of how best to express himself with the tools that were available to him. But he was too much a genuine artist to be typical of the new industry that was emerging. Ferdinand Zecca, on the other hand, in his quest to exploit whatever appealed to an audience, was a very recognisable forerunner of the showmen who would later come to dominate the cinema. He may not have mastered the flashback, but he understood perfectly the audience's appetite for sensation and spectacle. Showbusiness was in his blood. Born in 1864, he was the son of the concierge of the Ambigu theatre in Paris. When he followed his two brothers on to the stage, joining the Ambigu's repertory company of actors, it must have seemed less a career choice than a natural continuation of the only life he had ever known.

In 1899 he began to perform songs for the Pathé Brothers' phonograph business. A year later he was asked by the founder of the company, Charles Pathé, to organise the company's stand at the Universal Exhibition in Paris. 'Everything was perfect,' Pathé recalled in his memoirs.

So I asked him if he'd like to make films. He said yes. So I took him to our studios in Vincennes, where I asked him to make himself familiar with the process by helping out our director. He turned out to be so capable that at the end of a few weeks the director became *his* assistant. His limitless energy was inspirational.[1]

Under Zecca's direction, the Pathé factory turned out whatever the fairground market of the time was looking for – whether the 'trick' films that Méliès had pioneered, comedies, religious films or more sensational dramas like *Histoire d'un crime*. The simple strategy of copying whatever worked over and over again became a crucible for new genres.

In the contrasting characters of Méliès and Zecca lay the two poles between which the French cinema would oscillate: art and commerce. While Méliès was proud to think of himself as an artisan, Zecca was pioneering an industry that focused singlemindedly on the entertainment of the masses, choosing and varying its product range accordingly. His concern was to be neither original nor true to his craft, but to entertain, because entertainment had a reliable box-office value, whereas art often did not.

Behind him stood the world's first film mogul, Charles Pathé. So powerful is our notion of the primacy of culture in France that Pathé's single-minded devotion to statistics, figures and the laws of profit and loss come as something of a surprise. The cinema may have made him famous, but his memoirs suggest that he could as easily have made his fortune in some other field. He was a businessman, first and foremost.

Born in 1863, as a young man Charles Pathé travelled to South America to seek his fortune but, catching yellow fever, he returned to France. In his memoirs he would describe the start of his career as follows:

I had always intended to set up a small business. I was hoping that my mother would lend me some capital, but until August 1894 I had yet to find what that business would be. On the first Sunday of that month I went to the fair at Vincennes with not the slightest thought in my head that it was about to change my life.[2]

At the fair, he witnessed a performance of Edison's phonograph, which left him 'amazed like everyone else'. The fair's repertoire consisted of about ten wax cylinders on which were recorded various opera arias. Attached to the machine were twenty sets of headphones. Fair-goers could listen to a performance, which lasted about three minutes, for two sous:

As I listened, I calculated that the lucky owner of this phonograph could, in three or four hours, make a return of fifty or sixty francs. My mind was made up. At once I decided to do whatever I could to get hold of a machine and to exploit it.[3]

It's worth emphasising the source of Pathé's wonder, because it captures so well his character. What excited him was not the extraordinary feat of capturing the human voice, but the money-making opportunity that the new invention offered. He was an entrepreneur who had stumbled upon the perfect product. In another set of circumstances he might as easily have been remembered for Pathé vacuum cleaners or fridges.

At once Pathé gave up his job as a legal clerk and scraped together eighteen hundred francs to buy his own phonograph and accessories. With the regard for precision that was a notable feature of not only his memoirs but also his business life, he even recorded the exact date on which he gave the first performances of his new machine. On 9 September 1894, he set off for the fair of Monthéty, near Champigny, where in one day he earned two hundred francs, more than he had made in a whole month working as a clerk.

Soon Pathé had opened a shop in Vincennes selling phonographs, which he would import from London, to fairground exhibitors he had met at the fairs. He also began to make and sell his own recordings. He then went on to acquire, and to sell to his fairground clientele, examples of Edison's new invention, the Kinetoscope.

The high price of the films that went with the Kinetoscope created an incentive to develop a machine that could challenge Edison's monopoly. When the photographer Joseph Joly explained to Pathé in June 1895 his idea of building a machine to make Kinetoscope films, Pathé agreed to fund his development costs. It's worth stating, however, that at about the same time Pathé had funded another inventor to pioneer a special kind of typewriter for children. When the demand on his resources forced him to choose between the two ventures, he opted for the Kinetoscope camera as the one that was most likely to give a greater return. At every stage of his career, he was the unsentimental entrepreneur seeking to maximise the return on his investment.

Joly's acceptance of backing from another competitor broke up the partnership. Pathé took possession of the camera he had funded and tried, through his own efforts, to perfect it to shoot films for the Kinetoscope. Indeed, for some years Pathé believed that a film Joly had made in October 1895, *Bain d'une mondaine*, was the first French film. It was only many years later that he discovered that the Lumières, who had been making their own separate efforts to improve on the Kinetoscope machine, had managed this achievement months earlier, before Pathé's partnership with Joly had even begun.

The huge success that greeted the public exhibition of the Lumières' Cinématographe at the end of 1895 forced him to rethink again. He realised that the future of the cinema lay not in Edison's peephole but in the projected image, and he adapted the Joly camera accordingly.

Pathé's genius lay not in making discoveries, but in appreciating their commercial significance and then exploiting them. As impressed by the Cinématographe as he had previously been by the phonograph, he decided to make the most of the commercial opportunities the new invention offered. He persuaded his brother Emile, who had been the proprietor of a wine business, to go into partnership with him, founding the 'Pathé Frères' company on 28 September 1896. While Emile tended to the phonograph side of the business, Charles Pathé concentrated on the cinema.

In 1897 Pathé Frères received the backing of the industrialist Claude Grivolas, whose financial support Méliès had rejected. In December, Grivolas became a majority shareholder in the company, which was renamed the 'Compagnie Générale de Cinématographes, Phonographes et Pellicules'. The company then bought the patent for a 'Maltese cross' mechanism that pulled film through a camera more efficiently, and concluded an agreement with the Lumières to improve on their invention.

With its access to capital, the Pathé company was able to expand quickly in all the key spheres of the new business. It made cameras and projectors for sale worldwide, it produced raw film stock, and it made its own films.

I have always known what I wanted and I have always wanted whatever was the most easily achieved and the most profitable in practical terms. I did not invent the cinema, but I did industrialise it. Before Pathé-Frères the cinema was little more than a problem solved. But with us it became a formidable activity that, in engaging the interest of hundreds of millions of human beings, was worth billions of francs a year.[4]

Charles Pathé's importance to the cinema lay in establishing the basic business structure of the global film industry. While he was quick to seize a genuine opportunity, at the same time he possessed the businessman's caution, avoiding unnecessary risk. Focusing on the practical and the viable, he presided over a company that pioneered not a distinct artistic vision, but the ability to find a market.

The early history of the other major French film company to be established at the end of the nineteenth century, Gaumont, resembled that of Pathé. Its founder Léon Gaumont ran a company that made and supplied photographic equipment, the Comptoir général de la photographie. With the successful exhibition of the Cinématographe in December 1895, Gaumont instantly recognised the importance of the moving image and decided to develop a moving-picture camera and a projector to add to the firm's range of other optical devices.

Both Pathé and Gaumont established the commercial framework in which the pioneers who worked for them developed the potential of the new medium, but they themselves remained businessmen first and foremost. When in 1896 Gaumont allowed his secretary Alice Guy to make some of the demonstration films he used to help sell his moving-picture cameras, he did so on the express condition that she would not allow this activity to disrupt her secretarial duties.[5] It was only the discovery that these films had a commercial value that won her Gaumont's blessing to progress beyond these first very amateur efforts. She quickly graduated to become 'directrice du Service des théâtres de prises de vues'. Not only did she direct films herself, but she became responsible for overseeing story, casting, costume and scenery departments, and for engaging new directors to work under her. The assistants she hired included Ferdinand Zecca – who would soon join Pathé – Victorin Jasset, Louis Feuillade and Emile Cohl.

In effect, Alice Guy managed the nursery of the nascent French film industry, but it is her early departure from this nursery that – in marking a decisive shift from the old to the new world – has even greater symbolic value. Marrying Gaumont executive Herbert Blaché, she retired from her position in 1907 to accompany her husband to the United States, where he had been sent to establish a franchise for Gaumont's Chronophone process.[6] Although the French concerns continued to dominate the production of films, the rapid spread of the Nickelodeons meant that America now had by far the largest market in the world. As rival local producers sprang up to satisfy this market, the established French companies became more and more aware of fierce competition from the American cinema and the need to devise strategies to combat its growing power.

This competition itself became an important dynamic in the French cinema's subsequent evolution.[7] The growing output of single-reel films from the United States created pressure on French companies to produce a more ambitious multiple-reel product that could exploit an asset that American film-makers did not possess – a long history and a rich literary heritage.

Produced by a new company Film d'Art, but backed by Pathé, the showing of *L'Assassinat du duc de Guise* on 17 November 1908 at the Salle Charras in Paris marked an effort to find economic renewal in a prestige production. Based on a scenario by Henri Lavedan, a member of the Académie Française, and featuring actors from the Comédie-Française, this film version of a famous event in France's history represented a huge leap in ambition for a medium that had hitherto been considered little more than a fairground attraction. It featured not only a 'visual story' by a serious, respected writer, but also a score by one of France's greatest living composers, Camille Saint-Saëns. Fifteen minutes long, it was shown with three other '*oeuvres cinématographiques*' in a programme called *Visions d'Art*. *Le Temps* newspaper welcomed an 'experiment of great artistic interest'.[8] It would be typical of the French cinema's tendency – in the quest for ground on which it could best compete – to resort to cultural elitism, but it was a policy that backfired.

Although the audiences that made up the huge new American market were showing a taste for more complex narrative, they preferred simple, accessible stories, so that having a rich history and tradition – a 'usable past' as the American critic Van Wyck Brooks would later term it[9] – seemed a handicap rather than an advantage. The more the cinema came to assume the function of the theatre, providing substantial dramas rather than brief sketches, the more the content of any single film mattered. But it was the new American production companies, such as Biograph, Essanay or Vitagraph, that were best placed to understand the tastes of the American audience.

As the cinema entered its second decade, Pathé's response to this dramatically changed market was to make American-style films in America. In May 1910, the company released a western, *The Girl from Arizona*, and completed the construction of an American studio in Jersey City in the autumn. The other big

French companies followed suit, but in the long term the fierce competition from the American companies made their position unsustainable.

The rise of the film star would turn the cultural dynamic against them even further. For as the film historian Richard Abel observed, '[t]he new "gods and goddesses" . . . now had to be as American as the stories in which they appeared', a requirement that 'raised yet another barrier, further marginalising French films and excluding them from the world's most lucrative market'.[10]

France still possessed an unrivalled technical expertise, but it had lost the commercial initiative for good. It became effectively a kind of testing-ground for innovations that would be fully exploited in the American market. In 1911, Adolph Zukor bought the North American rights to Pathé's three-reel *Passion* (1911). Impressed by the successful run it enjoyed in his theatres, he helped to finance Louis Mercanton's production of *Queen Elizabeth* (1912) with Sarah Bernhardt. 'With *Queen Elizabeth* I expected to prove that the feature picture could be a success in America,' he recalled in his memoirs. But much more significantly, having confirmed the market potential with this French film, he intended 'to follow at once with feature films made here'.[11] In the wake of *Queen Elizabeth*'s success, Zukor formed Famous Players and hired Edwin S. Porter to make the first American-produced feature, *The Prisoner of Zenda* (1913), in New York. As other American producers quickly followed suit, France's final eclipse as the world's leading film-producing nation became inevitable.

For a French film industry that had already had its dominance snatched away by a resurgent Hollywood, the First World War must have seemed like the *coup de grâce*. Film personnel left to join the army, the studios themselves were requisitioned and the production of films severely disrupted.

It was perhaps symbolic of the general state of things that the world's biggest movie star Max Linder stopped appearing in French films to join the army. Then in 1916, when he was invalided out, he signed a contract to make films with Essanay in America, replacing Charlie Chaplin, who had moved on to better things at Mutual.[12] After he continued to suffer from ill health and made three unsuccessful films for Essanay at its studios in Chicago, the company dissolved his contract the following year. Recuperating in Hollywood, Linder met his usurper, who signed a photograph of himself: 'To the one and only Max, the "Professor". From his disciple, Charlie Chaplin, May 12th 1917.'

Pathé – still the biggest film company in the world, but not for much longer – reduced its production in France and relied on its subsidiary in America, until it was sold in 1923 to be merged five years later with two other companies to form RKO Pictures. The films that continued to be made in France were increasingly perceived as being dull and rather pedestrian: either patriotic scenarios in support of the war effort, or examples of 'filmed theatre' – unimaginative adaptations of stage works in the tradition of *L'Assassinat du duc de Guise*, but ultimately lacking its ambition.

Some figures provide a dramatic snapshot of the French cinema's decline in these years. According to Georges Sadoul, in 1910 about 60 to 70 per cent of all films distributed around the world originated in Parisian film studios.[13] Ten years later, the inexorable rise of Hollywood meant that France's share even of its home market was just 10 per cent.[14]

3

The Changing of the Guard

America may have taken away the French film industry's markets, but at the same time it provided a powerful example of what the cinema might be. When one reads French memoirs of the period, again and again one is struck by a sense of their stunned admiration for what the American cinema had been able to achieve. Jean Renoir recalled having no interest in the stagey French films that were shown during the First World War, but doing everything he could – like most of his contemporaries – to see the films of Charlie Chaplin. When he made *Nana* in 1926, it may have been based on a Zola novel, but he would cite Hollywood director Erich von Stroheim as a major inspiration. 'I didn't want to copy him,' he wrote in his memoirs, 'but I did want to pay him homage.' Chaplin, Griffith, Stroheim, De Mille, Ince – the giants of early Hollywood. These were the people who captured the imagination of a new generation of French film-makers.

One film from the period stands out as a landmark. Not Griffith's *Birth of a Nation* which had been banned in France, but Cecil De Mille's 1916 film *The Cheat*.

Out of the darkness, the face slowly emerges of one of Hollywood's early movie stars, Sessue Hayakawa. As the opening title explains, 'This is Haka Arakau, a Burmese ivory king to whom the Long Island smart-set is paying social tribute.' Wearing an Eastern tunic, he seems intent on some doubtlessly nefarious plan. But then, recollecting himself, he removes a brand from a brass pot at his elbow and blows gently on the hot coals to kindle the flames. Returning the brand to the pot, he heats it up until it is ready to impress his emblem on to the base of a figurine. As he sears the device into the ivory, the solitary

The Cheat (1916)

light from the pot, casting its sinister shadow, singles him out as the embodiment of the yellow peril. The next time he takes up that brand, he will use it on human flesh.

When the film opened in summer 1916 at the Omnia-Pathé in Paris, the world's first purpose-built cinema, audiences marvelled at what seemed to be a giant leap in film art. What impressed them was less the story itself than the way in which it was told – the extraordinary play of shadow and light that gave objects on the screen a liquid, dynamic quality.

The novelist Colette was among the film's many admirers, writing an ecstatic review:

In Paris this week, a movie theatre has become an art school. A film and two of its principal actors are showing us what surprising innovations, what emotion, what natural and well-designed lighting can add to cinematic fiction. Every evening, writers, painters, composers and dramatists come and come again to sit, contemplate and comment, in low voice, like pupils.

To the genius of an oriental actor is added that of a director probably without equal; the heroine of the piece – vital, luminous, intelligent – almost completely escapes any sins of theatrical brusqueness or excess . . . We cry 'Miracle!'; not only do we have millionaires who don't look as if they've rented their tuxedos by the week, but we also have characters on screen who are followed by their own shadows, their actual shadows, tragic or grotesque, of which until now the useless multiplicity of arc lamps has robbed us.[1]

If to a modern spectator it seems strange at first that the exaggerated use of light in *The Cheat* should be described as 'natural', it makes more sense once one realises that audiences were previously used to a cinema in which the blanketing of arc lights described by Colette meant that there were hardly any shadows at all.

French writers and film-makers embraced the film as a defining moment with remarkable unanimity. Expressing the opinion in 1925 that the cinema really began 'around 1915–16 with the appearance of the first good American films', the film-makers Henri Fescourt and Jean-Louis Bouquet commented that of these 'the most striking was *The Cheat*'.² In his book *La Naissance du cinéma*, published in 1925, Léon Moussinac commented that *The Cheat* 'rang out like a great blow of the gong'.³ In their 1935 history of the cinema, Maurice Bardèche and Robert Brasillach summed up the film as follows: 'When it was shown in France in the middle of the war, the audience was stunned and the producers astounded. It seemed as if everything that had been done before that time no longer counted.'⁴ The producer Pierre Braunberger, a boy of eleven when the film was first shown, recalled making a special trip to Paris with his parents in order to see it: 'It revealed to me a film language and influenced me hugely.'⁵

But Colette's review was finally more significant for what it said about the audience than about the film: she identifies a highly committed group of artists who were prepared to learn from the viewing experience and to emulate a group of film-makers they admired. The existence of a sophisticated, responsive and culturally aware audience was not only an important motivating force behind the change in French cinema during these years, but also one of the features that most distinguished that cinema from the ever populist and market-led Hollywood. Through individual passion and enthusiasm, the French cinema would regenerate itself in spite of the commercial obstacles.

Colette's article had been published in a new magazine called *Le Film*, which had been founded at the beginning of 1916 by

Henri Diamant-Berger. A war veteran, Diamant-Berger had been invalided out of the army the previous year and, benefiting from the kind of opportunity that war brings, had entered a badly disrupted film industry as the last-minute replacement for a director who had received his call-up.

In his memoirs, Diamant-Berger recalls his debut as a demoralising experience whose chief value was to serve as a wake-up call, acquainting him with the moribund state of French cinema:

This rather limited experience gave me a few ideas, which I shared with some young friends, Abel Gance, Jacques de Baroncelli, Jacques Feyder, Raymond Bernard . . . We knew that we had to rally a new generation if we were to recover from the mediocrity into which the French cinema had fallen. What we needed was a platform.[6]

So *Le Film* was born. Continuing to work as a director in the film industry, Diamant-Berger asked a young drama critic and novelist, Louis Delluc, to edit the new magazine. Delluc's combination of unflagging passion, energy and intelligence quickly put him at the heart of the film revival. A year after starting to edit *Le Film*, he began a weekly film column in the newspaper *Paris-Midi*. The year after that he published a collection of those columns in the book *Cinéma et cie*. When he founded his own magazine, he called it *Cinéa*, in the process coining the word *cinéaste*. Responding to the new American films, he developed the influential concept of *photogénie*, which identified the power of the moving-picture camera to invest ordinary, real objects with an extra quality, without eliminating their essential realness. 'The miracle of the cinema', Delluc wrote, 'is that it stylises without altering the plain truth.'[7]

It was in truth a theory of no great intellectual depth, articulating something that people must even then have instinctively understood – that some objects or people can be 'photogenic' – but the fervour with which the idea was expressed had great practical significance. For it forcefully implanted among a new generation of French film-makers the idea that the cinema existed not simply to tell a story, but had unique properties of its own, which it was the duty of the true film-maker to exploit. Theory mattered less than the passion with which its adherents would seek to put what was finally a simple idea into practice.

Abel Gance had an intuitive grasp of the potential of the cinema long before *The Cheat* was shown in France. Soon after the beginning of the First World War, he became a director for Film d'Art, but his attempts to use the medium in an imaginative way were constantly thwarted by the then director of the company, Louis Nalpas, who wanted him to turn out the conventional, unadventurous melodramas that fed the huge Pathé distribution machine.

Gance's great sense of himself as an artist made it more than usually difficult to endure such restrictions. Before the conflict began, when he was trying to eke out an existence as a writer, he had written a long tragedy for the stage, called *La Victoire de Samothrace*. Sarah Bernhardt had expressed her enthusiasm for the play, but asked him to write a shorter version. He did so, but the outbreak of war dashed his hopes.

After this glimpse of great artistic achievement, it was twice as difficult to come to terms with the banality of the film-making Nalpas demanded. It was a profitable but soul-destroying compromise that eroded Gance's sense of being a real artist. In March 1916 he wrote in his diary: 'The cinema has brought out a materialistic side in me that used not to exist. It will get only worse unless I make an effort of will to the contrary. I have been at Film d'Art for a year, during which time I have not had one interesting thought.'[8]

The perception drove him to fight against a betrayal of his previous ideals. If the cinema was not yet an art that could rival the theatre, if it was not yet worthy of his lofty ambitions, then he would make it so. 'I have to prove to myself that I am still the man who wrote *La Victoire de Samothrace*,' he wrote a few weeks later. Long discussions with Nalpas followed on how the tools of the cinema could be better used. But until the summer of that year, when *The Cheat* was released, Nalpas refused to allow Gance to put any of his ideas into practice. When Gance asked why they couldn't make 'psychological films, where instead of only action you can show feelings too', he was told that Pathé wouldn't accept it. With some sympathy for the constraints that Nalpas himself was working under, Gance recalled years later that Zecca, who continued to oversee Pathé production, did insist on a uniformity of style: 'We were told that if the camera cut off the actors below the knee, then the film would be rejected. The whole body had to be in the frame.'[9] There seemed to be less concern for the aesthetic quality of any individual film than for ensuring consistency of look between all the films on the production line. 'In those days, they virtually bought films by length. It didn't matter whether the film was good or bad, only the length mattered, and only that decided the price. Pathé was the firm who bought from Nalpas, and that was whom he had to satisfy.'[10]

But the success of *The Cheat* changed the climate, making producers more ready to take risks. Within weeks of its release in July 1916, Nalpas at last allowed Gance to depart from the prescribed formula to make the kind of 'psychological film' he had been arguing for. *Le Droit à vie* told the story of a young woman, Andrée, who is in love with stockbroker Jacques Alberty, but marries a wealthy financier, Pierre Veryal, so that she can pay off her dying mother's debts. After Veryal discovers that Andrée and Jacques are in love, he is wounded by one of his employees in a robbery attempt and, in his jealousy, accuses Jacques of the shooting. Jacques is put on trial, but acquitted after Veryal concedes his innocence.

In its style of lighting and its *ménage à trois* story with courtroom finale, *Le Droit à vie* resembled *The Cheat*, but Gance claimed that he did not see De Mille's film until some time afterwards. 'It did not influence me in any way. For over a year before the arrival of *The Cheat* in France I'd struggled to introduce the psychological drama between three characters. I've

35

been responsible for too many innovations in this profession for anyone to be able to contest the advance I made.'[11]

If the very need for this denial testified to the huge influence that *The Cheat* had over the French film industry, Gance quickly emerged as an extraordinary homegrown talent with too many ideas of his own to need to rely on others. Pleased with *Le Droit à vie*, Nalpas allowed Gance to make another psychological drama, *Mater Dolorosa*. On its release in March 1917, Emile Vuillermoz wrote in *Le Temps*: 'Let us remember the date of this film, for it is an important one in the life of this great child which is the cinema; it has yet to achieve its maturity, but it has already won its freedom.'[12]

The film established Gance as France's foremost film-maker, but what most haunted him was the war, in which many of his close friends were losing their lives. His successful career may have helped him 'to drown out its terrifying sound',[13] as he put it in his diary, yet at the same time it fostered thoughts on how he might document the conflict. 'The cemeteries turn away people every evening,' he wrote. 'First Act: Ruins. Second Act: Ruins. Third Act: Ruins. Everyone's unhappiness is the same these days. I'd like all the dead of the war to rise up one night and to return to where they came from, to their homes, to find out whether their sacrifice has been worth anything.'[14] It was the kernel of an idea for a film that Gance conceived as an indictment against the war: *J'accuse*.

Rejected several times as medically unfit for active service, Gance was recruited into the Cinematograph Section in April 1917. After some weeks at the front, which convinced him of the lunacy of attempting to film anything, he was transferred to Paris, where he had to unload ammunition trucks, and then to Aubervilliers, where he worked in a poison gas factory. 'Dante would have made it the eighth circle of hell,' he wrote in his diary.[15] Every day two or three workers died. With his own poor state of health, Gance feared that he would die too. But he was summoned before an inspection committee, which gave him a discharge.

Released from military service, he wrote a scenario for *J'accuse*, which Charles Pathé agreed to finance. '*J'accuse* will certainly make a huge impression in every country,' Pathé wrote to Gance in a letter dated 13 August 1918. 'I say "in every country" because I am convinced that this film will even be shown in the cinemas of enemy countries once the war is over.'[16]

J'accuse is long forgotten now, except among a few connoisseurs of the silent cinema. But even if it were better known, it would be difficult for a generation that did not live through the carnage of those years to appreciate the full significance of a film that not only chronicled the catastrophe but was an inseparable part of it.

After a brief prologue in which hundreds of soldiers form the words 'J'accuse', the film retreats into the past to depict the summer festivities taking place in a Provence village. Gance gives us a nostalgic vision of a lost paradise, idealising a peacetime that, when the sequence was shot, no one had experienced for four years. Against this background, he introduces his hero, poet Jean Diaz. Jean is in love with Marie, but she is married to François. The two men fall out over Marie, but with a string of tragic events that the outbreak of war precipitates, they become close friends, learning to put aside their differences. After four years of war, Diaz loses his wits. Discharged from the army, he returns to his village, where he challenges the inhabitants to justify themselves in the face of all the lost lives. A legion of dead soldiers rises up to march on the village.

To make the film, Gance rejoined the Cinematograph Section and returned to the front. In September 1918, he was with the French and US forces that took part in the Saint-Mihiel offensive, shooting material that he would use in the battleground sequences of *J'accuse*. He then went down to the Midi to film the peacetime sequences, but asked the army if he could borrow two thousand soldiers to film the Return of the Dead. 'These men had come straight from the front – from Verdun – and they were due back eight days later. They played the dead knowing that in all probability they'd be dead themselves before long. Within a few weeks of their return, eighty per cent had been killed.'[17]

J'accuse introduced many innovations in technique, but what finally makes it so memorable is the way it soaked up the atmosphere of a terrible moment in history that was still being lived. It was not just a film, but a unique, authentic document of a human tragedy, in which all its participants – whether director, crew, cast or extras – were in some way involved. A touching farewell scene takes the form of a series of stark, simple images. The hands of an unseen man and woman pack provisions into a kitbag, the woman slipping in a good-luck talisman; two glasses are raised in a toast to absent friends, one returned to the table empty, but the other still full, its owner too heartbroken to drink; in near-total darkness, a hand lights a candle for the safe return of a loved one; a child's tiny hands are enfolded in the rough, dirty palm of its father . . . This montage, which distilled the essence of what an entire nation had experienced in 1914, just as the March of the Dead captured the uncomprehending outrage of the survivors in 1918, owed as much to the truth of its perception as the technical virtuosity with which Gance filmed it. Ninety years on, it retains a raw, painful poetry.

Nearly three hours long, the film opened in Paris on 25 April 1919 to become part of that strange year of mourning and celebration. The headlines that day, as they were on most days through 1919, were dominated by the latest news from the Versailles peace conference. A year later, the film was shown in London at the Philharmonia Hall. The *Times* wrote of 'an allegory of war that is nothing less than inspired'. The *Daily Telegraph* applauded a film that 'puts its author at least on a level with Mr Griffith'.[18] The film perhaps emerged too soon after the war to be fully appreciated in its own right, but it also represented an important landmark for the cinema. As the London *Times* reviewer observed, 'The miracle has been achieved. A film has caused an audience to think.'[19]

J'accuse crystallised the moment at which the French cinema's reputation for thought began to take shape. There was certainly much less appetite for this kind of cinema across the Atlantic. In May 1921, Gance travelled to New York for a private screening of the film at the Ritz-Carlton Hotel. He hoped it would provide a platform for the successful exploitation of the film in the United States, but the big Hollywood companies who had shown interest in distributing it dropped out after the projection of a poorly prepared print. Gance begged D. W. Griffith to attend a subsequent trade show, which so impressed the American director that he persuaded United Artists to pick up the film.[20] But the version that was finally screened five months later, ruthlessly pared down to ninety minutes, was a travesty of the film that Gance had intended. The reviewer for the *New York Times* wrote:

To those who saw the original *J'accuse*, or have heard of it, it is necessary to say, first of all, that *I Accuse* is not the same thing. Changes that vitally alter the emphasis of the photoplay have been made. M. Gance's production was a terrific indictment of war. The phrase, 'J'accuse', ran dramatically through it . . . *I Accuse* is not an indictment of war. It is, inferentially, an indictment of Germany, and directly a sentimental appeal to patriotism. The scenes and subtitles of *J'accuse*, which made it a sweeping accusation of war and everyone everywhere who promoted it or profited by it have been deleted. And the inevitably tragic ending has been replaced by the usual 'happy' fade-out of the movies.

Now, of course, anyone has a right to make any kind of a war picture that suits him. But whenever film editors attempt to convert a completed photoplay of one kind into something entirely different they are likely to destroy the dramatic force of the original without gaining anything in its place. That's what has happened in the case of *J'accuse*. M. Gance's picture comes to a tremendous climax in its culminating accusation of war and false patriotism, but *I Accuse* does not accuse anything or anybody in its final scenes. Before they are reached, the stirring 'J'accuse' has been dropped. An anti-climax is the result.[21]

In the circumstances, it was hardly surprising if the film was not a success. Within days of its opening at the Strand, the manager of the theatre, Joseph Plunkett, confided his anxiety, reporting that he had received complaints that the film was too depressing and morbid, that two years after the war people no longer wanted to be reminded of it. Summing up the significant releases of 1921 at the end of the year, the *New York Times* reviewer commented that 'Abel Gance's terrific *J'accuse*' had been 'so emasculated before it reached the public screen under the title *I Accuse* that it must be counted as lost'.[22] The implication of the highly revealing piece was that *J'accuse* had fallen victim to 'that bogey-word of the motion-picture business, "highbrow"'. The writer commented on an anti-intellectual prejudice in the American film trade that led them 'to call everything that is beyond them "highbrow", and if any picture so condemned happens to be commercially unsuccessful, or yields only a modest profit on the money invested in it, they gloat over its misfortune and chorus, "You see, the public doesn't want that kind of stuff. It's too highbrow."'

Maybe it was this kind of fear that led United Artists to impose their crude cuts. In any case, by the time *I Accuse* reached the west coast, where it opened in the California Theater on 22 January 1922, it had been dragged even further away from Gance's original version. The French film-maker and Hollywood resident Robert Florey wrote that he was

very sorry that Abel Gance's drama had not been shown in its entirety as it had been in Paris. The projection of *J'accuse* lasted scarcely an hour, which gives you an idea of the number of cuts it suffered . . . Yet at the same time extra scenes were added to show the help brought to France by the American army. The film itself began with an address by President Harding, while the last scene showed us Jean Diaz and Marie Laurin living happily ever after.[23]

What was the through-and-through businessman Charles Pathé to make of this? His decision to support Gance's extraordinarily ambitious venture in the midst of the war was brave. And indeed, he went on to support the making of Gance's next venture, *La Roue*, a seven-hour epic that was years ahead of its time in its innovative use of the medium, introducing for example the rapid cutting that has been more usually ascribed to Eisenstein. But genius wasn't enough if it could not earn its keep.

Pathé knew that it had been a feat even to have *J'accuse* screened in the United States, regardless of how the distributors had torn the film to pieces once it was. Indeed, even before *J'accuse* received its first showing in the United States, he had seen more than enough evidence of the way the global film business had turned to make a historic decision.

In September 1920, the chief executive of France's biggest film company announced to his shareholders that Pathé was pulling out of film production. The decision marked a fundamental change in the nature of the French film industry from one with global reach to one that struggled even to defend its own national values. In his memoirs, he would explain why:

Henceforward, we had to face the fact that America, with its infinite resources, had conquered the global market probably for ever. The war had merely hastened a little the date of this inevitable supremacy. Favoured by the size of their home market, which in terms of box office receipts, was forty to fifty times greater than the French market, or roughly three-quarters of the global market, the Americans could pour huge sums into film production, get their costs back from their home market alone, and then dominate export markets in every country . . .

This reality became apparent in the course of my various trips to America. France's leadership in the cinema had depended solely on its head start, and was bound to disappear the day the Americans had finished establishing their own industry. That day had arrived . . .

Gradually I reached the conclusion that the production and distribution of films in this new era could no longer be financially viable. With our small home market, swamped with American films which had already paid for themselves in their own country, the films made in France were no longer making nearly enough in returns to justify the investment made. I'm aware that many of us have always hoped that our films might get substantial receipts abroad and above all in the huge American market. But this hope is illusory. Every now and then a high quality French film . . . can make some money among an up-market audience in Britain, America and elsewhere, but essentially the cinema will always be a spectacle for the masses; and, with only the rare exception, the American masses will never take to the French cinema, which is contrary to their psychology and tastes. To deny this, is to betray an ignorance of what the United States is really like . . .

So what was there left to do for a manufacturer concerned to ensure a reasonable return on his capital? He had to abstain from a ruinous or barely profitable activity and concentrate his efforts on money-making businesses . . . [24]

Pathé's decision marked a fundamental change in the French cinema, as this once huge industry – which had dominated the screens of the world – now had to adjust itself to a parlous new existence. At the time Pathé was accused of wrecking the French film industry, but really he was simply abandoning a ship that had already been sinking for some considerable time. He was doing what any sensible businessman, responsible to his shareholders, would do. Sooner or later, in the course of the 1920s, the other big companies that had dominated French film production followed Pathé's lead. It meant that any film-making activity which did occur in France henceforward tended to be ad hoc, in the hands of many small companies, individual financiers and enthusiasts, rather than the result of the strategic decision-making of a handful of large industrial concerns.

With the exception of Feuillade, who carried on until his death a year later, Gaumont stopped production in 1924, after reaching a distribution agreement with Hollywood's newly formed colossus, Metro-Goldwyn-Mayer. Its founder Léon Gaumont explained the logic:

In France I have fifty cinemas that must change their programme every week. Even on a rotation basis, at least twenty-five first features are needed a year, while we struggle to produce even four . . . I therefore have no choice but to get these films from the Americans – at a price, it should be added, cheaper than it would cost me to make them myself. [25]

With the same sense of corporate responsibility as Pathé, he declared: 'We have no intention of squandering the money of our shareholders.' [26]

But this sudden retirement of the big corporations did not mean the disappearance of the French film industry; it meant a metamorphosis of its structure into smaller, more flexible producing units that, for varying reasons, were ready to take the risks of production that the big companies no longer felt able to justify.

The ever-wily Charles Pathé sold the use of the Pathé name to a consortium of production concerns that, to the confusion of historians ever since, consequently called itself 'Pathé-Consortium'. Although Charles Pathé had a chair on its board, Pathé-Consortium was a separate company, which was obliged to pay Société Pathé-Cinéma – the legal name of Charles Pathé's company – a royalty of 10 per cent of its turnover. This risk-free deal was the business equivalent of having your cake and eating it.

Jean Sapène was the director of the daily newspaper *Le Matin*. He believed that a profitable synergy lay in publishing newspaper versions of the popular film serials. In 1919, with the actor René Navarre, he founded a film-production company called Cinéromans to produce such serials. He quickly turned Cinéromans into one of the most powerful production concerns in France, investing in features as the vogue for serials ebbed through the 1920s. Acquiring a studio at Joinville from Charles Pathé, he strove to build a Hollywood-style concern that would turn out mainstream, production-line entertainment. Its takeover of Pathé-Consortium in 1924 was an index of its newly dominant position in the industry.

In 1918, Abel Gance's old boss at Film d'Art, Louis Nalpas, left the company to team up with Serge Sandberg. Together they took over the Victorine studios in Nice, which they hoped to turn into a kind of Hollywood on the Riviera. In a letter to Sandberg, Nalpas wrote, 'In general terms, the approach I'll adopt for my films is the American one of focusing the action on two or three characters, with as exciting a setting as possible.'

Sandberg, meanwhile, had separately set up a company with the film distributor Louis Aubert. Called SIC (Société Industrielle Cinématographique), it bought the production company Eclair, with its studio at Epinay, some seven miles to the north of Paris.

Then there were the White Russians. Joseph Ermolieff had once headed the Pathé subsidiary in Russia. After the revolution he came to France, where he established a production company, Ermolieff-Cinéma, in 1920. When he left in 1922 to produce films in Germany, he was bought out by his business associates, chief among whom was fellow Russian exile Alexandre Kamenka. Swapping its trademark of an elephant whose trunk turns into a length of unfurling film for that of an albatross in a triangle, the company was renamed Albatros Film. Accompanying the new logo was a slogan that not only captured the essence of a survivor of the Russian Revolution, but described the state of the entire French film industry of the 1920s: '*Debout malgré la tempête*' (Still standing in spite of the storm).

One of the more adventurous of the new companies, Albatros Film would win a reputation not only for producing the ambitious projects of the Russian directors Alexandre Volkoff, Viktor Tourjansky and Serge Nadejdine, but also for supporting a new generation of young French film-makers that included Jacques Feyder, René Clair, Jean Epstein and Marcel L'Herbier. And it was at Albatros that the Russian-born art director Lazare Meerson began to develop a style that would anticipate the poetic realism of the next decade.

The spectacular Changing of the Guard that followed the war may not have made the industry as a whole any more profitable, or any more able to resist the Hollywood invasion, but it did produce a more flexible, open and varied environment in which the new generation could develop and flourish.

4

The Avant Garde

The principal members of the new generation of cineastes were Abel Gance, Germaine Dulac, Jean Epstein and Marcel L'Herbier, but always in the vanguard was Louis Delluc. In 1922 he made the first of the three films he would direct in his short life, *La Femme de nulle part*, but he was responsible for a hive of other activities that give one the sense of a film laboratory in which a new kind of cinema was being forged. With his natural publicist's flair for the memorable phrase, Delluc dubbed the group 'Impressionist', more to distinguish it from the Expressionist film-makers in Germany than to suggest any particular allegiance to the French movement of painters. In many ways a fairly disparate group of film-makers, what they had in common was a desire to forge a 'pure cinema' observing its own rules, free from the undermining conventions of the theatre.

An important part of Delluc's enterprise was to create new forums of intelligent appreciation. One of the magazines Delluc started, *Le Journal du Ciné-Club*, was linked to the ambitious idea of organising special film showings, where enthusiasts might gather to discuss the art of the cinema. The first such gathering took place at the Pépinière cinema on 12 June 1920. In the presence of an audience of seven hundred, the theatre and film director André Antoine gave a talk entitled 'The Cinema of Yesterday, Today and Tomorrow', which he illustrated with extracts from various films, including Gance's *Mater Dolorosa*. Other ciné-clubs soon proliferated, until there were about twenty in the Paris area alone.[1]

Equally important were the art-house cinemas that began to open during the course of the 1920s. In 1924, Jean Tedesco began to show films in Le Vieux-Colombier theatre. In 1926, the Studio des Ursulines opened with Pabst's *Joyless Street*. Its founders were the actors Armand Tellier and Laurence Myrga, who announced their goal, in unapologetically lofty terms, 'to gather our public from among the élite of writers, artists and intellectuals in the Latin Quarter . . . All that suggests originality, worth and commitment will have a place on our screen.'[2] In 1928, Jean-Placide Mauclaire opened Studio 28 in Montmartre, which likewise dedicated itself to supporting the new avant-garde film-makers.

The practical significance of these little cinemas is that they played a direct part in the film-making process, providing a means of exhibition and a support network for film-makers who did not have the backing of the mainstream industry. They were famously a showcase for members of the avant-garde like Man Ray, Marcel Duchamp and Luis Buñuel, but what finally distinguished them was not their commitment to any particular group, but their openness to anyone who sought to further the cause of cinema.

After Jean Renoir's first film *La Fille de l'eau*, which starred his then wife Catherine Hessling, had been rejected by the commercial distributors, he resolved to give up making films. But then he met Jean Tedesco, who had been screening extracts from the film without permission at the Vieux-Colombier. At first Renoir was furious, but then Tedesco invited him and his wife along to a screening. In his memoirs Renoir recalled the programme beginning with 'a rather tedious documentary about a power station' and a 'scene of general boredom', but when the extracts from *La Fille de l'eau* followed, they were greeted with several bursts of applause. After the showing, Renoir received an ovation:

For the first time in my life I knew the sweet smell of success. Jean Tedesco had placed us in the middle of the auditorium, in a position where the whole audience could see us. Catherine was recognised and the applause broke out again. The whole audience rose spontaneously to its feet. No, decidedly, we weren't going to give up film-making![3]

It's worth making the comparison between the group that gathered around Delluc in the 1920s and the New Wave of nearly forty years later. There's the same basic pattern – the enthusiasm for Hollywood cinema, the magazine articles setting out precepts for what cinema should be, and then the attempts of their writers to fulfil those precepts by becoming practical film-makers themselves.

When *The Cheat* came out, Delluc was impressed not only by the use of light, but also by the extraordinary new movie star on whom that light fell:

Of Hayakawa, one can say nothing: he is a phenomenon . . . I consider a certain kind of actor, especially him, as a natural force and his face as a poetic work whose reason for being does not concern me when my hunger for beauty finds there an expected chord or reflection . . . It is not his cat-like, implacable cruelty, his mysterious brutality, his hatred of anyone who resists, or his contempt for anyone who submits; that is not what impresses us, and yet that is all we can talk about . . . And especially his strangely drawn smile of childlike ferocity, not really the ferocity of a puma or jaguar, for then it would no longer be ferocity. The beauty of Sessue Hayakawa is painful. Few things in the cinema reveal to us, as the lights and silence of this mask do, that there really are *alone* beings. I well believe that all lonely people, and they are numerous, will discover their own resourceless despair in the intimate melancholy of this savage Hayakawa.[4]

What is fascinating about this passage is not the insight it provides into a long-forgotten movie star, but the emotional intensity and subjectivity that must have inspired successive generations of French cinephiles. Forty years later, François Truffaut would write of another great Hollywood actor's sudden rise to stardom:

Dean's acting is more animal than human, and that makes him unpredictable. What will his next gesture be? . . . When you have the good luck to write for an actor of this sort, an actor who plays his part physically, carnally, instead of filtering everything through his brain, the easiest way to get good results is to think abstractly. Think of it this way: James Dean is a cat, a lion, or maybe a squirrel. What can cats, lions and squirrels do that is most unlike humans? A cat can fall from great heights and land on its paws; it can be run over without being injured; it arches its back and slips away easily. Lions creep and roar; squirrels jump from one branch to another. So, what one must write are scenes in which Dean creeps (amid the beanstalks), roars (in a police station), leaps from branch to branch, falls from a great height into an empty pool without getting hurt. I like to think this is how Elia Kazan, Nicholas Ray, and, I hope, George Stevens proceeded.[5]

Many years separate these two passages, but in their celebration of the animal or 'cat-like' rather than the human, the intuitive rather than the intellectual, they share a remarkable affinity. Delluc may have died in 1924, but a generation later Truffaut was engaging in the cinema with the same passion and commitment, demonstrating the same practical agenda not simply to comment on but also to change the way films were made. Truffaut may not have been a film-maker when he wrote about Dean, but it must have been obvious to anyone reading this piece in 1956 that he was very soon going to become one.

One of the more significant landmarks in the avant-garde cinema that was taking place after the First World War was *Paris qui dort*, a short film made by a young journalist called René Clair.

The nightwatchman of the Eiffel Tower looks out over Paris. To his alarm, he notices that nothing is moving. He hurries down the hundreds of steps to find out what is going on. In the streets

Paris qui dort (1924)

48

he comes upon motionless cars and pedestrians who have been frozen like mannequins. The whole of the city is asleep. Only he, safe in his perch at the top of the tower, and the six passengers of an aeroplane that had been flying above the city, have been high enough to escape the effects of a mad scientist's sleep ray.

Paris qui dort is a charming film that eludes any attempt to categorise it. It contains elements of comedy, science fiction and documentary; it is a fantasy whose poetry lies in harnessing the extraordinary in the real. The nightwatchman invites the little group of air travellers, the only other people in the city to have been spared the sleep ray, to come back to his home. As we watch them picnic up in the airy heights, laying out their rugs amid the iron girders of the tower, much of the appeal of the sequence lies in the authenticity of the location. We feel exhilaration at this spectacular use of space, seeing for ourselves the real streets far below, knowing that the wind ruffling the edges of the rug comes not from some machine in a studio but from the Paris skies.

Paris qui dort (1924)

When the film was first shown, Clair wrote an article to explain what he had hoped to achieve with this startling debut: 'I believe that the cinema must be above all visual.'[6] When the Lumière Brothers tried to demonstrate the value of their new invention, they didn't photograph a still life or a conversation between two silent characters; they filmed life around them.

René Clair believed that French film-makers should build on the best of their own traditions, yet at the same time he was very aware of the traditions he wished to challenge. In the cinema, this meant escaping the influence of literary convention. 'Round about 1923, "purity" was on everybody's lips,' he later recalled. 'Pure cinema was the banner of a desperate though not completely fruitless revolt against the "anecdotal and descriptive" film.'[7]

Clair was only twenty-five when he made *Paris qui dort*. The film was financed by Henri Diamant-Berger, who had in 1921 struck lucky with his enormously successful production of *The Three Musketeers*. Two years on, however, the producer quickly became mired in cash-flow difficulties. It meant that *Paris qui dort* would be shelved for many months before it was finally completed and shown at the end of 1924.

During the day, Clair made a living as a journalist, writing a supplement on films for a monthly magazine called *Le Théâtre*, which had been founded by the director of the Théâtre des Champs-Elysées, Jacques Hébertot. Occupying a small office in the theatre, Clair was able to witness one of the most notable attempts in Paris to revitalise post-war culture. The theatre was home to Rolf de Maré's Ballets suédois, which in a modernist crusade to fuse together the different arts sought to incorporate into ballet contributions from some of the most innovative musicians, painters, writers and costume designers living in Paris. Collaborators included the painters Pablo Picasso, Francis Picabia and Fernand Léger. One of the productions during the company's first year at the theatre had been Jean Cocteau's play *Les Mariés de la tour Eiffel*, with incidental music by the group of composers that Cocteau had taken under his wing and called 'Les Six'.[8] The story of newlyweds who have to cope with increasingly absurd interruptions as they attempt to have their wedding breakfast on one of the platforms of the Eiffel Tower, it possibly provided some inspiration for Clair's subsequent film. Whatever the case, the daily ambience of Clair's working life at the innovative Théâtre des Champs-Elysées must have encouraged his determination to make a debut film that was equally progressive and daring in its challenge to the conventional.

As editor of the films supplement, he invited Jean Cocteau to express his attitude to the cinema. 'The cinema is in a cul-de-sac,' Cocteau observed. 'On the very first day, while everybody was still dazzled by this new invention, it took a wrong turning. People began to photograph theatre. Gradually, that theatre became cinematographic theatre, but never pure cinema.'[9]

The other writers and artists Clair interviewed included Fernand Léger: 'What I hope for in the future is the following: a cinematographic concept which can find its own medium. As long as the film remains literal or theatrical in origin, it will be nothing;' the poet Paul Valéry: 'What should be instituted is pure cinema art, or cinema reduced to its own media. That art must be opposed to those of theatre and of the novel, which pertain to words . . .' and the dramatist Sacha Guitry: 'As soon as cinema approximates to theatre by using stage methods, I detest it.'

Recalling the responses to these questions a quarter of a century later, Clair remarked on the unanimity of this 1920s generation that 'cinema is an autonomous medium of expression which must find its future within itself'.

The film company, Cinegraphic, which Marcel L'Herbier founded in 1922, provides a good example of the spirit at large. L'Herbier envisaged an enterprise that would pioneer the pure cinema that his contemporaries were discussing with such fervour. 'Soon Cinegraphic became a home for aspiring film-makers,' he recalled in his memoirs, 'the first creative workshop in the cinema.' But it was as much a showcase for the entire range of the decorative arts. Soon after its launch, L'Herbier declared the intention of Cinegraphic 'to support the research, experiments and projects that the poets, painters and musicians of our generation propose to us'.[10] This was surely another defining feature of the French cinema: not isolated and turned in on itself – like

Hollywood, marooned between the desert and the ocean – but an organic part of the wider artistic community.

L'Herbier might have added to his list architects, jewellery designers, couturiers, parfumeurs and restaurateurs, for the more renowned representatives of these trades occupied as important a place in his scheme. The new company's most ambitious production was *L'Inhumaine*, which L'Herbier described as 'a great mosaic of modern art'.[11] Its rather melodramatic story of a cold-hearted opera diva was overshadowed by L'Herbier's adulation of style. Made in 1924, the film boasted not one production designer, but five. While the architect Robert Mallet-Stevens created the modernist exterior of the house in which the diva lives, Claude Autant-Lara, Alberto Cavalcanti and Fernand Léger contributed interior decors with the cheerful excess that L'Herbier's thirst for experimentation encouraged. The fashion designer Paul Poiret created the costumes, working closely with the jewellers René Lalique and Raymond Templier. Jean Borlin of the Ballets suédois was invited to stage special dance sequences and the composer Darius Milhaud wrote an original score. 'It is undeniable that, with its list of prestigious names bringing together a wide range of talent in different fields, the film became a sort of miscellany of a new Art,' commented L'Herbier. 'It was what I wanted.'[12]

L'Herbier took pride in the lavish foretaste this avant-garde showcase offered of the famous Exposition Internationale des Arts Décoratifs et Industriels Modernes, which took place the following year. Indeed, the making of this definitive art deco film amounted to an exhibition in itself, although it attracted the participation of far more artists than there were tasks to go around. Celebrity visitors who had to be content with simply appearing as extras in a crowd scene included Erik Satie, James Joyce, Picasso, Man Ray, Ezra Pound and the dancer Vaclav Nijinsky, who had already begun his descent into madness. 'It was a somewhat pitiful sight to witness the decline of that idol,' recalled Cavalcanti.

He seemed unaware of the outside world, except for one fleeting moment when he saw an actor making himself up. Something seemed to stir within him and he appeared to be making an enormous effort to reach out for something which may have been the truth, trying desperately to hold on to his past life, at least for a few seconds. He didn't make it, however, and returned to his oblivion.[13]

Cinegraphic's next production, a film version of the Pirandello novel, *Feu Mathias Pascal*, was a co-production with Alexandre Kamenka's Albatros company. Cavalcanti designed the sets but also worked as assistant director, standing in for L'Herbier whenever he absented himself to attend one press conference or another. Although the experience gave the young Brazilian the opportunity to become a director in his own right with *Le Train sans yeux*, based on a novel by Louis Delluc, Cavalcanti's own account suggests that the film involved too many creative compromises to be a satisfying debut. Calling it a 'purely commercial venture', he characterised the project as 'a very bad story written by an intelligent film-man trying to be a novelist'. The experience was further blighted by the collapse of the production company, whose creditors confiscated the negative of the film.

Fearing for a career that looked in danger of ending before it had even properly begun, Cavalcanti decided to rely on his own resources to retrieve the situation. *Rien que les heures* was a spontaneous, improvised film, which he shot in 1926 with a handful of friends on the streets of Paris. His cameraman was Jimmy Rogers, who had previously worked in the studios of British International Pictures in London. It was a film made in reaction to the aspects of professional production that had so frustrated Cavalcanti during the making of *Le Train sans yeux* – whether dealing with producers, shooting in film studios or having to tell a conventional story:

This film does not contain a story. It is just a series of impressions of life in a city, although it does not claim to represent any single city. Every town would be the same were it not for the tourist sights that make them different.

An immensely influential film, first screened at the Studio des Ursulines, it is difficult to imagine how it could have been made without the avant-garde community to support it.

'Avant-garde' was a term that Cavalcanti thought inappropriate for a collection of individuals he considered too disparate to be a coherent school, but nonetheless he recognised the undeniable contribution they made to the cinema:

> In a complete lack of order and incredible confusion, the so-called 'avant-garde' managed to establish the important fact that the cinema was a new form of expression and should thus possess distinctive characteristics. The fact that the group was comprised of directors with the most varied tendencies only goes to show this. René Clair, Renoir and myself didn't form a unity, but gave a margin to the production of poetic films which had previously hardly been explored in French cinema.

One of the people to emerge from this 'margin' was Luis Buñuel, who, living in Paris during the late 1920s, had been trying to pick up whatever odd jobs he could in the film industry. In his memoirs, he describes giving a talk on the avant-garde cinema during a trip back to Spain: 'I brought along a few films to show – René Clair's *Entr'acte*, the dream sequence from Renoir's *La Fille de l'eau*, Cavalcanti's *Rien que les heures*.'[14] Soon afterwards, he and Salvador Dali discussed the exchange of dreams that would lead to his first film.

Un Chien andalou (1928)

54

'Our only rule was very simple,' recalled Buñuel. 'No idea or image that might lend itself to a rational explanation of any kind would be accepted.'[15] Although the outlandish images of *Un Chien andalou* were intended to defy any attempt at explanation, they seem inevitable, as representative of the human condition as Sisyphus rolling the boulder up the hill. Buñuel's comment that the images he and Dali agreed on seemed 'luminously right'[16] captures the paradox at the heart of the film. It articulates all the unconscious fears and longings of the human psyche, yet proceeds with a reassuring sense of order, irrational but not random. The chronological framework of the inter-titles – 'Once upon a time . . .', 'Eight years later . . .' 'Around three o'clock in the morning . . .', 'Sixteen years ago . . .', 'In spring . . .' – offer a firm narrative direction even if the connections do not make sense. It is a film of the avant-garde, yet contains all the emotional indulgence of mass entertainment, with images that could slot neatly into Hollywood melodrama: the arrival of the mysterious stranger (albeit dressed like a Vermeer milkmaid), a man pulling a gun, a corpse being found in the woods, a pair of lovers walking hand in hand into the distance.

Un Chien andalou was filmed over two weeks at the Billancourt studios, financed by money from Buñuel's mother. Once it had been completed, Buñuel recalled that he had 'no idea what to do with it'.[17] In any other city of the time – London, New York, Los Angeles – it would surely have been lost, assuming that Buñuel had managed to sustain the morale to make the film in the first place. But the avant-garde community in Paris gave it a life.

The biggest hurdle this kind of film-making faced was the technical complexity and extra expense of sound. At first, the omens seemed propitious. The resources required to make a sound film may have far exceeded those that Buñuel could expect his mother to provide. But the *succès d'estime* of *Un Chien andalou* drew the attention of wealthy new patrons in the form of the Vicomte and the Vicomtesse de Noailles, Charles and Marie-Laure, who provided Buñuel with a budget of a million francs to make a sound film, *L'Age d'or*. Their generous support seemed to open up a brave new world of artistically ambitious film-making. The hopes for what might be achieved were further fuelled when at about the same time Charles and Marie-Laure also succeeded in persuading their friend Jean Cocteau, the poet, painter and play-wright, to make a film. When the editor of the new weekly film page of *Le Figaro*, Richard Pierre-Bodin, saw the finished work at a private viewing, he was convinced that it would play a criti-cal role in determining the future progress of the sound cinema. Comparing Cocteau to Heine, La Fontaine and Oscar Wilde, he urged his readers to go and see the film when it came out. 'You will find yourself sometimes disturbed, sometimes baffled by its strangeness, but I defy you ever to be indifferent. Write to tell me what you think of it. But I warn you that you will strive in vain to persuade me that this work isn't important or beautiful.'

Praising the Vicomte and Vicomtesse de Noailles, Pierre-Bodin also wrote about the crucial patronage that had made such a masterpiece possible. In an exclusive article for the newspaper, Jean Cocteau himself explained how the gesture of his patrons enabled a creative freedom that was usually alien to the cinema: 'Through its need for huge, instant returns, the cinema, which ought to be the poet's best weapon, does not live up to its prom-ise: no freedom in this zone of perfect freedom! So when poets like Chaplin or Keaton take it up, they are constrained to limit themselves to provoking only laughter.' The expectations of con-ventional production, Cocteau argued, involved inevitable com-promise. But the aim of the Vicomte and Vicomtesse de Noailles was neither to make a financial return nor to win the approval of passing fashion, but truly to promote art for art's sake.

It is why I accepted their offer after having turned down so many others. For however enlightened the big film companies may be, simple decency obliges us not to expose them to unnecessary risk and to work for them with due care. But in this case, there is no need for care. Closing their eyes, covering up their ears, my patrons were discreet enough not to intervene in any way. The surprise of the work itself will be enough for them, whatever it may be and even if it should provoke society's condemnation.[18]

But the Noailles were not as above the fray as Cocteau would have liked to have believed. Soon their other great gesture towards free expression exposed the vulnerability of such patronage. *L'Age d'or* opened at the Studio 28 on 28 November 1930. Reports of how its content ridiculed the representatives of Church, Family and Nation provoked violent protests. On the evening of Wednesday 3 December, about thirty demonstrators from the League of Patriots and the Anti-Semitic League hurled ink at the screen and attacked members of the audience. On their way out, they then smashed up furniture and vandalised a display of pictures that included work by Dali, Max Ernst, Man Ray, Joan Miró and Yves Tanguy. The damage was estimated at 100,000 francs – about a tenth of the original budget of Buñuel's film.[19]

The following Sunday in *Le Figaro*, Richard Pierre-Bodin, the very writer who had a few weeks previously eulogised the enlightened patronage of the Vicomte and Vicomtesse de Noailles, launched a massive attack on *L'Age d'or*. In an open letter to the President of the French Board of Censors, he declared its continued screening to be 'a scandal without precedent', and demanded that it be banned, which it duly was three days later. Dropped by his friends, fearing excommunication and even expulsion from the Jockey Club, the then bastion of the French aristocracy, an embattled Charles de Noailles took refuge with his wife Marie-Laure in the country. Fearful that *La Vie d'un poète* would only further stoke the controversy, he asked Cocteau to stop showing the film in private and put off its release. The film made its public appearance at the Vieux-Colombier over a year later, the change of title, *Le Sang d'un poète*, an apt reflection of the costs of free expression.

Cocteau's film is an inward-looking, deeply personal work that explored the nature of poetic inspiration, tracing through loosely connected dream images a mysterious process that involved great suffering and defied the artist's efforts at rational control, yet at the same time – through startling transformations – enabled him to achieve a kind of immortality. An artist draws a face on an easel. When the mouth in the picture takes on a life of its own, he wipes it off with his hand to find with horror – in an image that recalls the stigmatic hand of *Un Chien andalou* – that the mouth has grafted itself on to his palm. No efforts to shake it off avail. The following morning, the artist encounters a statue that, taking on life, bids him to pass through a mirror. 'Try,' the statue urges him. 'Always try . . .' In *Le Sang d'un poète* the trick is achieved through substitution of the mirror by a vat of water. With a splash, the artist passes into the depths of the mirror. But twenty years later in his film *Orphée*, as if living up to the statue's injunction to constant experimentation, Cocteau returned to the mirror, this time achieving a far more seamless and convincing transition through the use of mercury.

Le Sang d'un poète is a rallying cry for the artist, capturing the anguish of creation, yet at the same time celebrating the power of the individual imagination. The dominating personality of Cocteau is always at the heart of the film – present in the narrator's voice, in the paintings, sculptures and masks, as well as the film images that he has fashioned, and in his interspersed handwritten notes, with the trademark star, that offer commentary. Describing the film as 'a realistic documentation of unreal events', Cocteau sets before us a representation of his own interior imagination. 'Every poem is like an emblem that needs to be deciphered,' a title explains at the beginning of the film. A second note then impresses the importance of this notion: 'The author dedicates this series of allegories to the memory of Pisanello, Paolo Uccello, Piero della Francesca and Andrea del Castagno, painters of emblems and enigmas.'

One of the allegories that it was possible to read in the film held a special appeal for aspiring film-makers: the truly imaginative artist is able to bend the cinema to his will, no matter how complex, costly or technical the medium may appear to be. Cocteau's cinema was an expression of his mind's eye that owed nothing to the cinema that had preceded him. He had received no training in film technique, but he knew what he wanted to see and to say.

Le Sang d'un poète could hardly be counted a commercial success. Confined to small art-house cinemas, only a very few people would see it. Badly burned by their experiences, its patrons Charles and Marie-Laure de Noailles refrained from sponsoring any further such productions. Cocteau himself, limiting himself to writing screenplays to be directed by others, would not make another film until *La Belle et la bête* nearly a decade and a half later. Nonetheless, *Le Sang d'un poète* provided an immensely potent example that others would seek to emulate – an alternative vision of the cinema that owed nothing to the practices of the conventional film industry but everything to the imagination of the individual artist. Across the Atlantic, where the medium was firmly in the thrall of Hollywood, the cinema attracted disdain rather than admiration from intellectuals. But in France, the engagement of artists like Cocteau meant that cinema would develop between the opposed, but more evenly balanced, poles of industry and art.

5

Sound

The French industry's efforts to embrace the new sound era had been shambolic. There had been many attempts to experiment with sound systems, going back as early as the Paris Exposition of 1900, at which three separate talking-film exhibits had been presented,[1] but the fragmentation of the industry after the First World War, with the effective retirement from the world stage of its two largest companies, Pathé and Gaumont, cut off the finance necessary to perfect these initiatives. Germany and America divided the spoils of the valuable sound patents between them. In June 1930, Tobis Klangfilm, Western Electric and RCA gathered together with the major production groups to agree territories of exploitation.[2] The fact that this meeting took place in Paris had obvious symbolic force, as yet one more example of the once all-powerful French industry yielding ground to its more successful post-war competitors.

The conversion to sound in France was a slow, piecemeal affair, where the initiative was firmly in the hands of American or German companies. The first theatres to receive sound systems were the large showcase cinemas of the Hollywood corporations. The smaller French chains, lacking the financial resources, had no choice but to spread out their investment over a much longer period. By the end of 1930, only 18 per cent of French cinemas had been converted to sound, compared to 63 per cent in Britain.[3]

Yet if the French film industry failed to regain its former economic dominance, it at least tried to take advantage of the huge opportunity that sound seemed to offer to build a profitable production industry in France behind the language barrier. But was that barrier really enough to make a difference in the long run? In a yet to be tested future market, an affirmative answer required an exercise of faith that seemed to be beyond pioneers like Charles Pathé and Léon Gaumont, who had seen their global dominance collapse in face of the Hollywood juggernaut.

At the end of 1928, a magazine, *Paris et le monde*, circulated a questionnaire among notables in the French film industry, posing the question of whether it would be a good idea for France to have its own Hollywood. Charles Pathé's response was to reiterate the economic argument he had outlined in 1920: Hollywood's home market, so many times larger than anyone else's, provided it with an unassailable advantage. For this reason 'and also because, in order to be both rewarding and profitable, French production must not be too important, I believe that the creation of a French Hollywood is not desirable'.[4]

This perception lay behind the downsizing of the French film industry that took place through the 1920s. The sudden loss of world leadership had had a profound effect on the psychology of the French film pioneers, causing them to resist the development of large film combines that were being constructed not only in America but also in other European countries such as Germany and the United Kingdom. But as the pioneers left the stage, the public craze for sound cinema encouraged their successors to be more ambitious.

The opening of *The Jazz Singer* in Paris in January 1929 was a much-written-about sensation. The talking picture wasn't really new. Previously, there had been countless attempts to master the technology. But it was *The Jazz Singer* that seemed to settle the issue once and for all. 'Of all the systems that have been presented to us up until now,' observed *Le Figaro*, 'the Vitagraph system, with which *The Jazz Singer* has been made, is unquestionably the best.' The film played to packed houses at the Aubert-Palace near the Opéra for the remainder of the year. It was seen in that one cinema by 545,893 people, grossing 8,555,000 francs (approximately £3 million in today's money).

It would have played in more cinemas if only there had been more cinemas equipped for sound. The film that finally replaced it was *The Singing Fool*, with Al Jolson again – 'a worthy successor to *The Jazz Singer*,' as the press advertisement put it.[5]

The decision of the *Figaro* newspaper in March 1929 to devote a weekly page to the cinema, called 'Figaro Film', reflected the resurgence of public interest in the medium. To mark the occasion, the veteran director Gaston Ravel wrote a piece in which he applauded the initiative as helping to develop 'an art which must become one of our principal national industries'.[6] Dismissing the narrow concerns of France's young avant-garde film-makers as 'juvenile', he argued for the construction of the kind of 'French Hollywood' that Pathé had warned against: 'The Cinema, which is still trying to find its voice in spite of clear progress, cannot limit itself to a narrow role; it must, above all, satisfy the varied tastes of a broad public.'

A more general mood of wounded pride and envy at what the American cinema had achieved, coupled with a determination to make up for lost ground, could be traced in the weekly round-ups of studio news, reviews and features that followed. 'WE NEED STARS!' declared the headline to one article some weeks later. 'I wonder why in France we have no idea how to create stars,' it mused. 'We should not forget that they offer a guarantee of commercial success, so attached are the public to the cult of personality. See how this system has been exploited by our friends the Americans, and even the Germans, to their great profit. But we possess neither stars nor the means to create them.'[7]

The tone of dissatisfaction persisted through 1929, an *annus mirabilis* of American and German talking pictures that threw into relief the conspicuous lack of French achievement. Towards the end of December, as *The Jazz Singer* finally completed its unprecedented forty-eight-week run at the Aubert-Palace, 'Figaro Film' ran – beneath the headline 'A SAD NOTICE' – the following article of national self-reproach:

At the entrance to a music hall recently converted, after the present fashion, into a cinema, passers-by could read: 'The Management would have liked to open this cinema with a French talking picture. BUT IT DOES NOT EXIST!'

This is quite correct. Since America has committed itself to the talkies, the French have not succeeded in making a single talking picture. The talking picture that was recently shown on the Boulevards was made at Twickenham studios in England with American equipment.* On 10 January, Parisians will be able to enjoy a new talking picture, in French with French actors. But the director is German and the film was made in Berlin.[8]

The piece went on to lament the absence of French directors, French writers and, above all, French producers. Such was the overwhelming hunger for a new French cinema when the old pioneers Pathé and Gaumont retired from the scene.

He was far too revered a figure to be the butt of any open criticism, but in such a climate Charles Pathé seemed like a dead hand. Since the First World War, he had presided over the systematic dismantlement of the Pathé empire. In 1920, he sold the US and British subsidiaries, Pathé-Exchange and Pathé Ltd, for a combined figure of nearly thirty million francs.[9] In the same year, he sold the production and distribution arms of his company, Pathé Cinéma, to Pathé Consortium. In 1927, he sold a controlling interest in his film-stock factory at Vincennes to Kodak for 135 million francs, the new name of the company, Pathé-Kodak, making it possible to continue to believe that he remained a force in the French film industry. When he gave up control of Pathé Cinéma itself two years later, he cited the arrival of sound as the principal reason – 'I was too old and too tired to take on such a challenge' – but in practice the retreat had begun long before. As a French historian of the Pathé empire put it, the goal that seemed most to motivate Pathé in his final years of running the company was 'an honourable exit and a well-deserved retirement'.[10]

Pathé's successor, Bernard Natan, was head of the aptly

* *Les Trois Masques*, directed by André Hugon.

named Rapid Film, which had started out as a small film services company before the First World War to become by the end of the 1920s one of the most ambitious production companies in France. In 1929, when Natan took over Pathé Cinema after a spectacular buy-out, his resemblance to a Hollywood mogul must have seemed to many a welcome promise of the kind of change that the French cinema so badly needed.

A Romanian of Jewish origin, he was born Nathaniel Tanenzapf, but changed his name to Bernard Natan in the same year that he became a naturalised French citizen in 1921. Having entered the industry as a chemist for Pathé in 1905, he established his own film laboratory, Rapid Film, in 1912. During the First World War, he fought in the French army. When he resumed the direction of his small company at the end of 1918, he discovered that the industrial landscape of the French cinema had totally changed. With the big companies in headlong retreat, he joined the new generation of entrepreneurs keen to fill the vacuum.

In 1924 he began to produce advertising films. In 1926, announcing a massive increase in his company's capital, he built a studio on the rue Francoeur in Paris to make feature films. Within the year, seven were put into production. The intention to make big-budget films that could command an international market became clear the following year when he produced *Education de prince*, with the Hollywood star Edna Purviance. More high-profile productions quickly followed, including in 1928 *La Merveilleuse Vie de Jeanne d'Arc*, which was one of the most expensive films ever to be made in France.[11]

Natan regarded the arrival of sound as the opportunity to build a mass-market, popular cinema that could at long last compete with the Americans, although the cost of embracing the new sound technology would require massive capital investment. The sheer scale of the enterprise demanded a policy of vertical integration, for in face of powerful American competition the only way that he could guarantee playing time for a substantial programme of his productions was to build an extensive distribution and exhibition network of his own.

So no sooner had Natan taken over Pathé in February 1929 than he began to build a circuit of cinemas: sixty, including some of the most prestigious sites in Paris, were acquired within a year. In June 1929, he bought the production companies Cinéromans and Pathé-Consortium-Cinéma, along with their studios at Joinville-le-point. At the same time he negotiated a deal with RCA to equip the studios with sound. Not content to wait for the conversion work to be completed, he sent the director André Hugon to London in September to direct *Les Trois Masques*.

A major coup was to sign up the veteran director, Maurice Tourneur. At the beginning of the First World War, Tourneur had left France for the United States, where he had become one of the most respected and influential figures in building Hollywood into the dominant global force that it became. Now he was back in his native country. The message was clear: he would help to do the same for Pathé-Natan.

At the end of the year, a short musical comedy, called *Chiqué*, went on the floor of the newly refurbished Joinville studios. Although it was not the first sound film ever to be made in France, it deserves a place in the history books as the first sound film to use a viable, commercially proven system. A steady and varied series of features then followed.

In February 1930, Marcel L'Herbier began to work for Pathé-Natan on his first sound production, *L'Enfant d'amour*, about a politician's mistress who keeps the existence of their love child secret rather than ruin his career. At about the same time, Jean de Limour directed *Mon Gosse de père,* about the complications that arise when a grown-up son resurfaces in the life of his roué father, who has just taken a young wife. An urbane comedy based on a play by Leopold Lemarchand, it was given international appeal by the presence of Hollywood star Adolphe Menjou, who made a parallel English-language version called *The Parisian.*

International box-office appeal was a key element in Pathé-Natan's strategy. It meant that its early talking pictures tended not only to rely heavily on proven stage successes, but also – in this time before effective dubbing – to be filmed in several different language versions.

The commercial pressures of the new sound cinema made Marcel L'Herbier regard his debut in the 'cinephonic art' with some foreboding.[12] Based on a play by Henri Bataille, one of France's most popular dramatists before the First World War, *L'Enfant de l'amour* was a well-made but conventional adaptation that L'Herbier was required to shoot in three different languages, with three different casts. 'One should not make three versions of a film when it is difficult enough to make one,' observed L'Herbier. 'But that was the idiotic effect of money . . . Our tyrant, money, made no allowance for the fact that, in crossing the Channel, the direction of a sentimental drama needed a completely different style. One does not break up with one's lover in London as one would in Paris.'[13] L'Herbier was left reconciling himself to the fact that the finished film – in all three versions – was the sort of 'filmed theatre' that he had always tried to avoid in the silent cinema.

Many commentators decried the mediocrity of the films that resulted in the early days of sound, with their over-reliance on the theatre, but a few recognised this dependence as an inevitable, perhaps even necessary phase. 'We believe firmly in the future of the talking picture,' wrote Jacques Darmetal, in 'Figaro Film' in April 1930, 'but we have yet to settle in and pass through all the stages of our apprenticeship.'[14]

Pathé-Natan's output during the early 1930s may not have been greatly memorable, but at least it helped to put in place the essential industrial infrastructure that would make more distinguished film-making possible in the future. Natan's significant contribution to the French film industry was to instil a confidence and daring that the battle-weary caution of the pioneers had long eroded. His belief in the future revealed itself in

his embrace not only of sound but also of the other new tech-
nologies. It was Natan who, in 1930, established a company to
develop the potential of television. It was Natan who bought
the rights to the wide-screen Hypergonar process of Henri
Chrétien, which would eventually emerge twenty years later as
Cinemascope.

But the breathtaking pace with which he created a Hollywood-
scale operation out of nothing filled Charles Pathé only with
horror. After the merger, he agreed to stay on as a director, but
within months became alarmed by the reckless rate of Natan's
spending. When his counsel of caution was disregarded, he
approached the bankers who had financed the takeover: 'I
explained frankly the perils to which Monsieur Natan was
exposing the company with his policy of acquisition at any price
. . . and that he needed to be dissuaded from his strategy of
unbridled production, which could only in the long run lead to
ruin.'[15] But ignoring his advice, the bankers continued to back
Natan. So on 26 May 1930, Charles Pathé resigned.

Ruin eventually came in 1935, when Pathé-Natan ran out of
credit and was declared bankrupt. Charles Pathé was able to say
'I told you so,' but it was Natan's leadership that procured the
capital investment needed to establish a native sound cinema in
France. Over the period, Pathé-Natan had made sixty films that
formed the backbone of French film production.

France's other big company, Gaumont, fared little better. Since
the very beginning of his career in the cinema – which was the
beginning of cinema itself – its founder, Léon Gaumont, had
devoted considerable efforts to establishing the talking picture.
When it finally arrived, he could not, however, claim any share
in the spoils, although he had worked longer on overcoming the
technical challenge than anyone else.

Even after the First World War, when he had become increasingly reluctant to invest in the production of films, he continued
to support the development of a workable sound system. On
15 June 1922, he gave a public demonstration of an improved

disc-on-sound system. When he had to concede that it was impractical, in January 1925, he bought into a double-track system developed by the Danish inventors Axel Petersen and Arnold Poulsen. Although this led eventually to the presentation of France's first sound feature, *L'Eau du Nil*,[16] the system was too cumbersome to offer any serious competition to the rival American and German companies. Gaumont's long-cherished dream to win the race for sound had come to nothing, but he knew that his company still had to equip its studios and theatres for the sound era, even if it was with systems that had been developed abroad.

Relinquishing control of Gaumont to a consortium of companies, supported by the Banque national de crédit, he announced his effective retirement on 17 April 1930: 'I've come to the conclusion that in spite of the best will in the world old age is upon me, and I am not up to the intense struggle that lies ahead.'[17]

The awkward name of the reborn company, Gaumont-Franco-Film-Aubert (GFFA), reflected the era of mergers that the need to embrace the expensive new technology demanded.

The cost alone of renovating its flagship cinema, the Gaumont Palace – fitted with the Western Electric sound system in 1931 – was forty-one million francs. But even greater expense would follow, as GFFA implemented an ambitious production progamme of French-language films to supply its ever-growing chain of cinemas. Behind the expansion lay the logic that sound would favour French-language production, especially at a time when no effective system of dubbing had yet been introduced, but GFFA so over-extended itself that the programme was abruptly called to a halt in 1934 after the company was forced into liquidation. It would be nearly ten years before another film was produced under the Gaumont name.

So few Paris theatres were equipped to exhibit sound films during 1929 that cross-Channel traffic swelled with French film-makers eager – but also fearful – to sample the new craze of the talkies in London, where the American film companies had already re-equipped their large first-run theatres. Prominent among these travellers was René Clair, whose two films for Alexandre Kamenka of Albatros – *La Proie du vent* (1927) and *Un Chapeau de paille d'Italie* (1928) – had helped to establish him in the forefront of the new generation of film-makers. 'The cinema must be above all visual,' he had declared when his first film, *Paris qui dort*, had first been screened.[18] Now the arrival of sound seemed to pose new obstacles to his dream of a pure cinema. During May 1929 he published a series of sceptical letters from London chronicling the new phenomenon. 'In London we can see that the Americans were not exaggerating when they spoke of the extraordinary attraction exercised on the public by the talking films. From noon till eleven o'clock at night people pour in successive waves into the crowded cinemas.'[19] The dominating tone was one of dread for what the talkies would bring. 'It is too late for those who love the art of moving pictures to deplore the effects of this barbaric invasion. All we can try to do is cut our losses.' It was not that Clair failed to recognise the creative potential of the sound film; he just feared the tyranny of 'hackneyed verbiage' that would prevent film-makers from exploiting that potential. 'I fear that the precision of verbal expression may drive poetry from the screen as it has driven away the atmosphere of dream. The imaginary words we used to lend those silent shadows were more beautiful than any actual words could ever be. The heroes of the screen spoke to our imagination with the complicity of silence. Tomorrow they will deafen us with their audible trivialities.'[20]

But when tomorrow came, Clair shot his own first sound film with a determination not to sacrifice any of the freedom of movement that the silent cinema had achieved. *Sous les toits de Paris* (1930) – *Under the Rooftops of Paris* – opens *over* the rooftops of Paris with a series of shots of the fantastically varied and eccentric collection of chimneys that the Paris skyline boasts. In their brevity and limited scope these shots set up, through

Sous les toits de Paris (1930)

contrast, the long travelling shot that follows, as Clair's camera slowly drops down from the heights on to a group of singers in the street below. The movement contains a wishful thinking that in this new age of sound the camera should remain free.

Commencing production in January 1930, Clair made the film for Les Films Sonores Tobis, a subsidiary established by the Dutch–German company that owned the patents in the Tobis Klangfilm sound system. Tobis believed that the best way to demonstrate the potential of sound was to make sound films themselves. With this purpose in mind, they took over Epinay Studios in March 1929, six months later showing off to the French press their new 'tower of Babel', where they made films simultaneously in many different languages. *Figaro* acclaimed 'this perfect organisation',[21] acknowledging German mastery of the new sound technology that had caused a sizeable community of French actors and film-makers to migrate to the German capital itself, where UFA had embarked on a policy of making French-language versions of its films. One of the early successes was *Die Drei von der Tankstelle*, a light romance about three men who fall in love with the same girl, which was simultaneously made in French as *Le Chemin du paradis*, with its original German star, Lilian Harvey. 'Is it a film?' began the *Figaro* review. 'No. It's a filmed operetta. And it's charming!'[22] Writing in the magazine *Candide*, the publisher Jean Fayard declared that it would 'open a new epoch for the talking cinema',[23] and in the film magazine *Pour Vous* Alexandre Arnoux declared it to be 'the first film operetta that is truly cinematic'.[24] Critics were impressed by the way in which it passed effortlessly back and forth between word and song, without lengthy scenes of static dialogue. René Clair, who had been writing the script of *Le Million* when *Le Chemin du paradis* opened in Paris at the end of 1930, admitted that he rewrote several scenes under its influence.[25]

The goal of *Le Million* was to achieve a *film sonore*, a *sound* rather than a talking film, which would, in the pursuit of cinema, harness the poetry of music but avoid the banality of dialogue. 'As it skips merrily on its way the characters frequently burst into song,' observed the *New York Times* critic, hugely impressed even if he was unable to overlook its hybrid quality.[26] 'This picture', he commented, 'may be referred to as a musical farce or tuneful operetta. But no matter what it is called, it is a scintillating entertainment.' Its worldwide success, which was quickly followed by that of *A Nous la liberté* and *Quatorze juillet*, established Clair as France's most acclaimed director in the early 1930s. In their *History of the Film*, first published in 1935, Maurice Bardèche and Robert Brasillach singled him out as 'the only film man in France whose work displayed both purpose and progress'.[27]

Clair was determined to use sound in a creative way, avoiding the stasis of lengthy dialogue scenes. In *Le Million*, for example, there is the celebrated backstage scene at the opera, where the protagonists chase after the coat that contains the winning lottery ticket. As the coat is passed back and forth, snatched by one person or another, a cheering crowd and a referee's whistle are heard on the soundtrack. It was a clever metaphor that made full use of the latest weapon in the cinema's armoury. Yet Clair's very devotion to pioneering a film style for the new sound age revealed its own limitations in a fear of dialogue that at times seemed to deny the reality that people do talk. His dislike of words meant that ultimately he was heading down a cul-de-sac. His camera may have been able to move freely, but the elaborately orchestrated film-ballets that he made for Tobis – *Sous les toits de Paris*, *Le Million* and *A Nous la liberté* – were gilded cages for characters who were allowed to speak only so long as they did so with a musical lilt in their voices. The direction their conversations took seemed determined by some hidden metronome that would soon propel them into yet another song. They were reduced, in effect, to charming but limited marionettes, condemned to live for ever in a sing-along, operetta world. Such a cinema could thrive in the early novelty years of sound, but offered no long-term future.

Tobis's expensive, prestige productions at Epinay provided a shop window for the Klangfilm sound system, but Hollywood put up powerful competition, seeking to use the new technology to entrench its dominance over the French market. The Hollywood company that had the most ambitious plans for production in France was Paramount.

During a visit to Europe in the autumn of 1929, its vice-president, Jesse Lasky, announced that the studio intended to build a production facility that would produce French-language versions of the studio's Hollywood productions:

I'll buy the rights of a book, a play or a script that I think suited to the French temperament yet which has the potential to succeed with the American public too. Our various departments will undertake the detailed work associated with the production of a talkie. The film is shot in America. The basic costs (of costumes, models, decoupage, etc) being established for the American film, I have a copy of it filmed in France with an entirely French cast, according to the original outline which the French producer need only follow to the letter.[28]

There was an unmistakably imperial tone to his manner as he issued such pronouncements, working out his European strategy in the suite of offices he kept in the Paramount Theatre on one of the Grands Boulevards. Indeed, earlier that year he had carried away the considerable plunder of France's top musical star

Maurice Chevalier, whom he had seen in a revue at the Casino de Paris.

Chevalier sang a number of songs especially for the large proportion of American tourists in the audience, and they were so captivated by his bubbling good humor and broken English I couldn't help thinking this ruddy-complexioned blue-eyed singer with a straw hat and infectious smile would have the same appeal for Americans in Paris, Texas, as he obviously did in Paris, France.[29]

A year after Lasky's visit, the old Cinéromans studios at Joinville and Saint-Maurice had not only been re-equipped with sound but also substantially enlarged, with six new sound stages.[30] In the short intervening period, Paramount's plans had become yet more grand. Joinville was to be the company's major base for European production, where it would produce local versions of its Hollywood product not just in French but in several other European languages as well. It was only natural to make the most of readily available capital to introduce economies of scale. At once, with this new multiple-language version strategy, a Hollywood major had established itself as France's largest production centre, in its first year of operation turning out fifteen films.[31]

The director Alberto Cavalcanti was an early recruit to Paramount's new film factory, where he arrived in 1930 to make a French version of the Dorothy Arzner film, *Sarah and Son* (1930). In his unpublished memoirs, he described the nature of the operation:

The newly established routine at Joinville was for the director to be shown the original film, to be given the script in French, then go to the floor to undertake the copy of the intimate scenes, as all the elaborate, spectacular stuff was to be duped from the model. This of course had to be done not only quickly (the schedules being twelve to fifteen days), but also very carefully, as these intimate scenes had to be fitted in the cutting-rooms into the original spectacular ones. The soundtrack consisted only of dialogue, although a so-called soundtrack was prepared for its background in Hollywood, which included the incidental music and the few noises in fashion then: telephones ringing, doors shutting, dogs barking and cars starting, running and stopping. We were not concerned with the re-recording and the copies were to be made in the USA.[32]

It was a crude system that placed an emphasis on strict fidelity to the original American film being copied, but nonetheless Cavalcanti remembered the experience as an important apprenticeship, which he considered to be of immense importance to the development of the still primitive French sound cinema. While he recalled many of his friends in the French avant-garde greeting the arrival of sound with dismay, his own willingness to work for Paramount put him in a position to appreciate its potential, however undistinguished the studio's output may have been:

Little I knew about the value of the lessons I was going to get. Only much later when sound in films started their improvement did I realise that the soundtrack included the three distinct elements, all of them having the same importance: words, music and noises. Talkies dealt primarily with words. The early attempts about noises had been negligible and music was still used as it had been in silent days, or it was borrowed straight from the Broadway musical comedies. Anyway to me it was quite a wonder to listen, not only to the new voices, but also to hear the voices on the faces I knew so well.[33]

While Tobis produced a handful of expensive films by top French directors like René Clair or Jacques Feyder, it used its own German sound engineers. The sheer scale of the Paramount operation, in which dozens of films were made a year, meant that even if the films themselves were of little consequence, Joinville became an important – if at the time little appreciated – nursery ground and laboratory for French film-makers. As Cavalcanti observed, 'Few people seem to have understood that Paramount very largely provided the basis for the creation of a sound film industry in Paris.'[34]

Contemporary commentators were awed by the sheer magnitude of the Paramount operation. Hailing the 'French

Hollywood', the reporter for *Ciné-Magazine* declared his astonishment to find himself, after just a twenty-minute car journey from Paris, 'in one of those magnificent Californian studios that we admired and envied so much, and rightly so until now'. What so impressed him were not only the more visceral qualities of Hollywood that so many other French commentators had written about before – its power, scale, energy and confidence – but also the single-minded purpose that lay behind such an extraordinary feat of organisation. 'At Joinville can be found the same discipline, order and precision that lay behind the great American successes. There is neither idleness nor panic. Everyone works hard over the length of a long day, but with calm.'[35]

Yet although the 'French Hollywood' of Paramount-Joinville might have impressed the reporters as a model of efficient organisation, all its best-laid schemes to reproduce French as well as other European versions of American films quickly disintegrated once it went into operation. Too often the American stories seemed absurd once they had been translated into a European context. The hurried production-line circumstances provided little opportunity for the effective assimilation of the material. 'I confess that I didn't even know who had translated the script!' commented Cavalcanti of his first film for Paramount, *Toute sa vie* (1930). After it had been finished he embarked at once on a second French version of an American original, *Les Vacances du diable* (1931).[36] He recalled: 'I felt incessantly while directing it how incredible the atmosphere of that very American [story] would appear to the French public.'[37]

Cameraman Osmond Borradaille, another of the many expatriate production personnel who had settled at Joinville, recalled that in the Paramount bar, 'one heard nothing but comments condemning the script . . . "It is impossible." "There are no such people in my country." "Something like that would never happen where I come from."'[38]

Abandoning Lasky's ambitious plan for remakes of American

films, Paramount-France substituted a programme of original productions. But these rushed films, which were still shot in only two weeks and corralled different language casts into short, inflexible schedules, were scarcely any better. After the initial novelty of talking pictures had worn off, Paramount's box-office receipts films plummeted. In an attempt to find new methods that might rectify the situation, Robert Kane, the American executive in charge of Paramount-France, held negotiations with the playwright Marcel Pagnol for a film version of his play *Marius*, which, after a record-breaking two-year run in Paris, was still playing to packed audiences.

In exchange for the rights to Pagnol's proven success, Robert Kane was forced to concede terms that turned standard Hollywood practices upside-down. Kane had wanted to use Paramount players already familiar to the cinema-going public, but Pagnol considered the proposal an absurdity, since he had shaped and rewritten the play around its original stage cast. Kane considered it an equal absurdity to produce a film without any recognisable box-office stars, but to an extent he was in unknown territory, unable to deny the continuing success of the play.[39]

Granting Pagnol effective 'final cut' over the production, Kane stipulated only that the film should be directed by the then Paramount employee, Alexander Korda, who had recently arrived from Hollywood, where he had directed films for First National and Fox. Although Pagnol was at first sceptical that an ex-Hollywood Hungarian director could capture the idiom of a play set in Marseilles, the cosmopolitan Korda turned out to be a powerful ally, as keen as Pagnol to depart from Paramount's standard production practice for the sake of a more artistically satisfying result. He elicited from the mostly Hollywood-trained crew such a painstaking respect for the original play that one of the stars of the film, Pierre Fresnay, would recall him as 'the vital presence, discreet and indispensable'.[40] *Marius* turned out to be not the product of an assembly-line operation that a

Paramount-Joinville film was originally intended to be, but a carefully crafted, handmade one.

When it was screened, the film ran over two hours. The Paramount executives were horrified by the lengthy dialogue scenes of a film that was forty minutes longer than the average Paramount production, but Kane kept his word that the French version should be exactly as Pagnol had intended.

He received encouragement from the successful release in March of a film adaptation of Marcel Achard's play *Jean de la lune*, produced by Albatros. Enjoying a six-month run in Paris, it was, in the words of a disapproving René Clair, 'acclaimed as a revelation, because [it] was filmed very nearly as if the camera had been trained on the stage of the Comédie des Champs-Elysées'.[41] But whatever it lacked in terms of cinematic qualities, it was a considerable advance in these early days of sound to bring a play to the screen without wholesale bowdlerisation. *Marius* later repeated Achard's box-office success, but however pleased Robert Kane must have been in practical terms, it served as much to demonstrate the viability of a native French cinema that Hollywood's commercial dominance could not displace.

Marius turned out to be a one-off experiment that Paramount found too contrary to its normal working practice to reproduce on a larger scale.[42] In any case, soon afterwards, with the introduction of effective dubbing,[43] the American studio would close down its French subsidiary as superfluous to requirements. But the film and the sequel, *Fanny*, that soon followed, launched Marcel Pagnol as a producer powerful enough to be able to build his own studio in Marseilles in 1934 and to establish his own distribution network.[44] Pagnol was then in turn able to help Jean Renoir, that most uncommercial of film-makers, to make *Toni* (1934), which was shot on location in the Midi, with the support of Pagnol's studio.

Rather than allow Hollywood to swamp the French film industry, as many had feared it might, the advent of sound seemed to offer film-makers an opportunity to take full advantage of

France's powerful cultural tradition, although the extent to which they placed their reliance on the novel or the stage drama would be a cause of considerable controversy among the film aesthetes and theorists, of whom there was never any shortage in France.

Pagnol was as enthusiastic a supporter of filmed theatre as Clair was an opponent. What they shared was the same indefatigable appetite to argue their contrasting views in print. Just days after seeing his first sound film in London – *Broadway Melody*, starring Bessie Love – Pagnol wrote an article arguing for the importance of a technical development that he believed revolutionised the art of the playwright:

> We will be able to write a scene spoken in whispers, yet make it heard by an audience of thousands, without any need to exaggerate the tone or strength of voice. It opens up a whole new set of possibilities, allowing tragedy or comedy to be expressed with a new psychological realism. In place of exaggerated cries and gestures, we will be able to achieve a wonderful simplicity and measure previously unheard of . . . For the first time playwrights will be able to write plays that neither Molière nor Shakespeare had the means to achieve.[45]

For Pagnol sound was the vital missing element that would allow the cinema to extend what the dramatist was able to achieve in the theatre. In his conception, it was not a separate art of its own but an improvement that would enhance the literary essence of a medium that expressed itself chiefly through speech.

Taking issue with Pagnol's 'shocking article' in the film magazine *Pour Vous*,[46] Clair insisted on the distinct nature of the cinema in terms that would have a familiar echo through subsequent film history:

> We know that the term, 'film author', lends itself to a great deal of argument. The public does not know of 'film authors' . . . It only knows – when it condescends to know them – of *metteurs en scène*, a title inherited, like everything else harmful to the cinema, from the theatre. For a long time people have been playing on words and getting away with it. Preposterous as it may seem, the writer who does nothing except

supply the plot is termed an *author*. But if the writer happens to make a film himself, based on his own scenario, he automatically becomes a mere *metteur en scène*. Under the pretext that the cinema – similarly to the theatre or literature – contains a number of incompetents, people pretend not to know that some film-makers are the true authors of their works, in as great and sometimes even greater measure than many dramatists or novelists are of theirs. And it so happens that the most memorable films have in fact been made without contribution from novelists or playwrights.

But Pagnol continued as fiercely to defend his conception of the cinema, in 1933 founding his own magazine, *Cahiers du Film*, to help argue the case. In the debate that raged between the two sides, Clair and Pagnol were effectively figureheads representing the two poles between which the early sound cinema developed: on the one hand, *cinéma sonore*, sound cinema; on the other, *cinéma parlant*, talking cinema. As significant as the divisions between the two sides were the energy and passion with which they argued their respective points of view. It was an example of a persisting film culture in France that seemed always able, even in the most unpromising circumstances, to foster a renewal.

6

A Personal Voice

In early 1930, when the first salvoes of the war over sound were being exchanged in Paris, Jean Vigo was in the south of France working on his first short film with the cameraman Boris Kaufman, brother of the Russian documentarist Dziga Vertov. Longing to make a career in the cinema, the twenty-four-year-old Vigo had come to Nice with the hope of getting experience in the Victorine studios. He had met the directors Leonce Perret and Rex Ingram, but there was no work to be found. Rather than continue to wait for an opportunity that might never come, he took advantage of a windfall from his father-in-law to buy his own camera. As the son of a once-famous anarchist, who had died in prison when he was only ten years old, he had learned not to place too much faith in institutions; the important thing was to seize the moment.

On 28 May 1930, *A propos de Nice* was screened for the first time at the Vieux-Colombier cinema in Paris. It was shown there again two weeks later before a ciné-club that called itself 'The Gathering of Avant-Garde Spectators'. For the occasion, Vigo wrote some notes to explain his thoughts on the cinema.

The blows exchanged over the importance of sound by René Clair and Marcel Pagnol, as well as many other film-makers, seemed ridiculous and irrelevant to Vigo. Setting down his notes in a spontaneous, sometimes irreverent style, he declared that he did not care whether the cinema was silent or talking, in colour or 3D. 'After all, would we expect a writer to tell us whether it was a goose-feather or a pen that he used to write his last novel?'[1] The important thing, he believed, was to work towards a *social* cinema. To work towards such a cinema would be 'to make use of the trove of subjects that contemporary life endlessly renews . . . It would be to avoid the overly aesthetic subtlety of a pure cinema . . .'[2] Attempting to define the phrase 'social cinema' more closely, Vigo reached the following formulation: 'social documentary or more exactly a documented point of view'.[3] In brief, Vigo was counselling a 'cinema with attitude' of the kind that has always posed problems for the commercial film industry, whose chief commitment has necessarily been the making of money.

With the support of a few sympathetic journalists, *A propos de Nice* became a much-discussed debut. Later in the year it would play at the Studio des Ursulines, and Vigo was invited to show the film at the Second Congress of Independent Cinema in December 1930. The prominent names who attended the Congress included Cavalcanti, Eisenstein and Germaine Dulac. Vigo must have experienced the warmth of recognition; but he was about to learn the hardest lesson, of which perhaps an already difficult personal life had given him some inkling: however much individual film-makers may applaud talent or genius, the film industry itself does not care. He may have established a small reputation for himself as an interesting new film-maker, but he still struggled to find work. Through Germaine Dulac, he received a commission to make a short film for Gaumont about the French swimming champion Jean Tauris,* but with no more substantial commission presenting itself he returned to Nice.

Vigo had a young wife and child to support, but project after project continued to fall through. In June 1931, financial hardship forced him to sell the Debrie camera with which he had filmed *A propos de Nice*. His circumstances were dispiritingly precarious, but he continued to show his enthusiasm for the cinema through the film club he had founded in Nice called 'Les Amis du Cinéma'.

Two years went by before Vigo enjoyed a decisive turn in his

* *Tauris, roi de l'eau* (1931).

fortunes. One of the admirers of *A propos de Nice* had been the actor René Lefèvre. Among his friends was the businessman Jacques Louis-Nounez, who wanted to invest in film production. Lefèvre recommended Vigo. After viewing *A propos de Nice* and meeting Vigo, Louis-Nounez was so impressed that he agreed to become Vigo's producer, and went on to secure a co-production deal with Gaumont-Franco-Film-Aubert for Vigo to direct a short film of twelve hundred metres.

On 24 December, Vigo began to film *Zéro de conduite* at Gaumont's Buttes-Chaumont studio, because of the tight schedule continuing to work even when he fell ill. A trade screening took place on 7 April 1933 at the Artistic cinema. In spite of a mostly negative response from the audience of journalists and exhibitors, the film was programmed to accompany the feature *La Maternelle*, but in the event had to be withdrawn when the censorship board refused to pass the film, which it considered subversive.

It was a massive setback, but Louis-Nounez continued to support Vigo. He proposed that the young director should now make a full-length feature, but on a safe subject. 'I've lost a lot of money,' he explained to Vigo's friend Albert Riéra. 'But that doesn't matter. He has a lot of talent, and I know what we must do. We must give him a really anodyne script. That way he'll do something really special, and the censors won't be able to interfere.'[4]

Nounez unearthed a script by an unknown writer called Jean Guinée, which told the story of a barge-boat sailor who marries a country girl. She dreams of the city, quickly tiring of life on board the barge. She runs away and is later found by the bosun of the barge praying in a small chapel. Vigo dismissed the script as middlebrow. At first he was reluctant to direct the film, but eventually saw a way in which he could make it his own.

Nounez convinced Gaumont-Franco-Film-Aubert once again to support the production. Vigo began to film in November 1933, but struggled with persistent illness, considerably worsened by a harsh winter. Immersed in the subject, he pushed himself to work on in the cold. François Truffaut would suggest that Vigo's fever even contributed to the brilliance of what he achieved. 'When one of his friends advised him to husband his strength, to hold back, Vigo answered that he felt he lacked the time and that he had to give everything right away. It seems likely that Jean Vigo, knowing the game was almost up, was stimulated by this measured time.'[5] Lying on what turned out to be his deathbed, Vigo himself confided to a friend, 'I killed myself with *L'Atalante*.'[6]

The trade screening of *L'Atalante* took place on 25 April 1934 at the Palais Rochechouart in the 18th arrondissement, where Vigo had been born twenty-nine years earlier. The response was mixed. Although several critics voiced their admiration for the film, the negative reaction of the exhibitors led Gaumont to insist that it be renamed after a popular song, 'Le Chaland qui passe', which was worked into the soundtrack at the expense of Maurice Jaubert's score.

Vigo was far too ill to offer any real protest. The film opened in the Colisée cinema on 12 September 1934, but closed at the end of the month because of the poor box-office. The film was later released into a few theatres in the provinces, but fared little better. Its fading existence seeming to mirror Vigo's own life slowly ebbing away.

Vigo died on 5 October 1934, having made a handful of beautiful, inspired films. Although they lacked the narrative drive upon which the commercial industry depends to exert its hold over a mass audience, they contained an unforgettable poetry for those who were discerning and patient enough to perceive it.

But his importance lay as much in what he represented. He was the cinema's Chatterton. Fulfilling the Romantic ideal – 'whom the gods love, die young' – he provided a powerful, immensely attractive archetype of creative purity. It is easy to understand why so many subsequent film-makers should have written about him, or even to some extent modelled their lives after him.

One of the first tributes to be written in English, weeks after

Vigo's death, was by Alberto Cavalcanti. He had only recently begun a new career in England at the GPO Film Unit, where he had the opportunity to make the kind of 'social documentary' that Vigo had argued for.

'*Zéro de conduite* is the only film about children in which no compromise of any kind is made with the sentimentality of the so-called commercial cinema,' he wrote in the magazine *Cinema Quarterly*.[7] 'Vigo had courage to show children as seen by themselves, and better still, grown-ups as seen by children.'

Going on to consider *L'Atalante*, Cavalcanti wrote with a clear understanding of the way Vigo's life dramatically epitomised the struggle of the individual artist:

The film is finished. Vigo falls seriously ill. Everyone round him knows that he is doomed. His wife and his friends do all they can to lighten his sufferings. Meanwhile, *L'Atalante* is put into the hands of the distributors. The surrealism of its story with a barge for a hero against a severe background of canals frightens the trade and it insists on making a box-office version.

A theme song is added of which the title is self-explanatory. *Le Chaland qui passe*. This title becomes the title of the film and as a final insult, close-ups of a popular music-hall artiste are superimposed more or less throughout. The mutilation of his work is a torture to Vigo during the last weeks of his illness.

Such was the life of one of the most gifted of young French directors. He could have made great films. He possessed enormous powers not only of imagination, but also of action. And above all, he had the gift of finding a true poetry in the world of the camera. This poetry of reality was his contribution, and it is the chief justification for films today. With the French film industry in its present state his loss is a serious blow. In the French studios such men as he are rare.

From a child in prison with his father, Jean Vigo developed into a man greatly in revolt against the injustices of his generation. Harassed ceaselessly by the Censors and the trade, he personifies the progressive film director in his fight against the stupidity and hypocrisy of the ordinary cinema-world.

Vigo's story may have played itself out during a particularly stifling period in the French cinema's history, when the mainstream commercial cinema, under the domination of the two big companies, Pathé-Natan and Gaumont, allowed little scope for anything different. But the tragic circumstances of his struggle to make films provided an immensely potent model of resistance for the cinema everywhere. His fate had archetypal value, wherever there existed a conflict of interest between the individual artist seeking to express a personal point of view and an entertainment industry whose chief goal was to return a profit to its investors. To this extent, however limited the recognition of his name may continue to be, he belongs not just to the French cinema, but to all our cinemas, and not just to his time but to all times.

The British film director Lindsay Anderson expressed a sense of this when he reviewed the London release of a restored version of *L'Atalante* in 1990.[8] He related an anecdote about a recent visit he had made to Britain's National Film School, where he had found himself startled by a talented young film director's ignorance of cinema history. 'I began to wonder how many distinguished names, knowledge of whom one would assume to be an essential for cinematic literacy, were unknown to the talented young of today. "Have you ever", I asked, "heard of Jean Vigo?" "Jean who?" he asked.'

Assuming an equal ignorance on the part of his readers, Anderson then proceeded to explain who Vigo was, what he suffered and how he died. Of *L'Atalante*, he wrote, it was 'a film which opposes, more wholly and more beautifully than any I can think of, the conception of cinema that largely obtains today – a cinema of sensation, of technical display, of coarse (however sophisticated) commercialism'. The National Film School, he urged, should bus their students up to the cinema to watch the film. 'Attendance compulsory.'

Some two decades previously, Anderson had made *If . . .*, a film that famously owed much to Vigo's inspiration, but we can trace the influence right to the very beginning of Anderson's engagement with the cinema. Even as an undergraduate at Oxford in 1947, writing for the university film magazine *Sequence*, he argued for the kind of personal cinema that Vigo represented:

The first duty of the artist is, not to interpret, nor to propagandise, but to create. And to appreciate that a genuinely creative work of art involves the willingness to jettison our own prejudices and viewpoints, and to accept those of the artist. If you expect all films about children at school to be realistic in style or sociological in approach, you will not be able to get much enjoyment from a fantastic, satirical masterpiece like *Zéro de conduite*. If you have forgotten that poetry, visual as well as verbal, is its own justification, you will call *L'Atalante* sordid and obscure.[9]

Anderson turned to Vigo again a decade later when he drafted a manifesto to help launch 'Free Cinema' at the newly founded National Film Theatre. The very first programme took place on 5 February 1956. Three short films were shown that evening – *Together*, by Lorenza Mazetti, *Momma Don't Allow*, by Karel Reisz and Tony Richardson, and Anderson's *O Dreamland*. In the accompanying programme, Anderson sought to summarise the common attitude:

> As film-makers we believe that
> No film can be too personal.
> The image speaks. Sound amplifies and comments.
> Size is irrelevant. Perfection is not an aim.
> An attitude means a style. A style means an attitude.

The words recall the 'documented point of view' that Vigo had argued for when he wrote notes for the screening of his own film *A propos de Nice* at Le Vieux-Colombier. Anderson made the connection explicit in the notes for *O Dreamland*, which, like Vigo's *A propos de Nice*, was a film about a seaside resort that he had made at his own expense and on his own initiative:

In this short record of some contemporary British ways of pleasure, all the sights and sounds are genuine, that is to say, unstaged. It must therefore be classed, I suppose, as a 'Documentary'. But it is unfortunate that this term has come to suggest little more than a miscellaneous assortment of instructional, informational, 'interest' or advertising shorts.

Perhaps the qualification 'social documentary', used by Jean Vigo when talking about *A propos de Nice*, will suggest the approach more clearly. Vigo said: 'Social documentary is distinct from the ordinary short film and the weekly newsreel in that its creator will establish his own point of view . . . it will dot its own i's. If it doesn't involve an artist, it involves at least a man.' British documentaries, on the other hand, rarely give the impression of having been made by human beings: they seem rather the well-turned product of a highly efficient, standardised industrial process. No rough edges. 'Please one – please all.' This at least cannot (I hope) be said about *O Dreamland*.

Although the Free Cinema programmes at the National Film Theatre ended in 1959, the tradition of 'Free Cinema' – a notion that Vigo would instantly have understood – carried forward into the style of film-making that Anderson, Reisz and Richardson were briefly able to pursue in the commercial film industry of the early 1960s. *Saturday Night and Sunday Morning*, *A Taste of Honey*, *The Loneliness of the Long Distance Runner*, *This Sporting Life* – all these films owe something to Vigo's example.

Arguably, it was the British New Wave of the 1960s that was even more true to Vigo's concept of a 'social cinema' than the French New Wave, which in its tendency to make a fetish of the cinema – what Vigo called the 'overly aesthetic subtlety of a pure cinema' – risked losing sight of the actual world that Vigo believed the cinema should reflect. But one tenet of Vigo that they embraced wholeheartedly was that the cinema should be personal.

It was a belief that accounted for a regrettable rejection of a vast part of their own film heritage. 'If you look at the history of French movies as the talkies began,' wrote François Truffaut, 'you find that between 1930 and 1940 Jean Vigo was almost alone with Jean Renoir the humanist, and Abel Gance the visionary, although the importance of Marcel Pagnol and Sacha Guitry has been underestimated by historians of cinema.'[10] It is an extraordinary suggestion of a wasteland that leaves out of the account – to name only a few of the more prominent names – the directors René Clair, Jacques Feyder, Marcel Carné, Henri Decoin, Jean Grémillon, Christian-Jaque, Jean Delannoy and Julien Duvivier, all of whom were making films during this period. But these directors were perceived as making industry films rather than personal films.

In the distinction lay a great rift that became almost a defining characteristic of the French cinema. Two opposed models of film-making existed sided by side, the one never achieving total ascendancy over the other. There was the industry, which observed the conventional standards of commercial production that were familiar around the world: a collaborative, creative team sought to build a product of mainstream appeal out of such proven box-office ingredients as the best-selling novel, the stage success, the star persona or the popular genre film. And then there was the cinema of personal expression, in which an individual film artist sought to realise *his* vision in celluloid, relying on the support of a technical team, but without necessarily any reference to those conventional box-office ingredients. While the monolithic nature of Hollywood made it very difficult for a film-maker of the latter kind to survive within the system, the French film industry was varied and disparate enough – open enough to the influence of a rich culture in which debate took place in many different forums, whether the ciné-clubs, art houses or magazines – to allow continual interchange between the two spheres.

The very process of interchange modified the character of the industry, making it more ready to accommodate the individual voice, whether from within or without, than its Hollywood counterpart. The film career of the celebrated dramatist and actor Sacha Guitry provides an example of this organic development.

His film *Le Roman d'un tricheur* (*The Story of a Cheat*) was a brilliant, ground-breaking work that demonstrated the huge potential of the cinema, but it was made by someone who had repeatedly dismissed the medium as a second-rate art. This paradox provides an important insight into the production history of a film that was itself all about a paradox. The hero of the story owes his life to a theft he committed when he was a child. Forbidden to have any supper as a punishment, he is spared the poisonous mushrooms that kill the rest of his family. The conclusion he draws is that cheating is the best way to get on in life, but he discovers that he can only cheat successfully when he does not try to cheat.

Sacha Guitry was the son of a famous turn-of-the-century actor, Lucien Guitry. Steeped in the traditions of the theatre, he had written his first successful play, *Nono*, when he was only twenty. By the time he directed his first feature film in 1935, he was able to look back on a hugely successful career in the theatre, as both playwright and actor-manager, that had lasted a quarter of a century.

His fame was such that he could have easily directed films much earlier had he not so disliked them. Indeed, he had been so outspoken in his attacks on the cinema that many people were nonplussed when he decided to involve himself in the medium.

One reason for his change of heart was his discovery in 1935 that the American studio Warner Brothers was making a film about the famous French scientist Louis Pasteur. Guitry had written the first dramatic account of Pasteur's life in 1918. Starring his father, the play had been so successful that it led to an English-language version that opened in New York five years later. Not wanting Warner Brothers to profit from the subject unchallenged, Guitry produced a film version of the play, which he shot in only nine days.*

But it was significant, too, that Guitry had in any case reached an obvious turning point in his life. Not only had he written nearly a hundred plays, but also he was fifty that year and had just married for the second time. His new wife, actress Jacqueline

---

* It opened in New York in early 1936 at the same time as the American film, thus benefiting from the shared publicity.

Delubac, was half his age, as Guitry pointed out himself, when he announced their marriage on his birthday, 21 February 1935: 'Today I celebrate my fiftieth birthday. Jacqueline is twenty-five. It is therefore quite natural that she should become my other half.'[11]

Flamboyant and audacious, Guitry, who epitomised the tradition of boulevard theatre, possessed the kind of facility that made it possible to dash off a play during an afternoon sitting at a marble-topped cafe table. His productivity was such that at one point his plays were showing in four different theatres in Paris at the same time.[12] The way that the film industry seemed to compromise such spontaneous creativity was one reason why he had held it in such low regard.

But this was not a Luddite prejudice against a new medium he did not understand, but a well-informed disdain for an invention that actually fascinated him. Indeed, Guitry already had practical experience of making a film. In 1915, with the support of the French government, he made a short documentary called *Ceux de chez nous* (*Those of Our Land*). Featuring Guitry's meetings with some of France's great musicians, writers, actors and painters, it was intended to counter German wartime propaganda by promoting the enormous contribution that France continued to make to European civilisation. His subjects incuded Sarah Bernhardt and his father Lucien Guitry, the painters Pierre-Auguste Renoir, Edouard Manet and Edgar Degas, the writers Edmond Rostand, Octave Mirbeau and Anatole France. When he turned up to film an elderly Auguste Rodin, he found the sculptor chiselling away at a block of marble dressed up in a black beret and his best suit. 'Tell me to stop when you're ready,' he asked Guitry, 'so that I'll know not to move.'[13] Another memorable sequence in this remarkable historical document is that of the young Jean Renoir standing by his aged father, occupying himself with the various chores that challenged the painter's arthritic fingers.

The film, which makes clear Guitry's high regard for cultural continuity and tradition, offered some explanation of why he should have suspected a medium that had next to no tradition, but it also served as an example of his adventurous, pioneering spirit. It made him determined to harness the full potential of the cinema, while remaining at the same time all too aware of its limitations. When he projected the finished film at the Palais des Variétés in November 1915, he devised a technique to offer the sound that the cinema still could not give: he and his first wife Charlotte Lysès, sitting to one side of the screen, spoke in synchronisation the words that they could be seen saying when they appeared in the film. But in spite of the audience's enthusiastic praise, Guitry was too sophisticated to regard this as other than a clumsy, inelegant solution; and too sophisticated over the years that followed not to notice the thousands of other compromises that the cinema involved, regardless of the considerable technical progress.

In practice *Pasteur* was more a return to the cinema than a debut, but it was an enthusiastic if sceptical re-engagement, which saw Guitry challenge the usual conventions. No sooner had he finished filming *Pasteur* than he went on – having a cast and film crew conveniently at his disposal – to make another film, *Bonne chance* (*Good Luck*), to showcase the talents of his new wife Jacqueline Delubac. Both films then opened together as a double bill in Paris at the Colisée cinema on 20 September 1935. They demonstrated the ease with which he could take to the new medium, but also the impressive range that enabled him to present to his audience in the same bill a sober profile of a revered French scientist, which the *Figaro* praised for its uncompromising devotion to the true story,[14] and a light comedy about an impoverished artist who shares a winning lottery ticket with a laundry girl.

From the outset, Guitry was determined that the industry should surrender to *his* way of working rather than the other way round. Even so, his expressed contempt for the cinema had been such that he felt a need to offer some explanation for the surprising new turn in his career. At a preview of the two films in Biarritz, he introduced the screening with a short speech: 'Ladies and Gentlemen, for ten years I've gone around France and Europe saying how awful the cinema is and now here I am appearing today on the screen!'[15] More flippant than serious in tone, his words seemed little concerned to suggest that he had had any genuine change of heart.

So what have I said about the cinema? That it weakens the performances of even the greatest actors. Now tonight I'm exposing myself to a comparison. But I don't think I'm risking very much: if you think I'm good, I'm very happy to have been wrong. And if you think I'm bad, then it's because I was right all along.

But his comment on actors was just one of many criticisms he had made about the new medium. On 24 April 1936, at just the time when he was making *Le Roman d'un tricheur*, Guitry broadcast on the French radio station, Radio-Cité, the text he had prepared for a lecture tour three years earlier called 'For the Theatre and Against the Cinema'.[16] The cinema lacked spontaneity, he argued, in its canning of actors' performances, rendering impossible the interchange between audience and performer, but also the organic improvement that resulted from that interchange. Aimed at a lowest common denominator rather than a discerning public, it observed 'the monstrous principle that the public knows nothing, understands nothing and refuses to think . . . And the perpetual fear of failing to please drives it to make every possible concession.' The result was a mediocrity, which had the added difficulty of spoiling an audience's taste for the theatre.

Guitry also railed at a mongrel product that was usually cobbled together from second-hand sources without developing a separate, inner life.

Do you know what your films are made out of, when they don't come from America? Out of old novels and plays, twenty, thirty, even fifty years old! Here's a brand-new invention unable to survive without our old plays! . . . I find most French films unbelievably poor. I cannot understand how such an extraordinary invention can be devoted to such asinine activity.'[17]

All these criticisms, which were fresh in his mind as he worked on *Le Roman d'un tricheur*, served as the grit that would produce a pearl. In later years Guitry would often content himself with simply recording his stage plays on film. Like Pagnol, he was too much a man of the theatre to care about the outcry of the cinephiles that he was producing 'filmed theatre' – he didn't mind 'filmed theatre' so long as it was also fine theatre. But *Le Roman d'un tricheur* represented a bold experiment, in which he attempted, free of the usual concessions, to raise the level of the cinema to an ideal of what it might be. He sought to address the shortcomings he had identified, but also to harness its intrinsic qualities.

Sacha Guitry's career can easily bring to mind that of Noël Coward, who was as much the king of the West End theatre as Guitry was of the Boulevard. Their box-office success was such that both men were able to dictate their terms to the film industry. But Coward, who had as little regard for the cinema as Guitry, was content to pass over the reins of the film-making process to his collaborators. *Brief Encounter*, for example, may owe its initial impetus to Coward's one act-play, *Still Life*; but Coward played only a minor role in its transformation, so it makes more sense to speak of it as a David Lean film than as a Noël Coward film.

By contrast, Guitry maintained as commanding a creative presence on the film set and in the cutting room as he had on the stage. He may have had little regard for the cinema, but he had thought too much about it to allow any creative abdication. Demonstrating a remarkable feel for the properties of the film medium, he moulded *Le Roman d'un tricheur* to his liking in every respect, even if he often did not know the technical words for what he wanted to achieve.

The film opens with Guitry signing his name on a white

board. In voiceover, he declares, 'I conceived and directed this film myself.' It was a much more significant statement than one might at first suppose. Guitry wanted to give his audience an assurance that his film was different from the usual cobbled-together, production-line entertainment that he considered to be typical of the cinema. *His* film would be an expression of the author's intentions, rather than the usual travesty of those intentions. Announcing his determination to make use of the unique properties of the cinema from the very outset, he then reverses the sequence, unwriting his name.

Le Roman d'un tricheur (1936)

Ten years later, Jean Cocteau, who happened to be a close friend and former next-door neighbour of Guitry, reprised the idea when he directed *La Belle et la bête*.

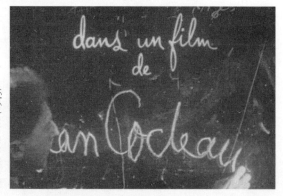

La Belle et la bête (1945)

94

While Cocteau's execution was spare and poetic, Guitry's pioneering introduction was generous and expansive. Having wiped away his name, he continues in voiceover, going behind the scenes to introduce both the production team and the cast. 'The music has been written by my friend Adolphe Borchard': we see Borchard playing some notes on a piano. 'Marcel Lucien recorded the pictures, assisted by Raymond Cluny': we see the two technicians preparing a set-up.

Le Roman d'un tricheur (1936)

And so on: the sound man, Paul Duverger, in his booth; the set designers Guerb and Ménécier arranging a piece of decor; the actresses Marguerite Moreno and Jacqueline Delubac; the singer Fréhel . . . Finally, the camera comes to rest on a man sitting behind a desk. He stands up promptly, as if put out by the interruption, and closes his office door, on which are written the words: 'Directeur du Film, Serge Sandberg'. Guitry brings spontaneity and immediacy by revealing the behind-the-scenes process of film-making. Escaping the sterile, hierarchical credits of cinema convention, with its carefully ordered list of box-office stars and supporting players, Guitry attempts to suggest the warmth and camaraderie of an actor-manager in the theatre surrounded by his onstage and offstage collaborators.

Whether consciously or otherwise, Jean-Luc Godard repeats the opening of *Le Roman d'un tricheur* in his own film about film-making, *Le Mépris*. The first image is of the film crew in the distance commencing a tracking shot. As they slowly approach, a voiceover enumerates the actors and film crew. Godard passes into the story proper by having his cinematographer Raoul Coutard tilt the camera downwards and then cutting to a corresponding high-angle shot of Brigitte Bardot and Michel Piccoli lying together on a bed.

Le Mépris (1963)

Guitry makes the transition into his fictional world through a shadow on a blank screen that turns out to be the blind of a cafe window. A shadow figure lifts up a glass of beer in silhouette and, with a cut to the opening scene, Guitry puts it down again in the persona of his character, the Cheat. He may have bemoaned the derivative nature of the cinema, with its dependency on old books and plays, but both his innovative use of film form and the command that he maintained over his material were helping to strengthen the alternative tradition of a cinema of personal expression that, with varying degrees of success, Gance, Cocteau and Vigo had pursued before him.

Le Roman d'un tricheur is based on the only novel that Guitry ever wrote, *Les Mémoires d'un tricheur*, which Gallimard published late in 1935. As Guitry embarked on production of the film only months later, it seems likely that he planned to transform the novel into a film from the outset. There is an organic relationship between the two, so that the novel, which is little more than a hundred pages long, seems like a sketch for the film that provides its full realisation. The book is illustrated by

Le Roman d'un tricheur (1936)

Le Roman d'un tricheur (1936)

some simple but charming line drawings that Guitry did himself. It is as if these drawings expanded and soaked up the entire narrative, so that it is impossible to disentangle the respective importance of text and picture. The words breathe life into the images; and the images breathe life into the words. The novel is best thought of not as a separate entity, but as the starting point for the venture as a whole.

The image of the 'Cheat' writing his memoirs at a cafe table provides the framework for a film whose images correspond to the voiceover narrative, yet are in themselves effectively silent, just as our memories of the past are silent. The device permits Guitry to use both word and image with an extraordinary fluidity and freedom. His tale of a reluctant cheat drawn inevitably to the gambling tables of Monaco allows scope for a raconteur's wit and digression, the essential charm of the film lying in the way it captures the idle fancies of the mind without being subject to the usual tyranny of conventional film narrative. Recalling his arrival in Monte Carlo for the first time, the narrator is able to break off from an account of his own adventures to muse with a gentle but perceptive wit on the nature of the gambler's town in which he finds himself. 'In geographical terms, it is a rock in the shape of a dog's head . . .' Passing effortlessly from conventional fictional narrative into documentary travelogue, Guitry maintains the underlying thread through the consistency of the narrator's voice, always alive to the ironies of existence, whether in his own life or in the people and places he observes.

Guitry uses images with as much ingenuity as words, but the sheer prevalence of those words challenges the ability of subtitles to do them justice. It is perhaps this simple fact that makes him a largely forgotten presence in the English-speaking world, although his combination of wit, style and accessibility ought to make him as well known as Noël Coward. In 1936, soon after the release of *Le Roman d'un tricheur* in a small art-house cinema in New York, *Time* magazine wrote, 'Noël Coward is not so penetrating a comedian or author as Sacha Guitry, but Mr Coward has the good fortune to write and act in English, the language which pays best.'[18]

In Britain or America it may be an all-too-rare pleasure to be able to see a Guitry film, but nonetheless he still has an enormous, if largely unappreciated, importance as the person who proved that word and image can be harmonious partners, and that the cinema can be as effective a vehicle for the expression of complex ideas as literature.

While the French have been able to find an honourable place for Guitry in their film tradition, it is perhaps significant that his most notable influence in the English-language cinema, where the industrial model has been more dominant, was on one of its more maverick talents. When at the beginning of the Second

World War Alberto Cavalcanti was working as a documentary producer at the GPO Film Unit, he hired a young French-speaking editor, Robert Hamer, to work on a propaganda film called *French Communiqué*, which described life on the Maginot Line in the early days of the conflict. When Cavalcanti moved on to Ealing Studios, he took his Francophile editor with him. There, Hamer eventually graduated to directing. In 1947, he made the crime drama *It Always Rains on Sunday*. A dark, brooding film that drew obvious inspiration from Marcel Carné and Jacques Prévert's *Quai des brumes* and *Le Jour se lève*, its box-office success enabled Hamer to embark on another production that, at odds with the social-realist style of film-making that the production head Michael Balcon encouraged at Ealing, turned once again to France for an appropriate model.

The whole approach and style of *Kind Hearts and Coronets* takes its inspiration from Guitry's film. There is the same framework of the chief protagonist sitting down to write his memoirs, the same delight in paradox, the same use of epigrammatic wit and irony to turn conventional morality on its head. Musing on some of the practical difficulties of committing murder, Hamer's 'hero', Louis Mazzini, reflects, 'It is so difficult to make a neat job of killing people with whom one is not on friendly terms.' And later, commenting on one of the many small deceits of social convention, he observes: 'Nine times out of ten, what is referred to as a matter of some delicacy, is in point of fact one of extreme indelicacy.' This was a use of language that Guitry would have relished.

Summarising what he had hoped to achieve with *Kind Hearts*, Hamer wrote:

Firstly, that of making a film not noticeably similar to any previously made in the English language. Secondly, that of using this English language, which I love, in a more varied and, to me, more interesting way than I had previously had the chance of doing in a film. Thirdly, that of making a picture which paid no regard whatever to established, although not practised, moral convention.[19]

Substitute the words 'French' for 'English', and it would be easy to imagine Guitry writing exactly the same of *Un Roman d'un tricheur*.

Reviewing the film in the *New York Times*, Frank Nugent commented on the inevitable curiosity one must feel about 'the kind of fellow who is not satisfied with writing, directing and starring in a picture, but must play seven or eight character roles as well. To Guitry, then, and blast his delightful impudence!'[20] It was with the same spirit of impudence that, in *Kind Hearts and Coronets*, Alec Guinness was cast in the roles of all eight members of the D'Ascoyne family.

Indeed, the shared sensibility of Hamer and Guitry makes the differences in their outlook all the more striking. Guitry's hero is a cheat; Hamer's is a murderer. Guitry's hero responds to the hypocrisy of the world with an amused stoicism, Hamer's with contempt. While the Cheat's reverses do not shake his fundamental belief in humanity, Louis Mazzini's disappointed idealism turns to a destructive cynicism. Irony is a distinctive characteristic of Guitry's cinema, but it was the irony of an insider who occupied a central position in French culture. He had known too much acceptance to be cynical. Working in a different, more industrialised system, where the tradition for a cinema of personal expression was far weaker, Hamer would never again have an opportunity to make a film with such freedom. Project after project that he proposed to Ealing would be turned down. *Kind Hearts* was a glorious exception to the rule. While Guitry belonged to an alternative but recognised tradition in his own country, in Britain or America the cinema of personal expression was always against the grain.

7

The Professional

If I was an architect and I had to build a palace to the cinema, I would put at its entrance a statue of Duvivier.

Jean Renoir[1]

To understand Renoir's comment it helps to imagine what his palace of the cinema would have looked like. To the extent that it reflected the 1930s French cinema in which he himself worked, it was a building designed to be accessible not to a select few but to everyone. In its combination of grandeur and simplicity, it possessed a classicism that other architects in Hollywood or London could emulate. It was the work of a team of artists, even if it was possible to discern a guiding hand that coordinated their efforts. It was dedicated to a mainstream, collaborative cinema that valued great stories, spectacle and stars.

It is a somewhat forgotten palace today because the generation that followed Renoir was as eager to pull down statues as put them up. Rather than value the two great traditions of film-making that had existed in France before the war – the popular, commercial cinema alongside the cinema of personal expression – they chose to champion the latter at the expense of the former. The denial of the past contained all the savagery of a revolution, whose after-effects continue today to compromise a proper appreciation of French film history.

The event that has come to symbolise the moment of rupture was not the storming of a prison but a polemical essay written by a young François Truffaut. Published in 1954 in the then recently founded film magazine, *Cahiers du cinéma*, 'A Certain Tendency in the French Cinema' launched a scathing attack on the 'tradition of quality' that had come to the fore in the main-stream French film industry of the 1930s.

The extent to which the essay serves as a kind of Bastille Day can be gauged by the fact that in 2004 the French Ministry of Culture celebrated the fiftieth anniversary of its publication in its annual bulletin of French achievements. On the Ministry's official website can be found the following account of its importance:

There exists an essay about fifteen pages long to which histories of the cinema accord a special place: 'A Certain Tendency in the French Cinema', written by François Truffaut, published in the 31st issue of *Cahiers du cinéma* in January 1954. It is a unique achievement: without question the only piece of critical writing to amount to a decisive break in the history of an art-form . . . [Truffaut] signed the death warrant of the 'Qualité française', and, with the same stroke of the pen, brought into being the 'Nouvelle Vague'.

In returning to the French cinema's *ancien régime*, this chapter will look at the film-maker that Renoir singled out as its most representative figure. Little known today, Julien Duvivier was once considered to be one of the world's greatest directors, although he was disinclined to claim a personal style or set of values. What mattered most to him was to find a good subject, whether novel or original script, that he could turn into a strong story on the screen. This approach accounted for a notably wide range of subject-matter.

Reluctant to be intellectual about the cinema, Duvivier talked about his craft infrequently, but when he did, he did so with the intuitive common sense of a practitioner. Asked in a 1962 inter-view about the then controversial distinction between a metteur-en-scène and an auteur, this is what he replied:

I think there are some *metteurs-en-scène* who are authors, some *metteurs-en-scène* who are only *metteurs-en-scène*, and some authors who are *metteurs-en-scène*. To give an example, a film by Pagnol, even if it's put on the stage by someone else, is always a Pagnol film. I've made lots of films with the same scriptwriter, for example Henri Jeanson, whom I like a lot, with Charles Spaak – but I think the film is still a film by Duvivier because the rhythm, the light, the framing, all the details that make up a film – that make a film a certain kind of art – mean that the author of the subject has less importance.

Writing about Duvivier in 1938, the British novelist and film critic Graham Greene rated him alongside Fritz Lang 'as the two greatest fiction directors still at work'.[2] Today it requires some effort to track down the mostly neglected films that would have provided a basis for this judgement, but to do so reveals an obvious master who lives up to Greene's estimate. To watch *Poil de Carotte*, *Pépé le Moko* or *Carnet de bal* at first makes it seem a mystery that Truffaut's generation had so little appreciation of his work. But the individualist dogma of the time – demanding directors who shot movies the way writers wrote books – made it inconvenient for this new generation to value a director whose approach represented the antithesis of the kind of cinema they wanted to achieve. Truffaut's generation had to pull down his statue – and the palace – to make space for the new cinema they wanted to build.

Solitary and reserved, Duvivier was a difficult person to get to know. Seeking to explain him, his friend Maurice Bessy – a journalist who had worked for Duvivier as a screenwriter – began his portrait on the stage of the Odéon Theatre in Paris, where during the First World War Duvivier made his debut as an actor:

Not a word escaped his lips. The prompter whispered his lines, whispered them again, almost shouted them to him. His fellow actors tried to help. But it was no use. He had fallen into a black hole. They had to lower the curtain. That was his first and last appearance. This fear, which Julien Duvivier never managed to overcome, entrenched a profound shyness, which he hid behind a mean character.[3]

Bessy traced the root of this shyness back to Duvivier's very conventional and strict *petit bourgeois* upbringing in the northern city of Lille, where he was born in 1896. Meals were eaten in silence and any show of intimacy discouraged. His grandfather owned a shoe shop, and his father was a travelling salesman.

The focus of family discussions was firmly on business and trade, with the artistic inclinations of the young Julien discouraged. 'I had a passion for the theatre,' he recalled, 'although I don't know where I got it from, since, through my childhood, I was never allowed to go there. It was only when I was old enough to go out on my own that I was able to get to know it. But before then, I would read about it, and that fired my enthusiasm.'[4]

It is easy to understand how the idea of becoming an actor might have appealed to him as a way of expressing the emotions it was so difficult to show at home, but that ambition crumbled with the disastrous night at the Odéon. Duvivier recalled that after the curtain had fallen, André Antoine, who was then the director of the Odéon, came backstage to comfort him. 'He said why are you crying? It's not your fault. You don't have the physique for this, you don't have the voice, you don't have what it takes. This is not a career for you . . . Come with me. Work with me in the cinema.'[5]

Duvivier was assistant to Antoine on *Les Frères corses*, as well as most of the other films that Antoine made during the First World War – *Le Coupable* (1917), *Les Travailleurs de la mer* (1917) and *La Terre* (1919). The apprenticeship with Antoine served to inculcate a regard for a psychological realism. Looking back, Duvivier agreed with Delluc's assessment of *Les Frères corses* that these early films were too 'theatrical'. But at the start of his career, to film theatre seemed enough. It was only later, as he learned the potential of film through practice, that creating cinema, as opposed to theatre, became a distinct, separate ambition.

In contrast to a Louis Delluc or a François Truffaut, Duvivier's ideas about the cinema developed through practice, rather than theory. As the only career he had was making films, it was important for him to keep working, which meant taking on projects for which he might not always have felt any great enthusiasm. His debut as a director in 1919 with a revenge drama called *Halcedama ou Le Prix du sang* was an assignment that he would not have chosen for himself, but it was an opportunity to learn more about his craft, and, as important, to work.

From the outset, Duvivier took pride in his professionalism. But as a practitioner rather than a theorist, he avoided making any great claims for the cinema as an art. Starting out as a director just at the point when the French film industry was in full retreat, it was perhaps natural that he should have looked elsewhere for a positive model of what the cinema could be. Impressed by a visit to London in 1921, he made no effort to hide how poorly he thought the French cinema came out in comparison: 'In England as in America, people realise that the cinema is an industry and not a child's toy or a dilettante's hobby . . . From the point of view of their equipment, the three main studios in London will soon have overtaken ours.'[6] The way forward for the French cinema, he recommended, was to adopt an 'Anglo-Saxon mindset, which means choosing simple, universal subjects'.

Prepared to move from one assignment to the next even if his heart wasn't entirely in it, Duvivier had already directed ten films when in 1926 he had the good fortune to find the kind of 'simple, universal subject' that most appealed to him. *Poil de Carotte* was the story of a neglected child who has an indifferent father and a harsh, unloving mother. It may have been based on Jules Renard's autobiographical novel, but Duvivier identified so strongly with the subject-matter that he made it his own. 'Poil de Carotte is every unhappy child who is victim to the ill feeling between his parents,' he commented of a subject that struck a personal chord. 'I've met him in the north of France, where I was brought up, and I've seen him living in the sunshine of the Midi.'[7] Unhappy in his marriage, Poil de Carotte's father Monsieur Lepic withdraws into himself, as his own unhappiness blinds him to the misery of his son, but gradually a close bond between the two is rebuilt.

A memory from the past that haunted Duvivier was that of being forced to leave Lille with his father soon after the outbreak of the First World War. Amidst the German bombardment, they set off on the road to Valenciennes, walking side by side without exchanging a word. When finally they stopped exhausted to rest by the roadside, his father, briefly touching him, whispered in the despair of the situation: 'My poor child, my poor child . . .' It was the one time that Duvivier could recall his father showing him any affection. Of the anecdote, Maurice Bessy commented, 'It took me thirty years to get it out of him, and Julien had the same trouble confiding the words to me as his father had saying them in the first place.'[8]

Duvivier's own experience of growing up had been one of longing for love but having to steel himself to live without it. The emotional repression of his childhood explained the pragmatism with which he could buckle down to the assignment and at the same time the special appeal of *Poil de Carotte*. 'One subject, always the same, pursued him through his life,' commented Maurice Bessy, '*Poil de Carotte*.'[9]

The 1926 silent version, starring Henri Krauss, Charlotte Barbier-Krauss, and André Heuzé in the title role, was a commercial and critical success that became an early benchmark of achievement for Duvivier, as he acknowledged in an interview with the film magazine *Cinémonde* in 1931. 'My favourite film? Without any doubt, it's *Poile de carotte*. Of all the films I've made, that's the one that has remained the most precious to me. I love films that have atmosphere, and *Poil de Carotte* is such a film. What have I done since? I've stagnated, to be honest.'[10]

Perhaps the frankness of the comment owed something to his knowledge that he was about to make the film again. The sound version, he explained, would not be simply a matter of synchronisation but an opportunity to attempt a total reworking. The result was another major success that helped to make Duvivier's name around the world. But even this second version did not sate his appetite for the story. During the Second World War, when Duvivier was working in Hollywood, he wanted to make an English-language version set in New England. He wrote an

Americanised scenario called *Nobody's Kid*, envisaging the role of the boy's father for Charles Laughton, whom Duvivier had directed in *Tales of Manhattan* in 1942. Although the project fell through, towards the end of the 1950s Duvivier once again tried to bring the story to the screen. This time his idea was to make a French version of the film in colour, with Jean Gabin playing the role of Monsieur Lepic, but Gabin turned the part down.

Had he decided otherwise, it might have provided an appropriate closing of the circle, because during the 1930s it was through the creation of the Jean Gabin star persona that Duvivier went on to develop the themes of exile, loneliness and rejection that he had first explored in *Poil de Carotte*. Their partnership dated back to Duvivier's film *Maria Chapdelaine* in 1934. Although Gabin played only a secondary role, actor and director discovered during the production that they shared a taste for the work of the novelist Pierre Mac Orlan. 'One day,' recalled Gabin, 'I was chatting to Duvivier about film ideas and I told him how much I loved [Mac Orlan's] *La Bandera*. He replied, "Me too! But although I've suggested the idea to several producers, no one wants to do it." When the subject came up again a few days later, we decided to take out an option together.'[11]

La Bandera tells the story of Pierre Gilieth, who is accused of murder. Fleeing France, he joins the Spanish Foreign Legion and is posted to North Africa, where he falls in love with a Bedouin girl, Aisha. But his nemesis arrives in the form of French detective Fernando Lucas who is determined to bring him back to France to face justice. The 'undertone of sadness and disappointment' that Greene recognised in Duvivier's work was evident. Like the misfit child in *Poil de Carotte*, Gilieth is condemned to live on the margins and his love for Aisha turns out to be a doomed love.

The success of *La Bandera* turned Jean Gabin into a star, establishing the type of the tragic victim of society that Duvivier would further develop in *La Belle Equipe* and *Pépé le Moko*. Gabin is the solid and decent proletarian, whom bad luck puts on the wrong side of the law. Usually fated to fall unhappily in love, he is prey to his emotions and cursed by a self-destructive streak that is as likely to express itself in violence against himself as against others. The persona was forged in Duvivier's films, but, suiting the fatalistic atmosphere of the late 1930s, Gabin carried it with remarkable consistency into the films he made with other directors during the period.

In *Gueule d'amour*, directed by Jean Grémillon, he plays ex-soldier Lucien Bourrache who, arriving in Paris, falls in love with socialite Madeleine Courtois (Mireille Balin). She plays with his affections and then rejects him in favour of a rich protector. Disillusioned, Lucien leaves Paris, opening a cafe in the provincial town where he had served in the army, but fate causes him to cross paths with Madeleine one more time: overcome by a fit of rage, he strangles her.

In Marcel Carné's *Quai des brumes*, based on another novel by Pierre Mac Orlan, he is a deserter who falls in love with Nelly, a girl he meets in an isolated seaside inn. To protect her, he beats up local gangster Lucien and kills her evil guardian Zabel, only to be gunned down before he can escape on a boat about to leave for South America. In the second film he made for Carné, *Le Jour se lève*, in 1939, he plays factory worker François, who is besieged by the police in his dingy apartment after killing a man in a crime of passion.

In Jean Renoir's screen version of Zola's *La Bête humaine*, he plays engine driver Jacques Lantier. Afflicted by a hereditary tendency to alcohol-induced violence, Lantier kills his lover in a fit of fury and then throws himself to his death from his train engine.

'I have never wanted to appear in whatever came along,' Gabin explained in 1939. 'I have waited for the right directors. With Renoir, Carné or Duvivier, I felt safe.'[12] As the screenwriter Charles Spaak, who wrote the script for *La Bandera*, put it, one could admire Gabin 'for the films he's made, but also for those that he's spared us'.[13] From 1936 onwards, Gabin was the most popular actor in France, but he chose judiciously, moulding his image after the model that he and Duvivier had first established.

If Gabin's star persona was an important engine driving the French cinema forward during the late 1930s, Duvivier played as vital a part in its construction. With *Poil de Carotte, La Bandera* and *Pépe le Moko*, he shaped the cinema of poetic realism that so dominated the French cinema in this period. Embroidering upon the mood and style of Duvivier, the films of Carné and Prévert developed a more baroque variant, which exploited Prévert's flair for language, paradox and the surreal, poetic image, but the root of the Gabin character was already there.

But if Duvivier was clearly a key contributor to French poetic realism, the fall from grace that he suffered in the 1950s hid the extent of the impact he also made on the British and American cinemas. In Britain, Graham Greene remembered his admiration for Duvivier when after the war he was invited by Sir Alexander Korda to write a screenplay for the director Carol Reed. A touching study of lonely, neglected childhood, *The Fallen Idol* observes the same psychological dynamic as *Poil de Carotte*. The son of an ambassador, Philippe may be a privileged child, but his mother is in hospital and his busy, distant father away on a trip. In their absence the boy is entrusted to the care of the Embassy's butler and housekeeper, Mr and Mrs Baines, who are trapped in a bitterly unhappy marriage. The failing relationship of these surrogate parents causes Mrs Baines to treat him with as much contempt as she sees her husband show him sympathy.

In its quiet way *The Fallen Idol* is a near-perfect film. It would be overshadowed by Greene's next collaboration with Reed, the more obviously crowd-pleasing *The Third Man*, but this too owed much to Duvivier's inspiration. Over ten years before, Greene had written an admiring review of Duvivier's compendium film *Carnet de bal*, about a recently widowed woman, Christine, who finds an old dance card from when she was young. In a story suffused with Duvivier's usual melancholy, she discovers varying degrees of disappointment as she traces her old partners. 'In one episode,' wrote Greene,

we have Duvivier's real greatness – the seedy doctor at Marseilles so used to furtive visitors and illegal operations that he doesn't wait for questions before he lights the spirit flame: the dreadful cataracted eye: the ingrained dirt upon his hands; the shrewish wife picked up in God knows what low music-hall railing behind bead curtains: the continuous shriek and grind of winch and crane. Nostalgia, sentiment, regret: the padded and opulent emotions wither before the evil detail: the camera shoots at a slant so that the dingy flat rears like a sinking ship. You have to struggle to the door, but you can run downhill to the medical couch and the bead curtains. There has been nothing to equal this episode since *Pépé*.[14]

Soon after Greene wrote this review, a world war intervened, dictating different priorities for the British cinema. But the return of peace coincided with the British rediscovery of poetic realism. *Quai des brumes*, which had first been shown in London in January 1939, was revived in 1944. In the *News Chronicle*, the film critic Richard Winnington hailed the 'revival of a great film, which I, like many others, consider to be the best French film ever made'.[15] When *Le Jour se lève* was revived in turn in May 1946, it became a small cause célèbre, with film writers reporting that it would be the last opportunity for the public to see a film that Hollywood had bought and intended to suppress so that it could produce its own inferior version.* The episode from *Carnet de bal* that Greene had so admired before the war would be reprised ten years later with the celebrated canted shots of *The Third Man*, in which he and Carol Reed evoked the same sense of corrosive corruption by extending the crooked, cock-eyed angles of the doctor's flat to an entire city. But Greene had already long ago drawn on the scene for his fiction. The crooked lawyer Mr Prewitt, who in *Brighton Rock* advises the gangster Pinkie while lamenting the degradation into which he has fallen, was a thinly veiled version of the seedy doctor.

* *The Long Night* (1947), directed by Anatole Litvak and starring Henry Fonda.

The debt to *Pépé le Moko* was as striking. In *The Third Man*, Greene and Reed transform the labyrinth of the Casbah – which provides the fugitive Pépé with a refuge from justice – into Harry Lime's underworld sanctuary beneath the sewers.

Their shared liking for Duvivier was a mark of the affinity that made Greene and Reed one of the most notable partnerships in the British cinema. Reed's own admiration of the French director was evident even before Korda paired him with Greene. The finale of his 1945 film *Odd Man Out* memorably reworks the ending of *Pépé le Moko*. In Duvivier's ending, Pépé is trapped by the police at the gates to the docks. Through the bars he can see Gaby, the woman with whom he has fallen in love, on board the ship that he had hoped would take them both to freedom. He stabs himself rather than face life in prison without her. In *Odd Man Out*, Kathleen is in love with wounded fugitive Johnny Macqueen. She succeeds in bringing him to the dockside. She had hoped that he would be able to escape aboard a departing ship, but now finds their progress impeded by the metal palings of a perimeter fence. As the police close in, she looses off a shot in their direction, knowing that their return fire will unite her with Johnny for ever. In *The Third Man*, meanwhile, Greene and Reed produce yet another variant on the *Pépé le Moko* ending. Cornered by the police in the sewers, Harry Lime's fingers reach up through the grille of a manhole cover to feel the breeze in the streets above. Rather than face capture, Harry quietly begs his friend Holly Martins to shoot him.

Of all the directors at work in the French cinema during the 1930s, it is Julien Duvivier who represents the point at which the classic French cinema and the English-language cinema came closest to each other. This is true not only for British cinema but also for Hollywood, on which he had just as substantial if as little appreciated an influence. The contribution he made is worth dwelling on, because it illustrates the distinctive characteristics of the two cinemas as well as the extent to which they could be dependent upon each other. Both the reliance and the difference are at their most apparent in *Pépé le Moko*, which inspired the Hollywood remake *Algiers* and cleared the way for that iconic example of the classical Hollywood style, *Casablanca*.

According to his own recollection, it was the actor Jean Gabin who first had the idea of filming *Pépé le Moko*, after reading the novel, which had been published by the writer Henri La Barthe in 1931 under the pseudonym 'Detective Ashelbe'.[16] He then took the idea to Duvivier, who was equally enthusiastic. The producers Robert and Raymond Hakim, who had just founded their production company Paris Film, agreed to back the actor–director partnership, in light of the considerable box-office success they had won with *La Bandera* (1935).

Duvivier spent a few days in Algiers location-hunting during September or October of 1936. He then returned to the city for a week in November to film exteriors. The stars, Jean Gabin and Line Noro, travelled with him, on board the ship *Ville d'Oran*, which features in the finale of the film. Noro would recall wandering with Gabin and Duvivier 'in the native quarters', where she was able to take inspiration from 'living models'.[17]

While Duvivier was the key creative and organising force, in the case of the Hollywood remake, *Algiers*, this role belonged to the independent producer Walter Wanger, who released his films through United Artists. Wanger bought the remake rights from MGM as a star vehicle for Charles Boyer, whom he had under a two-film contract. At the same time he bought the world distribution rights to the Duvivier film, withdrawing the prints in the United States to facilitate the release of his remake version. For all the impressive advance that the French cinema had made in the 1930s, the box-office logic was still such that a far greater return could be made by financing and distributing an American remake than by showing the French original, however superior it might be.

Wanger's whole approach was geared to the careful commercial exploitation of a proven property. He hired the writers James

Cain and John Howard Lawson to rewrite the original French story – just enough to meet the requirements of the Production Code, but otherwise following it as closely as possible. He then brought in John Cromwell to direct.

The film is a good example of how the contemporary convention of citing only the director's name in referring to a film so often leads to the burial of a film's true creative provenance.[18] Having just finished *The Prisoner of Zenda* (1937) for David Selznick, Cromwell was a veteran of Hollywood's factory system, where directors were either employees expected to direct the picture that their line producer had assigned to them, or freelancers who took on assignments with as much discrimination as barristers in England observing the cab-rank rule. He could be relied upon to implement Wanger's instructions, and not indulge any creative whims of his own. His reputation in the industry was as an actor's director capable of building the star value of his players. Hedy Lamarr, whom MGM had loaned out for the film, recalled Louis B. Mayer assuring her: 'As for your part, it is a good one. You lure a criminal to his doom. Even so, you will have the audience with you. John Cromwell will be directing. He is a women's director. He will nurture your beauty. The camera will always caress you lovingly. Cromwell is like that.'[19]

Wanger instructed the cinematographer James Wong Howe to shoot the film as closely as possible to the French model and, likewise, told the art director Alexander Toluboff to copy the sets so exactly that in the finished movie they are nearly indistinguishable. The same Vincent Scotto score provided the music soundtrack, and even Duvivier's location footage was retained to provide a documentary explanation of the Casbah in the opening scene.

Duvivier's original film was used less as an inspiration than as a blueprint. Boyer recalled that Cromwell 'would run a scene from the original and insist we do it exactly that way'.[20] The actor, who was a friend of Duvivier, dismissed the experience as 'a perfectly terrible way to work', but Wanger had sound business reasons for a procedure that made the usually uncertain and risky business of film-making just about as predictable and economical as it could be.

The technique inevitably recalls Paramount's 1930 plan to make European remakes of its American movies in France, when Jesse Lasky explained that the American original would provide a model that the 'French producer need only follow to the letter'. As we have seen, cultural difficulties caused the studio to abandon those attempts, but now here was Wanger trying the same experiment the other way round.

The trade press applauded the attempt. 'Walter Wanger's *Algiers* is the first picture ever made in Hollywood, adapted from a European success, that emerges an even greater success than the subject from which it was adapted,' declared the *Hollywood Reporter* on 24 June 1938. 'It is quite evident that Wanger instructed his writer, his director, his art director and cameraman to follow the French success as closely as it would be possible to do so. And they did, and further improved on it, bringing to Mr Wanger his greatest success in the production of screen entertainment. The picture is a certain hit before any audience.'

The emphasis of the article was on the Hollywood professionalism and discipline required. 'John Cromwell, the director, and John Howard Lawson, who adapted *Algiers*, did just what they were supposed to, and made a perfect adaptation.' The article was aimed at a readership of film-industry workers, who understood the strict framework of their trade, where it was the producer and the box-office that called the tune. As far as the *Hollywood Reporter* was concerned, the key criterion for accomplishment was whether a polished piece of entertainment would find an audience; whether it could be considered 'art' was irrelevant.

While the origin of *Algiers* was well known and openly reported within the industry itself, Wanger deliberately concealed the existence of the earlier French film from the wider public. In the credits of the film, the original novel of *Pépé le Moko*, by Detective Ashelbe, is cited, but not Henri Jeanson's and Julien Duvivier's film script, from which John Howard Lawson and James Cain drew their American version. When *Algiers* opened at the Radio City Music Hall in July 1938, the New York critics wrote about it as though it were a completely new film. The *New York Times*'s response is typical of the mostly favourable reviews:

John Cromwell, who has directed the film, has wound the drama's mainspring tight. Its seconds tick off like a pulsebeat in an accelerating rhythm of destiny – hopeless, inexorable, tragic destiny. Few films this season, or any other, have sustained their mood so brilliantly. Mr Cromwell has not done it alone, of course. The story was there, and the John Howard Lawson–James Cain adaptation of it, with its poetic economy of words and ample room within them for its players to build character . . . So you have it briefly; one of the finest directorial jobs, one of the most rewarding in its performances, clearly one of the most interesting and absorbing dramas of the season.[21]

The 'poetic economy of words' really belonged to the original *Pépé le Moko* script, which Lawson and Cain closely copied, and the 'finest directorial job' to Julien Duvivier – but the original creators had sold away their right to complain. After a week at the Radio City Music Hall, *Algiers* had taken $96,200 and was held over for another week.[22] It went on to be one of the biggest box-office successes of 1938.

Pépé le Moko drew obvious inspiration from the Hollywood gangster films of the early 1930s, most notably Howard Hawks' *Scarface* (1932), but that influence expressed itself in *mise-en-scène* rather than psychological depth of character. In *Scarface*, Hawks gives dramatic presence to each member of Tony Camonte's gang, through providing each with a memorable tic of behaviour that is repeated several times through the film. Perhaps most famously, George Raft, as Tony Camonte's sidekick Guino Rinaldo, is seen always tossing a coin. This gesture provides direct inspiration in *Pépé le Moko* for the character of gang member Jimmy (Gaston Modot), whom we always see catching a ball in a cup.

Duvivier also plainly felt on his mettle to rival the heightened style with which Hawks staged the gangland killings, but while the endless succession of such incidents in *Scarface* operates chiefly as an exercise in Hollywood spectacle – machine-guns rattling, windows shattering, cars crashing into one another – the one comparable scene in *Pépé le Moko*, where the gang members execute the informer Regis, is woven carefully into the fabric of a larger psychological drama. Duvivier was able to borrow and assimilate freely, producing a work of art that achieved creative independence from its models.

Whatever the superficial resemblances, the films seem to me more notable for exemplifying the difference between the two opposing traditions of the cinema to which they belong. Working in France's much more open system, Duvivier was able to attempt a realistic examination of a flawed but sympathetic character, while in the more regimented cinema of Hollywood Hawks had to produce the kind of polarised, moral drama that the Production Code encouraged.

Established as a cold-blooded killer from the opening scene, Tony Camonte is a monster, with no redeeming qualities of any kind. Although this fulfilled the requirement of the Production Code that 'the sympathy of the audience should never be thrown to the side of crime', it denied Camonte the human complexity that usually sustains drama. Less a recognisable human being than a dangerous freak of nature, Camonte belonged to the same category as Godzilla or the Creature from the Black Lagoon. If this was itself yet another tendency of the Code – that external spectacle should compensate for the absence of permissible inner human motivation – it met also the Hollywood need to satisfy a mass audience's preference for action over psychology.

It wasn't until 1941, when *Algiers* had exhausted its box-office potential, that the American public had an opportunity to consider the French original that Wanger had so carefully copied. *Pépé le Moko* was released in the United States in March 1941.

The *New York Times* singled out the film for the kind of frankness and realism of performance that American censorship made a rare occurrence in Hollywood films:

Jean Gabin's tough, unsentimental performance of the title role is much more credible and revealing than Charles Boyer's sad-eyed mooning as Pépé in *Algiers*; Mireille Balin is indeed more authoritative as a practical femme fatale than was Hedy Lamarr, and Line Noro certainly looks much more the part of a cast-off Algerian mistress than did Sigrid Gurie . . . Without criticising *Algiers*, which was an exciting film in its own right, it can be fairly said that *Pépé le Moko* tells the same story more trenchantly and with decidedly more true flavor. For, after all, it was made in a France which wasn't too squeamish about facts – the sort of facts, anyhow, which it contains.[23]

As the film made its way across the country, film reviewers in other newspapers and magazines unanimously echoed the praise. 'Ranks among the finest films ever made,' declared the *Boston Herald*.[24] And the *Hollywood Citizen* confirmed: 'Preceded by a delirious sort of praise from the East, it is gratifying to announce *Pépé le Moko* is as good as reported.'[25]

It must surely have been somewhere in the minds of the Warner Brothers executives who a few months later began to put together the project that would eventually become known as *Casablanca*. In December 1941, soon after Pearl Harbor, producer Hal B. Wallis – on the advice of his story editor Irene Lee – purchased the rights to an unproduced play called *Everybody Comes to Rick's*. It had been written by New York schoolteacher Murray Burnett, with Joan Alison. According to Burnett, its chief inspiration had been a visit he had made to Europe in the summer of 1938, during which he had witnessed Nazi persecution and the plight of refugees. Visiting Cap Ferrat in the south of France, he went to a nightclub where there was a black pianist. 'I said to my wife, "What a setting for a play . . ."'[26] But the play itself wouldn't be completed until 1941, after the German

Occupation of France, and – perhaps significantly – after the release of *Pépé le Moko* in New York.

Its content is familiar to us all from the worldwide success of the movie. American Rick Blaine is a disillusioned former lawyer who now runs a bar in Casablanca, French Morocco. A woman with whom Rick had had an affair in Paris some years before turns up in Casablanca with her boyfriend, Victor Laszlo, who is a Czechoslovakian on the run from the Nazis. The old feelings that Rick and Lois have for each other are rekindled, but in a spirit of self-sacrifice Rick makes Lois escape the city with Victor Laszlo.

The subsequent movie enlarged and elaborated upon this essential framework: Victor Laszlo, a wealthy anti-Nazi newspaper editor in the play, is transformed into a resistance fighter who has escaped from a German concentration camp; his American girlfriend Lois Meredith becomes his Swedish wife, Ilsa Lund; the evil police inspector becomes the corrupt but much more likeable Louis Renault. A flashback sequence is added, in which Rick recalls his romance with Ilsa in Paris.

It's impossible to know for certain the degree of conscious influence that *Pépé le Moko* might have had on the content of *Casablanca*, but it is worth making the speculation, because the parallels are so striking. The similarities are marked, in the detail as well as in the general theme. Both Pépé and Rick live far from home in a city in French-speaking North Africa. Both are under the investigation of the local police inspector, with whom they have a necessarily ambivalent acquaintance. And both look back with nostalgia to a happier past in Paris. The key motive force of the two films is the same – the arrival of a beautiful woman from Europe – as is the deeper metaphorical theme of an alien city as a pitiless prison whose exiled inhabitants long to get back to civilisation.

The influence of *Pépé le Moko* on the original play *Everybody Goes to Rick's* is necessarily tentative, but there is significant evidence that, via *Algiers*, Duvivier's film played an important part in the way that the play was translated into *Casablanca*. Right from the outset, the association was acknowledged, even playing a part in the decision of producer Hal Wallis to purchase the property.

In the process of making his mind up about the play, he circulated it to several studio staff for a second opinion:

Jerry Wald, an up-and-coming writer-producer, thought it might make a good vehicle for either George Raft or Humphrey Bogart, adding that it could be tailored along the lines of *Algiers*, which costarred Charles Boyer and Hedy Lamarr.

Jerry had gotten to the heart of the matter. This could indeed be another *Algiers* – a romantic story in an exotic setting. Two days after I received the play, I bought the rights to it for $20,000.[27]

On 31 December 1941, Wallis issued an inter-departmental memo to announce a change of title: 'Since *Algiers* had been such a hit, I decided on *Casablanca*.'[28] Two months later he tried unsuccessfully to borrow *Algiers* star Hedy Lamarr from MGM.[29] Two other stars he considered before finally settling on Ingrid Bergman were the French actresses Michèle Morgan and Edwige Feuillère.[30] To get hold of Bergman it was necessary first to persuade producer David Selznick, who owned her contract, that *Casablanca* would be a good vehicle for her.

Screenwriter Julius Epstein, who was then working on the script with his brother Philip, recalled having to pitch it to Selznick:

He was in his office having his lunch – soup on his desk. He never looked up from his soup as we started to tell what little story we had. I soon realised that we had told less than a half hour of story and we were floundering. Ingrid Bergman's character hadn't even come into the picture yet, and we wanted her for the starring role! So I said, 'Oh hell, it's going to be a lot of crap like *Algiers*. A lot of cigarette smoke and guitar music.' Selznick said, 'You've got Bergman!'[31]

Once again *Algiers* proved to be the 'open sesame'. In every department, it served as the benchmark for what everyone hoped *Casablanca* would be. To photograph the film, Wallis tried to secure the cinematographer of *Algiers*, James Wong Howe. When Howe turned out to be unavailable because of other assignments, Wallis instructed studio veteran Arthur Edeson to evoke the lighting style of *Algiers*, with 'as much contrast as possible'.[32]

But to what extent were the film-makers – whether producer, scriptwriters or actors – drawing on the original inspiration, Duvivier's *Pépé le Moko*? None of the key participants recalls the French film in their memories of *Casablanca*, but common sense suggests that they must have been aware of it to some degree. The word of mouth after the film's New York opening less than a year before, in March 1941, was such that the *Los Angeles Times* was a month later eagerly anticipating its arrival on the Pacific Coast. Under the headline '*Pépé* Popular in Eastern Run', the newspaper reported, on 8 April, that 'the original "unexpurgated" version of *Pépé le Moko* is proving one of the most popular money-makers ever imported from France'.

Three days later, Duvivier's film opened at the Esquire Theater, Los Angeles. 'The picture is outstanding, make no mistake about it,' reported John L. Scott. 'This is the feature from which *Algiers* was made in Hollywood. Personally, I'm sorry I didn't see the Gabin version first. It's almost impossible to compare the two features this way.'[33] A convenient focus for publicity was the fact that both the star and director of the film were in Hollywood at the time, re-launching their careers after the fall of France: Duvivier was directing *Illusions* for the producer Alexander Korda – a loose remake of *Carnet de bal* eventually released as *Lydia* (1941) – and Gabin was about to star in *Moontide* (1942) for Twentieth Century-Fox. Gossip columnist Hedda Hopper gleefully reported the two Pépés, Gabin and Boyer, running into each other at the French Relief headquarters.[34] Meanwhile the film was still playing at the World Cinema in New York, where it finally closed only on 8 June, four months after its opening.

The film may have been an art-house success rather than a mainstream one, exhibited in long runs in just a handful of small theatres, but it would inevitably have been of particular interest to film-industry workers. In practice, therefore, contributors to *Casablanca* were likely to have been much more familiar with the recently released French film than they would have been with its American remake, which had appeared so many years earlier. The more commercially dominant *Algiers* may have been adopted as a convenient term of reference among the box-office-minded Hollywood film community, but memories of the recently released *Pépé le Moko* would surely have been just as significant, if not more so, in the creative shaping of *Casablanca*.

Indeed, there are several characterisations, motifs or devices in that later film that find a plausible echo *only* in the Duvivier original. The use of the song 'As Time Goes By', for example. In *Casablanca*, it carries the dual signification of fulfilment and loss: it is the song that Sam used to sing when Ilsa and Rick were happy together in Paris, but later it becomes representative of their break-up, as Rick angrily tells Sam never to play the song again after he sings it at Ilsa's request. This scene, which is at the dramatic heart of *Casablanca*, recalls the sequence in *Pépé le Moko* – a sequence not present in *Algiers* – where the singer Tania (Fréhel) puts on the gramophone record of her younger self singing a nostalgic song about Paris. There is the same distinctive dynamic, of a song performed at a happier time in Paris now being sung years later, in exile, to signify the loss of that past.

But whatever the influences of the French film, *Casablanca* – as *Algiers* had done on a previous occasion – fashioned them into a fundamentally different kind of film, one that worked in Hollywood terms. In place of a naturalistic fidelity to truth of character and situation, it operates instead on the level of myth and fable, taking us on a moral journey of self-sacrifice and redemption. The value of Rick's character lies less in his plausibility as an individual than in his ability to embody desirable conduct. He's presented as a cynic, but only so that the audience can experience the thrill of seeing him revealed in his true colours. For his heroism is never in doubt, the fact of it carefully implanted in the audience's mind.

Early on in the narrative, Inspector Renault warns Rick not to help Laszlo:

RICK: What ever gave you the impression that I might help Laszlo escape?

RENAULT: I suspect that under that cynical shell you're at heart a sentimentalist. Laugh if you will. I'm familiar with your record. Let me point out just two items. In 1935, you ran guns to Ethiopia. In 1936, you fought in Spain on the loyalist side.

RICK: And got well paid on both occasions.

RENAULT: The winning side would've paid much better.

Rick is a two-dimensional character, but such two-dimensionality is an inherent feature of the cinema of the Production Code, which tends to impart meaning through symbol. As long as we respect its representative rather than naturalistic nature, then *Casablanca* – following the Aristotelian certainties of reverse, revelation and catharsis – proceeds to a satisfying conclusion. In rediscovering his love for Ilsa, Rick recovers from his disillusionment and, reawakened, has the strength to make the final sacrifice.

It is predetermined that in the famous final scene he will put Ilsa on the plane:

RICK: Inside we both know you belong with Victor. You're part of his work, the thing that keeps him going. If that plane leaves and you're not with him, you'll regret it. Maybe not today, not tomorrow, but soon. For the rest of your life.

ILSA: But what about us?

RICK: We'll always have Paris. We didn't have. We'd lost it until you came to Casablanca. We got it back last night.

ILSA: When I said I would never leave you . . .

RICK: And you never will. I've got a job to do too. Where I go, you can't follow. What I have to do, you can't be part of. I'm no good at being noble, but it doesn't take much to see that the problems of three people don't amount to a hill of beans in this crazy world.

It is a classic ending of Hollywood make-believe, but falls apart if one makes the mistake of opening the door to real life. Then it seems monstrous that Rick compels Ilsa to go off with a man she doesn't love. Even if Ilsa is willing to make the same self-sacrifice, what of Laszlo? Sooner or later, he will discover how Ilsa really feels. And then the two will have to endure a loveless marriage for the rest of their lives (divorce not being permitted under the Code).

The differences between the French cinema of the 1930s and Hollywood were so marked that even if Duvivier had directed the remake of *Pépé le Moko* himself – as had originally been the intention, according to Yves Desrichard[35]– it is unlikely that he would have made a positive difference. The near-remake he *did* make in Hollywood of one of his previous French films allows us to consider some of the difficulties.

Lydia (1941) was inspired by Duvivier's *Carnet de bal* (1937). Although it was as loose a reworking of that film as *Algiers* was a close imitation of *Pépé le Moko*, it shared the same structure of a woman trying to make sense of her life by recalling romantic encounters from her past. It was not the first Hollywood film that Duvivier had made. In 1937, he directed a musical extravaganza for MGM called *The Great Waltz*, based on a successful stage operetta of four years previously, which allowed little scope for his creative imagination. But *Lydia* must at first sight have seemed to offer the kind of artistic freedom that Hollywood seldom afforded. Not only was it loosely based on a film he had already made, but he co-wrote the original story. As significant was the fact that the project was being backed by the producer Alexander Korda, who possessed the rare combination of Hollywood expertise and European sensibility that, in films like *The Private Life of Henry VIII* (1933) or *The Ghost Goes West* (1935), seemed to offer a possible bridge between the two cinematic traditions. Perhaps no other producer working in Hollywood was better equipped to understand the working method and creative aspirations of a European-trained director.

But whatever Duvivier's initial hopes, in practice the basic realities of Hollywood were against him. Korda had to make use of his key asset, Merle Oberon, whose box-office power was at its height in the aftermath of *Wuthering Heights* (1939). Duvivier, therefore, had to exchange an ensemble team of players – where no individual actor's star value had priority over the story – for a Hollywood system of film-making that required strict subservience to such star value.

In *Carnet de bal*, the central character, Christine, links the different episodes: she is an observer, leading the audience through the different dramatic encounters, where the focus is as much on the individuals she meets. But in *Lydia*, the demands of Hollywood stardom require this dynamic to be reversed. The function of the Hollywood screen goddess – in this case, Merle Oberon – is not to offer a window on other people's dramas, but to stand immovably in the spotlight herself. As Lydia recalls the four men who loved her in the past, it is a thinly veiled excuse for her to bathe in the male gaze, *her* emotional drama the only one of any true consequence.

As we can appreciate from his French films, Julien Duvivier possessed a gift for translating emotional nuance and mood into visual terms, but the weight of Oberon's star presence represented a fatal handicap. If he was free in *Carnet de bal* to achieve a delicate balance of episode and character, in *Lydia* he must have felt as though he were expected to waltz on crutches.

While the distorting burden of Oberon's stardom chiefly accounted for the lifeless nature of the film, there were other contributory factors inherent in the Hollywood system of production. In *Carnet de bal* a series of haunting scenes shot on location in the Italian lakes form a memorable opening prologue. Real but dreamlike at the same time, they served perfectly to evoke the psychological state in which Christine succumbs to the tricks of memory that form the substance of the film.

But *Lydia* – like most Hollywood productions of the period – was totally enclosed in the studio, winter scenes being filmed with marble dust rather than real snow. While *Carnet de bal* inhabited a dream reality, *Lydia* belonged unmistakably to the world of the Hollywood sound stage.

Then there was the over-emphatic script, which, employing the broad brushstrokes of the Production Code, carried the production yet further from the psychological realism that Duvivier habitually brought to his French films. While most directors might have welcomed the opportunity to have one of Hollywood's most celebrated scriptwriters as a collaborator, Ben Hecht's work was rooted in a journalist's cynicism that ill equipped him for a lyrical romance relying so heavily on delicacy of sentiment. He could offer plenty of wit, and the professionalism of a long and successful Hollywood career, but not the kind of basic belief that Duvivier needed.

Duvivier would probably have preferred a different collaborator, but he was not in a position in which he could easily protest. In France he had driven the agenda, carefully determining his own creative partnerships, whether it was choice of writer, actor or technician, but in Hollywood he had to defer to Korda, whose need for box-office success inevitably subverted Duvivier's intentions.

It's interesting to look at United Artists' exhibitors' manual for the film. Duvivier is treated as being of minor importance. After the presence of Merle Oberon, fresh from her triumph in *Wuthering Heights*, the chief selling point of the film was Alexander Korda himself: his was the 'name above the title'. In the careful hierarchy of billing – the kind of economically sensitive issue that consumed endless memos in Hollywood – the exact wording was:

ALEXANDER KORDA
Presents
"LYDIA"
starring
MERLE OBERON
With

. . .

The supporting cast duly followed. Only then was the name of the director mentioned. The exhibitors' manual advised: 'Cash In On Korda Prestige.' Reminding the reader that Korda was the producer of such previous box-office successes as *The Four Feathers* (1939), *The Thief of Bagdad* (1940) and *That Hamilton Woman* (1941), it went on: 'Alexander Korda's reputation as producer of big-scale, momentous films has steadily been mounting with the appearance of one record-breaking picture after another. The Korda imprint on a picture has now come to be accepted as a certain identification of topflight film entertainment – and the fans know it!'

But few fans, by contrast, were expected to know of Duvivier. In an exhaustive book of tips that went through every possible publicity angle, he merited only a handful of paragraphs. In a suggestion for a possible newspaper feature on the director, one such paragraph observed:

The name of Julien Duvivier, the great French director who megaphoned *Lydia*, is one of the most outstanding and spectacular among motion picture directors since the birth of films. If you are in a situation where your local newspaper will have a readership interested in the directorial, artistic or technical side of the movies, publicity breaks on Duvivier will be easy for you and should be developed.

But for all the routine hyperbole, it was obvious that such a readership, interested in the 'directorial' side, was considered to be a rarity. The role of the director in the Hollywood system was to implement the producer's vision. To put forward his own vision required not only favourable conditions of working that were very rarely granted, but also a particular kind of talent that could master the language and demands of the Hollywood system in such a way as to turn its limitations into advantages.

If Alfred Hitchcock is the most obvious example of such a director, it is perhaps not surprising that he should have served an apprenticeship in a British studio system that possessed so many of Hollywood's structural features. At Gaumont-British, where he made seven of his films during the 1930s,[36] he enjoyed not only the support of a comparatively large, well-resourced studio and a continuity of production, but also the certainty of a well-defined, formulaic product – the suspense thriller – which chimed perfectly with what would be expected of him in America. It was a film-making background that was as much an aid to a Hollywood career as France's much looser framework of production was a hindrance.

Duvivier, who prided himself on his professionalism, tried as hard to adapt to the Hollywood way as, say, Renoir sought to resist it, but that does not mean that the system suited him any more than it did Renoir. Working within its confines, he found his artistic voice stifled.

8

The Art House

The audience that even the most popular French film-makers enjoyed in Britain and America was a limited one. It lay chiefly in the network of art-house cinemas that had come into being during the 1920s and 1930s. In Britain, the founding of the Film Society in 1925 paved the way for such specialist cinemas as the Academy, the Everyman and the Curzon, which opened respectively in 1928, 1933 and 1934. These were the cinemas where Greene would have discovered Duvivier, not in the circuits that regaled the mass audience on a diet of English-language, mostly Hollywood films. In the United States, an important landmark was the opening in 1936 of the Filmarte, in the old John Golden Theatre at 202 West Fifty-Eighth Street in New York. Born in Vienna in 1904, its founder, Jean Lenauer, had moved to Paris in the early 1920s and worked as a film critic for several French newspapers. With his first-hand knowledge of the French film industry, he was unusually well placed to identify and to secure for US distribution the most prestigious French films.

The inaugural programme for the new cinema promised 'a haven from all that is philistinism in the movie-at-large' and 'a rendez-vous for the cinema devotee to whom films are something more than an innocuous diversion'.[1] The occasion was celebrated by a now growing band of critics on the East Coast who wanted to take cinema seriously.

One such was Mark Van Doren, a poet and distinguished academic at Columbia University, who at the time contributed reviews to the *Nation*. 'A new theater has been opened in New York with the design of proving to interested persons that the studios of Europe are once more, after several years of faltering and eclipse, a challenge to Hollywood,' wrote Van Doren.[2] He went on to express his gladness 'that the facilities for seeing foreign films have been increased', and to celebrate the Filmarte's first presentation, *La Kermesse héroïque* (1935), as one of the 'most diverting' films he had ever watched.

The review in the *New York Times* was written by Frank S. Nugent, another of the more sensitive and thoughtful writers of the period, who would later make a reputation for himself as the screenwriter of several John Ford westerns. His piece suggests the great impact the film had, but also the considerable cultural hurdles that remained to be addressed.

A sly, gay and impious farce, typically Gallic in its conception and execution, it whipped its way past the State Board of Censors before that august body had time to recover from the news that the photoplay had received the Grand Prix du Cinema Français and some sort of a gold medal award of the Venice International Exposition of Cinematography. At first, we are reliably informed, the State Board had banned it outright. But then, hearing about its international honors, it reconsidered and leaned so far backward in its charity that the de Maupassant flavor of the piece has, miraculously, been preserved. Which is all to the good and will, no doubt, reflect undeserved credit upon New York's guides to filmic morals.[3]

If an overly moralistic and patronising censorship was one formidable barrier to appreciation, another was an unfamiliar language that required the kind of intellectual effort that audiences did not expect to have to make in a cinema. Nugent went to commendable lengths to anticipate such resistance: 'Do not, we beg you, be dissuaded from seeing it because the dialogue is in French. Even without the many English subtitles, *La Kermesse Heroique* would be clearly understood; like all great comedies, it speaks a universal language.'

The Filmarte's owner soon won a reputation for himself as an unusually articulate and trenchant advocate of a more intelligent cinema than Hollywood was prepared to provide. In February 1937, shortly after *La Kermesse héroïque*'s successful run at his cinema had come to a close, Lenauer wrote a letter to the *New York Times*, in which he took the producer Sam Goldwyn to task for claiming that there was no public demand for 'fine' pictures. *La Kermesse*, he argued, proved the contrary:

It was shown at private screenings to all the large distributors connected with the regular circuits and producers. And these executives loved it and raved about it. But when it came to booking the film and agreeing to show it they turned their thumbs down. 'You can't make money on a foreign picture, no matter how charming! The public won't stand for it. And look at that leading lady, Françoise Rosay. She's an old lady. That'll never do. There's no money in it.' That is, according to their method of handling. The Filmarte, looking for a film to open with, booked *Kermesse*. Its success is known. It ran at this theatre for fourteen weeks, during which thousands of people paid money to see it. They enjoyed it and the Filmarte returned a profit to itself and to the producer. Now, and only now, it has been booked through some of the major circuits, and is being advertised as 'direct from fifteen weeks on Broadway'.[4]

The Filmarte was a small theatre compared to the first-run houses for Hollywood movies – the Radio City Music Hall and the Roxy, for example, each had a capacity of approximately six thousand – but, with eight hundred seats, it was more than twice the size of most existing art houses. Its successful launch seemed to prove that the market for foreign films was larger than previously thought – not just an élite group of people with a taste for the esoteric, but a broader audience, more discerning and intellectually curious than usual, but nonetheless expecting to be entertained like any audience.

Lenauer now hoped that the film's distributor, the American Tobis Corporation, would prove that such an audience was large enough to allow *La Kermesse héroïque* – or *Carnival in Flanders*, as it was renamed for American audiences – also to enjoy a profitable life in the circuits, just like any other Hollywood film. 'Produced on a breath-taking scale of magnificence,' declared the front page of the lavish exhibitors' manual.[5] Its central message seemed to be: 'Anything Hollywood can do, the French cinema can too.' A long page of newspaper quotations not only pointed out the film's international accolades, but also sought to show that it possessed the Hollywood knack for universal appeal.

The quotes included Eileen Creelman of the *Sun*: 'A production which Hollywood might well covet for its own'; *Liberty Magazine*: 'This is recommended for people who love good pictures in any language'; and Frank Nugent once again in the *New York Times*: 'Technically equal, if not superior, to anything Hollywood has turned out this season.'

Summarising a whole page of similarly ecstatic quotes, the exhibitors' manual declared: 'The Most Unanimous Press Verdict Ever Rendered Finds *Carnival in Flanders* Guilty of Box-Office Perfection in the First Degree.' Finally, the distributors hoped to show that it was of little importance whether *La Kermesse héroïque* was a Hollywood film or a French film; what most mattered was that it was a good film.

Since no previous foreign-language film had enjoyed a comparable release in the US circuits, the distributors were to some extent in unknown territory. As the sound cinema was barely ten years old, perhaps it still seemed possible to dream of establishing a major new precedent in American cinema-going habits, but with hindsight the manual's obvious ignorance of the French cinema it was seeking to promote seems like an ill omen. 'American Tobis first to find René Claire,' it boasted, explaining that prior to directing the Hollywood film *The Ghost Goes West*, 'Claire' had produced the 'well remembered *Sou Les Toils de Paris*, *Le Million*, *A Mouse La Liberté* and *Le Quatorze Juillet* (4th of July)'.

In the event, *La Kermesse héroïque* was put into the RKO circuit of seven hundred theatres, but then withdrawn after little more than a day. The switch from art house to mainstream proved to be too big a leap to make. It was one thing to attract sophisticated audiences to an art-house cinema in New York, but quite another to create a genuinely mass market for such a film. The decision of the Catholic Legion of Decency at the end of the year to condemn the film for indecency confirmed its essential otherness.[6]

Anatole Litvak's *Mayerling* (1936) – which told the tale of the Habsburg Crown Prince Rudolph's doomed love for Mary Vetsera – would make a more successful attempt on the American circuits some months later. After a long showcase run at the Filmarte, its distributor, Pax International, managed successfully in early 1937 to book the film into some small theatres in the big cities. After breaking the house record in an art theatre in Pittsburgh, it came to the attention of Warner Brothers, which released the film into its own circuit theatres in the Pittsburgh area.[7]

Perhaps the most striking aspect of the publicity campaign was the kind of lesson the distributors had clearly drawn from the debacle of *La Kermesse héroïque*. The campaign manual contained a page of guidance for the exhibitors on how best to promote the film. While American Tobis had presented *La Kermesse héroïque* as a French film beating Hollywood at its own game, Pax International deliberately played down the French connection:

The key to the success of *Mayerling* is its unlimited audience appeal. The fact that it was produced overseas is no barrier. At the outset it has names which lead one to believe that this film masterpiece emerged from Hollywood. Do not mention that the film is French. This is absolutely unnecessary. Eighty per cent of the audience in New York City consisted of film-goers who had never before seen a French film. It is these very people who will leave your theatre with nothing but praises on their lips. It is this group that will send you the largest majority of your patrons. Bid for their patronage. You will get it. The largest paper in New York City, *The Daily News*, informed its readers in its review of *Mayerling*: 'Don't let the French keep you away . . . the English subtitles are concise translations of the dialogue, conveying satisfactorily the essence of the French conversation and fully interpreting the action of the tense drama. So, we repeat, don't let the language prevent you from seeing one of the finest dramatic films of the year.'

Mayerling can be sold as an American film. Let this be your guide.[8]

The manual further stressed the fact that the film's male lead, Charles Boyer, was already an established Hollywood star, while his young co-star Danielle Darrieux was working in Hollywood on her first film for Universal Studios and the director Anatole Litvak was also a 'Hollywood luminary'. This suggestion that a French film might more successfully masquerade as a Hollywood film, rather than trade openly on its own merits, was a mark not only of the inflexibility of the Hollywood exhibition and production system, but also of the persisting polarity between the two cinemas.

Through the following year, *Mayerling* would go on to play in nearly fifteen hundred US cinemas, achieving a gross of $250,000, modest for a Hollywood picture, but an extraordinary sum for a French import, especially considering that, in the words of the *Hollywood Reporter*, French producers 'used to consider a $5,000 advance important money'.[9]

The *Hollywood Reporter* went on, in the aftermath of *Mayerling*'s success, to publish regular stories on the French film industry's supposed resurgence. Its readers were given an overall profile of a national cinema that, of all the European countries, had made the most marked improvement in its fortunes. Five years previously, only three distribution outlets handled French films in the US. In 1938, that number had risen to more than twenty.[10] The average cost of French first features had risen from $57,000 in 1935 to $89,000 during the previous year, 1937.[11] In the coming year, 1938/9, according to the magazine, out of a hundred and fifty French films scheduled for production more than a hundred would be shown in the US.

The impression given was of a French industry that was not only building its presence in America, but also dominating export markets in Europe, rivalling even Hollywood. 'A check last week on the chief pictures in release in principal zones on the continent indicated seven French pictures getting the top spots as against three from Hollywood,' the magazine reported in July 1938.[12] And reports that France was planning to curtail dubbing permits for films imported from America intensified fears of the French film industry turning into a serious competitor.[13]

In the New Year the *Hollywood Reporter* carried a profile of the country's production that suggested a state of buoyant self-confidence. The increased returns from successful foreign exports were helping its producers to launch 'one of the most ambitious schedules in the history of the French motion picture industry'.[14] Able to command larger budgets, they were even persuading French stars to come back from Hollywood. In a typical story of the time, which suggested the French cinema's determination to project a distinct, uncompromising presence on the world stage, Jean Gabin was reported to have turned down an invitation from Louis B. Mayer to join MGM on his own terms. The wine he liked best, France's greatest star told Hollywood's most powerful mogul, didn't travel well.[15]

In March 1939, the *Hollywood Reporter* carried an article on the efforts of the French minister of education, Jean Zay, to pass a measure in the French parliament to impose a dubbing tax and end the double bill. 'The American film business in France is faced with one of the heaviest possible blows to its foreign income, which will cut off approximately 75 per cent of its business.'[16] Here were yet further worrying signs of France's determination to become a serious rival.

The magazine had already given a frank assessment of the situation in an editorial of a few months earlier:

Each foot of film, good or bad, that is turned out in Europe or the studios of any other nation, reduces the footage Hollywood has been supplying, and thereby reduces both the employment and the security of this business. So it behoves Hollywood and its creators to continue in their effort for BETTER PICTURES and more pictures, and to continue to deny participation by foreign film-makers, in so far as possible, in the production of pictures other than in Hollywood.[17]

The near-bellicose stance was rooted in a self-righteous belief in the superiority of Hollywood entertainment, which exhibitors around the world were presumed to prefer to their own local

product. In the wake of increasing attempts by foreign govern-
ments to limit the importing of Hollywood films, the US government made it clear that the industry had its backing. In a speech,
Nathan Golden, the chief of the Federal Bureau of Foreign and
Domestic Commerce, called American films 'the bread and but-
ter of foreign exhibitors', stating that Hollywood 'may be justified in taking a positive stand against merely narrow-minded
and punitive practices abroad'.[18]

The rise of the French cinema's reputation in the second half
of the 1930s was so rapid – and marked – that the curator of
the Museum of Modern Art's new film library, Iris Barry, felt it
necessary to add the following corrective note to her 1938 translation of Maurice Bardèche and Robert Brasillach's *Histoire
du cinéma*: 'It should be borne in mind . . . that the authors
write in 1935, when many remarkable films had not yet been
produced, and certainly before the present popularity of French
productions.'[19]

In truth, all the newspaper stories suggesting that the French
cinema was about to become a formidable new competitor to
Hollywood had about as much real substance as the Red Scare
in the time of McCarthy. The French films that very occasionally reached the major circuits – albeit even then for a very
limited playing – were freaks and oddities. The only other
French film in this period that could really match the success
of *Mayerling* was a documentary called *Cloistered* (1936). It
was the first time ever that the Catholic Church had allowed a
film crew into a convent. The director Robert Alexandre had to
secure the special permission of Pope Pius XI to make the film,
which followed the daily routine of the Sisters of Our Lady
of Charity of the Good Shepherd at Angers. With an obvious
appeal for America's twenty-five million Catholics (roughly a
fifth of the US population), it's easy enough to appreciate why
the circuits would have booked it, but it clearly did not offer
a reliable index to the box-office prospects of more typical
French films. Indeed, it arguably owed its mainstream success

to the ease with which it was able to suppress its Frenchness. Specially packaged for the US market, with a commentary by an American priest, *Cloistered* wasn't so much a French film as a Catholic one.

In practice, the popularity of French films was still almost entirely confined to a handful of art houses, but the location of these theatres in the major cities enabled them to exert a disproportionate degree of influence on public perceptions. The hopes of the French film industry that more films would, like *Mayerling*, gain entry into the big circuits, may have been disappointed, but nonetheless it was able to win powerful support from the East Coast intellectuals who, instinctively suspicious of the unbridled populism of Hollywood, were always ready to embrace a foreign import that seemed to offer a model for a more thoughtful, intelligent cinema.

Once upon a time it had been the German film industry that seemed to offer the most promising alternative model with the great films that came out of UFA during the 1920s. But with the rise to power of the Nazis in 1933, the French cinema showed itself more than ready to take the initiative. A major landmark for the influence of that cinema was *La Grande Illusion* (1937). For while films like *La Kermesse héroïque* or *Mayerling* – unusually sophisticated though they may have been – clearly belonged in the category of entertainment, *La Grande Illusion* seemed just as emphatically an example of great art that showed up Hollywood's trivial nature. The National Board of Review voted it the best film of the year, 'no matter where made'. Its magazine applauded 'an entirely unconventional film, deep and searching in its humanity'.[20]

Although Jean Renoir's films *Madame Bovary* (1934) and *La Marseillaise* (1937) had both had a US release, the French director was still a little-known figure in America. But an unprecedented six-month run at the Filmarte of *La Grande Illusion* – which opened in the cinema on 12 September 1938 – established him at last as a major international director.

'Very different, something for the mature and the grave young,' wrote John Mosher in the *New Yorker*.[21] An audience brought up on a diet of Hollywood was gently encouraged to rethink the conventions of what the cinema was and what it could do. Frank Nugent, who was perhaps the kind of mature and grave young man Mosher had been thinking of – he was thirty years old – commented in the *New York Times*:

For a war film it is astonishingly lacking in hullabaloo. There may have been four shots fired, but there are no screaming shells, no brave speeches, no gallant toasts to the fallen. War is the grand illusion and Renoir proceeds with his disillusioning task by studying it, not in the front line, but in the prison camps, where captors and captives alike are condemned to the dry rot of inaction.[22]

Nugent's review contained the implicit suggestion that perhaps Hollywood was the grand illusion too, Renoir's understated approach being more true to the texture of human emotion. 'The story ends sharply, with no attempt to weave its threads together. It is probably the way such a story would have ended in life.' In his comments on this 'strange and interesting' film, there's a sense of him drawing lessons that he would later apply to his own career as a screenwriter, contributing to the quiet humanism of such films as *Fort Apache* (1948) or *The Searchers* (1956).

Soon after the opening of *La Grande Illusion*, Nugent and Jean Lenauer were invited to discuss the relationship between foreign films and Hollywood in a radio broadcast for the New York station WNYC.[23] Nugent pointed out how the New York Film Critics' prize for the best foreign film had gone to France for two straight years – *Carnival in Flanders* in 1936, and *Mayerling* in 1937[24] – and, although the title of the programme was 'The Foreign Film and Hollywood', the listener would have been excused for assuming that foreign films *were* French films, because only French films were discussed.

But if the important breakthrough the French cinema had made in America during the second half of the 1930s was clear,

Lenauer, citing his old adversary, was careful to put this success into perspective:

Recently there has been a good deal of controversy about foreign films versus Hollywood. When Sam Goldwyn returned from Europe last year, he said: 'The crisis for the American picture is here. Foreign studios threaten the supremacy of Hollywood . . .' Now Mr Goldwyn is a man of great prominence in the movie world, and as a precautionary measure I don't think I should disagree with him. At the same time I do not believe that Hollywood needs to fear foreign producers – not even the French, who have made great strides in the last few years. I question whether the average American is interested in foreign films. I still feel their appeal is limited.

These comments represented a significant revision of his previous stance. Two years earlier, when – in the aftermath of *La Kermesse héroïque*'s long run at the Filmarte – he was arguing that exhibiting foreign films could be a profitable business, he didn't specify any limits. But now subsequent experience had shown where those limits lay. The people who watched French films in America, Lenauer stated, did not constitute a mainstream audience. They were people who were 'looking for the unusual' and were willing to 'go off the beaten track for their entertainment'.

The word 'entertainment' carried an important nuance. Lenauer did not think this different audience should be identified with the 'arty' or the 'so-called intelligentsia'. They expected to be entertained every bit as much as the mainstream audience; they were simply more inquiring and adventurous, prepared to make the effort to read subtitles and to engage with a story told in a strange language.

One can only explain such things by saying that it all boils down to the question of public taste. I think the average movie-goer is scared of a French picture – of any foreign picture. Once you get him over that mental handicap he is likely to do what some people did at the Filmarte when *Carnival* was running – come back ten and twelve times! Of course, this is an exceptional case and the only other foreign picture with a comparable record is *Mayerling*. Yet the receipts drawn by *Mayerling* from all over the country would be considered insignificant as against the box-office returns of a picture like *Alexander's Ragtime Band*.

To illustrate this boundary between the mainstream and what still remained a select audience, Lenauer cited the failure of *Carnival in Flanders* to work in the circuits and, subsequently, the need of *Mayerling* to masquerade as a Hollywood film for a French film at last to win a measure of circuit success: 'Because of Boyer, many people went to see it under the impression that it was an American film. Most of them liked it. But I am sure they would never have ventured in had they known the film was in French with English subtitles.'

It is true that Hollywood, aided and abetted by the US government, did go to great lengths to shore up its commercial advantage. In his book *Hollywood's Film Wars with France* Jens Ulff-Møller outlines the tactics that American industry employed, but his depiction of Hollywood engaged in an unprincipled, bullying campaign does not address the fundamental lack of appeal that French films had in America. His assertions that Hollywood refused to buy French films are made without any analysis of the actual market potential for those films. 'Despite successful productions such as *Le Crime de Monsieur Lange* (1936), *La Grande Illusion* (1937), *Quai des brumes* (1938) and *La Règle du jeu* (1939), French film production did not have the necessary political power to improve its position in the confrontations with the film industry of the United States.'²⁵ But much more critical was the absence of box-office power. Lenauer, who had played an important part in the critical triumph of *La Grande Illusion* in the United States, was discovering through bitter experience that, whatever the kudos a French film could certainly obtain in America, the financial returns were minimal as much on account of audience preference as any resistance from the industry.

In a particularly illuminating part of his discussion with Nugent, Lenauer went on to consider the differences between the two systems of film-making. At the heart of the Hollywood system was the star. Massive publicity meant that Garbo, Crawford and Gable were as well known around the world as they were in America. The international popularity of the Hollywood film was based on this fact. But such methodical and intensive promotion reflected the nature of a high-investment industry in which stars were tied to studios through long-term contracts.

In France a star was rarely signed for more than one film at a time, usually with a different producer. So while the cult of personality drove the Hollywood system, in France a star's appeal was an important factor, but only one of several factors. 'In France,' Lenauer pointed out, 'directors are as popular as stars. Men like Renoir, Duvivier and Guitry get equal billing with the players. Their names mean something at the box-office.'

Another fundamental difference lay in audience expectations: 'In France the public doesn't insist on having romantic stars. Or, at least, it doesn't see why middle-aged men and women are necessarily unromantic. If France doesn't actually practice the doctrine "Life Begins at Forty", at least it pretends that life doesn't end at 25 – as one is led to believe by Hollywood.' *Carnival in Flanders* was an example. The major star in the film was Françoise Rosay, playing the part of a middle-aged housewife.

Hollywood's tendency to standardise lay in its quest to appeal to as broad a market as possible. It made films that were 'calculated to be as entertaining in Timbuctoo as they are in Hoboken'. In France, a film was made principally for the French market and it was considered a bonus if it sold elsewhere, but the belief in Hollywood was that 'American pictures must sell to the world'.

The broadcast expressed the reality that French films had won enormous prestige but posed minimal economic threat. By the end of the 1930s, there were in the United States 200 small theatres that specialised in showing foreign films, but this was an insignificant figure compared to the total number of 17,500 theatres.[26]

The pattern of exhibition was such that a foreign film tended to have long runs, but with only a handful of prints being shared between the specialised theatres. A popular Hollywood film, by contrast, after enjoying an extended exclusive presentation in selected first-run theatres, would have hundreds of prints put into the exchanges for its general release. For the release of the 1938 Clark Gable film *Test Pilot*, for example, MGM put out 452 prints.[27]

In place of Hollywood's largely misplaced fear of foreign films, Lenauer expressed the hope that Hollywood might learn from them. He pointed out that they 'contain many new ideas, suggest new treatments, frequently provide new story material. *Algiers*, for example, was made from a French film *Pépé le Moko*, although I think it differed considerably from the original.'

But whatever Lenauer's hopes, Hollywood and the French cinema remained in effect mutually exclusive cinemas, each with its distinct set of characteristics. French films found an important role for themselves in the United States as a form of *avant-garde* pioneering a more mature, adult cinema, but they did so, with few exceptions, in the ghetto of the art theatres, the distinction between the two cinemas applying not only to the films themselves but to the people who watched them. While a 'general audience' went to large circuit cinemas that screened mainstream Hollywood films that had the approval of the Production Code, a specialised audience saw foreign films in small theatres that did not require such approval.

9

The Golden Age

Few French directors during the 1930s would have seen their careers in terms of the cinema of personal expression that the *Cahiers* generation of critics introduced as an increasingly popular way of thinking about the cinema. Instead, as a group they regarded the cinema as foremost a collaborative medium, in which their role was to coax the best out of screenwriter, cinematographer and performer. Displaying a solid respect for technique acquired through long apprenticeship, they espoused the basic values that their fellow professionals working in Hollywood or Pinewood would easily have understood. If the Cocteau of *Le Sang d'un poète* represented one pole of the French cinema, then Duvivier or Feyder represented the other.

Even if in Britain and America they struggled to break out of the ghetto of the art house, they demonstrated the same instinct to please a mainstream audience. That, rather than personal expression or experimentation, was their chief criterion of success. Yet at the same time their films demonstrated an impressive intelligence and individuality that so often eluded their British or American counterparts. They set a standard of taste and possibility for an otherwise much disdained medium. This was the perception that made the premieres of French films in the handful of London or New York cinemas that screened them eagerly awaited occasions.

In an article published soon after *La Kermesse héroïque* had its British premiere at the Studio One cinema in the presence of Jacques Feyder and Françoise Rosay, *The Times* summed up the nature of the achievement: 'The French cinema has always encouraged original minds to work for it. The *avant-garde* directors of the old silent days produced much of artistic and experimental value, but they failed in the long run because their efforts could be appreciated only by a small coterie of intellectuals. The directors at work today are managing to combine originality of style with popular appeal. It has been realised that artistic worth is not necessarily inimical to commercial success. Let Feyder's *La Kermesse héroïque* bear witness.'[1]

Jacques Feyder had started out as an actor at Gaumont before the First World War, appearing in small roles in films directed by the pioneer generation of directors Victorin Jasset, Louis Feuillade and Gaston Ravel. Possessing little patience for all the waiting around that acting in the cinema involved, he found himself increasingly fascinated by what went on behind the camera. So began an apprenticeship of the kind of breadth that only the cinema's early days afforded. 'Before the war, we did everything,' he recalled in his memoirs. 'We learned our trade. Scenario, editing, lighting, decor, camera, directing actors. We were true craftsmen. We ground our colours – or rather, our black and white – like the old painters. We threw together a film in two weeks, working fifteen hours a day. We were rough-and-ready pioneers, tough and resourceful.'[2]

In 1915 Feyder became an assistant to Gaston Ravel. When Ravel was conscripted into the army the following year, Feyder became a director in his own right. Through the remainder of the First World War, he directed a series of short films for the Gaumont production programme. It was in essence assembly-line work, but provided an invaluable training ground, in which Feyder was able to acquire not only a technical facility – as his comments above suggest – but also an understanding of dramatic rhythm and structure. Many of his films in this period were made in collaboration with the playwright Tristan Bernard, whom Feyder considered to be a major influence on his career, for encouraging a rigour of dramatic conception that far exceeded the usual practice of the early cinema.

The film that established Feyder as a leading figure in the

French film industry was *L'Atlantide*. Based on Pierre Benoit's best-selling adventure novel, it told the story of two French soldiers who discover the lost city of Atlantis in the Sahara desert. Producing the film himself, Feyder took his cast and crew to North Africa, where they filmed on location for eight months. 'It was the first big French film', he recalled, 'to break with the practice of studio fakery, exploiting the genuine Sahara landscape.'[3] Three hours long, the film offered a visual feast, but also drew immense narrative power from Feyder's eye for dramatic realism, authentic detail and atmosphere. With this extremely risky and ambitious personal venture, Feyder expressed a faith in the mainstream commercial cinema at just the point that the leaders of the industry, Pathé and Gaumont, had abandoned it as a lost cause.

Through the 1920s, at a time when the avant-garde were winning considerable public attention while failing to make films that could command a large audience, Feyder built his cinema around the conventional box-office virtues of story, star appeal and spectacle, but eschewed the formulaic in favour of realism of narrative and character. 'Jacques Feyder's importance at this time', commented René Clair, 'was to make quality films that appealed to everyone.'[4]

Feyder's belief in a popular, universal cinema made Hollywood an obvious destination for him, but his experience of working there was disillusioning. Given a contract by MGM in 1928, he directed Greta Garbo in the studio's last silent film, *The Kiss* (1929), and then Ramón Novarro in two talkies, *Daybreak* (1931) and *Son of India* (1931), as well as foreign-language versions of Garbo's first talkie *Anna Christie* (1929). In his memoirs, he recalled an inflexible, near self-sufficient system that defeated the best efforts of the European newcomer to make a distinctive individual contribution:

The Americans have all the equipment and people they need to make films. But from time to time, they tell themselves that they live in isolation, that they risk losing their edge in the too predictable routine of their assembly-line production and that it would be beneficial to bring in some grist from outside. In this way, they hope to put their own directors on their mettle, to throw into the mix some bright new ideas that might reinvigorate them without undermining their fundamental approach. The idea is to wake up film-makers whom commercial success has lulled into complacency and to forestall stagnation and decadence . . . Unfortunately, in practice, the system nearly always makes this effort pointless. It's not their fault . . . Nor is it the fault of the select few from Europe, who, setting off full of ideas and enthusiasm, gradually get bogged down. No. It's no one's fault. But the reality of such a process of transplanting, grafting and fusion involves more difficulties than one could possibly have imagined at the outset.

Feyder went on to describe a system of endless committees gradually grinding down any original point of distinction so that finally the result was 'a film that an American director would have made in pretty much the same way'.[5]

Feyder's portrayal of Hollywood suggested a place that was institutionally hostile to the individual touch. It was frustrating because the Hollywood goal of creating a cinema of universal appeal had been something he had always pursued in France. He shared the Hollywood regard for story, script and star – the difference was simply one of dramatic integrity. In France he was able to be true to the intrinsic nature of his chosen subject in a way that had not been possible in Hollywood.

When Feyder returned from Hollywood, he made *Le Grand Jeu*, which was released in 1934. It was a romantic drama that shared the North African background of his first great success, *L'Atlantide*. A disgraced Paris businessman who joins the Foreign Legion arrives in North Africa, where he meets and becomes obsessed by a singer who is the spitting image of his former lover. Screenwriter Charles Spaak, who would collaborate with Feyder again on the films *Pension Mimosas* and *La Kermesse héroïque* (*Carnival in Flanders*), wrote the screenplay from Feyder's original idea.

In filming the story, which introduced themes of estrangement and exile that would become increasingly popular in the French cinema during the 1930s, Feyder devoted as much attention to character as narrative, building emotional intensity through his attention to psychological detail. To this extent it was a precursor, if not an example, of a vague tendency in French cinema that would later be identified by the equally vague but persistent term of 'poetic realism', but it was also an example of a collaborative, workshop system typical of the French cinema of the period, where the final outcome depended upon the blueprint of a script, and where the chief difference from Hollywood lay less in method than in the greater importance the French cinema placed on dramatic consistency and plausibility.

The screenwriter Charles Spaak recalled:

After the construction of an important set for Le Grand Jeu, I accompanied Feyder along the African street that carpenters, masons, painters and workers of all kinds had put up in such a hurry. As I amused myself with the thought of the huge activity, with the involvement of so many different trades, that had been required to realise an idea that we had thought up in our quiet office, Feyder turned to me with a smile. 'The difficult time has arrived when the script which we conceived in peace and silence must pass from the intellectual sphere to the material one. To direct a film is to defend its meaning against all these people who work around us, and against the performers who are soon to take up their places on the newly finished set. It requires holding on to the original conception, which will threaten to slip away amidst all the comings and goings, the clouds of plaster and the sound of hammers. What a battle it was in the first place to get the material resources to film our story. And now what a battle it will be not to end up a prisoner of those resources.'[6]

In the Hollywood cinema, where the influence of the producer was so much greater, meaning was routinely hostage to spectacle. Otherwise, there was a considerable resemblance between the two industries, which shared the same collaborative model.

'The cinema is the work of a team,' asserted the director Christian-Jaque. Born in 1904, he had started out in the industry as a poster artist. Abandoning his studies as an architect, he then worked as a production designer until Julien Duvivier encouraged him to become an assistant director. He made his debut as a director with *Le Bidon d'or* in 1932, but his most popular pre-war success was the mystery thriller *Les Disparus de Saint-Agil* of 1938, based on a novel by Pierre Véry and starring Erich von Stroheim and Michel Simon. During the war, he would film another Pierre Véry novel, *L'Assassinat du Père Noël*, but his career was notable for a broad range of subject-matter that, pitched at a mainstream audience, encompassed thrillers, musicals, comedies, biopics and period dramas. 'I am incapable of specialising, of making the same film over and over again. I am eclectic, excited by variety and change.'[7] Expressing a preference as a spectator for action films and comedies, he cited Ernst Lubitsch and John Ford as important influences for him. But he clearly viewed his profession as that of fashioning well-made entertainment, rather than art. The key to a rewarding career, he believed, was not to take oneself too seriously. 'We are travelling players and bear-keepers. Our job is to inform, amuse and touch our audience.'[8]

During the 1920s, Claude Autant-Lara was a production and costume designer for Marcel L'Herbier and Jean Renoir. Between 1930 and 1932, he worked in America directing French-language versions of Buster Keaton shorts for MGM. It was an invaluable Hollywood training that helped him to direct his first feature, *Ciboulette*, scripted by Jacques Prévert after an operetta written by François de Croisset and Robert de Flers. But it was with the war that he emerged in the first rank of French directors, with his lavish productions of the Jean Aurenche and Pierre Bost scripts *Mariage de Chiffon*, *Lettres d'amour* and *Douce*. Highly ornate and studio-bound, these well-crafted adaptations were the products of a commercial French cinema in which the literary property was considered to be as much a dependable staple of production as it was in Hollywood. 'My goal as a film-maker is so simple that I hardly dare confess it: I want to see a beautiful story and to tell it well.'[9] This instinct for narrative, he believed, would be one of the chief casualties of the New Wave.

People who do not know how to tell a story try to deny its importance. That's what the adherents of *Cahiers du cinéma* try to do. But it's a dead end. For example, Jean-Luc Godard has never known how to tell a story, which is a very difficult thing to do successfully. The result is they try to stun their audience with fancy camera movements.

Born in 1890, Henri Decoin was a writer whose successful novel *Quinze Rounds* (*Fifteen Rounds*) won a prize for sports literature in 1930 and helped him to find regular work in the film industry as a screenwriter. In 1932, he went to Germany, where he supervised the French versions of double-language films produced by UFA at the Neue Babelsberg studios near Berlin. Returning briefly to France, he made his debut as a director in 1933 with *Toboggan*, which was made for Gaumont. Based on his own screenplay, it told the story of a has-been boxer who climbs back into the ring in search of former glory. But like so many other French film-makers and performers in this period, Decoin found that the German industry continued to offer the best prospects of sustained employment. Back on the Neue Babelsberg production line again, he learned to tackle a wide range of genres and to develop an eye for the box-office appeal of the film personality, taking advantage of the lesson he learned in 1935, when he directed seventeen-year-old actress Danielle Darrieux in *Le Domino vert*.

Marrying Darrieux in the same year, he directed her in a series of immensely successful films: *Mademoiselle ma mère* (1937), *Abus de confiance* (1937), *Retour à l'aube* (1938), *Battement de coeur* (1939) and *Premier rendez-vous* (1941). Carefully tailored to show off Darrieux's beauty and youthful vivacity, Decoin developed a brand of escapist romantic comedy that would see her mixed up in some absurd misunderstanding, from which a series of complications would ensue before all would be resolved in a happy ending. The style was that of a Lubitsch or Capra. Decoin's feel for lavish decor, carefully plotted narrative and polished performance made these films seems like the products of a French RKO or an MGM. 'Sophisticated, light, spiritual, unpretentious, the new film of Henri Decoin is conceived in the joyous tradition of the humorous American film or – if you prefer – the Boulevard comedy,' wrote the critic Maurice Bessy of *Battement de coeur*. 'A novel situation is elaborated with a number of amusing episodes, which a few talented performers animate without taking themselves too seriously.'[10]

Darrieux attributed to Decoin the success that she would enjoy as an international star. 'Without his advice, flair and influence, I would have remained a pretty girl who could sing appearing in only inconsequential productions and I would probably have left the profession pretty quickly. He knew how to give me a sense of what I could achieve and convinced me that I could take on serious dramatic roles.'[11] And Decoin himself knew how to switch to the different style that the changing mood of the box-office might dictate. In 1942 he directed Henri-Georges Clouzot's script of Georges Simenon's courtroom drama, *Les Inconnus dans la maison*. Featuring a powerful performance from Raimu as an alcoholic lawyer who gives up drink to defend a murder suspect, it was a dark, brooding film that reflected the sombre mood of the Occupation and anticipated several well-made thrillers that Decoin would direct in later years. But if such titles as *Entre onze heures et minuit* (1949) or *Bonnes à tuer* (1954) evoke little if any response outside France, it is because the changing critical climate conditioned international audiences to expect something else of the French cinema.

After a brief career as an actor in silent films, Jean Delannoy embarked upon a technical apprenticeship at Paramount's Joinville studios in 1930. Alberto Cavalcanti remembered him there as one of the 'good technicians in the cutting rooms who were glad, like I was, to handle sound'.[12] Delannoy rose to become chief editor at Paramount, working on over forty films. In 1933, he made his debut as a director with the musical comedy *Paris-Deauville*. Craft-conscious and exacting, he was, at the outbreak of war, one of the most prominent and sought-after film-makers working in France. He won international attention with his productions of Cocteau's *L'Eternel Retour* in 1943 and Gide's *La Symphonie pastorale* in 1946. Described by the *New York Times* as 'an intense, disturbing film', the latter won a *grand prix* at the first Cannes Film Festival and led to Delannoy receiving an invitation from David Selznick to remake the film in English with Selznick's then wife Jennifer Jones in the starring role. He turned the offer down, rightly fearing the kind of interference that he was spared in France. 'Here I am my own master, I am trusted,' he concluded.[13]

Looking back on his career in the early 1970s, Delannoy expressed the often-voiced preference of the industry director for a variety of subject-matter. 'I have attempted every genre and can say that I have never re-made a film . . . I like a change in inspiration. That means working with new collaborators. I seek this constant renewal in every sphere.'[14]

It was the kind of attitude that made him one of the special targets of the New Wave, whose championing of an auteur cinema was completely at odds with the production context in which he worked. His career in the commercial film industry depended upon his achieving box-office success for the projects that producers entrusted to him. It required respecting the economic value of the key box-office ingredients of star and story, containing any personal viewpoint within that framework. He was a commercial film-maker who knew how to hold, through the use of accessible but intelligent narrative, the attention of the large, mainstream audience that the New Wave struggled to reach.

The great achievement of the generation of French film-makers who came to the fore in the 1930s – the generation to which Delannoy belonged – was to make films that appealed to everyone, not just a narrow niche of the converted. By the end of that decade, the director Marcel Carné, who had established an extremely fruitful collaboration with the screenwriter Jacques Prévert, stood at the very pinnacle of what the French film industry could achieve. Capturing the mood of a weary, disillusioned country on the brink of war, his 1938 film *Quai des brumes* won every major prize of the year, both at home and abroad.[15] The path he took to reach this position had involved the long informal apprenticeship so typical of an industry career. As a child, he had been given a toy theatre, for which he wrote and put on plays. He went to the theatre and the music hall as often as he could, but was also mad about the cinema. He saw as many films as he could, but also joined a film-making club. When he was eighteen, he met the actress Françoise Rosay, who introduced him to her husband, Jacques Feyder. Taken on as an assistant on the production *Les Nouveaux Messieurs*, Carné did everything he could to make himself useful. ' If Feyder wanted someone to take away a chair that was annoying him, I would rush to do it . . . If a carpet had to be rolled up, or a vase switched from a table to a sideboard, I was always there.'[16] He asked Feyder if he could attend the editing of the film. Meeting the director every day at his apartment in Paris, he would travel with him to the cutting rooms at Billancourt. 'It was there that I spent whole afternoons learning how editing was able to impart life, rhythm and movement to the film – or the contrary.' But as important as this technical training was the clear affinity of outlook that he shared with his new mentor. Sometimes Feyder would invite him to a restaurant in the evening. 'We would talk endlessly, long past the time of the last metro.'

When the production was over, Feyder left France to work in Hollywood, where he stayed for three years. In this period Carné became a journalist writing about the cinema, and decided to make a little film of his own. He bought a camera and filmed young Parisians enjoying Sunday afternoon at Nogent on the Marne. The chief purpose of the exercise was to prove that he could make a film, but to his surprise the avant-garde cinema Studio des Ursulines booked the result. Playing on the same bill as Man Ray's *Le Mystère du château du Dé* and a documentary by Jean Painlevé, *Nogent, Eldorado ou Dimanche* was seen by

René Clair, who offered him a job as an assistant on *Sous les toits de Paris*.

Carné would later recall the unpleasant experience on this film of not fitting in to the long-established clique that had gathered around Clair. The lack of communication must have brought home to him the immense value of the rapport he had established with Feyder, who re-engaged him when he returned from Hollywood. Carné was assistant to Feyder on three of the most prestigious films to be made in France during the mid-1930s – *Le Grand Jeu*, *Pension Mimosas* and *La Kermesse héroïque*. As well as benefiting from the knowledge of Feyder himself, Carné was able to witness the work of such leading industry figures as production designer Lazare Meerson and screenwriter Charles Spaak.

A combination of this privileged insight into industry practice and the very best network that any newcomer could hope to have provided him with a fast track into directing on his own account. Françoise Rosay, who was one of the French cinema's biggest box-office draws in the wake of *La Kermesse héroïque*, offered to work in Carné's first film without payment. This commitment was enough to secure the backing of a producer, Albert Pinkevich. The subject he suggested, *Prison de velours*, was about a young woman who becomes, without realising it, the mistress of her mother's lover. Although the story was not of Carné's choosing, he was otherwise free to take the key creative decisions, which Pinkevich by and large accepted. Most providential of all these decisions was the choice of Jacques Prévert to write the screenplay.

The director and writer met for the first time at a private screening of *Le Crime de Monsieur Lange*, which Prévert had written for Jean Renoir. As Carné watched the film, Prévert's dialogue, with its striking combination of paradox, cruelty and tenderness, convinced him that he had found the perfect collaborator. Although Carné realised that they would have to accept the central protagonists in Pinkevich's suggested story, he knew that Prévert's genius for the offbeat, colourful character would make it possible to leaven the narrative of *Jenny* – as the film was eventually called – with some more interesting characters. 'Characters like the wicked hunchback Dromadaire or the arms-seller, who detests cruelty and likes only flowers, gentleness and little birds, were so striking that they caused one to forget the conventional nature of the plot.'[17]

The financial success of *Jenny* – it recouped seven times its cost, according to Carné – provided a solid foundation for the continuation of his career as a director. The reality of the French film industry, as with any commercial enterprise, was the requirement to make products that would achieve a profit-able return, but the collapse of the two big companies Gaumont and Pathé meant that, during the second half of the 1930s, the rigid, impersonal planned strategy of the corporation increas-ingly made way for a greater openness of thinking and indi-vidual initiative.

After Carné had completed *Jenny*, he was asked by Pinkevich to recommend a more established director that the company might support. Carné suggested Jean Renoir, since he had greatly admired *La Chienne*, *Toni* and *Le Crime de Monsieur Lange*. The commercial failure of these films meant that Renoir had yet to achieve any serious support from a mainstream audi-ence. Carné insisted that nonetheless Pinkevich should see the director. But when the meeting took place, Pinkevich was disap-pointed to receive from Renoir what he considered to be a com-mercially unappealing proposal to film a story about prisoners of war. Written in collaboration with screenwriter Charles Spaak, it was called *The Notebooks of Captain X*.

In his memoirs Carné recalled persisting in his support of Renoir. 'I can't comment on the merits of the story since I haven't read it,' he told Pinkevich. 'All I can say is that I know that over the last three years Renoir and Spaak have shown this screenplay to all the producers. If two such talented men are so desperate to bring this subject to the screen, it's because they have something special to say. They might not make a masterpiece, but it certainly won't be an insignificant film.' So Pinkevich saw Renoir again and, once he learned that the project had Jean Gabin's support, agreed to back the film. If the commercial subject and the star were important determining factors in the French cinema of the late 1930s, as notable a feature was the leeway for human interaction that Carné describes. In the event, Renoir repaid the hunch, with *La Grande Illusion* making a film that was not only a masterpiece but one of the most commercially successful of the period.

Jenny established the method of collaboration that Carné and Prévert would pursue through their ten-year-long partnership. As he wrote the script, Prévert would keep Carné posted step by step on the creation and the evolution of the characters. Meeting at a cafe, they would then exchange ideas on the script's progress, changing this or that aspect of it. Often Prévert would write a role with a particular actor in mind, which he would discuss with Carné. They found that usually they shared the same preferences, just as they complemented one another with their ideas for the script.

The kind of close organic collaboration that Carné describes in his memoirs brings to mind the British film-making partnership of Michael Powell and Emeric Pressburger. Powell may have been the director, and Pressburger the writer, but the symbiotic nature of the collaboration led them to share the credit for a creative process in which their respective roles were, in practice, interdependent. Maybe a similar solution would have helped Carné and Prévert to settle some of the inevitable questions about the authorship of their films.

Journalists always want to know which of us was responsible for what in the making of our films. We ourselves would find it very difficult to say for certain. Except for the dialogue, which Prévert wrote alone and I only occasionally modified, the development of the script and the choice of actors were a shared enterprise in which the importance of our respective roles varied from film to film. Our work together stopped once we had a final script. From that point, Prévert left me completely free to direct the film as I thought best.[18]

Carné felt particularly concerned to address the issue because of the hurt occasioned by the comments of the New Wave critics. He recalled in particular a comment of Truffaut, 'who declared that I "put into pictures the films of Prévert".' But it requires only a brief summary of the historical genesis of the films they made together to appreciate the inadequacy of such a simplification.

After the success of *Jenny*, Carné and Prévert went on to work with the producer Edouard Corniglion-Molinier, agreeing to film a subject that he suggested to them, the novel *His First Offence* by British writer Storer Clouston. Although the resulting film, *Drôle de drame*, was poorly received, it won the attention of Jean Gabin and Raoul Ploquin, the producer of French-language films at UFA, who both invited Carné to think of a subject for Gabin. The knowledge that a previous Pierre Mac Orlan novel, *La Bandera*, had helped to turn Gabin into a major star must to some extent have dictated Carné's suggestion of *Quai des brumes*, just as it is also surely natural to conclude that the iconic image of Pépé le Moko dying on the dockside had as much influence as the title of the novel in determining the switch from Mac Orlan's Montmartre setting to that of a port. The commercial considerations of film-industry production determined a creative path in which the star of the film, Jean Gabin, the director Marcel Carné, the screenwriter Jacques Prévert and the author of the original novel, Pierre Mac Orlan could all be said to have given the project significant authorial weight, but none decisively so.

When the completed script was sent to Raoul Ploquin it had become too dark and gloomy to win the approval of the propaganda department that now ruled UFA. Ploquin therefore agreed to arrange to have the project transferred to a French producer. Gregor Rabinovitch of Ciné-Alliance agreed to take over the venture on the strength of Gabin's involvement, although he too was disturbed by the relentlessly dark nature of a screenplay whose most sympathetic characters were an army deserter, a painter who commits suicide and a teenage girl who takes refuge in a dilapidated bar to escape the attentions of her perverted guardian. He insisted that the script should be rewritten to be more positive, but had to back down when Gabin expressed his faith in the project as it stood. The balance of power in the French film industry was such that the authority of a producer could be challenged in a way that was rarely possible in corporate Hollywood, where actors and directors, invariably tied to long-term contracts, were individually dispensable in a production programme that each year consisted of not just a handful of films, but dozens.

After *Quai des brumes*, Carné was invited by the producer Joseph Lucachevitch of Imperial-Film to direct a film starring Annabella, who was then the number one box-office star in France. This time Carné suggested as an appropriate vehicle a book called *Hôtel du Nord* by Eugène Dabit. 'If Annabella's happy, I'm happy too,' replied Lucachevitch.[19]

As Prévert was abroad, Carné turned to Jean Aurenche to provide an adaptation of the novel and Henri Jeanson to write the dialogue. Filming, which began in the summer of 1938, was disrupted by the political crisis that followed the Nazi invasion of Czechoslovakia. Several members of the crew, as well as the male lead Jean-Pierre Aumont, were called up. But the Munich agreement of September brought the respite needed to finish the production.

In February 1939 Carné embarked on the filming of *Le Jour se lève*. It emerged out of a contract that the producer Pierre Frogerais signed with Carné, Prévert and Gabin to make a mutually agreed subject. Gabin wanted to film a novel about a building-site foreman called *Martin Roumagnac*, but both Prévert and Carné found it dull. Prévert wanted them to make a script he was writing called *La Rue des vertus* about a gangster who returns to France with new ideas that a visit to the New World has inspired. But when Carné read a three-page synopsis by Jacques Viot about a factory worker who barricades himself into his room after killing a man, he was so impressed by the original construction of a story that began at the end and told itself in flashback that he decided this should be the project they pursued.

Through the mutual trust, respect and friendship of what had now become a close team, Carné was able to win the agreement of his collaborators. Gabin was doubtful about the project, but agreed to do it because Carné was directing it. Prévert was reluctant to abandon his script, but nonetheless, swallowing his pride, put it aside to work on building Viot's synopsis into a full-length scenario.

This was the professional compromise of film-makers who did not pursue the cinema of personal expression that the New Wave championed, but instead one of shared inspiration, whose great achievements lay in an affinity of outlook between close collaborators. The loose framework of the French film industry in the late 1930s, allowing a fluidity and ease of association, enabled such collaborative partnerships to mature and grow. The strength of the Carné films lay in his close working relationship not only with Prévert, but also with his favourite stars, Gabin and Arletty, the art director Alexandre Trauner, the composer Maurice Jaubert, and so on. A consistent nucleus of collaborators, who were bonded together more through a concordance of attitude than any contractual obligation, made it possible for ideas to emerge all the more strongly, out of the collective awareness of one another's tastes and qualities, and also to refine those ideas from film to film.

Often voted the best French film ever made, *Les Enfants du paradis* (1945) illustrates well the process of mutual inspiration that seemed to guide Carné's collaborative team. The film is an example of Jacques Prévert's screenwriting at its finest, yet the initial idea came from the actor Jean-Louis Barrault, with whom

Prévert and Carné had previously worked on the film *Drôle de drame*. Carné recalled that he and Prévert encountered their old friend strolling along the Promenade des Anglais in Nice. It was 1943, when the director and screenwriter were looking for a new subject in the aftermath of their extremely successful production, *Les Visiteurs du soir* (1942). In a cafe, where the three went to catch up on one another's news, Barrault told them an anecdote about the famous nineteenth-century mime, Baptiste Deburau. Although it seemed too slight to provide the basis for a film, Carné was so fascinated by the idea that he travelled to Paris to research the background in the Musée du Carnavalet. Here he found the wealth of material on the Boulevard du Crime and the theatre of Deburau's time that convinced everyone that it would be possible to make a strong film.

From the outset, Prévert wrote a script that assumed that Jean-Louis Barrault would play the part of Deburau. Prévert had no pre-existing story on which to build, but here too Barrault's involvement in the project suggested a solution. The previous year Barrault had starred in an ambitious, big-budget production called *La Symphonie fantastique*, in which he played the nineteenth-century French composer Hector Berlioz. Set in a similar period and milieu to *Les Enfants du paradis*, the film provided Prévert with an excellent model. Barrault's role as Berlioz – described in the film as 'a martyr to his art' – helped Prévert to develop the character of the mime artist Baptiste, but also offered a precious storyline.

Berlioz marries actress Henriette Smithson. They have a son together. Impatient with her husband's lack of success, and suspecting that he has fallen in love with singer Marie-Geneviève Martin (also known as Marie Recio), Henriette leaves him, taking their son Louis with her. Many years later, Berlioz is at last successful and living happily with Marie, but he misses his son Louis. Discovering that Louis won't see his father because of her, Marie decides that she must go away so that father and son can be reunited, but she is still deeply in love with Berlioz and, secretly attending his concerts, continues to watch over him.

Les Enfants du paradis makes a wholesale raid on this story-line. Baptiste is in love with the beautiful Garance, who joins the company of the Funambules theatre, but through his shyness he loses her. When Garance gets in trouble with the police, she leaves Paris under the protection of a rich count. Baptiste marries fellow actress Nathalie, with whom he has a son. Years later, Garance returns to Paris. Deeply in love with Baptiste, she attends the Funambules theatre to watch him perform on stage each night, but is deterred from attempting to revive their relationship when she discovers that Baptiste has a son. Not wanting to come between them, she goes away once again.

Prévert transformed the source material, investing the at times rather moralistic melodrama of *La Symphonie fantastique* with a truth of character and poetry that were all his own, but what is finally so striking about *Les Enfants du paradis* is the network of interdependent influences: the film cannot be said to have taken definitive shape from the decisive lead of any of the key contributors, but is best understood as the shared effort of them all. It is not Prévert's film, nor Carné's, nor Barrault's, although in the absence of any one of them it could not have existed at all.

An industry film rather than an individual's film, *Les Enfants du paradis* represented the essence of the collaborative nature of the French cinema at its finest. It was narrative-driven, popular cinema that, aimed at a large mass-market audience, was built around the conventional box-office values of star and story. The kind of director's personal expression that critics would later increasingly single out as a prime criterion of value was the exception rather than the rule, but nonetheless the director working in this system was likely to enjoy a far greater freedom than in Hollywood to guide the collective effort without interference.

10

The Spirit of '36

As an industry, the French cinema of the 1930s led an against-the-odds existence of continuous crises. After the collapse of Gaumont in 1934, a government report reached the conclusion that film production in France was deplorably incoherent.* It was entrusted to hundreds of small under-capitalised firms, a large percentage of which went bankrupt each year; the few large firms which had seemed on the way to a coherent structure had likewise just failed.

The Popular Front government, which came into power in June 1936, held another inquiry. In a series of sessions between December 1936 and May 1937, it painted an equally bleak picture of a film industry that, in economic terms, was completely dominated by foreign – especially American – companies. Pierre Wolff, a playwright and film critic for *Paris Soir*, expressed sentiments fairly typical of most of the witnesses the inquiry heard:

The French cinema is dying. There's no doubt about it. I can point to the cinemas in Paris, among them the very best and most prestigious, that never show a French film. Never! The Paris, the Lord Byron, the Avenue, the Balzac, the Cinéma des Champs-Elysées, the Cinéma de l'Etoile, the Elysée 79. These are very important theatres, but they never show a French film. It is appalling. The great competitor to the French cinema is the dubbed film. A dubbed film costs hardly a thing. Just a thousand francs to rent a dubbed Hollywood film. It might not always be a success in Paris, but it goes down well everywhere else. The upshot is that French films are left behind.[1]

* The report was written by Guy de Carmoy and presented to the Conseil National Economique in July 1936.

French films were popular with audiences but they were expensive to rent, so it was always tempting for an exhibitor to put on a cheap American film instead. It was significant too that fewer people in France went to see films. The country may have built a reputation for itself as a great film loving-nation, but the cinema was in practice a pastime for a small, largely city-based minority. In 1937 only 7 per cent of the French population went to the cinema, compared to 40 per cent in the United States.[2] In America, according to figures cited before the Renaitour inquiry, the average film had a box office return of eight to ten million francs, while in France the figure was a tenth of this sum.[3]

This basic economic fact not only limited the scope of the French film industry, whose resources prevented it from attempting a cinema of spectacle on the scale of Hollywood, but also made it an inherently precarious activity. Addressing the inquiry, the new minister of education and culture, Jean Zay, spoke of the institutional failings of an undercapitalised and unregulated industry that had led to the collapse of fifty-two film companies in 1935, and sixty-five in 1936.[4] Lamenting 'this beast with a thousand nameless heads', Zay advocated some kind of state intervention, but – deplorably incoherent itself – the government collapsed before it could do anything at all.

Deplorable incoherence was somehow the prevailing condition in 1930s France, but it was also at the heart of a great paradox. In terms of things that could be measured – audience figures, box-office receipts, investment – the French cinema fully justified the terminal gloom of the commentators, but at the same time, in terms of creative inspiration and sophistication, it had produced – and continued to produce – some of the most memorable films in the world. It is difficult not to conclude that, for all the genuine economic distress of the industry, this deplorable incoherence had at least one beneficial effect. The absence of solid authority – in which no powerful Hollywood-style moguls existed to impose an orthodoxy or to stifle individual enthusiasm and initiative – allowed a very broad and diverse cinema to develop.

While Hollywood seemed hermetically sealed by design from contemporary reality, the fractured, individual nature of the French film industry, in which not just production, but distribution and exhibition too, were in the hands of many small concerns, made the cinema unusually responsive to external circumstances. The sheer size of the big Hollywood companies resulted in a tendency for central diktat, whether it took the form of the rigidly imposed self-regulation of the Hays Code or the corporate conservatism of executives anxious to appeal to a world market and to retain the support of their shareholders. While Hollywood tended to offer a rose-tinted view of the times, the French cinema was free, in its disorganised and decentralised chaos, to offer a more direct engagement.

Through the decade, the cinema acted as a barometer to a political and social cauldron. The Stavisky scandal of 1934 provoked a series of violent demonstrations which culminated on 6 February in right-wing anti-parliamentary riots in which seventeen people were killed.* The next day the Radical party prime minister Edouard Daladier resigned. When the Communist Party organised a demonstration two days later at the Gare de l'Est, there were nine more deaths. The turmoil eventually led to a public alliance of the liberal and left-wing parties, the broad *front populaire* that the Communist leader Maurice Thorez – after a suitable nudge from Moscow – called upon in October 1934 'to combat Fascism and for Work, Liberty and Peace'.

A huge rally of this new Popular Front took place on Bastille

---

* A Ukrainian, Jew, Alexandre Stavisky was a fraudster whose financial dealings implicated many politicians and prominent figures of the period. In January 1934, the French police found him fatally injured from a gunshot wound, leaving public opinion divided as to whether his death was suicide or a police execution. The affair became a focal point for the widespread malaise, unrest and xenophobia that affected the decade.

Day 1935. Ten thousand delegates of the various organisations that supported the Popular Front took a solemn oath 'to remain united, to disarm and dissolve the seditious Leagues, to defend and develop democratic liberties and to ensure peace for humanity'.[5] The leaders of the Radical, Socialist and Communist parties, Daladier, Thorez and Léon Blum, marched side by side. Here was a political force whose goal was not only to take on the fascists but also to usher in huge progressive change. Nearly a year later, a Popular Front government, with Blum as prime minister, was voted in with a mandate to implement a raft of social legislation that included paid holidays, shorter working hours and collective bargaining rights. This was France's New Deal, the cause – among progressives at least – of huge idealism and hope.

The American journalist William Shirer was able to offer a first-hand account of the Popular Front's rise to power. Writing in his book *The Collapse of the Third Republic*, he commented:

There was something in the atmosphere fostered by the Popular Front which writers, philosophers and historians, as well as Leftist politicians, later looked back to as *L'Esprit de 1936*, the Spirit of 1936. For the poor there was a feeling of liberation. At last they felt a sense of participation in the life of the nation. They had helped to elect a Parliament and government that shared their aspirations and had tried to achieve some of them.[6]

L'Esprit de 1936 was as inspirational a force as, say, the 'Dunkirk spirit' was in Britain half a decade later. A renewed sense of political commitment and hope percolated through into a film community where there was no strong hierarchy to deter the idealistic initiatives of individuals. The future director of *Les Enfants du paradis*, Marcel Carné, had, at the request of the Communist Party, filmed the Popular Front Rally of Bastille Day 1935 with his own camera. He recalled in his memoirs that as the elections of the following year approached, he was invited to use the footage to make a film depicting the progressive struggle of the French people. Having signed a contract to direct his first feature film, he reluctantly had to decline, but Jean Renoir was happy to step into his shoes.[7] 'In 1935 the Communist Party asked me to make a propaganda film, which I was delighted to do,' he recalled. 'I believed that every honest man owed it to himself to resist Nazism. I am a film-maker, and this was the only way in which I could play a part in the battle.'[8]

La Vie est à nous (1936) seems a notable exception to the Renoir oeuvre both for the manner in which it was shot and for the crude and polarised stances it takes. Although Renoir did shoot some sequences himself, his critical role was to bring together footage which had actually been shot by a large team of other film-makers – Jacques Becker, Jacques Brunius, Henri Cartier-Bresson and many others who received no credit at all. Flung together very quickly from a large collection of assorted scraps, and supplemented with reconstructed scenes featuring actors sympathetic to the cause – Charles Blavette, Jean Dasté, Gaston Modot – it was a polemical rather than considered work of circumstance which promoted the Communist Party's role as principal crusader against the evils of fascism.

The upheavals of the time led film-makers into a political engagement. In Renoir's case it had begun with *Le Crime de Monsieur Lange*. When shooting on the film commenced in October 1935, the exhilarating events of Bastille Day a few weeks previously would have still been uppermost in his mind. He had himself attended the rally with his assistant Jacques Becker. It was Becker who had brought the original story idea for *Le Crime de Monsieur Lange* to his notice. Written by Jean Castanier, a member of the radical theatre company the Groupe Octobre, *Sur la cour* told the story of a group of print-shop workers who set up a cooperative after the disappearance of their unscrupulous 'patron'. Becker had wanted to direct the film himself as his first feature, but the producer André Halley des Fontaines did not feel confident enough to entrust the direction to someone with so little experience, and turned to Renoir instead.

In this way Renoir was brought into a project that he had

not initiated but for which he nonetheless felt huge sympathy. The story of a workers' cooperative was itself made in the kind of cooperative spirit depicted in the film. Jean Castanier, who had written the first draft script with Renoir, stayed on to be an assistant on the production. At Renoir's suggestion, Prévert, another member of the Groupe Octobre, joined the team to perfect the script. It was a marriage of such distinctive creative personalities that it doesn't seem far-fetched to regard it as having been yet another alliance in the spirit of Blum and Thorez. Of their partnership, Renoir commented:

I constantly said to him, 'Well, old man, here we have to improvise,' and the film was improvised, as were all my films, but with Prévert's constant collaboration. I'm sure that it would be impossible to know the origin of which ideas were mine and which were Jacques'. Actually, we found everything together.[9]

Le Crime de Monsieur Lange amounted to an allegory, with a revolutionary twist, of the wild hopes that the Popular Front had instigated. The unscrupulous proprietor Batala represented the old order that the progressive new forces would sweep away. Some weeks after its opening at the Aubert-Palace cinema in Paris on 24 January 1936, the critic Roger Leenhardt described it as 'a film clearly inspired by Communism (1936-style)'.[10]

Within weeks of the premiere of *Le Crime de Monsieur Lange*, Renoir was at work on *La Vie est à nous*. Once again the whole spirit of the enterprise was – in 1936 style – to play down individual roles. The film is described in its opening credits as 'made collectively by a team of technicians, artists and workers'. Nowhere is Renoir singled out as the director.

Exhibited just weeks before the parliamentary elections of 1936, the film has the feel of a kind of primitive party political broadcast. An impassioned assembly listens, with fervent expressions of hope, to the oratory of the Communist party leaders, behind whom loom giant posters of Marx, Lenin and Stalin.

Some of the film's staged scenes seem to lean on recent history.

For example, one sequence shows a group of Communists coming to the rescue of a newspaper vendor who is being beaten up by Fascist thugs for selling the Communist Party newspaper *L'Humanité*. This scene would have been shot just weeks after a notorious incident in which one of the leaders of the Popular Front, Léon Blum, had been attacked and badly injured by Fascist thugs from Action Française. A group of construction workers came to his rescue.[11]

The film was shown in private at the Panthéon cinema in Paris on 7 April.[12] Three days later, Paul Vaillant-Couturier, editor of the Communist Party newspaper *Humanité*, celebrated the film as a '*coup de maître*' that, in its depiction of the people's struggle for 'bread, peace and freedom', offered an example of what the French cinema might become once it had been freed from the 'enslavement of money'.[13] The same issue ran an advertisement promising that the release of the film would take place 'very soon', but the French censors refused to grant the visa necessary for its public exhibition, so that the ban of the film itself became the occasion for yet another of the French Communist Party's endless crusades.

In the week leading up to the first round of the parliamentary elections (on 26 April), *L'Humanité* carried daily adverts urging its readers to take appropriate action. 'The censorship board has forbidden the public exhibition of *La Vie est à nous* because it reflects the life, struggles and aspirations of the French people,' it declared on 23 April. 'Protest by joining Ciné-Liberté.'

Established a few months previously, Ciné-Liberté was an association of film-makers, workers and spectators who believed in an independent, progressive cinema. It took its name from Radio-Liberté, a similar initiative that had been set up in the field of broadcasting. Its supporters included such prominent figures as Henri Jeanson, Jacques Feyder, Louis Jouvet and Gaston Modot, who like Renoir probably regarded it as a vehicle to make a political stand in a time when neutrality was no longer acceptable.

On 24 April, *L'Humanité* announced the details of Ciné-Liberté's campaign to help *La Vie est à nous* beat the ban. 'The great organisation that is Ciné-Liberté, which, with Jean Renoir, Henri Jeanson, etc., fights for a people's cinema, has decided – in keeping with its aim of making known the cinema's potential – to present *La Vie est à nous* in private showings to its members.' Readers were invited to subscribe to the organisation, 'in order to see this great film of the people, in order to fight for the freedom of the screen'. A week later, the newspaper wrote of the organisation's intention itself 'to produce films of genuine public appeal, to bring together audiences sick of the platitudes of bourgeois films, to support independent production and to combat censorship'.

Over the next two years, some documentaries and perhaps most notably Renoir's dramatisation of the French revolution, *La Marseillaise*, would emerge out of the Ciné-Liberté initiative. The movement eventually ran out of steam as disillusionment with the Popular Front movement grew. In the event, it did little more than dent the public appetite for 'bourgeois' entertainment, whether Hollywood or the mainstream French cinema. But if it failed in its ambition to forge an alternative progressive cinema for the masses, its impromptu existence was an index of the speed with which an alternative framework of opinion could spring up in France to challenge the prevailing orthodoxy.

Looking back many years later, when he was interviewed for the ORTF TV programme *Gros Plan*, Jean Renoir was able to give his own naivety some historical perspective:

It was a time of enthusiasm. A great firework display before the catastrophe. During this marvellous moment we could believe that France's divisions were at an end. We could believe that we could achieve a kind of union, a union of all French people from all their different classes and backgrounds. We could believe that we had got over all that endless division in French society that had endured since the Religious Wars.

Renoir's romance with the Popular Front would continue

through two more films. *Les Bas-fonds* (1936), which was based on the socialist realist play by Maxim Gorky, was made soon after the Popular Front government had come to power in June 1936, shot during August and September, then released in December. *La Marseillaise* was made soon afterwards through the participation of Ciné-Liberté and the Communist Party trade union the CGT, but perhaps most of all 'the people'. A film about the people, it was intended to be made by the people for the people. With a subvention of fifty thousand francs from the Popular Front government, the rest of the money was raised by public subscription. In March 1937, the magazine *Cinématographie française* explained that the film was intended to demonstrate 'that the people can create an important work of this sort without the aid of "capitalism". This demonstration film represents the start of a new age in film production, in which employers and finance will have no place.'[14]

But the report turned out to be over-optimistic. By the time filming had begun in August 1937, the first Popular Front government of Léon Blum had fallen and the great hopes of the previous years were beginning to turn into disappointment.

Duvivier's *La Belle Equipe* (1936) – made just as the first Popular Front government was elected – turned out to be a prescient anticipation of the disillusionment ahead. Together five unemployed men form a cooperative to restore and run a *guinguette*, financing the venture with money won in a lottery. But bad luck and dissension thwart the group's idealistic vision. One of their number, Mario, a political refugee from Spain, receives a deportation order. Then another, Tintin, falls through the roof just as he raises up a workers' flag to celebrate the *guinguette*'s restoration. Finally, the two remaining members of the group, Jean and Charles, fall out over a woman.

Famously, Duvivier shot two endings. In the original script, the argument between the two men comes to a head on the day the *guinguette* opens. In a struggle, Jean shoots Charles dead. 'It was a good idea, a good idea,' he laments. 'Too good to work.'

But the producer Arys Nissotti, perhaps mindful of the huge support that the newly elected Popular Front government still enjoyed, insisted that Duvivier film a happy ending, in which Jean and Charles repair their differences and shun the woman who has come between them. Both endings still survive. The downbeat ending that today is usually shown not only reflects the dramatic logic of the story, but also represents the way history actually turned out.

As the Depression deepened, the Popular Front government of Léon Blum came under increasing pressure. The financial and business community moved their capital out of the country, and the government was forced to devalue the French currency by 30 per cent in the hope of attracting capital back – but to no avail. Blum compared this flight of capital to 'desertion in wartime. If every Frenchman had done his duty we would have nothing to fear.'[15] When Blum sought emergency powers to cope with the financial crisis, the Senate voted against him. Faced with an impasse, he handed in his resignation on 22 June 1937. The words of Jean Gabin might easily have been ringing in his head: '*C'était une belle idée*. It was a good idea, a good idea. Too good to work.'

11

Breaking the Rules

By the time the Popular Front government had come to power, Jean Renoir had achieved considerable prominence in France, but he was barely known in the English-speaking world. Few of his films were exhibited in England or America. When they were, it was rarely because anyone had any idea who he was. The reason why New Yorkers in late 1934 might have gone to see *Madame Bovary* at the tiny Acme Theatre in Union Square was Flaubert, not Renoir. 'Turned out by a capable French director,' the *New York Times* believed that the film might give an American audience 'at least a faint idea of why the publication of Gustave Flaubert's masterpiece of *Madame Bovary* created such excitement in literary and social circles in France'.[1]

When *Toni* reached New York two years later, it was described as 'Marcel Pagnol's latest Gallic film production'.[2] Brought up almost exclusively on a Hollywood diet, English-speaking audiences had not been schooled to discern a director's voice, but the lack of recognition was also because Renoir's often elliptical style challenged the very concept of what the cinema was. In the *New York Times* Frank Nugent described Renoir's adaptation of Gorky's *The Lower Depths* (*Les Bas-fonds*), which reached the United States in September 1937, as 'a strange drama, all the stranger for its surface unsuitability to the cinema'. It was a film in which 'nothing happens', but nonetheless he observed, 'If Hollywood could do nothing half so well, we should be content.'[3]

Ignored by most, greatly respected by a few, Renoir seemed too different to gain any serious hold until *La Grande Illusion* perfectly captured the Zeitgeist of a Europe that seemed on the verge of another war. Opening in the United States just before the Munich Agreement, at the Filmarte, 12 September 1938, it brought him at last the kind of commercial success and international recognition that had eluded him through most of the 1930s.

Renoir took advantage of his change in fortune once again to establish his own film company. The name, Nouvelles Editions Françaises (NEF), which sounded more like that of a book publisher, suggested his continuing devotion towards a cinema of personal expression. The commentators of the period noted the control that this new venture allowed him to exert over every sphere of the production, which was a remarkable departure from the usual practice of the mainstream industry. 'Word from Paris has it that Jean Renoir, best known as a director, will not only direct but will also write, produce, distribute and star in his next film,' wrote a reporter for the *New York Times* in February 1939, shortly before the production began.[4]

From the American perspective, it was extraordinary. Theirs was a cinema in which large corporations dominated, Hollywood providing a glitzy facade for an assembly line. While personalities may have been the essential commodity of this factory, it was the impersonal demands of the profit motive that drove the enterprise. The one company that seemed a notable exception was United Artists, which had been formed in 1919 by film pioneers Chaplin, Griffith, Pickford and Fairbanks. Twenty years on, it distributed the films of Hollywood's most prestigious independent producers, including Samuel Goldwyn, David Selznick and Walter Wanger. The NEF had been created with the specific purpose of producing and distributing Renoir's own films, but, as Renoir put it, the 'far-off goal was to form something like a French "United Artists"',[5] which would afford film-makers more creative independence and freedom than the prevailing practices of the French film industry made possible. It was a development that echoed the aspirations that he had already expressed under the umbrella of Ciné-Liberté. At the end of January 1939, he gave a lecture at the London Film Institute Society, in which he expressed some of his hopes for a new kind of film-making. During the trip, he met the great documentary film-maker Robert Flaherty, whose career-long struggles with the commercial industry must have evoked considerable fellow feeling. They discussed the possibility of Flaherty releasing his films through the NEF, once the company had become firmly established. Renoir also hoped to attract the participation of France's most successful director, Julien Duvivier.

But even for the much more loosely organised French cinema, Renoir's new venture was a decisive departure from the usual trinity of Script, Star and Director that sustained the industry. The hugely successful *La Grande Illusion* demonstrated these three central pillars around which most French feature productions were constructed – director Jean Renoir, writer Charles Spaak, box-office stars Jean Gabin and Pierre Fresnay. But as circumstances provided him with increased freedom, Renoir's natural inclination seemed to be to revert to the model of the 1920s avant-garde cinema in which the author-director was clearly at the heart of the venture from the very outset.

The first project that Renoir's new company announced was *La Règle du jeu*. It was an ensemble piece of several well-known performers, but every aspect of the production was infused with Renoir's sensibility, which he spread through his command over the chemistry of personal relationships. There was something essentially organic about his approach to the film-making process. This can be seen in the choice of people who made up his team, which was notable for its nucleus of friends and family. The production manager was his younger brother Claude Renoir; the editor of the film was his partner Marguerite Houllé, who had long been known in the French film industry under the name of Marguerite Renoir; the script girl was his new love and future wife Dido Freire; and an assistant cameraman was Alain Renoir, his son by his marriage to Catherine Hessling. Many other members of the production team were people he had worked with before and felt comfortable with – the production designer Eugène Lourié, the composer Joseph Kosma, the cinematographer Jean Bachelet, the sound engineer Joseph de Bretagne, to name just a few. This network of pre-existing relationships formed a rich soil.

The cinema for Renoir was a process of soaking up the influences of environment and culture, which were then reflected back in the films that resulted from the interaction. It was directly opposed to the notion of the international box-office film, as he explained during his lecture in London:

The Englisman could only interest the French by telling them stories of what was happening in his homeland, by trying to make them love and understand his country. If he tried to describe to them the Rue de la Paix, they had a right to retort that they knew that street better than he did. In the same way, a French film was not good because it was international, but because it was typically French.[6]

In *La Règle du jeu* Renoir reflected back the society that he saw all around him, which in 1939 – to use Renoir's memorable phrase – was 'dancing on a volcano'. His engagement with contemporary events meant that fact and fiction were inextricably entwined, to the extent that behind *La Règle du jeu* can be found a haunting and parallel true story.

A leading actress of Vienna's prestigious Burgtheater, Nora Grégor, played Christine, the Austrian-born bride of the Marquis Robert de la Cheyniest, played by Marcel Dalio. Enjoying a privileged and opulent lifestyle, the couple are at the heart of Paris's high society, yet at the same time outsiders. While Christine must live in a country that is not her own, Robert is a Jew at a time when anti-Semitism has begun to take hold in France as well as Germany.

The characters take shape out of immediate history. Grégor's own recent experience gave her a direct insight into their uneasy existence. Of Jewish descent, at the end of 1937 she had married the former Vice-Chancellor of Austria, Prince Ernst Rüdiger von Stahremberg. An astoundingly wealthy aristocrat, who owned thirty-six castles, Stahremberg led the kind of complicated romantic life that his fictional counterpart in Renoir's film would surely have recognised. Determined to 'deserve' his new wife, the Marquis Robert de la Cheyniest attempts to engineer a dignified farewell to his long-term mistress, but finds that life resists such tidy solutions. Stahremberg had long been romantically linked to Grégor, but it took years to have his marriage to his first wife, Countess Marie-Elisabeth Salm-Reifferscheidt-Raitz, finally annulled. The Jewishness of his new bride then effectively put an end to his political career as the leader of Austria's paramilitary and fascist party, the Heimwehr. In spite of his authoritarian politics, Stahremberg had been an outspoken opponent of Hitler.

The German annexation of Austria in March 1938 forced the couple to flee the country. While the Nazis set about confiscating their property, they both began to hunt for temporary jobs in Paris, intending in the longer term to move on to the United States. It was in Paris that Renoir first met von Stahremberg. 'He and his wife were in a state of great disarray,' he recalled. 'Everything they believed in was collapsing.'

Their glamorous but nonetheless painful dislocation can be traced in the society pages of the period. Soon after their arrival in Paris, they attended a reception in an hotel on the Place de Palais Bourbon. The guests of honour were the Duke and Duchess of Windsor – themselves exiles of a kind. At the end of the evening, the Princess Stahremberg – Nora Grégor – got up to sing, 'Auf wiedersehen . . . Vienna, oh my Vienna . . .' And according to Le Figaro's society reporter, 'No one thought to try to stop the tears that shone in her eyes like hidden diamonds.'[7]

'One could write a novel about the state of mind of those exiles,' commented Renoir.[8] Instead, he seems to have put much of what he might have written into his film. The prince and his collapsing world must surely have reminded him of Captain von Rauffenstein, the aristocrat commandant of the prisoner-of-war camp in La Grande Illusion, who clings on to an outdated code of honour and privilege that he knows cannot survive the war. With his burnt and crippled body patched together with bits of steel, he is a symbol of a lingering but broken past that the values of a totally changed society will soon efface.

La Règle du jeu is a return to the theme, depicting the loss of innocence that follows the final destruction of this old world. Christine, according to Renoir's conception of the character, was an out-of-date romantic who must 'suddenly face the ugly realities of life'. Recalling *La Règle du jeu* in his memoirs, Renoir explained a method of creation that relied on building a story after real-life models. 'I was content to use the appearance of Nora Grégor, her look of "birdlike" sincerity, to shape the character of Christine. Once again I started from externals to arrive at the creation of a character or a plot.' Grégor's Austrian accent further helped him to develop his conception of an outsider struggling to find her bearings in an unfamiliar society. 'I had the impression that this accent was the tiny barrier, the tiny curtain that kept her apart from her entourage.'[9] Concerned to stress the importance of an abiding aesthetic principle, he appealed to the example of his father, Auguste: 'I need observation as a point of departure. My father, who mistrusted imagination, said: "If you paint the leaf on a tree without using a model you risk becoming stereotyped, because your imagination will only supply you with a few leaves whereas Nature offers you millions."'

A long interview with Renoir conducted by the New Wave film-maker Jacques Rivette in the late 1960s brought out this fusion of reality and make-believe well. By far the greater part of the interview took place in a windowless viewing theatre, where Rivette and Renoir discuss projected sequences from the film. But about halfway through, Renoir returns to the country house where *La Règle du jeu* had been made, nearly thirty years previously. Assuming his old role of the Marquis Robert de la Cheyniest, the actor Marcel Dalio comes out on to the terrrace to greet Renoir, addressing the director by the name of the character he played in the film: 'Ah, Octave . . . It's so kind of you to come to see me after such a long time.'

They sit down on the front steps together.

'I know this terrace so well,' he continues.

'How so?' asks Renoir/Octave.

'It must be because I'm at home here.'

'Yes, you're at home . . . You're Marquis Robert de la Cheyniest, and Dalio too.'

'Yes, and Dalio too.'

When the actor asks why he was chosen to play the Marquis, Renoir answers, 'I work through memory. I'm not very good at making up things, but I have a good memory. And once I knew lots of people in the aristocracy who were like you.'

'Luckily for me!'

'And I knew your character extremely well. And you knew him too. You knew him, and you were able to get inside him.'

'Little by little, it should be said. I was born here! And in six weeks I became the Marquis de la Cheyniest.'

In the film, Christine is the daughter of a great musician, while Renoir himself plays her oldest friend, Octave. 'That girl,' Octave explains to his friend André Jurieux, 'is like my sister. We grew up together. Her father, old Stiller, was the greatest conductor in the world, but also the very best of human beings.'

A published commentary on *La Règle du jeu* explains the reference in a footnote as follows: 'Although no celebrated musician by the name of Stiller exists in reality, Mauritz Stiller (1883–1928) was one of the great film-makers of the silent era.' Possibly, Renoir was thinking in part of Stiller, but even here there was a closer real-life model.

Although Nora Grégor had become the Princess Stahremberg in 1937, she had previously been married to a concert pianist called Mitja Nikisch. Her father-in-law, Arthur Nikisch, was renowned as one of the world's great conductors during the first decades of the twentieth century. Of Hungarian descent, Nikisch was director of the Leipzig Opera and a principal conductor of the Berlin Philharmonic. In 1913, he made the first ever commercial recording of Beethoven's Symphony No. 5. When he died in 1922, one of his disciples, Sir Adrian Boult, wrote a long tribute, lamenting a loss that was 'comparable to the loss of the dies at the Mint or the destruction of the standard measures at Greenwich'. In these words we can find some of the admiration that Octave feels for Christine's father.[10]

The house party slowly descends into chaos, reflecting a society that has lost its moral bearings. Caught up in the confusion, Octave and Christine share a brief moment of nostalgia for a better time when Christine's father was still alive to provide a standard of excellence, beauty and good authority. In their imaginations they are once again children, who are able to put their faith in the grown-up world.

'Your father passed by without looking at us. And we hid behind the door. The musicians of course were already standing. And, in the chamber, there was applause.'

Christine is pleased to share the illusion. 'The atmosphere of great days.'

'And your father . . .' continues Octave. 'Such presence! He crossed the stage and at once everyone fell silent, even the King. Then he took up his baton from the first violin in the usual way. And as in a dream . . .'

At this point the dream crumbles, as Octave reaches the part in his memory that it is pointless for him to try to reconstruct. He can take up the conductor's stick, but he does not know how to use it. Realising that he will never be able to live up to the example of his hero, he has no choice but to confront his own failure.

As the son of a great painter, Renoir himself would have been able to imagine this fate of falling short. Perhaps he once feared it for himself, especially in the early years of his career, when his attempt to make films was such a struggle, with so little return, that it seemed principally a means of squandering the fortune that his father's genius had provided. Only with the recent successes of *La Grande Illusion* and *La Bête humaine* did his reputation at last seem assured.

Mitja Nikisch had the same problem of how to come out from behind the shadow of a famous father's reputation. He started out as a concert pianist, but his real passion was for the dance music of the Weimar republic. His jazz group, the Mitja Nikisch Tanz-Orchester, was described by one prominent musician of the time as 'the best dance band ever heard in Berlin'. It provided the music for the 1931 Nora Grégor film, . . . *und das ist die Hauptsache!? (That's All That Matters)*. When he married the star of the picture, he must have anticipated a bright future. But with the new decade, fate took a cruel turn. First, the rise of Nazism took away his career; and then Prince von Stahremberg took away his wife. In 1936, Nikisch committed suicide.

In the film, Renoir's hapless innocent, André Jurieux, who does not know how to play the rules of a jaded and decadent society, seems as much a victim of the time. He makes his own attempt at suicide after Christine greets with indifference his grand gesture of flying across the Atlantic for her. This suicide attempt fails, but his eventual death, when the enraged game-keeper Schumacher shoots him, mistaking him for the poacher Marceau who is after Schumacher's wife, seems nonetheless inevitable. Recalling the scene, Renoir commented, 'The Gods demand their sacrifice.'[11] Jurieux seems as helpless as the rabbits slaughtered in the earlier hunt, caught in the trap of unavoidable circumstance.

These traces of ghosts from a vanished world linger in the intimate relationship with reality that allowed *La Règle du jeu* to capture the atmosphere of its time with such accuracy. In a seamless blend of the personal and the political, Renoir's depiction of private decadence amplified his own sense of disappointment in France; the exhilaration he had felt at the election of the Popular Front government had to yield, only two years later, to the shabby compromises of the Munich Agreement.

Renoir's active commitment to the struggle against fascism

expressed itself not only in the films he made during this period, but also in his journalism. In 1937 he began a weekly column for the new Communist evening daily *Ce Soir*, which was edited by the writer and poet Louis Aragon. A persistent theme in his writing was the growing menace of militarism in Europe. While he made clear his special fondness for Germany, he lost no opportunity to point out the evils of the Nazi regime that had taken the country over. His unflinchingly frank comments amounted to a programme to wake up a society that he regarded as sleepwalking into disaster, to get it to take notice before it was too late. Often he reflected on the essential absurdity of Hitler and Mussolini that the world preferred to disregard. Writing one week about Mussolini's hat, with its extravagant tassel and bobble, he observed, 'If the craftsman who made this headwear had the least sense of humour, he would have to laugh. What should bother us is that millions of men do not laugh, and that the opposite of farce is calamitous tragedy.'[12]

If some of the tragic-comic tone of *La Règle du jeu* is suggested in this remark, it was Munich that brought home to Renoir that his warnings had fallen on deaf ears. The column that he wrote immediately afterwards expressed the depths of his disillusionment:

I was a little less proud to be French this week, when I saw the crowds on the streets of Paris welcome our president's return from Munich. So, the Germans are entering the Sudetenland. Will our newspapers publish, as they did after Vienna, photographs of the sort of courtesies that Hitler's followers are bound to pay to the Sudetenland Jews? Will we once again see old men made to clean the streets on their knees in the mud? And women forced to wear degrading badges in public?[13]

The following months would dent Renoir's faith in France even further, as the Popular Front crumbled into meaninglessness and the Franco dictatorship was officially recognised, in February 1939, after the defeat of the Republic in the Spanish Civil War.

It was with the bitter taste of Spain and Munich that Renoir began to conceive *La Règle du jeu*. With its intimation of approaching disaster, the film has a prophetic quality. 'You know, you're not a fool,' the Marquis tells Octave. 'You're a poet. A dangerous poet!'

But the poet's message turned out to be too difficult for people to accept – many of them, after all, had cheered Daladier on his return from Munich. 'Not since the landing of Lindbergh has Le Bourget known such enthusiasm,' wrote *Le Figaro* the day after the French prime minister's return. 'From lunchtime the aerodrome was invaded by a joyful crowd pouring out of buses, trams, taxis and cars.'[14]

Renoir would recreate the rapturous reception the reporter had described a few months later, in mid-June 1939, when he filmed the opening of *La Règle du jeu*:

We have just reached the tarmac of Le Bourget airport where we are trying to clear a path through the crowds, who have come to greet the great airman André Jurieux – André Jurieux, who has just achieved an extraordinary feat: he has crossed the Atlantic in twenty-three hours, a performance unmatched, my dear listeners, since Charles Lindbergh.[15]

By a paradox, even as Renoir was pondering the shame of Munich, he himself was enjoying the same taste of public adulation that had greeted Lindbergh and Daladier. No French film in 1939 could have been more eagerly awaited than the first effort of his new independent production company. He was on a roll. His most recent film *La Bête humaine* had opened in Paris to huge acclaim over Christmas 1938. Then in the New Year, he won the award for Best Foreign Language film for *La Grande Illusion* from the New York Film Critics' Circle. To mark the occasion, on 8 January 1939, NBC broadcast a special trans-atlantic interview with Renoir and one of the stars of the film, Erich von Stroheim. The following month, just days after Renoir had commenced shooting his new production, he learned that *La Grande Illusion* had become the first ever foreign-language film to receive an Academy Award nomination for Best Film.

La Règle du jeu was meant to build on this success. Costing five million francs, it was the most expensive film yet to be produced in France.[16] An inventive and varied press campaign, which began a week ahead of the film's release, offered some measure of the great hopes for a film clearly conceived as a radical departure from the conventional production. To whet readers' appetites, the campaign team issued a crossword competition three days before the opening night. The winners were to receive free tickets to see the film. Typical of the clues were 5 Across: 'A foreign princess and star who has just created a magnificent role with enormous feeling.' Or 5 Down: 'Son of a great painter, he has won his own acclaim as a director.'[17]

But the acclaim was about to come to an abrupt end. On Wednesday 28 June, the finished version of the film, running an hour and fifty-three minutes, had its first private screening. The reception was ominously muted. The next day the film was screened again before the French minister of culture, Jean Zay, and the jury responsible for choosing an annual *Grand Prix* for best French film. Up until that night, Renoir could have considered himself a prime contender to take the prize, but it quickly became apparent that this was no longer a realistic expectation. When the award was announced ten days later, the winner was Marcel Carné's *Quai des brumes*.[18] The fact that *La Règle du jeu* wasn't even named among the runners-up for the award was a major setback, after all the expectation.

Amid the atmosphere of dissatisfaction that followed the private screenings, the executives at Gaumont, who were the distributors of the film, expressed their view that it should be cut. At first Renoir refused, relenting only when he was warned that otherwise it would be a box-office failure. Working with Marguerite Renoir, he pared it down by thirteen minutes, trimming shots here and there through its entire length.

On Friday 7 July, Renoir attended the premiere of *La Règle du jeu* at the Colisée cinema. The film was greeted with cries of derision. One of the spectators set the back of a chair alight with a newspaper, protesting that any cinema that showed the film ought to be burned down. Others whistled and booed.[19] Dismayed by the hostile reaction, Renoir walked out early, taking refuge with some friends in a nearby cafe.

The controversy surrounding the premiere helped to attract sizeable audiences over the weekend, but they responded no more favourably. 'At every performance I attended I could feel . . . unanimous disapproval,' recalled Renoir.[20] Dismayed by the continuing negative reaction, the managers of the two Paris cinemas in which the film had opened for the exclusive first run asked him to cut the passages that appeared to give the most offence. Desperate to save the film, he quickly agreed. Shorn of yet more minutes, it continued to play through August, but the long summer break, and now the fear of an imminent war, meant that it did so to largely empty houses.

The toast of the film world at the beginning of 1939, Renoir was responsible for the summer's biggest flop. Analysing the reasons for the film's failure years later, he concluded:

People go to the cinema in the hope of forgetting their everyday problems, and it was precisely their own worries that I had plunged them into. I depicted pleasant, sympathetic characters, but showed them in a society in the process of disintegration, so that they were defeated at the outset, like Stahremberg and his peasants. The audience recognised this. The truth is that they recognised themselves. People who commit suicide do not care to do it in front of witnesses.

La Règle du jeu announced itself as a *divertissement*, an entertainment, but the sustained political and social commitment of Renoir's preceding films made it hard to doubt its serious purpose. The epigraph from *Le Mariage de Figaro* that opens the film suggests the model that Renoir had in mind. Performed in 1784, Beaumarchais's play was ostensibly a comedy – one perhaps more familiar to us today through the opera that Mozart and Da Ponte made from it. But if its story of a master's thwarted attempts to take advantage of his servant's betrothed has long since been safely assimilated into the canon of establishment culture, the original play, with its unmistakeable attack on the class system, was regarded as a hugely influential and subversive work that helped to pave the way for the French Revolution.

As a deeply divided France began in July 1939 to mark the hundred and fiftieth anniversary of that revolution, the parallels between the two times must have seemed more than usually marked. There was the same great release of chaotic, unpredictable energy, the same atmosphere of civil discord and external danger, the same maelstrom of rallies, marches and expressions of solidarity.

But at the last minute the mood had turned, the imminence of war breeding a show of resolve. The frivolous Cupid that on the day of the film's premiere smiled at the readers of *Le Figaro*'s 'What's On' page, advertising *La Règle du jeu* to be 'a film unlike the others', made a sharp contrast with the newspaper's front page, where the lead story concerned the efforts of Britain and France to negotiate a defence pact with the Soviet Union, with a photograph beneath showing model-boat enthusiasts conducting trials of miniature battleships on a pond in the Tuileries. Another article, a whole week ahead of the occasion, was already looking forward to the Bastille Day celebrations. 'Fifty-two English planes will take part in the fly-past,' claimed the headline, in a display of the Anglo-French unity that had become a familiar theme during the last days of peace. The clear agenda was reassurance and the projection of strength. 'In France, one thing always manifests itself at the last minute more clearly than anything else: the Frenchman is a patriot . . . When he sees that his country is really in danger, then nothing will prevent him from sacrificing everything to it.'[21]

Now that the country was limbering up for war, the pressing need was for examples of valour and determination, not indictments of decadence. By chance the Warner Brothers movie *Confessions of a Nazi Spy* opened in Paris in the same week as *La Règle du jeu*. Based on a true story, this account of how the FBI broke up a Nazi spy-ring in America was the first

DES CUIRASSES « MINIATURES » EVOLUENT
DANS LE BASSIN DES TUILERIES

Le Figaro, 7 July 1939

major Hollywood film to be openly hostile to the Nazi regime. Welcoming a 'masterpiece', *Le Figaro* considered it to be a film of current significance that 'must be seen', because 'it dares to tell the truth, the whole truth and nothing but the truth'.[22] When the newspaper reviewed both films together in the same column, Renoir's seemed irresponsibly inconsequential in comparison, a wilful disregard of duty during the nation's hour of need. Dismissing the whole 'bizarre spectacle' as 'one long succession of errors . . . a heavy-handed fantasy with woolly dialogue', the reviewer puzzled over what exactly the director had hoped to achieve.[23]

The priority for France in the summer of 1939 was to rekindle some self-belief. In this context, it is easy to understand the disappointment of Jean Zay, the Minister of Education and Culture, when he viewed the film just before its opening. Long before the resort to guns and bombs, the fascist dictatorships and democracies had been engaged in a fierce propaganda war. The Venice International Film Festival became an important battleground. In 1937, Renoir's *La Grande Illusion* won a prize at the festival for 'Best Artistic Ensemble'; but the widespread view that it had been denied the top prize for political reasons seemed to be confirmed when both Germany and Italy banned the film soon after the festival. There was an even greater uproar the following year when the festival's highest award, the Mussolini Cup, was awarded jointly to Leni Riefenstahl's *Olympia* and an overtly fascist Italian film, *Luciano Serra Pilota*, which had been made under the supervision of Mussolini's own son, Vittorio. So the French government backed efforts to organise a rival festival that would promote democratic values.

As Zay began to think about the possible French entries for the first Cannes Film Festival, to take place over the first three weeks of September 1939, he must have hoped that Renoir's new film would provide a propaganda weapon to equal *La Grande Illusion*. But while the earlier film had offered a passionate plea for peace between the nations, *La Règle du jeu*, with its depiction of a society blundering into disaster, suggested that its director had lost faith in the ability of his country to maintain such a peace. Negative in tone, it offered a view of France that no government could possibly sanction. Hence it was an inevitable absentee from the list of official French films chosen for the new festival.[24]

The plethora of spy dramas that reached French screens during the second half of the 1930s were not the kind of films to win awards, but they expressed the need of a threatened nation to project an image of strength. In *Deuxième bureau* Jean Murat plays French spy hero Captain Benoit, who manages to get hold of the plans for a new aeroplane engine. The success of the film spawned the sequels *Les Loups entre eux* (1936), *Homme à abattre* (1937) and *Capitaine Benoit* (1938). In *Marthe Richard: Espionne au service de la France*, set during the First World War, Edwige Feuillère is a young French spy who seeks to avenge the death of her parents before a German firing squad. In his role as the brutal German officer responsible for their execution, Erich von Stroheim gave a performance that was as two-dimensional as Von Rauffenstein in *La Grande Illusion* was complex and nuanced. In another First World War story, *Soeurs d'armes* (1937), Josette Day plays Léonie Vanhoutte, who spies for the British army during the German occupation of northern France and Belgium. In *Double crime sur la ligne Maginot*, Victor Francen plays the French captain who foils the attempts of German spies to discover the secrets of the Maginot Line.

When the film reached America in May of 1939, two years after its original release, the reviewer for the *New York Times* wrote: 'The shots of the great concrete fortress – reputably taken within the Line itself – create an overpowering impression of its cold, forbidden reality and its subterranean strength. Victor Francen as the veteran captain gives an excellent performance of hard-grained excellence.'[25] This was the view of France that Zay wanted to project, not Renoir's image of a decadent society, however true it may have been.

La Règle du jeu was still playing in Paris when war was declared on 3 September 1939. It was only the closure of the city's cinemas, which occurred with the commencement of hostilities, that brought its run to an end. Over the coming weeks the city's cinemas gradually reopened, but the establishment of a wartime censorship authority meant that Renoir's film had no hope of making a return. In October 1939, the authority explained that films considered to be 'depressing, morbid, immoral or having an undesirable influence over the young' would be unlikely to be allowed to be shown in France, regardless of their artistic merit.[26] Other notable casualties of the measure included Carné and Prévert's *Quai des brumes* and *Le Jour se lève*.

'The failure of *La Règle du jeu* so depressed me that I resolved either to give up the cinema or to leave France,' Renoir wrote in his memoirs.[27] Soon after the disastrous premiere, Renoir set off for Rome, where he was invited to make a film version of *La Tosca* and, at the request of the Italian government – in effect, Mussolini himself and his film-mad son Vittorio – to give a series of lectures at the newly opened film school, the Centro Sperimentale di Cinematografia. Although the French government looked favourably on a visit that it hoped would help to improve Franco-Italian relations, anyone who had read Renoir's scathing comments on Mussolini in the columns he had written for *Ce Soir* would have been astonished by his readiness now to accept the dictator's hospitality. The newspaper's editor, Louis Aragon, for one, did not trouble to hide his disappointment in his old columnist, ending a review of *Espoir*, André Malraux's film about the Spanish civil war, as follows:

I'm writing these words for you, Jean Renoir, who left Paris without wanting to say goodbye to me . . . for all those who are weak and cowardly . . . for all those who had despaired of France too soon and whom perhaps I will never again be able to look at calmly after this film, and this war, and the great Passion of the Spanish people, my brothers.[28]

La Règle du jeu marked a major crisis in Renoir's career, and also in his personal life, the two aspects in practice being indivisible. Accompanying him to Rome was not his companion and editor of the last ten years, Marguerite Houllé, but his new partner, Dido Freire, who would eventually become his second wife. Through some strange synchronicity of the times, his difficult life in 1939 seems reflected in the film he had just made. There are obvious touches in the character of the Marquis Robert de la Cheyniest, who is caught in a transition between two women that is both messy and painful, despite his best efforts to make it otherwise. But in her profound disillusionment with the way life has turned, Christine offers an even more revealing snapshot. Years later Renoir would interpret her character and actions with a considerable degree of fellow feeling:

As a young woman, she was probably very naive . . . So her romantic nature, her belief in pure love, ever-lasting love, is suddenly replaced by the brutal reality of physical desire. Her choice becomes that. Since life is like that, she says to herself, 'Let's go with it. I'll make love with the first person who comes along. I might not really love him, but I'll do it all the same, because those are the rules of the game, and I want to follow the rules.'[29]

Renoir was naive enough to think that the Popular Front government could prosper, naive enough to think that his films could change society and even stop a war. The reception of *La Règle du jeu* brought home to him the foolishness of such hopes. There was no end to the strange bedfellows that the rules of the game seemed to demand. While Renoir was still in Italy, he was greeted with the news of the Nazi–Soviet Pact, signed by Ribbentrop and Molotov on 24 August 1939. Even more shocking to him must have been the French Communist Party's support for the agreement. Two days later, the offices of both *Humanité* and *Ce Soir* – for which Renoir had written so many columns attacking fascism – were closed down in the interests of national security. His disillusionment was complete.

At the end of *La Règle du jeu*, after the disastrous house party in which his best friend André is accidentally killed, Octave says farewell to the poacher Marceau, who has just been dismissed from his job as a servant to the Marquis. The scene expresses well the bewilderment and dislocation that Renoir himself must have felt in 1939 at a world that was being turned upside-down without good reason, although everyone had their reasons.

'What will you do?' Octave asks the poacher.

'Oh, go back to the woods. Do odd jobs here and there. And you?'

'Oh, me. I'll go back to Paris, and try to sort myself out.'

'Oh well, perhaps we'll meet again one day.'

'That would astonish me. But then, one never knows. Anything's possible.'

In the course of a year all Renoir's hopes and plans had foundered. He was a man trying to pick up the pieces, coming to terms with a now rootless and dispossessed existence. When war was declared, he joined the Army Film Service, who ordered him back to Italy, in Renoir's own words, to establish 'artistic contact between the two countries through the cinema'.[30] In practice, this meant resuming the production of *La Tosca* and the lectures at the film school. But there would soon be more brutal disruptions. After Germany's invasion of Belgium and Holland on 10 May 1940, he returned briefly to Paris, only to be on the move once again with the Fall of France the following month. The fact that he relocated with Dido to his father's old home in the south of France was in itself an indication of his wish for continuity, but there were now very few options left open to him.

'Of course Jean believes his duty is to stay here,' Dido wrote to their friend, the American documentary director Robert Flaherty, 'but in my opinion it is quite useless as he will not be able to work for a long time, and in every way it is tragic for him to be idle.'[31] With the active encouragement of both Flaherty and Dido, Renoir resolved at last to make the journey to America. All that he had seen and suffered in France over the previous two years seem more than enough to explain why, having settled in America, he should have chosen not to return. It was in his nature to put down firm roots.[32] Once this had occurred, he could not be easily re-transplanted.

12

The Occupation

Upon his arrival in New York in early 1941, Jean Gabin was asked to describe the state of the French industry he had left behind. He replied that the studios had been badly damaged, production had ground to a halt and actors were conducting a campaign of passive resistance, not wishing to participate in the kind of films that the Nazis would have them make. When he was asked to comment on the French cinema's future prospects, he 'just shook his head in a gesture of sadness'.[1]

According to the consensus of opinion, the French cinema was finished – it would become a propaganda vehicle for the Nazis. In fact, it would go on to enjoy one of its most fertile periods, producing films that are today acknowledged to be among its great classics – *Les Visiteurs du soir* (1942), *Les Anges du péché* (1943), *Le Corbeau* (1943), *Lumière d'été* (1943), *Les Dames du Bois de Boulogne* (1945), *Les Enfants du paradis* (1945). In the words of Philippe d'Hugues: 'The blossoming in less than three years of an exceptional number of films made it possible to speak of a "Golden Age" of French cinema, especially when the extraordinarily difficult circumstances in which these films were made are taken into account.'[2]

An important reason, he maintained, was 'the lack of competition, certainly the lack of Hollywood competition'. Other commentators support this conclusion. Louis Daquin, who was one of a new generation of directors to come to the fore during the Occupation, commented: 'Isolation and the absence of the Hollywood cinema allowed directors and technicians, who had previously been unable to ignore an American approach that offered technical perfection but no style, to rediscover a source of inspiration that was truly French.'[3] Georges Charensol, writing in the immediate aftermath of the war, was even more insistent. In a piece entitled 'Renaissance du cinéma français', he wrote: 'Why was France able to achieve so much after 1941? Because it was cut off from America. Forced to rely on itself, denied both the influence and competition of Hollywood, our cinema rediscovered its former glory.'[4] Pierre Billard, focusing on the work of Marcel Carné and Jacques Prévert, perhaps the most representative film-makers of the period, commented of *Les Visiteurs du soir* that 'it was unlike any American film, indeed it was in many respects (rhythm, language, understated direction and writing) the opposite of an American film.'[5]

Yet these claims that the absence of Hollywood films allowed the French cinema during the Occupation to flourish and to develop a truly native idiom take no account of the fact that it had already achieved both these things in the immediately preceding period, at a time when Hollywood competition was intense.

The French cinema of the Occupation has been called the 'cinema of paradox'[6] because, in spite of the Fall of France, it survived this period of supreme difficulty, creating some of its finest works. But a less acknowledged aspect of the paradox is that, for all its isolation from Hollywood, during these years the French cinema came to resemble its briefly absent rival all the more closely.

After the Armistice of 22 June 1940, France was divided into a northern zone under German authority and a southern 'free' zone, ruled by the newly established Pétain regime, which chose the spa town Vichy as its new seat of government. Joining the exodus from occupied Paris, many of the leading French film-makers regrouped on the Côte d'Azur. Unable in these early days to conceive how production could resume at the major studios clustered around Paris, they imagined a new beginning in the south, Hollywood seeming to provide a natural archetype for their plans.

In his memoirs, Marcel L'Herbier recalled entertaining fellow directors Jean Renoir, Henri Decoin, Marc Allégret and Raymond Bernard in his Antibes garden, discussing a 'project whose goal was no less than to build a vast studio complex at Valbone with a view to creating a French Hollywood'.[7] Indeed, even before the Armistice, this notion of a southern retreat removed from wartime troubles had already been on the agenda. In January 1940, *La Cinématographie française*, under the headline 'We must make films. But where?', ran a piece extolling the virtues of Marcel Pagnol's new studio near Marseilles. With its modern facilities, as well as the extensive and varied terrain for outdoor filming, here was a place where it was possible to film without all the wartime disruptions and dangers of the Paris studios.[8]

But it was in the interests of Germany to put the Paris studios back to work again. Not only did the cinema offer an important means of pacifying a defeated population, but it was also one of the many industries in France that Germany intended to corral in support of its own economy and war effort.

With this purpose, the occupying authorities passed a measure on 16 August 1940 requiring each industry to dissolve the trade unions and employers' associations that had existed before the Armistice and to re-form instead as a 'Comité de l'Organisation'. Each Committee was to comprise representatives from the various branches of its industry, who would serve under a government-appointed commissioner.

The Vichy government was, of course, required to cooperate with Germany under the collaborationist terms of the Armistice, but the German directive provided the opportunity at last to implement measures that had first been advocated under the Popular Front government, but had never become law owing to opposition from various factions within the industry.

Establishing a 'Service du Cinéma' to supervise its film policy, the Vichy government appointed as its first director Guy de Carmoy, the civil servant who had written the report recommending legislation for the film industry under the Popular Front. De Carmoy then, in turn, appointed the film producer Raoul Ploquin to run the Comité de l'Organisation de l'Industrie Cinématographique (COIC). An important qualification for the role was that Ploquin had long experience of working with the German film industry. Between 1927 and 1939 he had been based in Berlin, where he had made French-language films for UFA.

Both the Service du Cinéma and the COIC were expected to consult with the Propaganda Abteilung, a division of the German information ministry, but their central brief was to foster a cinema that could serve the Vichy policy of *redressement* – the restoration of national pride and morale following the debacle of 1940.

Rather than expect the French film industry to produce propaganda on their behalf, the German authorities focused instead on taking economic advantage. In October 1940, a Paris-based production company, Continental Films, was set up to work closely with the German-controlled distribution company, L'Alliance Cinématographique Européenne (ACE). At the same time a nationwide exhibition network was created – the Société de Gestion et d'Exploitation de Cinéma (SOGEC) – through the compulsory purchase of circuits which had previously belonged to Jewish owners. The result was the sudden appearance of a large vertically integrated corporation, after the model of Germany's state-controlled UFA.

Dr Alfred Greven, a former First World War pilot who had been a friend of Field Marshal Goering, was appointed to run this new entity. Although he had close connections with the Nazi party, Greven was first and foremost a professional film producer, who had worked at UFA during the 1930s. But at the same time, as an officer in the Propagandastaffel – the propaganda division of the army – he had responsibility for the general film policy of the occupying authorities. His dual role turned him into the single most powerful figure in French wartime cinema.

Raoul Ploquin had known Greven at UFA's Neue Babelsberg studio in Berlin. In 1935, they had worked together on the UFA dual-language production *Domino vert / Der Grüne Domino* (1935), the French version of which had starred Charles Vanel and Danielle Darrieux. After the war Ploquin recalled that as soon as he knew that he would be the director of the COIC, he got in touch with Greven to enquire after his intentions:

He said he wanted to help me to get the French film industry working again. Continental, with its production programme and the chain of cinemas it had requisitioned, would be a great aid for our profession. He went to great lengths to assure me that Continental's films would avoid any political content and that any form of propaganda would be rigorously excluded . . . And I must acknowledge that on these two points he kept his word.[9]

The recollections of the screenwriter Charles Spaak, who wrote three scripts for Continental, confirms Ploquin's account. In a magazine article published after the war, he wrote:

It's very difficult today to speak objectively of any Germans, but not all of them were torturers. The difficult thing for us was precisely the fact that among them were some extremely civilised men who in the pursuit of their duty behaved in a way that seemed entirely honourable. Whatever the mysterious reason was or the personal motive I don't know, but Greven wanted the French cinema to survive and that it should be distinguished. Greven was a German, but he loved the cinema.[10]

A sophisticated man who was as much a Francophile as he was a cineaste, Greven seems to have regarded his new post as an opportunity to make films free of the crude propaganda that had long marred German production. Certainly, his attitude would incur the disapproval of Goebbels, who, after seeing *La Symphonie fantastique* (1942), a Continental production about the life of the composer Berlioz, wrote in his diary:

Greven is going about this in entirely the wrong way. He seems to think it's his job to raise the quality of the French cinema. But it's not for us to provide the French with good films, and especially not to give them films with a nationalist flavour. What the French need are frivolous films, empty, and even a little stupid, and it's our job to see they get them. It's not our job to develop their nationalism.[11]

Yet however appalled Goebbels may have been by the high quality of the films that Greven produced, it was hard to counter-mand him without undermining the larger commercial purpose of Continental. The occupying power viewed the French cin-ema as the spearhead with which the film industry of a 'Greater Europe' would compete in world markets.[12] As a producer at UFA during the 1930s, Greven had witnessed the collapse of the export market for German films after the rise to power of the Nazi Party. He knew that the logic of the situation was to build on the huge prestige that the French cinema had won for itself in the pre-war years. The 'empty', 'stupid' films that Goebbels advocated would not have found a market.

Even more pressing was the need to make up for the absence of Hollywood films from the screens of Occupied Europe. In his book on the French cinema during the Occupation the film historian Jean-Pierre Bertin-Maghit explains the reasoning:

To promote the quality of the French cinema became necessary, because it was the only cinema capable of matching English-language production, which had been excluded from Europe . . . The French cinema was intended as the bait which would enable German films to be distributed through occupied Europe: in return for one French film the distributor would have to take three or four German films as well.[13]

In effect, an amalgamated German–French industry would use the advantage of its size to carry out an equivalent of the Hollywood practice of block-booking, according to which the big studios sold their entire programme of films on the strength of a handful of prestige productions.

The tendency of the kind of European expansion that Germany envisaged was for the industry as a whole to take on the struc-tural characteristics of Hollywood. Yet at the same time, as Bertin-Maghit has observed, 'the creation of Continental simply

continued an already existing Franco-German tradition of collaboration in the cinema'.[14] German companies had played a
major role in French production ever since Tobis had produced
René Clair's first sound films at their French studios at Epinay.
The German-owned ACE was a major distributor of French
films, and there was also a substantial industry of dual-language
feature production based in Germany itself. While Paramount-
France had turned out to be a short-lived experiment in the production of multiple language versions, UFA's Neue Babelsberg
studios continued to churn out films in both French and German
– using the same script and decor – through the 1930s.

For France's leading film actors, therefore, 'Berlin-Babylone'
was a familiar place. Jean Gabin made his screen debut there in
the dual-language production *Chacun sa chance / Jedem seine
Chance* (1930). A list of other actors who passed through the
Berlin studios would amount to a roll-call of the most familiar
names in 1930s French cinema – Madeleine Renaud, Arletty,
Charles Vanel, Marcel Dalio, Pierre Blanchar.

The future director Henri-Georges Clouzot worked as a screenwriter at Neue Babelsberg between 1932 and 1934. After the war
he would comment, 'My taste for light and dark, I owe to the
Germans.'[15] As the political climate changed, many producers
began to shift their base from Berlin to Paris, but no sudden sever-
ance of the link ever occurred. Even after Hitler's rise to power in
1933, many of France's leading directors continued to work there.

Produced by Tobis at Epinay in 1935, *La Kermesse héroïque*
is remembered as a great classic of the French cinema, but its
star Françoise Rosay also appeared in a German-language version (*Die klugen Frauen*), attending its premiere at the Capitol
Cinema in Berlin in the presence of Joseph Goebbels. In 1938,
her husband Jacques Feyder directed her in another Tobis
double-language version, *Les Gens du voyage / Fahrendes Volk*,
which was made in Munich. But even at this point, when Europe
feared an imminent war, their presence in Germany was hardly
exceptional. In the same year, to take just one example, Louis

Daquin was in Berlin directing *Le Joueur* (1938), the French version of a double-language production of Dostoyevsky's *The Gambler*, with Pierre Blanchar and Viviane Romance. The last French film to be shot at Neue Babelsberg, just weeks before the outbreak of war, was *L'Héritier de Mondésir* (1939). Albert Valentin was the director and Jacques Becker his assistant.[16]

In the film industry, 'collaboration' between Germany and France had been a reality long before the policies of Vichy gave the word a pejorative sense. This fact clearly facilitated the speed with which Greven was able to acquire the services of the leading stars and directors of the French film industry.

Rather than follow in Deanna Durbin's footsteps at Universal, Danielle Darrieux now became the biggest contract star at Continental. 'As I had, like so many of my colleagues, made films in Germany before the war, I wasn't quite sure what this company was meant to represent.'[17] Continental was careful to play down the German connection. Neither Greven's name nor that of any other German producer appeared in the credits of its films. On the surface it appeared to be a French enterprise. As Jacques Siclier – a regular wartime visitor to the cinema – observed: 'The films produced by Continental were to our eyes as French as any other films, belonging to familiar genres, made by well-known film-makers, with performances by stars, actors and actresses that we loved.'[18]

But crucial to this perception was the absence of the kind of propaganda element that was, however, present in the weekly newsreels.* As Siclier recalled, these received an unambiguously hostile response:

For the four years of the Occupation, audiences treated the newsreels with an instinctive mistrust. We had to put up with them because they

---

* In the Occupied Zone, audiences for the first part of the war watched the German-produced *Actualités mondiales*, and from August 1942, *France-Actualités*, made under the joint supervision of Vichy and the German occupation authorities.

were part of the programme. But soon the whistles and the catcalls from the audience made it clear that they hadn't been fooled. We didn't go to the cinema to see real life distorted through propaganda; we went there to escape real life. For this reason, the intrusion of the news into cinema entertainment was badly received.[19]

The agenda for Greven at Continental, as for the other producers of French films, was as far as possible to leave the war behind – a retreat from reality that caused them to embrace the make-believe and escapism of Hollywood more than ever. Greven would make frequent trips to Portugal to get hold of Hollywood films, 'to which he was very partial'.[20] Hollywood was a source of both inspiration and rivalry. According to the writer Philippe Esnault, when Greven tried to persuade Jacques Prévert to work for Continental, he promised 'no politics, but total freedom. The one aim was to compete with the Americans.' Turning down the offer, Prévert replied that Greven had already lost. 'Because you don't have any Jews working for you. Look at Hollywood: the cinema would be impossible without them!'[21]

Indeed, Greven seems to have drawn inspiration from Hollywood as regards not only the content of Continental's films but also his own personal style. Keeping a close eye on every stage of production, he dominated the activities of the studio in the manner of the most powerful Hollywood mogul. According to the reminiscences of those who worked with him, he could often be ruthless, taking full advantage of the powers of coercion that his position within the Nazi hierarchy gave him. When Danielle Darrieux's fiancé was imprisoned in Germany, she recalled that Greven 'blackmailed me: if I wanted to spare the person I loved serious trouble, then I had to agree to make *Caprices* and *La Fausse Maîtresse*, two feeble comedies which however amused audiences during those dark years'.[22]

Yet in pursuit of what he considered to be Continental's best interests, he was equally prepared to disregard Nazi Party doctrine. Although Vichy legislation had forbidden the presence of Jews in the film industry, Greven – perhaps mindful of Jacques

Prévert's comments – chose to feign ignorance of the Jewish origin of one of his screenwriters, Jean-Paul Le Chanois, whose real name was Jean-Paul Dreyfuss.[23] He also gave another Continental screenwriter, Carlos Rim, a laissez-passer, which he was able to use to get the child of his Jewish wife to the comparative safety of the Free Zone. The screenwriter Jean Aurenche even recalled Greven lamenting the absence of good scripts 'because of the absence of Jews in France and Germany', and asking him if he could put him in touch with some good Jewish screenwriters.[24] Jacques Siclier summed up Alfred Greven as follows: 'An iron fist in a velvet glove. His authoritarian manner was in pursuit of his own conception of the cinema. He seems to me to have ruled over Continental like Irving Thalberg ruled over his fiefdom in Metro-Goldwyn-Mayer.'[25]

These comments provide a useful way to think of Continental as a whole. A huge concern, which would produce thirty films over a three-year period, it was effectively the Metro-Goldwyn-Mayer of the Occupation. Both its size and the political circumstances in which it operated required the company to adopt an essentially Hollywood approach to production.

The films that emerged were a French version of the 'dream factory'. They ignored the reality of the German Occupation in the same way that Hollywood films ignored, for example, the reality of sex, adultery or unpunished crime. In order to avoid controversy, they sought the refuge of genre. It was a tendency that the absence of Hollywood films inevitably encouraged, for the French cinema now had to satisfy the appetite for escapist fare and spectacle that had once been Hollywood's special province.

It is worth bringing out this point by considering specific productions. According to Jacques Siclier's classification of the output of Continental's production, the two largest categories were comedies (eleven) and thrillers (seven).

The very first Continental film to appear was the mystery thriller *L'Assassinat du Père Noël* (1941), directed by

Christian-Jaque. Based on a story by Pierre Véry, it recalled *Les Disparus de Saint-Agil* (1938), which Christian-Jaque had made with the same writer shortly before the war. While *Les Disparus* was essentially a 'whodunnit' set in the enclosed world of a boarding school, Continental's repetition of the formula carried the audience even further away from the contemporary world to a remote mountain village in the Savoyard.

Harry Baur plays Cornusse, an old craftsman who makes dolls and wooden globes that depict a world he's never seen. His young daughter Catherine lives a dream existence, a kind of 'Sleeping Beauty' longing for the arrival of a knight in shining armour who will carry her away. As her father puts it, 'She lives more and more in a fairyland.' When the baron of the village returns after ten years abroad, the rumour spreads that he has leprosy. He is shunned and abandoned by his staff, but his predicament prompts the previously passive Catherine to come to his aid, volunteering to be his servant: 'It is bad to abandon someone who is ill.' She seems to act from an innate conscience as alert as she appears to be asleep, but also from the instinct that her 'knight' has finally arrived. The baron tells her that she must return to her father, but before she leaves, in an act of faith, she kisses him in spite of his supposed leprosy.

The film takes its title from a parallel story strand, in which Catherine's father dresses up as Father Christmas, but fails to turn up at the party that he is supposed to attend. Later some children stumble upon the corpse of Father Christmas in the snow, with a bullet in his back. Although at first everyone believes Cornusse to be dead, it turns out to be a stranger wearing the Father Christmas costume, and Cornusse is discovered alive at the baron's castle.

When the baron himself is found tied up in Cornusse's house, he explains that Cornusse had visited him in his castle, where he fell asleep. So the baron took advantage of the opportunity to dress in Cornusse's costume in order to deliver a pair of golden ear-rings to Catherine as a Christmas present. But on his arrival at Cornusse's house, he was knocked out and the costume stolen.

The mystery is, as the title for the post-war American release of the film succinctly put it, *Who Killed Santa Claus?* It turns out to be the local pharmacist, who sought to eradicate the pestilence that the baron supposedly brought to the village. But the emotional heart of the film lies in the fairy tale of Catherine, or 'Beauty', finding her prince.

In the film's final scene, Cornusse gives a globe to an invalid child. Asked what the little Chinese children speak about, he replies: 'They speak of France and little French children. And also of a beautiful princess who had been asleep in a little chair for many years. In her sleep she would always have the same marvellous dream of a Prince Charming who would one day wake her up and bring her happiness.'

L'Assassinat du Père Noël, the first film to be both conceived and executed during the Occupation, was characteristic of that cinema's retreat into a fortress of the imagination, where resistance – even in this production financed by the invader – was offered through a combination of fantasy and allegory. The standard mode of Occupation cinema was to act as though the Germans were not there – to 'send them to Coventry' – yet at the same time to offer protest through the use of metaphor. Allegories lose their force to the extent that we attempt to pin them down to definite meaning, but it would have been natural for a wartime audience to find in *L'Assassinat du Père Noël* a message encouraging them to look forward to the day when a saviour would help France to rise again, would 'wake her up and bring her happiness' – even if in 1941 no one could have anticipated that the saviour would take the form of an Anglo-American army landing on the Normandy beaches, three years hence.

At first sight it seems extraordinary that such a film should be the production of a German-financed company that had, after all, been founded in the aftermath of France's defeat to further the interests of the occupying power. But although there is no shortage of examples of the fundamental evil of the Nazi regime, the Occupation authorities paid as much regard to practical expediency as Nazi dogma.

It seems implausible to suggest that the Germans were blind to such allegory; much more likely, they simply tolerated the mildly rebellious sentiment as the understandable need of a defeated country to lick its wounds. The subjugated population was welcome to imagine some far-off resurrection, just as long as such dreams did not undermine compliance with the day-to-day reality of the present. To the extent that the cinema provided a harmless outlet for such sentiments, the vagueness of such allegorical rebellion probably suited both the occupied and the occupiers – the latter were ultimately much more afraid of French men and women's deeds than their thoughts. The different agendas of the Occupation forces, the Vichy government and the film-makers themselves were able peaceably to coexist through this kind of everyday collusion.

The key point is how the necessity of having to deal with such issues obliquely rather than directly nudged French film-makers into a Hollywood way of thinking. In America the studios had been living with the draconian censorship of the Hays Production Code ever since the advent of sound. After assuming responsibility for the Production Code Administration in 1934, Joseph Breen made it clear to his staff that he regarded the code as 'a full mandate to enforce respect for all law and all lawful authority'.[26] This included political authority. As Gregory Black has observed, 'Anything that might be construed as overt criticism of the government, the free-enterprise system, or the police and courts, was Breen wrote "Communistic propaganda" and was hereby "banned from the screen".'[27] The result was that allegory had long been second nature for anyone in the Hollywood system who wanted to make a serious political point. Retreat into the past was an obvious strategy. The British producer Alexander Korda adopted it when he made *Lady Hamilton* in a still neutral America in 1940. When Admiral Nelson warns, 'You cannot make peace with dictators!' it was obvious who was really meant, even if under attack from isolationists, Korda later asserted that no contemporary parallels had been intended.*

The French film-makers of the Occupation may no longer have been able to see Hollywood films,† but once they found themselves having to work in a closed system that replicated so many of Hollywood's features, it was only natural to emulate a closed Hollywood style. This was evident not only in allegorical films set in the past, but also in the resort to formulaic genre. Whether the hero of a romantic comedy was trying to find love or the hero of a thriller trying to solve a mystery, this kind of story, even if the setting were contemporary, could operate in a space of its own, easy to insulate from the controversial issues of the day.

An equally significant factor was longing for the Hollywood cinema itself, which the editor of *La Revue du cinéma*, Jean-Georges Auriol, had defined as 'something to make the heart race, full of life and action, as often energising as it was escapist, sometimes extravagant, sometimes refined – a product as exciting as champagne'.[28] It is easy to understand why in the grim, depressing reality of the Occupation, audiences might have wanted some of this stuff, and why French film-makers would seek to make up for the sudden lack of supply from abroad.

Citing Marcel L'Herbier's *L'Honorable Catherine* (1942) as a notable example, Philippe d'Hugues identifies a robust genre in Occupation France of 'pseudo-American ersatz comedies

* In September 1941, Korda was summoned before a Senate committee which had been established to investigate allegations of Hollywood war-mongering. The Japanese attack on Pearl Harbor a few weeks later spared him undue embarrassment. See Charles Drazin, *Korda: Britain's Only Movie Mogul* (London: Sidgwick and Jackson, 2002), pp. 237–42.
† But although Hollywood films did become extremely scarce after the Fall of France, they were not forbidden in the Free Zone until October 1942.

that flourished during that time to make us forget Capra and McCarey'.[29] The comment captures a key motivation for a cinema that represented as much an escape from – as an allegorical engagement with – France's wartime problems:

The audience's need for escape, their desire to turn their backs on a cruel, nasty and grinding reality; it was a desire to take refuge in other times and other settings, in the imagination or in the past, in the company of characters, real or fictional, who enjoyed glittering, glamorous lives that would help them to forget all the bombing, cruelty and restrictions of the Occupation.[30]

With its privileged, well-resourced position, Continental may have led the way in forging such an escapist cinema, but its efforts were typical of the wider French film industry as a whole.

Soon after *L'Assassinat du Père Noël*, Continental released the comedy-thriller, *Le Dernier des six* (1941). Based on *Six hommes morts*, a novel by the Belgian thriller writer Stanislas-André Steeman, it was directed by Georges Lacombe, but the film's chief distinction came from its script by Henri-Georges Clouzot. Creating a kooky girlfriend sidekick for the detective hero Wenceslas Wens – a character who had not existed in the original novel – Clouzot fashioned a witty, light and fast-paced script that recalled the MGM *Thin Man* films of William Powell and Myrna Loy.

Greven was so impressed by Clouzot's work that he offered him a job as head of Continental's script department. Joining the staff at the beginning of 1941, Clouzot took advantage of the new position to acquire the rights to Georges Simenon's *Les Inconnus dans la maison* – a deeply sombre novel which offered a disenchanted view of a decaying and corrupt pre-war French society. Deserted by his wife years previously, small-town lawyer Hector Loursat lives with his teenage daughter, Nicole, in a dilapidated house, drowning his sorrows in drink. When a corpse is discovered in the house, Nicole's gang of friends is suspected. Nicole's boyfriend Emile is put on trial for the killing, and Loursat, who has not worked for years, agrees to take on the case. As Loursat's moral sense slowly reawakens, he uses the trial to expose the degradation of a town that has allowed its young to grow up without guidance or direction.

It's easy to read the film as an allegorical attack on the decadence of the Third Republic. But the choice of subject-matter was, as José-Louis Bocquet observes, an index of Clouzot's personal tendency 'to dive into the darkness of the human soul',[31] rather than an attempt at an anti-French propaganda that Continental had never intended in the first place. Indeed, the evidence suggests that Greven, in the interests of box-office appeal, tried to encourage Clouzot to tone down his notably bleak outlook. After *Les Inconnus dans la maison*, Clouzot had wanted to adapt another of Simenon's dark novels about bourgeois life. *Le Voyageur de la Toussaint* tells the story of a young man who returns to his home town after inheriting a fortune to find the place in the terrified grip of an overbearing, mafia-like family. Greven turned down the subject.* He explained to his chief scriptwriter, 'It's hard to make the public accept such a savage attack on bourgeois society after the already bitter indictment we offered in *Les Inconnus dans la maison*.'[32]

Clouzot would later recall *Les Inconnus* as the film 'that made me decide to become a director', but the project that Greven actually assigned to him for his directorial debut suggests Greven's own wish – in the manner of a typical Hollywood mogul – to marshal Clouzot's talent within a framework of solid entertainment values.

L'Assassin habite au 21 (1942) was a sequel to *Le Dernier des six*, which Greven had decided to make after the box-office success of the first film. Shot in May 1942, the film adopted the same light tone, but was striking for Clouzot's extraordinary command of the film medium. The memorable finale – in which

---

* But it would be made in 1942 by a French company called Cinex. Directed by Louis Daquin, it features early appearances by Simone Signoret and Serge Reggiani.

the heroine realises the identity of '*l'assassin*' with the sudden insight that there are not one but three killers, all with the same name – was executed with a visual brilliance that rivalled Hitchcock. As Suzy Delair, Pierre Fresnay's co-star in the film, observed of Clouzot, 'He already had an impressive command of his craft. He worked out all the camera movements and planned it all in advance. He could do everything.'[33]

Greven's respect for Clouzot's ability would cause him eventually – much against his better judgement – to allow the director a free hand to make the film he wanted. The result was the notorious *Le Corbeau* (1943). Based on a true pre-war incident in which a provincial French town suffered a campaign of anonymous poison-pen letters, it offered a pitiless depiction of French society that the clandestine Resistance magazine *L'Ecran français* condemned as promoting 'the twisted ideology of the enemy'. In an unsigned article, the actor Pierre Blanchar attacked Clouzot for offering a vision of France in which 'the inhabitants of our little towns are no more than degenerates who deserve nothing better than servitude'. The film, he went on, in a clear allusion to Continental, 'produced and encouraged by hidden German interests, fed anti-French propaganda'.[34]

Yet the reality was very different. Far from being the work of a 'toadying lackey', *Le Corbeau* was, according to Clouzot himself, 'the first film where I had total freedom'.[35] Summoned before an anti-Collaborationist tribunal after the Liberation, Clouzot gave the following explanation for making the film:

I'll tell you exactly why I made it. I was fed up with the terrifying climate of denunciation in which we lived, with all the anonymous letters. I should say that Bauermeister, who was head of production, thought it was too harsh and disturbing a subject. So I had to fight with Greven, who told me it was a very dangerous film . . . But I was determined to make it. It was a revolutionary film which fascinated me. In the end, he said, 'OK. Be it on your own head. Make it.'[36]

Clouzot's differences with Greven over *Le Corbeau* would cause him to leave Continental shortly before the film's premiere in October 1943. Although the film enjoyed a successful release, it was undoubtedly an embarrassment for Greven. When Continental's marketing department promoted the film with the slogan, 'The shame of the century: anonymous letters', the Gestapo in Paris ordered the company to halt a campaign that threatened to undermine its supply of informers. UFA then subsequently refused to distribute the film in Germany, on the grounds that the film 'did not suit the German character'.[37]

When Jean Cocteau saw the film, he wrote in his journal, 'Clouzot's film is extraordinary. It demonstrates once again the effectiveness of the author-director. A really biting film like bits of Maupassant or Zola. Each disturbing, violent image pushes to the very limit.'[38]

The comments get close to the true nature of Clouzot's crime, which was to have broken away from the genre of *Le Dernier des six* and *L'Assassin habite au 21* to make a personal, auteur's film, when the system that prevailed during the Occupation expected positive, upbeat entertainment in the Hollywood style. Rather than provide audiences with an escape, Clouzot had plunged them right back into their troubles.

In terms of production at Continental, Clouzot was the exception that proved the rule. Indeed, with our knowledge of the films he went on to make after the Liberation, it becomes even more easy to appreciate the tension between his personal inclinations and Continental's policy of producing high-quality but essentially conventional entertainment.

The studio's association with Georges Simenon provides a good example of where the limits lay. Although the Clouzot-chosen subject *Les Inconnus dans la maison* proved to be a box-office success, Greven – as we have seen above – vetoed Clouzot's plan to offer 'such a savage attack' through an adaption of *Le Voyageur de la Toussaint*. Instead, in March 1942 he bought the rights to make films based on Georges Simenon's character Maigret. Rather than challenging society, the inspector was a representative of the Establishment who could be relied upon to work within its frameworks. The venture was a return to the lighter tone of the two Detective Wenceslas Wens films with Pierre Fresnay. Over the next two years, Albert Préjean would play the character of Maigret in three Continental films – *Picpus* (1942), *Cécile est morte* (1943) and *Les Caves du Majestic* (1944).

In every sphere, Greven made plain his intention to build a Hollywood in Occupied France. It was apparent not only in the choice of subject-matter, but also in his attempts to establish the whole paraphernalia of a film factory, with a long-term production programme and a roster of contract stars whose personalities could be developed in a series of star vehicles.

Appearing within days of Continental's founding on 16 November 1940, a new fan magazine, *Vedettes* (Stars), seemed to pick up on the agenda. In an opening preface, an anonymous editor promised:

We will not discuss politics of any kind. We will not preach to you. We will give you only the breath of fresh air that we all need – a rich, invigorating breeze perfumed with all the flowers of our country, a breeze that allows you to relax after all the tiring daily struggles. Paris will stay Paris. It will live up to its mission – its vocation even – to sow the seeds of hope, good taste and charm.

On the cover was a photograph of France's biggest box-office star, Danielle Darrieux, cuddling her dog. In the light of the star's recent highly publicised return from Hollywood, there was a natural subtext for the keen followers of her career. Circumstances meant that she was no longer going to be fulfilling her contract at Universal, but it didn't matter, because she was now going to become just as big a star at Continental.

Even the title of her debut film for the new company suggested plans for the kind of long-term association that had been rare in pre-war French cinema but was a commonplace in Hollywood. Directed by her ex-husband Henri Decoin, the romantic comedy *Premier rendez-vous* had its premiere in August 1941. Looking at the film today, one is immediately struck by the transatlantic feel. In this blatant star vehicle, it is Danielle Darrieux who has her 'name above the title' – the two words of which themselves display the kind of whimsy we associate with Hollywood's golden age, filling the screen in an extravagant, flowery hand, a heart dotting the 'i' of 'Premier'. Although Decoin is credited as director and screenwriter, that phrase 'un film de' – which was a regular practice of French cinema long before the New Wave generation – is absent. Nothing is permitted to dim the aura of the star. Equally absent – as in all Continental films – is the German name of the producer, which would of course serve only to taint the brand. But the name of Continental itself is prominent. The production programme of the company had sufficient scale and coherence to mean that in the fullness of time a Continental comedy would evoke the same kind of recognition as, say, an MGM musical or a Warner Brothers gangster picture.

Danielle Darrieux plays an orphan girl Micheline, who answers a lonely hearts ad in a newspaper. She runs away from her puritanical orphanage to meet the person she hopes will be her Prince Charming. But the writer of the ad turns out to be a lonely old schoolteacher, Nicolas Rougement. Touched by Micheline's charm and beauty, Nicolas pretends that he has come on behalf of his nephew Pierre. He hides the runaway orphan in his house at the private school where he teaches. Eventually Pierre (played by Louis Jourdan) – who is really Nicolas's former pupil, not his nephew – turns up at the school and, after the misunderstandings usual in this kind of comedy, falls in love with her. The police discover Micheline's hide-out and return her to the hated orphanage, but Pierre's friends at the school club together to secure the funds for her education, enabling her to leave. Nicolas becomes her legal guardian and she is free to marry Pierre.

A set-piece scene captures the overall flavour of the film. Still hidden away at the school, Micheline, happy to have found her Prince Charming, spontaneously begins to sing to Pierre, who plays along on the piano. It is the title song: 'Oh, how sweet but troubling / That moment of our first meeting . . .'

But her singing gives away her hiding-place. The schoolboys, overhearing her, rush to the window of their dormitory: one takes out a violin to accompany the stranger's beautiful voice, another a guitar. Elsewhere in the school grounds a teacher exclaims, 'So delightful!' The make-believe nature of the scene and the soft-focus way in which Darrieux is lit recall standard Hollywood practice.

The film was clearly a conscious attempt to build on the success of *Battement de coeur* (1940), the previous film in the Decoin–Darrieux partnership, which – made just before the German Occupation – had been, in Darrieux's own words, 'an equivalent of the great American comedies'.[39] But after the fall of France there was, as we have seen, even more incentive to satisfy the appetite of a Hollywood-deprived audience with this kind of film. '*Premier rendez-vous* catered to the nostalgia for the American comedies,' observed Jacques Siclier. 'In 1941, [Darrieux] personified a young generation that still wanted to believe in happiness and romance in spite of a historical reality that was crushing its hopes and dreams.'[40] The logic of the situation was to encourage a make-believe, escapist cinema. The cute persona of Darrieux was as much an emblem of the Occupation as the Busby Berkeley musical had been of America's Depression.

Premier rendez-vous had a special showing in Berlin in the presence of Goebbels. Greven's taste for American-style promotion caused him to organise a notorious visit of Continental's stable of stars to Germany for the occasion. The party, which included top box-office stars Danielle Darrieux, Albert Préjean, Viviane Romance and Suzy Delair, set off from the Gare de l'Est on 18 March 1942. Dr Dietrich, in charge of the Propaganda Staffel office in Paris, accompanied them. In Vienna, they attended a performance of Richard Strauss's opera *Salome*, conducted by the composer. In Munich, they watched G. W. Pabst direct the film *Paracelsus* (1943). Then, in Berlin, after dinner with Joseph and Magda Goebbels, they attended the performance of *Premier rendez-vous*.

Back in Paris, the stars gathered for one more publicity event on the terrace of the Propaganda Staffel building at 52 avenue des Champs-Elysées, where the press were invited to celebrate their return. The magazine *La Semaine* covered the occasion under the headline: 'Hollywood no longer counts, say the French stars on their return from Germany.'[41] The carefully orchestrated publicity tour itself was of course part of the plan to replace Hollywood, demonstrating Greven's access – in the words of the famous MGM slogan – to 'more stars than there are in the heavens'.

After *Premier rendez-vous*, Greven put Darrieux into two more romantic comedies, *Caprices* (1942) and *La Fausse Maîtresse* (1942) – in the former she played opposite Continental's other leading star, Albert Préjean. And he would undoubtedly have put her into many more such pictures had not Darrieux, according to her own account, refused to cooperate any longer.[42]

The opening of *Premier rendez-vous* coincided with the publication of yet another new film magazine, *Ciné-mondial*.[43] Once again Danielle Darrieux was on the cover. Produced with the support of the Propaganda Abteilung and the German embassy in Paris, it was intended to promote the new Franco-German film industry that seemed to be emerging.

Inside was a letter of welcome from Raoul Ploquin, the president of the COIC:

I am pleased to welcome the creation of a film magazine that addresses itself to the broad public. It's not just chance that the birth of *Ciné-Mondial* should coincide with a general upturn in French film production. Our studios, which for many long months were shut because of wartime difficulties, have resumed their activity. With effective assistance from the Occupation authorities, the French film industry is at present working flat out: nine films have been completed, nine are in production, and twenty-five projects, which have received the approval of the French censorship board and the German authorities, will follow shortly. The reorganisation of the French cinema is not an idle boast. For the first time all the sectors of the French industry are being coordinated through the creation of a unique institution:

the COIC, which has an immense task ahead of it, which can be successfully achieved only through the discipline and understanding of an extraordinary art-form that is both an instrument of culture and a means of effective propaganda. It is unquestionably the most important form of communication with the public in our present time. We know that *Ciné-Mondial* will always want to encourage good films and raise the standard of French production, refusing to allow that crude, overly vulgar work should poison the spirit of the French public.

In the reform of France, the cinema has a very important role to play. The films of this new era must bring optimism and encouragement to the large number of people who go to the cinema every week. In a word, the French cinema must be constructive.

A part of the artistic life of our country, the French cinema must play a vital role in the collaboration of the European peoples. Let us not forget that the cinema is a means of universal expression and that, in spite of the difference in languages, the best films of one nation are projected and appreciated in all the other countries of the world. It is through the cinema that different peoples will learn better how to know, respect and love one another. The role that the cinema will play in the Europe of tomorrow is huge. France must take up its true place in the European cinema. *Ciné-Mondial* will help it to do so.

The letter amounted to an effective statement of the film policy of the Vichy regime. It may have been formulated on the basis of collaboration with the occupying power, yet at the same time it amounted to a sincere effort to re-establish a healthy cinema in support of the French national interest. But one of the striking features of Ploquin's statement is its evocation of the language of the Hollywood Production Code. Here are the opening paragraphs to that document:

Motion picture producers recognise the high trust and confidence that have been placed in them by the people of the world and that have made motion pictures a universal form of entertainment.

They recognise their responsibility to the public because of this trust and because entertainment and art are important influences in the life of a nation.

Hence, though regarding motion pictures primarily as entertainment without any explicit purposes of teaching or propaganda, they know that the motion picture within its own field of entertainment may be directly responsible for spiritual or moral progress, for higher types of social life, and for much correct thinking.[44]

There may have been differences in emphasis – Hollywood, for example, clinging with a near-religious insistence to the word 'entertainment' – but the sentiments were the same. Both Vichy and Hollywood considered the cinema to be 'a means of universal expression'; both Vichy and Hollywood assumed that the influence of the cinema over a mass audience was of such importance that they had a duty to ensure that it was used to encourage positive values. Just as Vichy's National Revolution sought to rebuild a positive image of France after the calamity of defeat, Hollywood's embrace of the Code amounted to a *redressement* too, albeit with the ultimate motive of safeguarding its commercial interests. 'To be constructive', to promote 'correct thinking': for the first time, the French cinema and Hollywood shared an explicit moral agenda.

Vichy's recognition of cinema as the key tool with which to promote the values of the National Revolution won film-makers the kind of official support they had previously struggled to find. After the anarchic 1930s, in which production companies seemed to spring up and vanish overnight, the Vichy government intervened to give the French cinema the kind of organised system of production that had long existed in Hollywood. As Bertin-Maghit has observed, 'With the creation of the COIC, the cinema ceased to be looked upon as an art; it was now an industry.'[45] It was a similar recognition of the industrial scale of Hollywood that had led to the creation in 1922 of the Motion Picture Producers and Distributors Association, the organisation responsible for the Production Code. The two organisations were natural counterparts, Raoul Ploquin watching over the cinema under Vichy in the manner of a French Will Hays.

From its establishment, the COIC controlled access to this industry through the issue of a 'professional identity card', which – by a Vichy law of 26 October 1940 – anyone wishing to work in the cinema had to have. Notoriously, this measure served as a practical instrument with which to implement Vichy's racist law, excluding Jews from the film industry, but at the same time it enabled the COIC, which required producers to demonstrate sound finances and professional standing, to engineer a leaner, more competent industry. In 1942, there were fifty-seven production companies operating in France, compared to the 330 that had existed in 1937; and the number of distributors had dropped from 419 to fifty-two.[46]

The introduction of a state film bank in May 1941, the 'Crédit National', provided another means with which to support – but also control – production. The new 'Crédit National' could advance a maximum of fifty million francs or 65 per cent of the production as a loan, if the project was approved by the COIC.[47]

Other measures included the abolition of the double programme, which increased the profitability of the features; support for the making of shorts; a simplification of the tax tariffs on cinemas; and an audit system that made it possible to keep a reliable nationwide record of box-office receipts.

A COIC policy statement of May 1942 shows how the organisation used such powers in pursuit of an active and careful management of the industry, setting production quotas and rationing the scant supply of materials and film stock – but it also suggests the prevailing sense of national purpose. Specifying a production plan that would run from 1 May 1942 until 30 April 1943, the document announced that forty-three companies would make seventy-two films, a quota calculated to conserve film stock, to satisfy the demand of the French market and to increase the quality of production:

This quota of 72 productions is determined above all by the amount of available film stock. It is why no film will be permitted to exceed a length of 2,800 metres [approximately one hour and forty minutes]. And the number of copies that can be made from each film will depend on the quality of the completed production . . .

The Service du Cinéma and the COIC have done everything in their power to sustain the activity of the French film industry. In return, we have the right to demand that producers live up to what is expected of them.

It is not acceptable to make films solely in pursuit of profit. Producers must meet the demands for quality, as much on the level of art and technique as from the perspective of national purpose.

Film stock is scarce. So we expect producers and directors to use it wisely. It is inexcusable to waste even a metre of film.

Marshal Pétain's government is ready to encourage French film-making of boldness and excellence that lives up to our artistic heritage and reflects the true nature and talent of our country . . .

We must not lose sight of the fact that the cinema is a key ingredient in our national propaganda.

Everyone must keep in mind the national and social role it can play in the renewal of our country.[48]

With the Occupation, France's previously anarchic film industry had suddenly become one of the most regulated in the world. Yet another instrument of control was a new double visa censorship system. All films had to be submitted for the approval of the Service du Cinéma, which, in consultation with a 'Commission de contrôle cinématographique' (film control committee), would issue a provisional visa on the basis of a preliminary scenario, and then a final visa on the basis of the realised film – although even then, as the ultimate overseeing authority, the Propaganda Abteilung in Paris had the power to intervene if it chose. The procedure paralleled that of the Production Code Administration in Hollywood, which monitored scripts before production, but issued a seal only after viewing the finished film.

The cumulative effect on the French cinema of all these Hollywood-style measures of control was naturally to encourage a more ordered, artificial and polished cinema. Scripts, which had to run the gauntlet of not only the COIC but also the Commission de contrôle cinématographique and the Crédit National, became more highly worked. The proviso concerning a film's duration, which – with only a very few exceptions – kept length down to a maximum of a hundred minutes, encouraged a more tightly constructed, faster-paced exposition in which the balance between narrative and character shifted towards the former.

The tight control of film stock also had an impact during the shooting itself. There was less scope for improvisation, more emphasis placed on thorough rehearsal and the pre-planning of shots. Location shooting, for which many directors had shown a taste during the 1930s, became increasingly rare. The tendency now was to shoot in the studio, where chance events, costly in terms of precious materials, could be minimised. The result was that the French cinema became less naturalistic than it had been before the war, more contrived. Its previous artisanal nature was giving way to the film factory. Hollywood films may have been banned but, paradoxically, working practices and modes of production resembled Hollywood more than ever.

Just as the Code, to quote Richard Maltby, 'forced Hollywood to be ambiguous, and gave it a set of mechanisms for creating ambiguity',[49] so Vichy provided a practical framework for French film-makers to forge a more allegorical cinema. If both these closed systems could allow the creation of such works of genuine creative achievement as *Les Enfants du paradis* or *Casablanca* (1942), it was because both Pétain's National Revolution and the Hollywood Production Code were essentially reactive, rather than imposing rigid dogmas of their own.

The attraction of Pétain's National Revolution lay more in the absence than the practice of a coherent political doctrine. The great appeal of its figurehead, Marshal Pétain, was precisely the fact that he did not belong to the breed of politicians who had allowed France to fall into the abyss. A revered figure, he had built his reputation on the defence of Verdun during the First World War, when he had revealed himself to be a humane general prepared to take every effort to safeguard the lives and improve the conditions of his men.

Hugely popular, he featured regularly in the newsreels, the commentator reporting on his latest appearance to dispense comfort and compassion to France's suffering people in hushed tones of respect. Through the Occupation, huge crowds regularly turned out to greet him.* He was perhaps France's biggest film star after Danielle Darrieux.

Under his huge personal authority, the Vichy regime implemented a clearing-away – a *nettoyage*, to use the word endlessly repeated in Vichy newspapers – of discredited groups, whether politicians or foreigners, falling back in this spirit of *redressement* on France's most enduring institutions and values. No longer the République française, but L'Etat français, defending the Family, the Church and the Land. 'France will become again what she should never have ceased to be: an essentially agricultural nation,' he declared in April 1941.[50] He prized not the intellectual but the peasant who, as the historian Julian Jackson has argued, represented for him 'hard work, discipline and tradition'.[51] What Pétain had in mind was a pre-industrial picture-postcard France of the *ancien régime*, god-fearing and proud, invincible in its folklore, handicraft and cheeses.

The vision had its counterpart in the attempts of American fundamentalist opinion to turn the clock back during the 1920s, when, in the words of historian Richard Hofstadter, the 'older, rural and small-town America, now fully embattled against the encroachments of modern life, made its most determined stand against cosmopolitanism, Romanism and the scepticism and moral experimentalism of the intelligentsia'.[52] The Production Code was Hollywood's way of placating such sentiment.

As far as the French cinema was concerned, the advent of Pétainism caused several pre-war films to be stigmatised as decadent and defeatist – *Quai des brumes* (1938), *La Règle du*

---

* Pétain's last public appearance in Paris, on 26 April 1944, can be seen in Claude Chabrol's compilation of the Occupation newsreels, *L'Oeil de Vichy*. Adopting his habitual pose as saviour-grandfather, he addressed a vast cheering crowd from the balcony of the Hôtel de Ville: 'I cannot speak to each one of you individually, it's impossible, there are too many of you.'

jeu (1939) and *Pépé le Moko* (1937) – but nonetheless the very vagueness of this new conservatism created a vacuum in which individual artists could still operate. As long as their work was considered *constructif*, they still enjoyed a large measure of freedom – more, arguably, than the film industries of Germany's adversaries, which were obliged to produce active propaganda in support of their countries' war efforts.

In his letter to *Ciné-Mondial*, Ploquin referred to the cinema as 'a means of effective propaganda', but in practice, as citizens of a country that had been defeated yet was now officially neutral, France's film-makers were spared the pressure to make the kind of crude propaganda that active engagement in the war would have required. Germany may have turned France into a giant prison camp, but part of the *grande illusion* of Vichy was that within their barracks the inmates were allowed to put on their own shows – as long as they didn't insult their captors and obeyed their own commanding officer.

While most film-makers were content to take refuge in far-removed imaginary worlds, there were a few who offered a direct and positive expression of the conservative agenda. *Le Voile bleu*, directed by Jean Stelli in 1942, offers a notable example. 'This film is dedicated to all those women who have sacrificed the pleasures of life for other people's children,' announces a prefatory title. 'For children whom they protect and defend and one day must leave for ever even although they may love them as much as if they were their very own.'

Starring Gaby Morlay, the film tells the story of Louise Jarraud, who loses her newborn child soon after she has learned of the death of her husband in the First World War. Compelled to earn her own living, she becomes a children's nanny. Henceforth, she devotes her life to the children in her care, sacrificing herself repeatedly for their sake, offering them the love and affection that their own parents – symbols of a decadent between-the-wars France – often fail to show.

The years go by, bringing us to the film's finale. Louise lives alone now, old, ill and apparently forgotten. But then she breaks her arm in a fall and has to go to hospital. There the doctor recognises his childhood nurse and organises a party for her. All the children she once looked after, now adults, turn up to express their love and gratitude.

The Pétainist agenda does not make the film any less touching. Conventional in its values, it nonetheless possesses the tenderness of genuine emotion, providing themes of sacrifice and loss with which the wartime population of France could all too easily identify.

Reported by Jacques Siclier to be 'the greatest commercial success of the French cinema during the Occupation',[53] it was a perfect example of the highly conventional and populist cinema of the time. It is little surprise that it should have been remade in Hollywood after the war. Filmed in 1951, with Jane Wyman in the Gaby Morlay role, *The Blue Veil* won its star a Golden Globe and a 'Best Actress' Oscar nomination, and anticipated – arguably even helped to pave the way for – the now celebrated Douglas Sirk melodramas of the 1950s.

Le Voile bleu or *The Blue Veil*: Vichy propaganda or Hollywood melodrama? In practice, there was not so much difference between the two.

13

Irreconcilable Differences

The last year of the Occupation weighed heavily on the French film industry. On the one hand power cuts and the scarcity of materials made film-making increasingly difficult, while on the other air bombardment and raids by the German occupation forces, searching for members of the Resistance or absconders from the 'Service du travail obligatoire' – a scheme that required French men to work in German factories – caused cinema attendance to plummet. Production fell sharply from seventy-eight films in 1942 and fifty-nine in 1943 to only twenty-one in 1944.[1] Nonetheless, these disruptions seemed merely temporary setbacks to an industry that had, against the odds, emerged from the Occupation years considerably strengthened.

To this extent the French cinema became a victim of its success, drawing from its wartime survival unrealistic expectations of what it could expect to achieve in peacetime. In its efforts to protect and strengthen the industry it had developed, it displayed a notable militancy. The Blum–Byrnes agreement of 28 May 1946 provided a focus. While Hollywood had wanted to return to the pre-war agreement of 1936, which set a quota of 188 dubbed films a year, the French proposed a new system which would organise a new quota according to screentime. The Americans accepted the principle, but while the French had wanted an allotment of seven weeks in every thirteen during which only French films could be shown, this figure was whittled down during the negotiations to only four.

In the wider framework of the talks – whose chief purpose was to agree a $650 million aid package for the ruined French economy – the concession was understandable, but in the film world it caused consternation. At a press conference held on

14 June 1946 at IDHEC, the new national film school that had been one of the achievements of the Occupation years,* a delegation of industry representatives, including Jean Grémillon, Claude Autant-Lara and Louis Jouvet, declared their dissatisfaction with the accord and their intention to fight against the 'American invasion'.

Blum gave this response: 'I have to admit that had it been necessary in the greater interest of France to sacrifice its film industry, I would have done so without hesitation.'[2] As Pierre Billard has commented, it was the frank and courageous reply of a genuine statesman. Less understanding, Philippe d'Hugues has described it as the 'typical reaction of a turn-of-the-century intellectual full of contempt for the cinema',[3] a comment that seems to ignore that it was Blum's government of 1936 that made the first serious attempt to identify and to address the French film industry's problems. But it is certainly true that Blum's remark revealed the failure of an older generation to understand how central the cinema had become to the expression of France's cultural identity.

The path to France's cultural exception began in the furious reaction to the Blum–Byrnes accords, which refused to accept the legitimacy of purely economic arguments. From July 1946 French cinemas began to exhibit a backlog of films, which included many of Hollywood's most accomplished works: *Citizen Kane* (1941), *The Little Foxes* (1941), *The Maltese Falcon* (1941), *Casablanca* (1942), *Double Indemnity* (1944), *The Big Sleep* (1946). After years of deprivation, the French public flocked into the cinemas to welcome back Hollywood films. While the distributors and exhibitors were pleased to have such profitable products, they nonetheless resented the block booking system that forced them to take mediocre films as well as high-quality ones. It caused sufficient resentment for them to

---

* The Institut des hautes études cinématographiques was founded in September 1943 under the presidency of Marcel L'Herbier.

make common cause with the French film producers, who feared the impact Hollywood's return would have on the viability of indigenous production. Amid a financial crisis in which production costs had rocketed and investors were shying away from an industry that seemed an increasingly poor prospect, pressure was fast building for some kind of counter-measure.

On 19 December 1947 a 'Comité de Défense du Cinéma' (committee for the defence of the cinema) was established. Its members included well-known directors, screenwriters and actors, but also, in a rare display of unity, the heads of the three key branches of the industry – production, distribution and exhibition.[4] So often divided in the past, the whole film industry was presenting its case with complete unanimity.

Two weeks later, on 4 January 1948, there followed a well-organised demonstration in which French film stars, including Jean Marais, Simone Signoret and Serge Reggiani, as well as some of the industry's most prominent directors, led a ten-thousand-strong contingent of industry workers on a protest march from the Madeleine to the Place de la République.

The route was chosen to contribute to the political message. It passed by some of the most impressive cinemas on the Grands Boulevards, yet – as the reporter for *L'Ecran français* observed – '35 out of 40 cinemas on average show American films'.[5] Several of the demonstrators' banners pressed home the point, singling out the 'bad American films' that threatened their livelihoods and demanding the renegotiation of the Blum–Byrnes accords.

L'Ecran français, which devoted a double-spread feature to the protest, adopted a stance of unambiguous support for its aims. The magazine may have been heavily reliant on Hollywood to fill its pages but it nonetheless made the most of any opportunity to subvert Hollywood's prevailing values.

To take the issue devoted to the demonstration as an example, after the coverage of the demonstration itself the next full-page feature was devoted to Hollywood's longest-enduring rebel, Charlie Chaplin: '*Monsieur Verdoux* has come to Paris! Chaplin greater than ever!' Then there followed a double-page spread on the fortunes of black jazz musicians in Hollywood cinema. In the context of that week's highly publicised protest against the Blum–Byrnes agreement, it was difficult not to read into the piece a topical subtext.

'A victim of the American cinema: Jazz emasculated and betrayed,' ran the headline, the article itself going on to provide a hard-hitting indictment of the racism that had kept a generation of talented black musicians off America's screens:

Blacks are welcome to polish shoes, work as servants or pick cotton . . . But it's another matter to admit that they receive applause, even if it's only for their music. Stop right there! Back to your brushes! Back to your kitchens! Back to your fields!

The bitter sarcasm betrayed a common feeling. After all, wasn't the French cinema every bit as much a victim, struggling as hard against the dominant ideology to make its voice heard?

It was a week for underdogs that gave Charlot's arrival in France in the guise of a Frenchman a strange timeliness. *Monsieur Verdoux* is a respectable Paris bank clerk who is made redundant during the Great Depression. He is driven by the cruelty of the world to murder wealthy widows in order to support his invalid wife and child. It was easy enough to draw the appropriate parallels.

This latest battle of the French cinema against Hollywood was fought much more over social and cultural issues than commercial ones. It was as if the leaders of the campaign had given up pretending that they could possibly compete in this arena. The non-conformist, distinctive voices of Hollywood cinema – Charlie Chaplin, Orson Welles (who had written the original idea for *Monsieur Verdoux*), Preston Sturges – continued to be applauded; it was the middlebrow mass that became the focus of French ire.

In February 1948, the Comité de Défense du Cinéma published its manifesto. It is worth quoting at length, because the expression of high ideals was so typical of the French cinema's enduring tendency through the years to justify itself in cultural rather than commercial terms:

In the contemporary world, the cinema – scarcely fifty years old – has in both the artistic and industrial sphere achieved a pre-eminent position.

Every great nation finds in the cinema a means of expression and an aid to expansion appropriate to the modern age. To make and show good films: for a modern people, it's a mark of their greatness and vitality.

France, which has over the centuries been able to exert an exceptional influence through so many artistic activities, must once again take up its rightful place.

On the world's screens, which each day beckon into dark theatres more than fifty million people, the French film must give citizens of every continent a diverse picture of our country.[6]

The issue touched a raw nerve in which the cinema became a symbol of France's perennial fears concerning the onward march of American culture. The Communist leader Maurice Thorez joined the bandwagon. On 18 April, in a speech that was as opportunist as it was hysterical, he denounced Hollywood 'which thanks to Léon Blum invades our screens' and 'which, not content to take jobs away from our workers, literally poisons the spirit of our children, our young men and women, in order to turn them into the docile slaves of American billionaires . . .'[7]

The intervention served to fuel an already emotive debate in the press, which now turned into a national crusade for the renegotiation of the Blum–Byrnes agreement. As a result the French government requested a new round of talks and, in September 1948, a revised four-year agreement came into force. The quota of French screentime was raised to five weeks out of every thirteen and the number of dubbed films was limited to 186 films a year, of which the allocation for American films was 121.

But such measures did nothing to stem the undeniable public demand for Hollywood films, nor make French films any more profitable than they were before. Having conceded the cultural importance of a national cinema, the French government had no choice, therefore, but to put in place the machinery of long-term state subsidy. In the same month as the revised agreement, the Centre National de la Cinématographie (CNC) – in effect a successor organisation to the wartime COIC – began to administer a production fund established by the 'Loi d'aide temporaire à l'industrie cinématographique' (law for temporary aid to the film industry). The word 'temporaire' was wishful thinking. In 1955 the Loi d'aide gave way to the 'Fonds de développement de l'industrie cinématographique' (development fund for the film industry), which in turn yielded to the 'Compte de soutien financier' (financial support fund). These measures envisaged some notional time in the future when such economic support for the industry would no longer be needed but, in practice, the cultural exception had come into existence long before it had even been given a name.

It was built on disappointment. If, on the basis of its pre-war and wartime record, it was possible for the French film industry to imagine that it could establish a healthy export market for itself, it soon discovered that such hopes were a chimera. *Les Portes de la nuit* (1946), Carné's follow-up to *Les Enfants du paradis* (1945), was a notorious example. Its colossal budget of $400,000 reflected its ambition to break into the American market. But the original stars of the film, Jean Gabin and Marlene Dietrich, who had name-recognition value for transatlantic audiences, pulled out at the last moment and RKO, which had a tie-up with the French producer of the film, Pathé, withdrew its support. Mired in production difficulties, the budget spiralled to $800,000, making it easily the most expensive film in French cinema history up to that time – yet with its two tyro stars, a young Yves Montand and Nathalie Nattier, both completely unknown in America, it lacked the most basic box-office ingredients for transatlantic success.

As the post-war French cinema engaged in largely futile efforts to take on Hollywood, suddenly they found themselves having to face a completely unexpected rival.

The *New York Times* began its review of *Rome, Open City* (1945) as follows:

It may seem peculiarly ironic that the first film yet seen hereabouts to dramatise the nature and the spirit of underground resistance in German-held Europe in a superior way – with candid, over-powering realism and with a passionate sense of human fortitude – should be a film made in Italy. Yet such is the extraordinary case. *Open City (Città aperta)* . . . is unquestionably one of the strongest dramatic films yet made about the recent war.[8]

James Agee in the *Nation* echoed this sense of having been bowled over by an exceptional, unexpected experience. Praising the film's 'immediacy', he observed, 'You will seldom see as pure freshness and vitality in a film, or as little affectation among the players.'[9] Indeed, what impressed him was the fact that the performers were not 'players' in the traditional sense. The greatest virtues of the film were precisely those that could not be replicated on a Hollywood sound stage:

It was made on a good deal less than a shoestring; mainly without sets or studio lighting; on varying qualities of black-market film. All sound, including dialogue, was applied later. The author and director had a good deal of movie experience; nearly the whole cast was amateur. The result is worthless to those who think very highly of so-called production valyahs . . . But plenty of people realise a point that many others will never understand and that there is no use labouring: some professional experience is exceedingly useful and perhaps indispensable, but most of the best movies could be made on very little money and with little professional experience. Judging by *Open City*, they can be made a great deal better that way.

Yet this wasn't a message French film-makers seemed ready to hear. More organised, more professional, they had built an industry that, seemingly intent to fight Hollywood on its ground, paid more attention to 'production valyahs' than ever. *Les Portes de la nuit* was an example. The role they had once played as an alternative to the Hollywood system was compromised because, in their pursuit of grandeur, they had assumed too many of the attributes of that system.

By contrast, the Italian films seemed raw and immediate, offering a view of a continent from which the Americans – unless they had been in the armed forces – had been cut off during the last four years.

Among American film reviewers, who had been so enthusiastic about French cinema before the war, a kind of French-weariness set in. The French films that began to return to the screens of New York's art houses were certainly accomplished, but if anything all too recognisable, old, no longer so diverting.

The first French film to be released in the United States after the war was Jacques Becker's *Goupi mains rouges* (1943), which opened in the Fifty-Fifth Street Playhouse in December 1945. James Agee, who didn't get round to seeing the film until two months later, confessed in the *Nation* that he had put off going to see a film that, in the event, had much to admire, because he was 'as usual set on edge by the kind of finishing-school, French-table, cultural chitchat to which so many American enthusiasts are aroused by anything from France'.[10] When Pagnol's *La Fille du puisatier* (1940) opened in New York a few months later, once again there were the usual respectful reviews, but there was no longer the excitement of discovery that characterised the reviews of Pagnol's pre-war films. It seemed merely an example of the French cinema picking up from where it had left off.

The French film renaissance of the 1930s was entering the difficult baroque phase. *Les Enfants du paradis* may today have entrenched its position as prime contender for the title of 'best French film ever made', but its reception upon its first showing in the United States was lukewarm. Reviewers had to acknowledge an obviously impressive achievement, but in their respectful praise one can discern the boredom of critics who had seen it all before.

When Bosley Crowther observed in the *New York Times* that

the 'strong philosophical disposition of the French film director Marcel Carné to scan through the medium of cinema the irony and pathos of life . . . has apparently not been altered by the tragic experience of the last few years',[11] the subtext of his comment seemed to be that he rather wished it had. He went on:

Obviously such an Olympian – or classical – structure for a film presumes a proportionate disposition to philosophise from the audience. And it assumes a responsibility of dramatic clarity. Unfortunately, the pattern of the action does not support the demand. There is a great deal of vague and turgid wandering in *Les Enfants du paradis*, and its network of love and hate and jealousy is exceptionally tough to cut through.

Somehow, in its very ambition, the film seemed to challenge the bounds of what movie entertainment was.[12] Writing in the *New Yorker*, John McCarten wrote:

The plot is one of infinite complication, which tries to follow the love affair of a dreamy pantomimist and a readily accessible lady but keeps getting tangled up with half the population of Paris. Whenever the action shows a tendency to flag, M. Prévert breaks out a fiesta, and if you are as intolerant of fiestas as I am, I don't think you're going to have much fun sitting through the noise and the confusion.[13]

Even the much more enthusiastic James Agee, who considered the film to be 'close to perfection of its kind', attributed to the story an 'over-ripe grandiloquence', openly suggesting that his liking for the film betrayed a lapse of taste: 'I do suspect that unless you have a considerable weakness for romanticism, which I assume includes a weakness for the best of its ham, this will seem just a very fancy, skilful movie. But if you have that lucky weakness, I think the picture can be guaranteed to make you very happily drunk.'[14]

In the French context, this extraordinary super-production, made during the darkest period of the Occupation, was considered to be a tribute to their resistance, a source of national pride – in the words of Roger Régent, a 'masterpiece . . . of incredible technical virtuosity', a 'monument' and 'the splendid crown' to France's distinguished wartime cinema.[15] But in the United States, it was treated as no more than a grand but over-intellectual divertissement. In terms of the cinema's future progress, *Rome, Open City* seemed important, *Les Enfants du paradis* irrelevant. French cinema may have been as accomplished, decorative and elegant as ever, but this miraculous new Italian cinema *mattered*. When they went along to see the next new Pagnol or Carné or Guitry, the American critics knew they could expect a civilised evening of intelligent, characteristically Gallic cinema, but the Italian films, with their human warmth and immediacy, seemed to transcend national boundaries.

The film that replaced *Rome, Open City* after its long run at the World in New York was Luigi Zampa's *Vivere in pace* (1946). It too won rapturous praise. And the string of extraordinary films continued with *Shoeshine* (1946), *Paisà* (1946), *Bicycle Thieves* (1948), *Miracle in Milan* (1950), *Umberto D* (1952) . . .

With their non-professional actors and intense, contemporary stories, so different from Hollywood, these Italian films were taking the cinema somewhere new. When De Sica's *Shoeshine* opened in New York in the summer of 1947, Agee called it 'about as beautiful, moving, and heartening a film as you are ever likely to see'. By coincidence, in the same piece he reviewed Marcel Carné's *Les Visiteurs du soir* (1942), released in the United States as *The Devil's Envoys*. At certain moments, when it gave a glimpse of what the Middle Ages must have been like, he thought it 'wonderful' and 'elaborately beautiful', but he went on,

I was forced to realise anew, as I watched it, just how boring unalleviated beauty can be . . . most of it is like a required reading of *Aucassin and Nicolette*, translated into Middle High Marshmallow. It is a discouraging sign that *The Devil's Envoys* won a French Critics' award. That goes far toward helping explain why the best movies in the world, and in many years, are being made in Italy.[16]

The Italian cinema not only mattered but also possessed the

traditional entertainment values that American audiences understood. The social and contemporary significance of these films would finally have meant very little had they not also possessed a visceral dramatic appeal. The intellectuals might celebrate the 'new realism' of *Rome, Open City*, but there was also the more basic star appeal of Anna Magnani. Her bare-legged image provided a focal point for the publicity posters, which also carried the following prominently displayed words: '*Life* says: "VIOLENCE and PLAIN SEXINESS project a feeling of dangerous struggle that Hollywood seldom approaches!"'

While the French cinema seemed icily remote and sepulchral, something belonging behind a glass screen like the *Mona Lisa* in the Louvre, the Italian film-makers demonstrated an instinctive feel for the popular idiom. *Rome, Open City*, which grossed $1,200,000 at the US box-office,[17] went on to play in circuit cinemas that had never previously shown a foreign-language film.

'Italian importations are running away from the field as box-office winners in the foreign language trade,' reported *Variety* in April 1948. 'Top b.o. status of the Italo pix is a marked reversal of pre-war form when they ran a poor second to French films which practically blanketed the sure-seater trade.'[18]

The following month, the French trade magazine *Cinématographie française*, which closely followed the fortunes of French films exhibited in New York, ran an article under the headline, 'Italian films eclipse the French cinema in the United States.' Making an attempt to explain why, it also cited the universal appeal of the Italian films, commenting that French films by comparison seemed only to interest intellectuals or snobs. 'It is clear that films like *La Belle et la bête*, *L'Idiot* or *Farrebique* do not appeal to a typical American audience.'[19]

Once the French film industry had hoped that the pre-war prestige of its films would help to build an audience in the United States. Now it was beginning to appreciate that this prestige actually operated as a barrier. French films were perceived as too arty and intellectual ever to appeal to more than a tiny élite. Where once French film-makers had aspired to narrow the gap between the two cinemas, now they had to come to terms with the fundamental differences that separated them.

Under the terms of the renegotiated Blum–Byrnes agreement, Hollywood companies had to submit to currency controls that restricted the amount of box-office profits that they could remit back home. But they were allowed to invest this money in French-made co-productions. The situation bore a direct parallel with the Anglo–American film agreement that the British Board of Trade had negotiated a few months earlier. It, too, was based on a twin policy of limiting the amount of box-office revenue that Hollywood could remit and of encouraging those blocked revenues to be invested instead in local production.[20]

In the case of the British film industry, the policy enjoyed a measure of success. Within weeks of the agreement, the British producer Alexander Korda had embarked upon a production programme of four films for the Selznick Releasing Organisation and signed another deal to make *The Elusive Pimpernel* (1950) for the Samuel Goldwyn Company. Both partnerships would turn out to be very difficult, but *The Third Man* (1949), with its British crew and Hollywood box-office stars, did at least offer an example of the potential of such cooperation. A year later, MGM had established its own British production centre with the opening of its studio at Borehamwood. Other Hollywood companies also began to build on their already substantial holdings in Britain, firmly establishing a tradition for investment in British production that would carry on well into the 1960s.

But no such sustained cooperation occurred in the case of the French film industry. Hollywood's reliance on the French market did not provide a sufficient incentive to invest in an industry that it regarded as too alien in its approach towards the cinema ever to make co-production successful. This wasn't simply a question of language. The Italian industry, for example, building on the international success of the neo-realist films, was able to attract major investment from Hollywood during the same period. Because its producers were more ready to acknowledge the traditional ingredients of box-office success in American terms – entertainment value, star appeal – there existed a common understanding for future progress.

By contrast, the French cinema in the post-war years seemed less inclined to seek a *rapprochement* with Hollywood than to entrench its difference. Someone who was well equipped to explain the conflict between the two opposing concepts of the cinema was the director Robert Florey. He had begun in the French film industry as an assistant to Louis Feuillade, but then settled in Hollywood during the early 1920s. There he made a number of avant-garde films,[21] but also established a career as a prolific director for the major studios, including Paramount and Warner Brothers.

Becoming an intimate part of the Hollywood social scene, he was a friend of Fairbanks, Pickford, Valentino and Chaplin, yet at the same time a prominent figure in the French expatriate community, maintaining close links with his native country. At the end of 1948, soon after the revision of the Blum–Byrnes agreement, Florey contributed a long piece to *Cinématographie française*,[22] which focused on the failure of French critics to understand the nature of a director's working life in the big American studios.

Apart from a small handful of 'director-authors', Hollywood directors, he stressed, neither contributed to a film's script nor chose its subject-matter. They were just one of many cogs in a very large machine. To keep working in what was a fiercely competitive job market, directors had no choice but to take on assignments for which they often had very little natural sympathy.

Now in the reviews of the Paris critics, the producer of the film – the man who imposed the subject on the director – is never blamed; the name of the screenwriter is hardly ever mentioned, and it is the poor director who nearly always carries the can for everything they find wrong with the film.

By contrast, he thought that the American critics, who were more familiar with the production-line circumstances in which Hollywood films were actually made, offered far more constructive insight and sympathy.

The return to France of the wartime Hollywood exiles Clair, Renoir, Ophüls and Duvivier served further to highlight the conflicting natures of the two systems. Clair's time in Hollywood only strengthened the nostalgia he felt for the cinema of his pre-First World War childhood. It provided the subject for the first film he directed in France upon his return from Hollywood in 1946.

Set in turn-of-the-century Paris, *Le Silence est d'or* (1947) was a homage to the pioneers of the early cinema, but at the same time an example of the conflict between the two major traditions into which that cinema subsequently divided. Co-financed by Pathé and RKO, Clair presided over both the French and English-language versions of the film. While *Le Silence est d'or* enjoyed considerable acclaim in Europe, it was poorly received in both Britain and America. Georges Charensol and Roger Régent, who wrote a book on Clair in 1952, ascribed the poor reception to a difference of taste between the Anglo-Saxon and French audiences: 'American and English audiences were united in the view that there was not enough action and that the theme of an old man in love was interesting only to Latins, who attach excessive importance to such matters.'[23] In words that seem to capture not only the sentiments of Clair himself but also their own – as well as the post-war Paris film milieu in which they were writing – Charensol and Régent went on to comment: 'This hard lesson taught Clair that it is useless to try to appeal at the same time to both a Latin audience and an Anglo-Saxon one.'[24] If the lack of commercial reward caused Hollywood to show little interest in such Franco-American co-productions, creative dissatisfaction seemed to be as much a factor from the French perspective.

Although Clair's huge reputation meant that he counted among the few directors working in Hollywood able to have significant control over their films, his own estimate of the contemporary American film industry confirmed Florey's account:

Among the four or five hundred films made each year in California how many have any individual style? How many give the appearance of being the work of an original artist? It's by a kind of superstition that we continue to cite the names of American writers and directors. With few exceptions, these names mean no more than those to be found on bank notes, which can change with the value of the notes being any different. Regardless of the big letters and fanfares that accompany the credits on the screen, the names you find there are usually little more than the employees of a corporation directed by an all-powerful and anonymous board.[25]

After the disappointment of *Le Silence est d'or*, Clair was released from a contract to make another film for RKO in America, but was presumably content to make a permanent return to a France that, according to the consensus on both sides of the Atlantic, offered a far more favourable climate to the 'director-author'.

But of all the French exiles in Hollywood, Clair had enjoyed perhaps the smoothest path. The Chaplinesque style of his films had turned him into an international, highly sellable commodity. Not only had he long been lauded in America as one of the world's top film directors, but, even before he had arrived in the United States for the first time, he had already made a successful English-language film, *The Ghost Goes West* (1935), and had one of Hollywood's most powerful agents, Myron Selznick, to represent him.

Max Ophüls, by contrast, was barely known in the United States. Shortly after his arrival in the autumn of 1940, his film *De Sarajevo à Mayerling* (1940) opened at the Little Carnegie Theatre, New York. But it made little impression and, when he arrived in Hollywood, he struggled for several years to find work. 'America was certainly not as I had imagined it, and for quite a time I was very depressed,' he later recalled.

I couldn't understand the workings of the Hollywood machinery, till one day a big-time executive said to me with a friendly pat on the shoulder: 'Our studios are producing a lot of cheaply made money-spinners just now: thrillers, Westerns and so on. But one day the Board of Directors may decide to embark on Quality Production. That is when we shall need you.' His words were true, which meant that waiting for my chance I might well starve.[26]

Ophüls was only finally rescued in 1946 when Preston Sturges, who had seen *Liebelei* (1933), persuaded Howard Hughes to let Ophüls direct his script, *Vendetta*. Soon after disagreements with Sturges over how the film should be made,[27] however, Ophüls was dismissed. Robert Siodmak, who had known Ophüls in Germany and France, then recommended him to the film star Douglas Fairbanks, Jr., who was producing for Universal his own screenplay, *The Exile* (1947), a swashbuckling romance in the style of his father's films.

The contemporary reviews of the film were perhaps the inevitable response to the production system of which Clair complained. No one expected a director's contribution to be of any consequence in this system, and therefore no one looked for it. 'In a not precisely perfect exemplification of that hardy saw, "like father, like son," Douglas Fairbanks Jr. makes an earnest debut as a producer in *The Exile*,' wrote the *New York Times*.[28] In conclusion, it commented: 'Having chosen to film the work in sepia, Mr. Fairbanks has given it a pleasant pastoral tone.' This was about the extent of the modest praise, but Ophüls himself was not mentioned once, the authorial presumption in Hollywood's producer-centric system being in Fairbanks' favour.

Writing in *Time*, James Agee considered *The Exile* to be 'one of those shy wildflowers which occasionally spring up almost unnoticed in the Hollywood hothouse'.[29] He thought the story to be 'a pleasant little fraud', but '*The Exile* is also Young Doug's first fling as a producer, and he has concealed most of the fraud with both legitimate and handsome cinematic tricks'. Elaborating, he explained how 'the direction saves the day by insisting on a witty, natural reading. Fairbanks has also inflicted an extreme lilt on the rhythm of the film.'

For today's film-viewing generation – by long-established convention attributing priority to the director even in the most questionable of circumstances – it seems extraordinary that Ophüls should have been so disregarded, even to the extent that what was clearly his province – the direction of the film – is treated as yet another aspect for which the star-producer might as well take the credit. But this was perhaps the inevitable result of Hollywood's producer-led system, in which, with a few exceptions, the director was regarded as just a cog in the machine.

The lack of appreciation Ophüls experienced in the United States was the other side of Robert Florey's coin: knowing how very little control directors usually had, American critics tended not to make the assumption of their French counterparts that he should be held to account for a film's failings, but they had yet to develop a critical language with which to tease out the qualities for which the director did deserve credit.

Ophüls made three more films in America, *Letter from an Unknown Woman* (1948), *Caught* (1949) and *The Reckless Moment* (1949). According to Ophüls' own account, once he began working, he enjoyed considerable freedom on these films. *Letter from an Unknown Woman*, at least, would have been recognised for the visual masterpiece it was in a more director-aware film culture. But instead, once again Ophüls barely made it on to the radar of appreciation. The film was acknowledged by the *New York Times* to be 'handsomely put-together', but – belonging to the then much derided genre of 'woman's picture' – was dismissed as 'pseudo-Viennese schmaltz'.[30]

As far as any presumptions of authorship were concerned, once again they were in favour of the producer-star. Describing the film as a 'moist-handkerchief romance', the *New York Times* observed: 'Apparently that's how Miss Fontaine wished it, for not only is she the picture's star but she and her husband, William Dozier, produced it with John Houseman's aid. And apparently, too, as producer she was biased toward herself as star, for it cannot be stated too strongly that the picture is largely

Miss Fontaine's.' The visual illiteracy that characterised so many reviews of the period meant that Ophüls' writing with the camera, his extraordinarily fluid and inimitable *mise-en-scène* – and perhaps it is telling in itself that there should be no direct English equivalent for this phrase – went unnoticed.

In 1950, Ophüls returned to France to direct a film version of Balzac's *La Duchesse de Langeais* for the producer Walter Wanger, for whom he had made *The Reckless Moment*, but the project fell through. 'As nothing came of it, I finally got tired of drawing my salary in idleness and I enthusiastically seized the chance of filming another famous Schnitzler subject: *Der Reigen*, a favourite story of mine.'[31]

Ophüls had managed to establish himself as a director in America, but the drift back to France was nonetheless natural. In a film culture that attached so much more importance to his métier, it was easier there not only to avoid idleness and to find subjects of his own choosing, but also to enjoy the wider appreciation and understanding that he failed to find in the United States. If Hollywood provided generous financial support, it was finally the cultural support of France that mattered even more.

Of all the French directors to work in America during the 1940s, Julien Duvivier was perhaps the most suited to adapt to the Hollywood system. Not only had his career in France already been notable for an unusually wide breadth of subject-matter, but he also displayed, in Henri Jeanson's words, the kind of 'love of a job well done' that Hollywood prized.[32] He had obvious creative flair, but also prided himself on a rigour and discipline that enabled him to complete projects within budget and on schedule.

Significantly, he did not arrive in Hollywood as a refugee – like Renoir, Ophüls or Clair – but was invited to come by MGM before the war: the move had been a positive choice. *The Great Waltz*, which he made in 1938, may have been a studio assignment rather than a subject of his own choosing, but nonetheless he relished the challenge of making a film on the Hollywood scale:

I had all the resources I needed. I was given 2 million dollars to make my film, which is a lot of money even for Hollywood. *The Great Waltz* will be one of the big films of the year and I can feel only flattered that its direction was entrusted to me.[33]

But at the same time he understood the considerable creative compromise that his work in Hollywood required. 'In France I have always had freedom more or less and artistic control over my films. It is obvious that a director in Hollywood does not enjoy the same privileges.'[34]

It was why, after *The Great Waltz*, he returned to France to make *La Fin du jour* (1938). The story of a group of elderly actors dwelling on their past successes or failures in a retirement home, the film boasted some of the most distinguished actors of the French cinema and stage, but lacked a genuine box-office star in the Hollywood sense of the term and did not belong to any obvious genre. Possessing none of the mainstream attractions of a Hollywood production, but nonetheless hugely entertaining, with Duvivier's usual sense of drama and atmosphere, it was ideal fare for the sophisticated patrons of the Filmarte, where it opened in September 1939 – but, as Duvivier knew, of no interest whatsoever to a more general English-language audience.

His return to Hollywood during the war was a natural transition for him. That he quickly found his feet there is no more surprising than that Renoir or Ophüls should have struggled. For he *did* understand the workings of the Hollywood system, even if he was no more prepared to sacrifice himself to it in the longer term. At the end of the war he came back to France and – after a brief sojourn in England to make *Anna Karenina* (1948) for Alexander Korda – successfully re-established himself in the French film industry, never to return to Hollywood again.

In the late 1940s, the French film industry and Hollywood went through a kind of divorce, as though they had each discovered too much about their partner to make cohabitation any longer bearable. The renegotiated Blum–Byrnes agreement may have sought to encourage continued cooperation, but the experiences of Ophüls, Renoir, Clair and Duvivier help to explain why such cooperation was so limited in practice.

The export successes of the French cinema during the 1930s had established the hope that it might be able to compete with Hollywood commercially. During the Occupation, aided by its European collaborator, Germany, the French cinema used the breathing space of isolation from Hollywood to build the industrial infrastructure that might have turned this hope into reality. But the commercial disappointments of peacetime had caused the agenda to move on yet again. Rather than attempt to compete with Hollywood on its own ground, the French film industry began instead to identify and defend the values of its own artisanal, director-centric system, which led to even more regulation and state control.

By contrast, the monolithic facade of Hollywood was beginning to fragment. In October 1940 the five integrated major studios, to avoid the full consequences of the US government's anti-trust suit, signed a consent decree that outlawed blind selling and reduced block booking to groups of not more than five films. As a result, 'the majors cut back production overall to concentrate on top features'.[35] Departing from the safe genres of the past in their quest for prestige production, the studios began to take chances for which there had previously been no commercial incentive.

The opening of *Citizen Kane* in March 1941 was acknowledged by most serious critics in the United States as a major landmark in Hollywood's history. Both the New York Critics Circle and the National Board of Review chose it as best film of the year. In an editorial, the *National Board of Review Magazine* emphasised the significance of such universal acclaim. It showed

the reward that can come to a producer for courage and persistence. Courage in backing an unpredictable talent in an untried field, and persistence in vigorously continuing that backing in the face of old traditions and adverse pressure. Mr Schaefer of RKO risked a lot when he gave Orson Welles the chance to be Orson Welles on the screen. In return he has gained enormously in prestige . . . And the whole film industry has gained something in the unforeseeable influence an unrestricted new creative force may have in the growth of the motion picture art.[36]

John Huston's *The Maltese Falcon* and Billy Wilder's *Double Indemnity* soon followed. They were both examples of how Hollywood film-makers were learning that it was possible to make intelligent, sophisticated films within the framework of Code cinema. At the same time, however, the Production Code itself seemed to be demonstrating a new flexibility. According to Billy Wilder, he was warned by his studio, Paramount, that the Hays Office would not approve a film adaptation of James M. Cain's novel, but he decided to write a script nonetheless. To his surprise they then not only passed the script but also pronounced the finished film to be 'the best crime-doesn't-pay subject yet'. Philip Scheuer, who interviewed Wilder for the *Los Angeles Times*, listed the 'movie don'ts' the film violated, observing that the adulterous affair at its heart was a taboo 'so unmistakable that even a Hays warden couldn't miss it'.[37] But the Production Code Administration had evolved to the point where it was increasingly prepared to trade literal observation if the film as a whole could be considered to meet the overall objective of the Code to raise moral standards.

'Finally, like the great French cinema, it is adult,' Philip Scheuer wrote of *Double Indemnity*. Fritz Lang's *Scarlet Street*, which was made the following year for Universal, helps us better to appreciate the comment. Taking advantage of the new ground that *Double Indemnity* had opened up, it was based on source material that would previously have been considered unfilmable in America – the Georges de La Fouchardière novel that Jean Renoir had made in France as *La Chienne* back in 1931.[38]

Starring Edward G. Robinson, who had played the insurance agent in *Double Indemnity*, *Scarlet Street* offered the same themes of adultery and murder. Married to a nagging wife, Christopher Cross (Edward G. Robinson) falls helplessly in love and has an affair with gold-digger Kitty (Joan Bennett). With her lover Johnny Prince (Dan Duryea), Kitty manipulates Cross into stealing from his employer. When Cross finally discovers how he has been betrayed, he kills Kitty, loses his job and, down-and-out, wanders the streets haunted by guilt.

Like *Double Indemnity*, the film received the approval of the Hays Office, presumably for offering the same crime-doesn't-pay message. But its position at the very limits of what was possible came into focus on 4 January 1946 when, three days before its advertised opening in New York, it was refused a state licence by the New York State Board of Education on the grounds that it was 'immoral, indecent, corrupt and tending to incite crime'.[39] The ban was finally lifted on appeal and the film passed with minor cuts, but the significant point is that now Hollywood films were daring to challenge the boundaries, not just French ones.

It was significant, too, that Universal were – as the *National Board of Review Magazine* might have put it – allowing Fritz Lang to be Fritz Lang. The studio's response to the Consent Decree had been to acquire prestige films by financing independent production units. *Scarlet Street* had been made by Diana Productions, whose directors were Walter Wanger, Joan Bennett and Fritz Lang himself. Other new independent production companies came into being at about the same time, providing a framework at least for some of Hollywood's more established directors to enjoy greater creative freedom. Among the more notable examples were John Ford's Argosy Pictures, formed in 1945, and Liberty Films, formed by the directors Frank Capra, William Wyler and George Stevens the following year.

Yet if in the immediate post-war period Hollywood's increased flexibility did lead to a more European style of production, it is important to point out that this change was a direct response to trading conditions. The fundamental heart of Hollywood – commercial and oriented towards a mass market – remained unchanged. It requires only a brief consideration of Orson Welles's career after *Citizen Kane* to appreciate this. Welles was left free to make *The Magnificent Ambersons* (1942) as he chose, but after disastrous preview screenings, RKO cut more than fifty minutes without Welles's participation or approval. *Lady from Shanghai*, made for Columbia in 1946 but released only in 1948, would suffer a similar fate. To find the freedom to make films as he wished, Orson Welles had no choice but to drift into exile, just as Fritz Lang, who was able to direct *Scarlet Street* without interference, still had to allow Universal, on the grounds of 'censorship requirements' and 'commercial value', to impose cuts that he did not want.[40]

With its usual market efficiency Hollywood would turn films like *Double Indemnity* or *Scarlet Street* into a new genre, which the French – with their usual cultural percipience – would be the first to identify: *film noir*. The relevant article,[41] in which Nino Frank re-coined a phrase that had first been used of the dark French poetic realist films of the 1930s,[42] captures the huge impact Hollywood cinema was having on post-war French film culture – however much this may have angered French film producers:

The appearance of half a dozen fine works made in California compels us to write and affirm that American cinema is better than ever. Our film-makers are decidedly manic depressive.

Seven new American films are particularly masterful: *Citizen Kane*, *The Little Foxes*, *How Green was My Valley*, plus *Double Indemnity*, *Laura*, and, to a certain extent, *The Maltese Falcon* and *Murder, My Sweet*. The first three are exceptional; but we cannot consider them if we want to focus on typical Hollywood productions. Instead let's look at the other four.

They belong to a class that we used to call the crime film, but that would best be described from this point on by a term such as criminal adventures or, better yet, as criminal psychology. This is a major class of films which has superseded the Western . . .

. . . The detective is not a mechanism but a protagonist, that is the character most important to us: accordingly the heroes of *Maltese*

Falcon and *Murder, My Sweet* practice this strange profession of private detective, which (in the US) has nothing to do with bureaucratic function but, by definition, puts them on the fringe of the law – the law as represented by the police and the codes of gangsters as well. The essential question is no longer 'who-done-it?' but how does this protagonist act?

In this manner these 'noir' films no longer have any common ground with run-of-the-mill police dramas. Markedly psychological plots, violent or emotional action, have less impact than facial expressions, gestures, utterances – rendering the truth of the characters . . . after films such as these the figures in the usual cop movie seem like mannequins.[43]

If this critical receptivity was in itself a vital aspect of France's open cinema, I believe a corresponding obtuseness among US critics played a major role in hindering the progress of the postwar French cinema in the United States. The real battleground for the French cinema was not Hollywood but New York, whose art theatres dictated the potential of the only realistic market that French films had. Its importance as the chief cultural arbiter for the nation as far as foreign films were concerned is reflected in the statistic that the average foreign film, even two years after its initial New York first run, still took 60 per cent of its US revenues from that one city. By comparison, when it came to Hollywood-produced films, New York accounted for just 10 per cent of the domestic gross.[44]

The film columns of the *New York Times*, therefore, enjoyed a disproportionate influence, but the newspaper's chief film critic Bosley Crowther, in spite of his position pivoted between Hollywood and Europe, still offered a viewpoint that was oriented towards the dominant Hollywood model. The more one becomes acquainted with his column, the more one begins to appreciate the frustration that many French film-makers must have felt at the failure of understanding or sympathy that so often greeted their work in these years – as well as the desperate need for some new critical framework or theory that might better explain to the *New York Times*'s audience of intelligent film-goers the more personal and individual nature of film-making in France.

Every now and then that frustration would be expressed through attempts by French film-makers to engage in a debate with Crowther. But these exchanges served only to emphasise that American film culture was as imprisoned in the mentality of a closed system as Hollywood itself. In early 1948, under the headline 'Snows of Yesteryear', Crowther wrote that the appearance in New York of *Farrebique* (1946), *Le Corbeau* (1943) and *Passionnelle* (1946) within the same week 'briefly aroused wistful memories of activities in this line in years gone by'. But the main purpose of the piece was to offer a lament:

For as much as this Francophile flurry gave a fleeting illusion of old times and possibly stirred some passing fancies that the Golden Age of French films might return, the evidence on this occasion, and for several months, has not encouraged much hope. Except for a few delayed chef d'oeuvres from the dead past, the pickings have been slim. And this is the more depressing in view of the notable fact that there has been a strong revival of interest in foreign pictures since the war.[45]

Attempting to single out a common failing in these latest French films, he alighted upon the 'disposition toward dejection and surrender to the wretchedness of life'. They tended to be 'dour and defeatist', lacking 'the vitality and urbanity, the unrestrained vigor and wit, of the films which distinguished French production in its true – and departed – Golden Age'.

Some weeks later, Jacques Chabrier, the representative of Pathé Cinema in New York, wrote to the *New York Times* to take issue:

The great tradition of French pictures, which you say in your article . . . 'distinguished French production in its true – and departed – Golden Age', is, in my opinion, more than anything else, putting our heart into the making of a film. The pictures which you see now are still in that same tradition.

It is true that many of the post-war films shown here have had a grave note. However, the people who are making these films continue to express themselves as before.[46]

Chabrier was defending a cinema that accommodated the individual, personal voice of its film-makers rather than compelling compliance with the latest fashion or mood. The key phrase was 'putting one's heart' into the making of a film, with its unspoken reproach that the Hollywood tradition was 'selling one's soul'. Firmly occupying the high ground, Chabrier saved his final barb for the last paragraph: 'As far as the French producers are concerned, I do not believe they have wistful memories of the Golden Age you refer to, which was not so golden for them – they never made one cent out of the American market.'

It was a familiar pattern: the French sense of artistic integrity versus the ever-present commercial imperative of the American film business, which even the critics – who were themselves part of that business – respected.

Crowther's response to the emerging reputation of the French director Robert Bresson provides another opportunity to consider the gulf. When Bresson's debut feature film *Les Anges du péché* opened at the Paris Cinema in New York in 1950 (seven years after it had been made), Crowther's column billed it as a 'French Film by Jean Giraudoux'.[47] According to a Hollywood attitude that regarded film-making as a collaborative enterprise and relied much more than the French cinema on the pre-existing literary property, it was natural to give creative precedence to the famous playwright who had written the screenplay.

In April 1954, *Journal d'un curé de campagne* (1950) opened in New York at the Fifth Avenue Playhouse. It was a few months after Truffaut had first broached the 'politique des auteurs' in *Cahiers du cinéma*,[48] but firmly entrenched in the traditional Hollywood mindset that such thinking had yet to penetrate, Crowther complained of 'the veil of mysticism that strangely enshrouds the whole film'. He felt, however, that it 'may not be blamed on M. Bresson. The late George Bernanos . . . wrote the original story, which is the basis of the film.'[49]

The conflict between the two different concepts of film-making became more evident when Bresson himself wrote a letter to the *New York Times* a few weeks later to complain about the mutilation of his film:

I have the terrible surprise to hear that my picture, *Diary of a Country Priest*, has been entirely mutilated by the distributor, who took on himself to cut out a considerable number of scenes, in order to shorten the picture of a whole half-hour!

My producer here in Paris is cabling the distributor asking him to put back the picture in its entirety. But I am not at all sure that it will be taken into consideration.

What I am sure of is that it is impossible (I have tried it myself) to cut even one scene of the film without making it absolutely un-understandable. I had built it with utmost care and precautions. And every little detail is indispensable. Besides, a picture is also made of proportions, rhythms . . .

I do not need to tell you how upset I am and how your article (in which you say: 'We followed the picture as closely as we could, ears open and eyes darting diligently over the English subtitles for the dialogue. And still we could not catch the pattern . . .') seems to me sadly justified!

I feel my hands are tied from this side of the Ocean. It is not very gay to think that you and the American public are judging me on a work that can hardly be called mine anymore.[50]

While Bresson clearly regarded himself as the self-evident author of the film, Crowther's response displayed the kind of disregard for a director's importance that once again suggested a Hollywood mentality. The editing of imported films, he wrote, 'is delicate because the practice is a quite frequent and usually tacit one and because – for all the good reasons there may be for it – it may naturally be misconstrued'.[51]

Crowther was attempting to be even-handed, but his own obvious sympathy for the distributors' position, with the bias of that word 'misconstrued', betrayed an attitude that regarded films less as a fully fledged art that could be compared to literature or the theatre than as entertainment products rolling off the conveyor-belt of the film factory.

Representing the film distributors' view, he went on: 'They say that most such pictures that reach them need "editing". They say the foreigners have the inclination to make their pictures "too long" and that trimming and sometimes rearrangement are often essential to satisfy the American taste.' He explained that when he contacted the Fifth Avenue Cinema, which had shown the Bresson film, a representative explained that the cinema had agreed to do so only on condition that the distributor made the cuts that were made. 'The trimming was done to eliminate scenes which were felt superfluous and tended to retard the pace. The sole aim was to make the picture more presentable to New York audiences.'

For all Crowther's efforts to appear impartial, his final comments, in the essentially imperialist stance of Hollywood's dominant ideology, made it quite clear to which side he finally belonged:

Whether the material cut from it would have helped to clarify the theme which this writer found very bewildering is something we cannot say. Presumably, more elucidation by way of material should facilitate a better understanding, but the nature of this picture is such that more material of the sort that is in it might well only complicate it more – that is, for one to whom its contents and its reckonings are essentially abstruse.

It was an example of the market mindset that had made the butchery of French releases near routine, as distributors sought to make them conform more closely to the expectations of audiences accustomed to Hollywood narrative. The first US release of *Les Enfants du paradis*, for example, had been pared down from 183 to 144 minutes.[52] But it was a long tradition that could be traced all the way back to Gance's *J'Accuse*.

The wilful refusal of the French cinema to embrace such a market mindset and the associated virtues of a coherent business strategy were perceived in the United States as being the key obstacles to its success. 'What French producers mostly suffer from', commented *Variety*, in an article on the film crisis of 1948, 'is an inability to get together on any project, to organise under one banner and, having nominated a chief, abide by his decisions. Each one prefers to remain independent and scramble against the others as best he can.'[53] The French film industry would easily surmount its then severe difficulty in financing films if only its producers 'operated like an American major, meaning a production plan and schedule, a talent stable and a worldwide distributing organisation instead of being satisfied with national returns supplemented by meagre foreign outright sales'. If only the French producers brought in 'businessmen to direct their operations', then they 'could graduate from artisans into industrialists'.

Jacques Tati's first feature, *Jour de fête*, encapsulated the conflict between the two attitudes. Shot during the summer of 1947 in the Loire village of Sainte-Sévère, where the music-hall comedian had taken refuge during the war to avoid conscription into the Service du Travail Obligatoire, it grew out of a short he had made called *L'Ecole des facteurs* (*School for Postmen*). The spontaneous, do-it-yourself nature of the production made it seem recklessly casual even to the 'artisans' who supposedly ran the French film industry. To make the film, Tati went into partnership with Fred Orain, a former sound engineer who had been the production manager of *Les Enfants du paradis*. Directing the film himself, Tati employed a handful of professional actors, but most of the cast consisted of inhabitants of the village, whom Tati had got to know during the war.

The decision to shoot the film in an untried colour process called Thomsoncolor – when not even the established film industry had begun to compete with Hollywood's Technicolor productions – contributed to the quixotic quality of the enterprise. Fortunately, the precaution was taken to film also in black and white, because in the event adequate prints could not be struck from the Thomsoncolor negative. Armed with production plan and schedule, no American major would have embarked on a path that left so much to chance, but then no American major would have been able to produce the spontaneous charm that resulted. *Jour de fête* effortlessly epitomised the struggle between the industrial and the individual that characterised the contrast between the two cinemas.

A travelling fair arrives in a country village. Among the carnival attractions is a mobile cinema, which shows a documentary about the American postal service. Inspired by the spectacular modern methods of delivery shown in the film, the village postman, François, seeks to match the American feats of speed.

Built around the comic highlight of François's super-fast round, *Jour de fête* elaborated the gags that Tati had worked out in *L'Ecole des facteurs*, but his affectionate depiction of 'La France profonde' was just as memorable. Tati revealed an extraordinary eye for the rural beauty of the setting, which he integrated seamlessly into the comic purpose of the film. A tractor pulls a fairground caravan and trailer along the country lanes to the village, a phalanx of roundabout horses poking their noses over the tailboard. At the sight of this outlandish apparition, a pair of real horses in a meadow gallop away in alarm to the furthest corner of their field. As the tractor arrives in the village, a gaggle of geese in the road force it to slow down. The two fairground workers joke over the prospect of a meal, one miming a knife being sharpened, the other putting a napkin under his chin. Tati's comedy arose out of a perception of how people actually behaved, his 'gags' offering true observations of absurd but real patterns underlying the familiar.

The fair turns out to be a source of dangerous novelty, putting ideas into François's head that he would have done better to ignore. When his attempt to copy the American postmen ends in disaster, he gives up his bicycle and joins the farm workers harvesting hay in the fields. The old lady, who gives him a lift on her wagon, advises him: 'Let the Americans do things in their own way. That's not a reason for you to go any faster. Good news can wait.' François learns to accept that the modern delivery methods that had so excited him are an unwise intrusion into the slow but more natural rhythm of the village's traditional way of life.

Many felt that the French cinema had a similar lesson to learn. Rather than attempt to ape the Americans, it would fare better if it was true to its more artisanal nature, fostering methods that arose naturally out of its own culture and traditions – although, in truth, Tati's artisanal approach was a challenge even to the French film industry. At first, the distributors showed no interest in a film that contained a series of comic incidents but had no strong narrative. So Fred Orain arranged a series of previews in the Paris suburb of Neuilly. It was only the enthusiastic response of audiences to these that at last persuaded a distributor to take on the film.

Varied and disparate, French producers relied on the CNC (which US distributors regarded as being in the hands of anti-American Communist fellow travellers)[54] to provide some strategic direction. The idea of forging an international corporation that could take on Hollywood in film markets around the world died with the disappearance of Alfred Greven. After the Liberation, the production, distribution and exhibition interests of Continental were confiscated by the French government, which regrouped them into the state-owned holding company UGC.

Under the direction of the producer André Halley des Fontaines, whose previous films had included *Le Crime de Monsieur Lange* (1935), *Dernier atout* (1942) and *Falbalas* (1945), UGC produced a mere handful of films each year. Some, like *Monsieur Vincent* (1947) and *Journal d'un curé de campagne*, were of commendable quality, but the overall output demonstrated not a Continental-style production plan with which to take on the might of Hollywood, but rather the tendency of the French cinema to revert to the small-scale. The industry was not so different from what it had been during the 1930s, except that now the government was committed to protecting it.

14

Accursed Films

In France, every time an attempt is made to
organise, to adopt systems, the individual rebels
and slips in between the gears of the mechanism.
One result of this is that crooks easily get the upper
hand, but another is the formation of underground
élites – a vast hidden force with a spirit of
contradiction that is the very basis of the spirit of
creation – beyond the reach of the official élites.
For centuries this has been the French rhythm.

Jean Cocteau[1]

Tati's postman in *Jour de Fête*, slipping into the gears in spite
of his best intentions, was a hapless, inadvertent example of
the French rhythm, but at about the same time another aspiring
film-maker, operating outside the conventional framework of
the industry, made the challenge to the system more purposeful
and explicit, providing an invaluable model for the underground
of which Cocteau wrote. Born Jean-Pierre Grumbach in 1917,
Jean-Pierre Melville famously changed his name in homage to
the American novelist Herman Melville. As Grumbach, he had
enjoyed a prosperous middle-class upbringing in Paris. When he
was only five, he received a film projector. A year later, he was
given a film camera. He was a 'Pathé Baby' baby. It was during
Melville's infancy that the great pioneer industrialist of the cinema, Charles Pathé, had reached his conclusion that in the new
age of Hollywood, commercial feature-film production was not
really a sensible business, but he could see a market in providing
amateur film equipment. Using a 9.5mm gauge, the 'Pathé Baby'
projector was introduced in time for Christmas 1922. Marketed
under the slogan, 'The Cinema at Home', it gave a second life to

Pathé's huge catalogue of films, which were reduced to the new 9.5mm format. The following year a hand-cranked 'Pathé Baby' camera was introduced.

The energy with which Melville began from the age of seven to make films was matched only by his appetite for watching them. In the 1920s, he recalled, he would see four or five films a week on his Pathé Baby projector. 'It was *l'amour fou* completely. The basis of my cinematographic culture.'[2] Then, with the coming of sound, he transferred his passion to the cinemas on the Paris boulevards. Through the 1930s he was watching films from first thing in the morning until late at night. The focus of his interest was the classic Hollywood cinema of the period. He would later produce his own canon of sixty-three Hollywood directors from 'before the war', whom he felt few European directors of the same period could match. 'It's impossible to find ten men – just one Russian, one or two French. All the Germans were in the USA.'[3]

Melville's passion for the cinema was abruptly interrupted when he was called up for military service in 1937. After the defeat of France, he joined the Resistance. In this decision can be found a continuity with the kind of film-maker he became, wishing always to create the circumstances of his own freedom rather than wait for it, but it also determined the subject of his first feature film.

Just forty pages long, *Le Silence de la mer* was a wartime novel that became a symbol of French resistance. Written by Jean Bruller under the pseudonym 'Vercors', it was first published in February 1942 by the underground press Editions du Minuit. It told the story of an old man and his niece who have a German officer billeted with them. In spite of their growing respect and affection for their unwanted guest, who is an empathetic and cultured Francophile, they make an act of resistance by refusing to speak to him.

The first, clandestine print run was only a few hundred copies, but the circulation quickly snowballed both within and outside France. A year later a second edition was published in London by a press that called itself Les Cahiers du Silence. Miniature copies of the slim volume were air-dropped into occupied France. The appearance of an abridged English-language version of the story in *Life* magazine in October 1943 helped to establish its fame. A full-length translation, by the English writer and critic Cyril Connolly, was then published under the title *Put Out the Light* in February 1944. It was this version that Melville first read when he was in London with the Free French. 'From the day I was given the Vercors story,' recalled Melville, 'I was absolutely determined that it would be my first film.' The success of the book, which, by the end of the war, had sold over a million copies in seventeen different languages, offers some measure of Melville's presumption. He had never made a feature film before, he hadn't even worked in the film industry, yet here he was seeking to make a film of the celebrated famous French novel of the war.

In more ordinary times the odds would have been massively stacked against him, but the special circumstances of *Le Silence de la mer* turned his outsider status into an advantage. The implicit targets of Vercors's book were French writers and artists who had continued to pursue their literary careers during the Occupation. The French cinema itself was an obvious example of such creative compliance and compromise. For all its glittering wartime achievement, its existence had depended upon cooperation with the Occupation authorities in a way that contradicted the gesture of passive resistance that inspired Vercors's story.

Melville was not only a newcomer unblemished by such past associations, but also a former member of the Resistance. He was able to offer an appealing authenticity that chimed in with the nature of a novel that – for all its subsequent commercial success – had been conceived as a spiritual crusade. Vercors may have routinely rejected the offers of other film companies, but Melville's personal commitment meant that he was much more difficult to turn away. The effort of courtship became a drama in itself that offered an echo of the original story, the aspiring young film producer now seeking to overcome the novelist's silence. Aware of its publicity value, Melville did not hesitate to release the correspondence, which showed how he finally won Vercors's conditional cooperation after an initial refusal. It helped to feed a legend that took shape even before the film was released. In May 1948, the *New York Times* published this account of what had happened:

When young Melville came to him and asked for the film rights, Vercors refused him summarily and absolutely. Melville was stopped – but for several months only. He pleaded his case in a letter to Vercors.

'I know I will make a film of *Silence of the Sea*,' he wrote, 'which will not betray the spirit of your work. The love, the respect which I bear for it are the guaranty.'

Vercors replied to Melville:

'You must understand this: *Silence of the Sea* no longer belongs to me alone. Its extraordinary success is not due to its qualities alone. It is due to circumstances. I must recognise that the love which certain people had, and which they still have, for it made it a masterpiece. In this it slips away from me, just as the image of a god before whom the multitude fall prostrate slips away from the sculptor who carved it.'

Melville countered with a proposition that may be unique in film history.

'I am one of those men you describe who feel so deeply for your book,' he answered, 'and I have decided to play a card that might seem very risky to you. You cannot stop me from filming *Silence of the Sea*, if I so wish. You can only stop me from showing it in public. Very well. I will take the entire risk. I will make the film. If you don't like it, I will burn it. If, on the other hand, you like it, you cannot refuse me the right to show it publicly.'

Finally, fourteen days after the correspondence had begun, Vercors wrote to Melville:

'No misunderstanding! I authorise you nothing. I promise you nothing, not even hope. I shall not grant you the movie rights unless, after a private showing, you have the approval of a selected jury . . . I will follow your work with sympathy.'[4]

For all the expressed caveats, Vercors's admiration for Melville was already such that he permitted the young film-maker to shoot the film in the house where he had both written and set the original story. Here was an obvious kindred spirit. *Le Silence de la mer* was an underground novel, which Vercors had had to publish himself without any support from the established publishing industry. Now Melville was making what was effectively an underground film. Because he was refused membership of the film union, on the grounds of lack of experience, he set up his own production company. Denied any allocation of scarce materials through the CNC, he bought old film stock on the black market (although he told the *New York Times* that he got it from an 'American cousin'). His 'budget' was what he was able to scrounge from friends and relatives. His 'crew' comprised an assistant director, electrician and a cinematographer who had never shot a feature before. And his 'stars' were a Swiss actor, Howard Vernon, who since the end of the war had played small character roles – often as a German officer – in French films, a painter, Jean-Marie Robain, who had never appeared in a film before, and a nineteen-year-old drama student, Nicole Stéphane, who had none of the conventional box-office value of a star even if she did possess the possibly compensating attraction of being the daughter of a Rothschild.

Necessity dictated shooting on location rather than in the studio, and the use of unknown actors rather than box-office stars, but the very limitations contributed an authenticity. Melville, who took pride in the maverick nature of the production, probably wouldn't have wanted it any other way. 'It was the first time anyone had tried to oppose the unionised structure of the French industry,' he commented twenty years later,[5] recalling that the CNC had greeted the completion of the production with a fifty-thousand-franc fine.

When the private showing before the chosen jury of Resistance members eventually took place in October 1948, Melville had done everything he could to turn the odds in his favour, making the film with respectful fidelity but also considerable flair, and arousing a blaze of publicity in the process. Even his public commitment to burn the film in response to a negative verdict seems not so much foolhardy as the kind of gambler's gesture that, whatever the verdict, could only help to launch his career in a gambler's profession. Making movies, after all, was as much about taking chances as anything else.

In the event, the film received a positive response from all but one of the twenty-four members of the jury. It went on to receive its public premiere on 22 April 1949, Melville securing a distribution contract from independent producer Pierre Braunberger, who had supported many of the avant-garde film-makers of the 1920s.

The camera closes on a distant temple, set against a background of scudding clouds, as the letters of the name, M-E-L-V-I-L-L-E, appear on the screen one by one to the toll of a bell. Then the initial M, fashioned out of celluloid, is swiftly animated on the screen from left to right, as though Melville himself is signing his signature with a hidden hand. If the effect is to suggest Melville's aspiration for authorship in the cinema, the film nonetheless goes to lengths to emphasise the importance of the original book on which the film is based.

Le Silence de la mer (1949)

In a prologue we see a member of the Resistance covertly pass on a suitcase to a comrade. The man then opens the case to find beneath some folded clothes the famous underground newspapers *Libération* and *Combat*, and then, buried even deeper beneath these newspapers – as if to suggest the ultimate symbol of wartime resistance – a copy of Vercors's *Le Silence de la mer*. Taking the book out of the case, the man turns the first page. The image then dissolves to the credits for the film, which are displayed on the turning pages of a book. The effect is to suggest the extreme fidelity of the film to the book, even although this prologue itself is a departure, anticipating the Resistance thrillers that Melville would make later in his career.

The book provides the word-for-word voiceover narrative to which Melville's images provide a visual correspondence. So exact is this correspondence that Melville's occasional departures from Vercors's text have all the greater weight. In one of his nightly visits to the library, the German officer von Ebrennac speaks of the great literary tradition of France and the equally impressive musical tradition of Germany. Although the two countries have been at war with each other, in this shared poetic spirit there should be the basis for a perfect marriage. Citing the tale of *Beauty and the Beast*, von Ebrennac goes on to reflect upon how winning over France's proud heart will be all the more meaningful for her initial resistance. But Melville divides the scene after the first mention of marriage, so that this discourse on how Germany must win France's heart takes place over two evenings rather than one. In between, he interpolates his own imagined outdoor encounter between the old man's niece and von Ebrennac, as they chance upon each other in the snow. As they walk towards each other, he intercuts between the two figures, on the same path but heading in opposite directions, with the camera tracking back in the same identical manner. The likeness of these twinned tracking shots brings out the extent of the affinity between the two, one that the war has blighted by setting them on opposed paths. In other circumstances, the sensitive young woman might have fallen in love with the officer; here, she must shun him, which she does by walking past without even acknowledging his presence. Melville then cuts to a winter sun hanging low in the sky behind leafless trees – warmth frozen in winter. It is a beautifully rendered sequence although it serves to bring out and amplify an idea that is already there in Vercors's original story.

Melville's feel for cinema goes astray only when he seeks to go beyond what is already there. The other most significant departure from Vercors's text involves a trip that von Ebrennac makes to Paris, during which he discovers that his comrades do not entertain the equal partnership between France and Germany that he has dreamt of. Instead, they envisage France's

Le Silence de la mer (1949)

permanent subjugation and spiritual enfeeblement, with all the great writers of her past, as well as her present, being banned from publication.

In a chilling scene, which has no counterpart in the novel, Melville adds a second reason for von Ebrennac's disillusion-ment during his stay in Paris. He visits an old comrade who is an SS officer working at the Kommandantur in the place de l'Opéra. The scene opens with the pair laughing light-heartedly. But then, noticing a report on his friend's desk, von Ebrennac asks what is the significance of Treblinka. 'Let's not talk about that,' comes the reply, 'it's not for the faint-hearted.' But von Ebrennac is nonetheless permitted to open the report. As he reads out aloud its details of the improvements being made for the more efficient

Le Silence de la mer (1949)

conduct of mass executions in the death camp's gas chambers, the camera slowly tracks in on his comrade's desk, until it holds a photograph of Hitler in extreme close-up. As von Ebrennac finishes with the date of the report, 'Treblinka, 21 March, 1941', his comrade observes ironically: 'The start of spring.'

The sequence is staged with considerable style, but Melville's wish for a bold graphic statement about the evil of the Nazi regime warps the content, introducing a false note into a story that is otherwise notable for its realism. It is difficult to accept that the highly cultivated and humane von Ebrennac would have a friend belonging in the ranks of the fanatical and feared SS, while the distortion of history is even more glaring: the imagined meeting of the two friends takes place in the early summer of 1941, but the extermination camp of Treblinka did not open until a year later, in 1942.

The way in which Melville inserts the episode into the existing framework of the novel's narrative does yet further damage. The consistent focus of the Vercors story is upon the relationship between the victorious occupier, Germany, and a proud but vanquished France. During the Paris trip, von Ebrennac learns from his comrades that Germany intends France's complete humiliation. That is his chief discovery. The episode remains in the film, but now it takes place at a party of German officers that follows von Ebrennac's discovery about Treblinka and the murderous nature of the Nazi regime. The result is that he seems to have a desperately skewed sense of importance, when, at the party, he reacts with despair at their support for the Nazi suppression of French culture. Compared to what he has just learned about the regime's acts of genocide, the censorship of France's great writers now seems trivial.

Melville's sacrifice of psychological realism here offers an early index of a director who prized the emotional over the intellectual, the dramatic over the documentary. The cinema he would go on to develop was an increasingly aestheticised and referential one of myth and fable, favouring intensity of mood over objective reality. This passionate cinephile, who had changed his own name out of admiration for an American writer, would build much of his later identity in his assimilation of an adored Hollywood cinema into a French sensibility.

Le Silence de la mer was made at the very start of Melville's career, before this identity took hold. But even though it is more a case of sensitive interpretation than independent authorship, it represents the opening of an important new pathway leading to the cinema of the auteurs. For Melville's near-total involvement in, and control of, all stages of the production process, and his ability to fashion a polished, professional production without such conventional elements as studio or star, proved the extent to which film-making could lie within the scope of an individual rather than an industry.

Jean Cocteau attended the first night. With his belief in the individuals who defy the system, he would have admired Melville's achievement, but would also have been struck by the inspiration the film drew from the fairy tale that he himself had filmed with great success only shortly before. As the German officer von Ebrennac expresses the view that it is France's destiny to bring out Germany's better side, *Beauty and the Beast* provides him with the perfect parable:

Poor Beauty! The Beast holds her at his pleasure, captive and powerless – at every hour of the day he forces his oppressive and relentless presence on her . . . Beauty is all pride and dignity – she has hardened her heart . . . But the Beast is something better than he seems. Oh, he's not very polished, he's clumsy and brutal, he seems very uncouth beside his exquisite Beauty! But he has a heart. Yes, he has a heart which hopes to raise itself up . . . If Beauty only *would*!

This is the film's only explicit allusion to the fairy tale, but *Le Silence de la mer* is a retelling of the same story in all but name. Just as the Beast asks Beauty every night to marry him, so the nightly discourses of von Ebrennac – in which, at the Beast's hour of nine o'clock, he comes down to the library of his silent, uncompromising hosts to speak of his love of France – are the same act of courtship. Each evening the uncle and niece refuse to respond to his overtures, but always he takes his leave with the same respectful 'I wish you a good night.' There is also, in essence, the same resolution. Having finally recognised the evil intentions of Nazi Germany, von Ebrennac commits himself to the near-certain death of a posting to the Eastern Front. As he takes his leave, at last the niece utters 'Adieu!' As in the original tale, it is death that finally brings love to fruition.

An irresistible speculation is whether Vercors's original 1942 story might have inspired Cocteau to make his own version of *Beauty and the Beast*. Published accounts suggest that it was his protégé Jean Marais who at the end of the war asked him to make a film of the Leprince de Beaumont story,[6] but the then celebrity of Vercors's Occupation reworking might well have put the idea in the air.

At the end of *Beauty and the Beast*, the Beast dies, to be resurrected as the handsome Prince, who is then able to marry Beauty. It offered an appealing symbol of the creative metamorphosis by which the same story can take different forms – something Cocteau availed himself of in *Beauty and the Beast*, as well as *L'Eternel Retour* and *Orphée* – but it also prefigured an alliance. In Melville, Cocteau had found a young suitor who had

defied the restrictive conventions of the film industry, much as
Cocteau himself had done with *Le Sang d'un poète* twenty years
previously.

It is easy to appreciate why Cocteau might have wished
to work with him. Melville had captured the original text of
Vercors with considerable fidelity, yet at the same time demonstrated a sense of cinema that gave the story independent life
in the film medium. As enticing was an approach to film production that seemed to sidestep the creative compromises that
most producers usually required with their reliance on expensive studios and stars. To this extent, their agreement to make
Les Enfants terribles together seems natural, even if it is difficult
to be entirely sure how the collaboration began. According to
Melville, Cocteau 'telephoned me the day after he saw *Le Silence
de la mer* to tell me he wanted me to film *Les Enfants terribles*'.
According to Cocteau, he had always turned down requests to
film the novel, but he accepted Melville's 'because I thought his
maverick style would give the production some of the feel of a
16mm movie'.[7]

In spite of Melville's later insistence that the project was not
undertaken at his initiative, he had strong personal reasons
to become involved. He had attended the Lycée Condorcet
in Paris, where Cocteau's story begins. 'Like all pupils of the
Lycée Condorcet, I took part in those snowball fights in the Cité
Monthiers, and we had all read *Les Enfants terribles*. We considered it our book.'[8] So whichever of them actually suggested
the idea, an adaptation of *Les Enfants terribles* was the obvious
project to bring them together.

The marriage that followed was a fruitful but difficult one.
Perhaps the hesitation both men expressed about the origin of the
film can be attributed to the uncomfortable coexistence between
two collaborators who had the same wish to assert total command over their material. Jean-Pierre Melville may have established his reputation in the cinema through the largely faithful
adaptation of a celebrated novel, but he was no more prepared

to be an acolyte than Cocteau was to compromise his artistic vision. Cocteau probably assumed that the young director's role would in practice be that of a technical assistant. There was an obvious precedent. When Cocteau had made *La Belle et la bête*, his assistant was the young film director René Clément, who had just directed his first feature, *La Bataille du rail*. Melville was far too much a maverick spirit to defer in this way, even if the irresistible creative force of Cocteau was nonetheless clear in the recollections of those who were involved. Claude Pinoteau, who was an assistant director on the production, commented: 'I think the situation is pretty clear. Melville was the technical director, if I can put it that way. He already possessed that flair which he would show later as regards angles and shots, but without a doubt the film was totally impregnated by the work and personality of Jean Cocteau.'[9] Pinoteau observed too the hold that Cocteau seemed to have over the actors. 'Very often when Jean-Pierre said, "Cut", the actors would look first at Cocteau to see if the shot had his approval, which naturally irritated Jean-Pierre.'

Although the actors liked to have Cocteau on the set, Melville's obvious discomfort at his presence was such that Cocteau chose to absent himself for a while. Twenty years later, Melville acknowledged the diplomacy of the gesture, remembering Cocteau's comment, 'One must always know just how far one has the right to go too far.'[10] With the passage of time it was possible for Melville to admit how difficult he must have been. 'I was very stubborn, with no taste for compromise. I was producer, director and adapter of the film – even though I did put Cocteau's name on the credits as co-adapter – and I absolutely refused to be opposed, directed or controlled in any way.'[11]

At stake was the creative ego of a remarkable young producer/director whose new way of working, free of the usual studio controls, was precious enough for Cocteau to make the necessary concessions, even if later he couldn't resist the comment, 'The novel *Enfants terribles* passed through Melville without the slightest shadow, almost as if he were the author.'[12] His attitude to the collaboration was clear from the publicity notes he wrote when the film was screened in America. Here was an opportunity to resume, without compromise, the kind of deep personal creative engagement with the medium that he had not enjoyed since Charles and Marie-Laure de Noailles bankrolled *Le Sang d'un poète* twenty years previously.

> [Melville] represented for me an independent in a profession a thousand times too subservient to technique. He agreed to follow me, to truly remain faithful to the novel, and to see it through with me, hand-in-hand, every step of the way. Thanks to this truly cooperative attitude, I was able to have a hand in the filming, to select my actors and settings, and to avoid falling into the error that it is necessary to change everything in a book, and to render it unrecognisable in order to reach a wide audience.[13]

With hindsight the difficulty of the collaboration between the two men – and the wish of *both* of them to be authors – was symptomatic of the fault-line that was beginning to open up between two different kinds of cinema. In this battle, at least, Melville and Cocteau stood firmly on the same side. What was of the most lasting significance was not the specific content of *Le Silence de la mer* or *Les Enfants terribles*, but the way in which Cocteau and Melville together were opening up the possibility of a cinema that could express itself with a greater freedom than the dominant model permitted.

It was impossible for any serious artist to disregard the practical shortcomings of the medium. 'The cinema has happened back to front,' Cocteau observed. 'It began with huge audiences, when all other artistic schools have begun with small ones. It was just a very few copies of Rimbaud's books that were banned and burned, but today there are endless reprints of his work.'[14] What was needed for the cinema was the equivalent of a small press. That was the virtue of Melville's do-it-yourself method of making films.

But the battle for a cinema of personal expression needed to be fought not only in the way films were made, but in how they were seen. The fault-line opening up was as much one of reception as production. Cocteau took encouragement from the immediate post-war growth of the ciné-clubs, whose members might return to see a film several times. It was a significant development, he thought, because previously the cinema had been regarded as 'little more than a watering hole where you stop off to refresh yourself with a pint of beer'.[15] Now there was scope for proper appreciation.

The year 1949 was a pivotal moment. There was the opening of *Le Silence de la mer*, there was the collaboration between Cocteau and Melville on *Les Enfants terribles*, but equally significant was the 'Festival du Film Maudit', over which Cocteau presided at Biarritz in the summer. The idea behind the festival was, in Cocteau's words, 'to try to give new life to masterpieces that an inhospitable reception had denied an audience when they first appeared'.[16] Included in the programme was an eclectic mix of films old and new such as Jean Vigo's *L'Atalante*, Nicholas Ray's *They Live By Night* and Visconti's *Ossessione*. To the extent that the most obvious common characteristic of the films was the lack of regard that they had received from commercial distributors, the selection may have been a touch arbitrary, but it served to bear witness to the serious point of the festival: that a film had a poetic value regardless of the success of its commercial exploitation. It was about respect in the cinema for the poetic voice that might not be able to win the mass audience to which the film industry was wedded.

In the preface to the festival programme, Cocteau explained that the festival's name had been inspired by the term *poètes maudits*, which Mallarmé had used in the late nineteenth century to designate poets such as Baudelaire, Verlaine or Rimbaud, whose verses flouted the expectations and tastes of conventional society. Neglected during their own lifetimes, they would be celebrated by a later age for the modernity of their poetic inspiration.

Implicit in the chosen title of the festival was an attack on the limiting horizons of the established industry:

The time has come to honour the masterpieces of film art which have been buried alive and to sound the alarm. Cinema must free itself from slavery just like the many courageous people who are currently striving to achieve their freedom. Art which is inaccessible to young people will never be art.

Both *Le Silence de la mer* and *Les Enfants terribles* could easily have found a place in the programme of a festival that was so intent on celebrating work that defied the expectations of mainstream exploitation. The iconic nature of the book on which it was based meant that *Le Silence de la mer* enjoyed a good audience in France, but there was little interest beyond. 'A good majority of the scenes take place in a living-room with little or no action on the part of the characters,' observed the Paris correspondent of *Variety*. 'The pic will definitely run into trouble in the States since the dialogue, the most important thing in the picture, will be lost to American audiences.'[17] Blind to the extreme sensitivity with which Melville's camera was able to register the emotional significance of a fleeting regard or even a trembling hand, the review dismissed the film as 'a still photograph rather than a moving picture'. Although it was another example of 'living-room cinema', *Les Enfants terribles* won the US release denied to *Le Silence de la mer* on the strength of Cocteau's reputation as France's foremost artist and poet. But it was clear from the largely uncomprehending reactions that the film was no less accursed than *Le Silence de la mer*. As *Newsweek* observed, the general response of the US daily press to the film could be 'characterised by fits of repugnance, on the one hand, and ardent advance-guard salutes on the other'.[18] The US title, *The Strange Ones*, seemed particularly appropriate.

But the accursed films that played in Biarritz would soon become more fashionable than anyone could possibly have anticipated. Ten years later they would resurface in the films of the French New Wave, winning over critical opinion with such success that in truth the term 'accursed' served better to characterise the contempt with which many of the most respected figures of the established French film industry suddenly came to be regarded.

A striking feature of this eventual success was an often con-suming cinephilia that Melville more than anyone pioneered, although it required a break from the elitist Cocteau for him to forge his own Hollywood-allusive style. Nicole Stéphane recalled an incident during *Les Enfants terribles* that suggests the path that Melville wanted to follow. 'I was once called into his office at 2 a.m. and he said, "You must play this scene like Bette Davis – more exaggerated." I looked at him in horror. He wanted me to . . . "camp" it up. I said, "No. I won't do that – never."'[19]

The collaboration with Cocteau had been a mixed blessing. It won him public attention, but took him down a marginal path that, as Nicole Stéphane's reminiscence suggests, was at odds with the popular Hollywood cinema that most stirred him. Melville's next film was an attempt to adjust the balance. Starring singer Juliette Greco, *Quand tu liras cette lettre* (1953) was a melodrama about a young woman who, having given up her vocation to become a nun, protects her sister against the preda-tory advances of a local gigolo. Although Melville undertook the assignment to prove that he was a professional capable of direct-ing a commercial film, he used the generous remuneration he received to build a small studio that was a mark of his continuing non-conformist spirit. Situated on the rue Jenner in south-east Paris, it consisted of two small sound stages, two cutting-rooms, a dressing-room and a projection theatre. Melville lived with his wife in a flat above. Scraping together the production finance bit by bit, as he had done before with *Le Silence de la mer*, here, over the next two years, he made the film that, perhaps more than any other, ought to be considered the crucible of the New Wave.

Made outside the system, it was another 'accursed' film, yet at the same time offered a wholesale, unrepentant plundering of Hollywood lore. With his trenchcoat and hat, the eponymous hero of *Bob le flambeur* (1956) dresses like an American gangster and drives a Plymouth convertible. His life is as much dedicated to style as it is to gambling. He serves as an alter ego for Melville himself, who made a personal trademark out of his Stetson and liking for American cars, but also surfaces powerfully in Godard's *A bout de souffle*. 'Après tout, je suis con,' muses Michel Poiccard in the very opening line of the film. Striking up a pose after the fashion of Humphrey Bogart, the image-conscious Michel Poiccard recalls Bob le flambeur emerging on to the street after a night's gambling. Bob looks at himself closely in a shop-window mirror. 'A real hood's face,' he declares, as he straightens his tie.

A bout de souffle is as much a homage to Melville as it is explicitly dedicated to Monogram pictures. When Melville makes a cameo appearance as the famous visiting novelist Parvulesco, surrounded by admiring reporters who question him on his philosophy, he is re-enacting his real-life role as mentor to the New Wave – outside the group, but inspiring it decisively.

'What's your greatest ambition in life?' asks Patricia. 'To become immortal and then die,' Parvulesco replies. The exchange captures Melville's regard for image well. But if he introduced the constantly alluding, film-conscious style, he was equally responsible for its fusion with a contemporary reality. In *Bob le flambeur*, he may have filmed the lights of Pigalle as though he wished he were in Times Square, but he invested Paris at the same time with its own living mythology. Melville's narrator's voice introduces the opening of the film. After a slow, lingering pan over the Paris skyline, he announces, to the image of the Sacré Coeur basilica,

Bob le flambeur (1956)

'Montmartre is both heaven and . . .' He then breaks off for a long pause that accompanies a sequence of an elevator making the steep descent downhill, before resuming his narration with the image of the Métro station at Pigalle: '. . . and Hell.'

Writing his own original script, filming with a small crew using hidden cameras in the streets, casting unknowns rather than stars, Melville carried forward the aesthetic of necessity that he had already established in *Le Silence de la mer*, anticipating most of the practices that would become identified with the New Wave.

The paradox was that in attempting to emulate a Hollywood style, he displayed an aestheticism that could hardly have been more French. Narrative was secondary to mood and ambience, so that the typical Melville character regarded even the shortest distance between two points as an opportunity for display. In *Le Doulos*, Jean-Paul Belmondo's last act after being shot in the back is to adjust his hat in an extravagant mirror, while in *Le Cercle rouge* Yves Montand puts on a dinner jacket and bow-tie to go out on a heist. Melville may have declared his allegiance to the Golden Age of Hollywood, but he ultimately fashioned a cinema of *haute couture* that owed as much to the Faubourg Saint-Honoré as it did to *Scarface* or *The Public Enemy*, prefiguring not only the New Wave but the *Cinéma du look* of twenty years later.

Le Doulos (1962)

15

A Changing Culture

The backlash against France's *tradition de la qualité* cinema occurred in the United States long before François Truffaut 'signed the death warrant' with 'A Certain Tendency of the French Cinema' in *Cahiers du cinéma* in 1954.[1] In its very artistry and sophistication, the kind of cinema that had seemed vital before the war became easy to ignore afterwards, not because its films were in any way less accomplished, but because they were *too* accomplished. In their polished perfection, these products of France's film establishment offered nothing exciting, nothing new, but served chiefly to block the natural process of renewal and regeneration that the war had deferred.

With hindsight, the lack of interest in the French cinema that the US critics showed after the war seems like a barometer, predicting the reaction that would soon follow in France itself. Perhaps necessarily, that reaction came from outside the film industry. There were the films that Tati, Melville or Cocteau made so against the grain of the established conventions, 'accursed films', but equally important was the culture of appreciation upon which Cocteau had remarked. The ciné-club movement of Louis Delluc and Ricciotto Canudo had helped to give rise to the avant-garde cinema during the 1920s; as Pierre Billard observes, this movement – as well as the avant-garde cinema to which it gave rise – dissipated with the advent of sound, but it would resurface after the Liberation with all the greater force.[2]

The new film magazines that proliferated along with the ciné-clubs provide another index of the intensity of interest that the cinema provoked in the immediate post-war years.[3] As René Prédal observes, the amateur footing of many of these periodicals meant that they tended to be short-lived, but significantly, the handful of magazines that did last long enough to achieve an influence were founded in the same cinephile spirit.[4]

Perhaps the most famous of them all, *Cahiers du cinéma*, declared its intent to take on the role of Jean-Georges Auriol's *La Revue du cinéma* (1929–31, 1946–9), which was revived in 1946 only to fold shortly before its founder's death in a car accident in 1950. In *Cahiers'* opening issue, an editorial praised Auriol for a magazine that had expressed itself in 'forthright terms whose sole concern was the cinema, its art and its technique'.[5] *Cahiers* would seek to follow this example.

The principal commercial magazine of the period, *L'Ecran français*, for which a number of *Cahiers* contributors, including André Bazin, had previously written, stood out for its intelligent, often passionate engagement with the cinema, but – as René Prédal points out – had built its circulation of over a hundred thousand out of a broad constituency, which included 'a few cinephiles who would today be reading either *Cahiers du cinéma* or *Positif*, the industry itself – above all exhibitors who would today subscribe to *Film français* – and a mass readership who could read in its pages features on the stars'.[6] It carried an in-built partiality towards the French film industry and felt a duty to defend it.

With the magazine under the control of the Communist Party, its partisan stance became only more extreme with the advent of the Cold War, making it increasingly difficult for film-writers who did not share its left-wing views to contribute. The rift came out into the open when André Bazin published a piece in the August 1950 issue of the magazine *Esprit* entitled 'The Soviet Cinema and the Myth of Stalin'. The Communist Georges Sadoul, who was a regular contributor to *L'Ecran français*, answered back, accusing Bazin of having sold out to the 'bourgeois Hollywood reactionaries'.[7]

Ceasing to write for *L'Ecran français*, Bazin was forced to abandon a platform that he had hoped – with the idealism that characterised so much of his writing – could help win broad support for a popular avant-garde of the cinema. It had been in *L'Ecran français*, at the end of 1948, that Bazin had written what was in reality, as Jean-Pierre Jeancolas observes, 'the manifesto for a new movement which would lead a little more than two years later to the birth of *Cahiers du cinéma*'.[8] Called 'In Defence of the Avant-Garde', the purpose of Bazin's piece was to promote the cause of yet another new ciné-club, Objectif 49:

Some of us have recently sought to bring about a kind of avant-garde in the contemporary cinema and have founded the ciné-club Objectif 49 with this idea in mind.

It's the cinema's serious weakness, but also its unique opportunity, that it is committed to the entertainment of a very large public. While all the traditional arts have since the Renaissance developed a refinement that appeals to a small privileged élite, the cinema in its very essence belongs to the masses the world over. Any aesthetic experimentation based on a narrowing of its audience is therefore doomed from the outset.

. . . If we apply the label 'avant-garde' no longer to a small group of people with an exclusive set of aesthetic values, but to whatever in the cinema expands the possibilities of the medium, then the first avant-garde film-maker was Méliès. So too Griffith, Feuillade, Abel Gance, Stroheim, although they never sought to make other than commercial films.

. . . It's *this* kind of avant-garde which is still achievable, and which we should try to find and support.[9]

The mission of Objectif 49 was to single out, without political or nationalistic bias, those films that represented a genuine aesthetic advance in an inherently popular medium. But in practice, the tendency was to privilege a small élite group of directors in a Hollywood whose hegemony *L'Ecran français* tended routinely to attack. The future of the cinema lay with such men as Orson Welles, Preston Sturges, Alfred Hitchcock and William Wyler, who were pushing back the frontiers of the medium, making Hollywood the key source of inspiration for those who cared about the future of the cinema.

It was this concept of a popular avant-garde that accounted for a novel alliance between Hollywood's previously much derided mass entertainment industry and the cinema of personal expression. 'Objectif 49 was much more than a ciné-club,' observed one of its founders, the film-maker and critic Roger Leenhardt. 'We wanted to turn it into a campaign for a "new" cinema and to rehabilitate the "accursed films".'[10]

In the spring of 1949, the new ciné-club organised its first showings, which included films by Orson Welles and Roberto Rossellini, a series of American film noirs and some of the early shorts of Alain Resnais. It then went on in the summer to organise, with Jean Cocteau, the Festival du Film Maudit at Biarritz.[11] After a second Biarritz festival in 1950, the ciné-club folded. Its crusade for a popular avant-garde continued in *Cahiers du cinéma*, but the fact that *Cahiers* enjoyed a circulation of only four thousand rather than the hundred thousand plus of *L'Ecran français*, in which Bazin had first set out his manifesto, meant that its arguments were addressed from the outset not to the mainstream audience at which the Hollywood films championed by Bazin aimed, but to a small élite, making this notion of a popular avant-garde seem all the more incongruous. To this extent, *Cahiers du cinéma* actually marked the failure of Bazin's initial hopes. But the fact that it did not have to address any obvious interest group other than its own narrow constituency of cinephiles gave it an enviable freedom. Its élitism and independence may have meant a small circulation, but they provided the ideal nursery for a new generation of revolutionaries.

Evident from its earliest issues was a natural regard for a personal cinema, but also a Hollywood cinema. So far from considering the two to be incompatible, as conventional opinion had long held, it strongly promoted the view that the latter had immeasurably opened up the possibilities for the former.

While the image of Gloria Swanson in *Sunset Boulevard* (1950) graced the opening issue of the magazine, the very first essay was dedicated to a film-maker who had come to the fore working within the Hollywood system. Jacques Doniol-Valcroze's article on the director Edward Dmytryk argued that he belonged to a new generation, able to benefit from a film language that Orson Welles had brought to a pinnacle of perfection with *Citizen Kane* (1941): 'The young man who chooses to express himself with neither pen nor paintbrush but with film and a camera no longer needs to make up a grammar of vocabulary.'[12] Notable was the total conviction with which Doniol-Valcroze went on to identify the films of Dmytryk with the individual Dmytryk. Pointing out that the director had Ukrainian parents, but was born in Canada and brought up in the United States, he observed: 'Dmytryk is the sum of his origins. From his Slav blood he has retained ardour, torment and passion; from his Anglo-Saxon blood, the taste for technique, a sense of rhythm and a preference for the morality tale.'

An Anglo-Saxon reading these words nearly sixty years later is likely to find them fanciful, projecting on to Dmytryk the excesses of an engagement that was more romantic than analytical, but the cult of the personal ruled out a more objective appraisal. The notion of the *caméra-stylo* was a central tenet of faith for the magazine, which it would pursue with religious intensity. Although the term had famously been coined by another of *Cahiers*' contributors, Alexandre Astruc, in a piece he wrote for *L'Ecran français* three years previously,[13] Bazin himself had expressed the idea in essentially the same terms as long ago as 1946. In an article for *L'Ecran français* on 'The New American Cinema', he wrote:

Just as a writer's style implies a previous possession of the necessary resources of language, or a painter's style the techniques of painting, so the style of a great director is formed out of a similar control over the means of cinematic expression, rendered as easy to use as a pen through the formidable organisation of the Hollywood studios.[14]

The idea of the *caméra-stylo* was inherent in the importance that the French cinema has long accorded to the creative role of the director. But what made *Cahiers* so revolutionary was to suggest that it was Hollywood – more usually characterised as the film factory that crushed individual expression – which had at last perfected the *caméra-stylo* ideal.

From the outset, it was clear that *Citizen Kane* marked a kind of 'cinema year zero': there was before *Kane*; and after *Kane*. Adopting this stance, the agenda of the first issue seemed to be to establish the Hollywood cinema of the 1940s as the driving creative force in the cinema's renewal. In the second of the two principal essays, André Bazin argued that Hollywood cinema had developed depth of focus into 'a key tool of direction; a dialectical advance in the history of film language'.[15] While deep focus had been a feature of the early French pioneers, Lumière, Zecca and Feuillade, it was essentially no more than a recording tool, which enabled maximum readability of the image at a time when the cinema had yet to develop a language that could express narrative through montage. Since all the events in the film drama unfolded as on a stage, it was important to be able to see everything that happened on that stage. During the 1930s Jean Renoir had made some notable attempts to harness the technique in France, but it required the technical resources of Hollywood – and specifically, the experimentation of one exceptional cinematographer, Gregg Toland, in films such as Welles's *Citizen Kane* and Wyler's *The Little Foxes* (1941) and *The Best Years of Our Lives* (1946) – to demonstrate its full potential as a sophisticated tool with which to impart meaning. This Hollywood advance had made it possible for the contemporary film-maker to be as complete an artist as the most ambitious painter, writer or musician.

A kind of joyous fervour at this discovery inspires the first issues of *Cahiers du cinéma*, which perhaps helps to explain why what was essentially a theory of film language would inspire so much dogma about artistic inspiration: once the existence of this wonderful new language had been established, it became only natural to single out those individuals who made full use of it. The magazine's quest became to celebrate the total film-maker, who used film language in such a way that it freed the cinema from the literary sources on which it had traditionally been dependent.

It's perhaps an irony, when one considers that Bazin's supposed defence of the 'bourgeois Hollywood reactionaries' contributed to his departure from the Communist *L'Ecran français*, but there was a notably Marxist cast to his writing. He took a historical materialist approach that presented the cinema as an art-form undergoing a journey through different stages of development to the perfect mode of expression. But while the Marxists had to concede that the perfect society was still some way off, Bazin wrote as though the perfect cinema was only just around the corner, and maybe had even already arrived.

In the third issue, André Bazin wrote a long essay on Robert Bresson's third film, *Journal d'un curé de campagne*. Adapted from a novel by Georges Bernanos, the film told the story of a young priest who is dying from a fatal illness. Taking up residence in an unwelcoming parish, he persists in his faith, in spite not only of the injustices that are heaped upon him, but also his own uncertainty and loneliness.

Bazin argued that the film opened a new stage in film adaptation. Until then, the cinema had attempted a substitution of the novel, as though translating it into another language. But Bresson's film built, on the foundation of the novel, an entirely new work: 'not a film comparable to the novel, or "worthy" of it, but a new aesthetic entity'.

In Bresson, a new champion of the cinema of personal expression had been found, to stand beside Jean Cocteau. Bresson had been a painter, whose interest in the cinema had been encouraged by René Clair. After a long struggle to interest producers in the project, he made his first film, *Les Anges du péché*, in 1943 in collaboration with the writer Jean Giraudoux. Set in a Dominican convent, which took in women criminals as novices upon their release from prison, it told the story of a young sister who strives with formidable dedication to save the soul of an unrepentant novice. Already evident was a spare style that focused on the characters caught in the spiritual struggle, avoiding any extraneous decoration or dramatic emphasis. *Les Dames du Bois de Boulogne* followed two years later. Based on an episode in the Diderot novel *Jacques le fataliste*, with dialogue by Jean Cocteau, it told the story of a rich society woman who plots a revenge against her lover, who has grown tired of her. It too was remarkable for an economy of expression that subjugated the conventional show of the cinema to a rigorous exposition of the intention and situation of the principal character.

Bresson's uncompromising goal was to bare the inner life of his protagonists, eliminating all those elements that might distract from this purpose. The logic of this kind of film-making led him to discard all the staple ingredients of the conventional cinema – glamour, suspense, emotionalism, detailed narrative, star appeal. *Journal d'un curé de campagne* marked an important turning point. His previous two films had used well-known actors, but the nature of their profession, always involving stepping into other roles, and their public status as film stars blurred the truth of the specific characters that Bresson wished them to articulate. To play the priest, then, Bresson chose an untrained actor, Claude Laydu, who was a practising Catholic. For a year before filming began, Bresson met him every Sunday to impress upon him his conception of the character.

The film writer Jean Douchet, who witnessed the filming, was struck by the total control that Bresson exerted. 'He demands such-and-such an intonation; he listens; he modifies. He works on the actor as the sculptor models his clay.'[16] The method seemed calculated to discourage the independent conception of the role that an actor would normally bring. The requirement was less to act than to surrender oneself completely to Bresson's vision.

Roland Monod, who played the pastor in Bresson's next film, *Un condamné à mort s'est échappé* (1956), gave an insight into

278

the approach. A journalist who had for a time studied theology, he was chosen not for any acting experience but for a background that would help Bresson to narrow the gap between his model and his conception of the character. 'Forget about tone and meaning,' Bresson advised Monod. 'The film actor should content himself with *saying* his lines. He should not allow himself to show that he already understands them. Play nothing, explain nothing.'[17] Bresson would go through the lines over and over again to explain the tone of austere simplicity that he wanted. Then, when shooting, he would repeat the take as often as necessary until he achieved the exact effect he had been searching for. Even then, Monod recalled that, dissatisfied with the sound in a particular sequence, Bresson brought his actors back to dub their lines in a sound studio: 'There, phrase by phrase, word by word almost, we spoke our lines after their author – ten, twenty, thirty times over, trying to match as exactly as possible the intonations, the rhythm, even the tone of his voice. There is no paradox in saying that in the end Bresson played every part.' Here was the embodiment of the *caméra-stylo* style for which the *Cahiers* writers had been calling. 'Robert Bresson works alone,' concluded Monod, 'and the team about him – technicians and actors – must accept this as an imperative need of his talent and character. They exist simply as instruments: only Bresson creates.'

Reading Bazin's *Cahiers* piece on Bresson, one has the impression that the appeal of the director for Bazin lay as much in the exclusivity of his vision as in the vision itself. The very assertion of a viewpoint became the presiding value. It was a blinkered concept that not only denied the collaborative nature of the cinema, but also disregarded the vital economic framework that made such activity possible. It is a valuable exercise to identify and appreciate the great artistic talents in the cinema, but in its endemic confusion of the industry with the individual, the championing of the auteur has been responsible over the last sixty years for burying as many reputations as it has unearthed. The damage started early. An inherent part of Bazin's idealisation of the pure auteur – who could create rather than simply translate – was to devalue the achievement of those who failed, in terms of the theory, to reach this higher state of being. In an essentially feudal system that placed the director at the pinnacle, such lowly vassals as screenwriters – more often than not intermediaries between the original source material and the director – were easy targets. The most prominent in the French film industry of Bazin's day were Jean Aurenche and Pierre Bost. Together they had written such then celebrated films as *La Symphonie pastorale*, *Le Diable au corps* and *Jeux interdits*. But Bazin's new hierarchy would dismiss them as of secondary importance, no matter what their actual achievement.

'After Robert Bresson,' he concluded in his article, 'Aurenche and Bost are no more than the Viollet-Le-Duc of film adaptation.' Viollet-Le-Duc was a nineteenth-century architect whose reconstructions of medieval cathedrals had won him a widespread reputation in France for second-rate, derivative art.

Three years later, in 'A Certain Tendency of the French Cinema',[18] Bazin's young protégé François Truffaut would turn the irreverent comment into an assault against the whole 'tradition de la qualité' of the French cinema; although its extreme polemical nature made the piece a key text in the emerging *politique des auteurs*, the core philosophical content had already been stated in Bazin's earlier article. The new style of criticism would in practice require film-makers – whether writers, directors or even actors – to be judged not on what they had actually done but by the degree to which they lived up to the preferred model of exclusive authorship. There was a touch of zealotry about this new approach.

The creed Bazin had developed was hugely seductive for a group of young acolytes who had no practical experience of the film industry, but were determined to become film-makers themselves. The vein of wishful thinking that led them to believe that they might be able to make films as freely as they expressed themselves in their writing served only to reinforce the philosophy. A year after Bazin's piece on Bresson – in a statement that was then as radical as today it seems banal – Eric Rohmer, writing under the name Maurice Scherer, declared, 'Hitchcock is not only a very clever technician . . . but also one of the most original and complex *auteurs* in the entire history of the cinema.'[19]

The emphasis Bazin placed on Hollywood's decisive role in the formulation of this higher language made the quest to find auteurs in Hollywood an obvious next step, although it required applying the French concept of a director-centric cinema to a system in which the producer still dominated. Bazin's much later criticism of Truffaut and Rohmer, in 1957[20] – that they had turned the *politique des auteurs* into 'a dogma that involves the infallibility of the *auteur*' – suggests that he realised that he had opened up a Pandora's box, but by then it was too late to close it.

Barely a year after its first appearance, *Cahiers* found itself facing a major new rival. Like *Cahiers*, *Positif* was conscious of defending a certain tradition. Just as *Cahiers* had dedicated itself to the memory of *La Revue du cinéma* of Jean-Georges Auriol, the opening editorial of *Positif*, in May 1952, expressed an intention to carry the torch of Gilles Jacob's recently defunct *Raccords*.

Its words are worth quoting, because they epitomise the strength of a notably resilient and self-supporting film culture. 'Why we fight,' announced a headline to the editorial, implying a commitment that would sustain the enterprise in spite of the lack of any obvious business sense. Disdaining to feign ignorance of all the casualties that had preceded it, the editorial went on:

You will say, yet another film magazine and yet another editorial, but so many of these magazines are bound to disappear . . . What does it matter that the market is free when you have run out of subscribers? Your magazine will be here today, gone tomorrow, so what's the point of buying it?[21]

The riposte the editorial then made to such thinking was as resolute in refusing the relevance of commercial concerns. The magazine would survive because it would make itself too important not to. 'Besides the interest of its contents, the magazine will provide a voice for the sizeable public we are. It may be a minority public, but the minority is always right.'

This frankness about the precarious nature of its own existence was typical of a magazine that showed a far greater sense of realism and open-mindedness than *Cahiers du cinéma*. But it shared the same passion for Hollywood, the same determination to chart the key features of cinema's principal wonderland.

With its eleventh issue, the magazine embarked upon a major survey of all aspects of Hollywood's system:

On the aesthetic level, its success has been and remains one of the most brilliant . . . But Hollywood is above all a provider of entertainment. Enormous resources and the talent of many individuals lie behind this remarkable success . . . But we should not belittle these films any more than we should make original artists, as we have too often tended to do in France, out of technicians who only bring their considerable skill to genres chosen for their profitability.[22]

The magazine's readiness to offer a corrective to the cult of the auteur was typical of its empirical approach. While *Cahiers* seemed more concerned to establish a set of principles for an ideal of what the cinema should be, *Positif* sought to engage with what it actually was.

Yet both magazines were celebrating Hollywood in a way that would have seemed inconceivable to the practical film-makers of an older generation – like Clair, Florey or Duvivier – who had had experience of working there. Now Hollywood was being embraced not as a system that was inherently hostile to the creative film-maker, but as a rich source of inspiration. The desire of the new generation was not to compete against Hollywood but to learn from it.

That it *was* a new generation requires some emphasis. In 1952, the year of *Positif*'s launch, Gilles Jacob – who had founded

Raccords as a student publication while studying for entry to the Ecole Normale Supérieure – was just twenty-one. Bernard Chardère, the founder of *Positif*, was twenty-two. Of the leading figures at *Cahiers du cinéma*, François Truffaut was twenty, Jean-Luc Godard and Claude Chabrol (who had been a friend of Gilles Jacob at the Lycée Louis-le-Grand) twenty-one, Eric Rohmer thirty-two, and André Bazin, who is often portrayed as the mentor and father figure of the *Cahiers* critics, not so much older at thirty-four.

The fault-line of the war served only to make the gulf between the generations seem even wider. The writers at *Cahiers* and *Positif*, who had for the most part come of age several years after the Liberation, were free of the prejudices and struggles of a notably turbulent past, but also had little acquaintance with the practical difficulties that faced the French film industry.

Established directors, who found it increasingly difficult to make the films they wished, felt little sympathy for a Hollywood cinema that they perceived as offering grotesquely unfair competition. The experience of one of the best-known directors of the period offers an example of the general sentiment. After the release in 1950 of his Simenon adaptation, *La Marie du port*, Marcel Carné spent many months seeking finance for another project with a contemporary setting. Eventually he gave up, instead accepting an offer to direct an expensive international production of the Alexandre Dumas novel *La Reine Margot*, although eventually this venture fell through too.

While a generation of young aspirants who had no practical experience of the film industry were indulging themselves with notions of the *caméra-stylo*, Carné was finding his own opportunities for personal expression harder to achieve. In an interview with *L'Ecran français* at the end of 1951, he vented some of his frustration. 'For some time now it is no longer the director who proposes subjects to the producers as was the custom before the war. Now it's the producers who suggest the subject to you.'[23]

Nor did he hesitate to single out Hollywood as the prime cause

for the industry's ills: 'The number one problem is unquestionably the invasion of our screens by the American film. It is this
that is responsible for the present situation.' The sheer financial
power of Hollywood, which enabled it to undercut the French
product, gave it complete dominance over the French market.
There might notionally be a quota, but the Hollywood companies were able to help exhibitors flout it, even offering to pay
their fines.

The *loi d'aide* had been introduced to support the French cinema, but Carné felt that it did not help people like himself. 'I'd
even go so far as to say it helps not to belong to the industry if
you want to be sure of work. This is not a paradox . . . During
these last two years, amateurism in the cinema has prevailed.'
They may not have been eligible for the fund, which was meant
for 35mm production, but among these amateurs Carné would
presumably have counted the first efforts of Eric Rohmer, who
had in the same period made two shorts on 16mm, *Journal
d'un scélérat* (1950) and *Présentation ou Charlotte et son steak*
(1951). Carné believed that the subsidy law, which was then
being reappraised by the government, needed to include a proviso about quality – if only appropriate criteria could be agreed
as to what 'quality' was.

Two years later, Truffaut launched his blistering attack on
the *tradition de la qualité* cinema to which Carné belonged,
but Carné's comments make clear the antagonism that already
existed between the established generation and a younger generation seeking to break in. The Hollywood cinema, which his
generation perceived as a threat, was the *de facto* nursery for the
next.

In the United States, the natural sympathisers of the *Cahiers* writers were to be found not in the Hollywood they so admired, but
among outsiders mostly hostile to Hollywood, whether rebels on
the margins of the Hollywood community or East Coast intellectuals. These were the first American voices to feature in *Cahiers*.

In August 1951, Herman G. Weinberg began to contribute to *Cahiers* a monthly 'Letter from New York', in which he sought to keep its readers informed of the latest film developments across the Atlantic. Weinberg, who had been a manager of the Filmarte before the war, was then working for the Film Library of the Museum of Modern Art. A dedicated cinephile, he had contributed articles to the film journal *Close-up* during the 1930s, and was also an experimental film-maker himself: at the time of his first contribution to *Cahiers* he had just finished a short film called *Knife Thrower*.

The following month, the magazine published a piece by a young Kenneth Anger called 'Modestie et l'art de film'.[24] Anger had come to France after his avant-garde film *Fireworks* (1947) had won the 'prix du film poétique' at the 1949 Festival du Film Maudit at Biarritz. Encouraged by Jean Cocteau, Henri Langlois and Pierre Braunberger, he made a short film in 1950 called *La Lune des lapins*, although it would not surface in a finished version until many years later.[25]

In his article Anger championed 16mm film-making, which freed the cinema from the paraphernalia of industrial film-making – the studio, the scenario department, the large film crew. 'The dream of a personal cinema, free and pure, is achievable on the basis of modest means.' The piece amounted to a practical manifesto that some of the *Cahiers* critics would pursue in their lives as film-makers, yet at the same time showed the total disregard for Hollywood that characterised most of the American independent film-makers of Anger's generation.

Anger's own journey to France was itself partly a result of the difficulty he had experienced in Hollywood of achieving individual expression. Brought up in Los Angeles, Anger had appeared as a child in several Hollywood films, including Max Reinhardt's production of *A Midsummer's Night Dream* (1935). Turning to film-making while still in his teens, he made the homoerotic *Fireworks*. But no framework of appreciation existed in Hollywood for an approach that dumbfounded even the more liberal and encouraging members of the film community there. In the late 1940s the film star Gene Kelly presided over a salon that sought to offer support to young film-makers. One night, Anger presented *Fireworks*. Kelly's then wife Betsy Blair recalled the 'amazing shock' the film caused:

We watched in stunned silence this fascinating surreal homoerotic essay on film. Occasionally there was an audible gasp, but at the end there was an awkward moment of silence. Gene leapt to the rescue, put his arm around Kenneth Anger's shoulders, and took him into the study, where he congratulated and thanked him . . . When they came out we had all collected ourselves enough to be polite. Kenneth Anger took his film, shook Gene's hand and left. As soon as the door closed behind him, there was shrieking and hysterical giggling at the memory of the cascades of candle sparks erupting from the sailor's crotch. It was actually rather callous and childish behaviour, but we were in a state of astonishment.[26]

The strength of the French magazines lay in their ability to be a crucible of ideas that would operate as a driving force for future cultural activity. Contributors to *Cahiers*, for example, were confident of being able to influence and win a place in the film-making community they criticised. But no such organic relationship existed in the United States.

Born in Lithuania, Jonas Mekas emigrated to America in 1949 after completing his studies at the University of Mainz. On his arrival in New York, the prevalent attitude towards the cinema seemed to him to be one of aesthetic disregard and complacency. When in 1955 he started a new magazine, *Film Culture*, its name seemed pointedly to single out what his adoptive country lacked. As he observed in his first editorial, 'Cinematic creation tends to be approached primarily as a production of commodities, and large sections of the public – to whom film-going is still merely a mode of diversion – remain unaware of the full significance of filmic art.'[27] In expressing its ideas for a new generation of American cinema, *Film Culture* often cited the example of the new generation of young film-makers in France, but there was a fundamental difference. The *Cahiers* critics may have reacted against the *tradition de la qualité* of an older generation, but when they began to make feature films in the late 1950s, they did so within an established cultural framework, however much they may have challenged and modified it. If total divorce from Hollywood seemed the only realistic operation for an equivalent generation of film-makers in America, it was because Hollywood seemed to operate completely outside culture, with no other purpose than to make money.

In France, however much the new generation of would-be film-makers may have railed against their elders, there was always significant interaction between them and the prevailing establishment. Not only did they have patron saints among the film-makers of the older generation – Cocteau, Renoir, Bresson – who provided active support and encouragement, but the evolving post-war infrastructure of cinema in France encouraged their aspirations.

In 1953, the *loi d'aide temporaire* was modified to include a *prime à la qualité*, which could be awarded to films 'of a kind that helps the cause of the French cinema or opens up new perspectives in film art'.[28] Coming into effect from May 1955, the measure announced a clear resolve in public policy for cultural criteria to take precedence over purely commercial considerations, predisposing the CNC to support the more innovative and artistically ambitious programmes of the new generation.

The measure effectively eased several of the *Cahiers* critics into their film-making careers. Chabrol's first feature *Le Beau Serge* (1958) cost $84,000, but he received a *prime à la qualité* from the CNC of $70,000. Before the film was even distributed in France, the grant and advance foreign sales paid off all the costs with a considerable surplus, so that Chabrol was able immediately to launch himself into his second feature, *Les Cousins* (1959).

Beneficiaries of the kind of mature cultural continuum and infrastructure that didn't yet exist in the United States, the new film-makers in France were also able to rely on support from a film industry that was sufficiently diverse, small-scale and arti-sanal in its nature to contain some responsive figures. François Truffaut was able to make his first feature, *Les Quatre cents coups* (1959), with the support of his father-in-law Ignace Morgenstern, who was head of Cocinor, one of the country's largest distribution companies.

It was Pierre Braunberger, meanwhile, who in the late 1940s supported Alain Resnais's short films on famous painters.[29] He also produced Jean Rouch's influential feature *Moi, un noir* (1958) and in 1956 co-produced with Claude Chabrol the first film of Jacques Rivette, *Le Coup du berger* (1956). The exist-ence of the *prime à la qualité* must have considerably encour-aged his involvement, but equally important was a general sense of a film culture that was a long-established tradition in France. After all, Braunberger had been supporting this kind of alter-native, avant-garde film-making since as long ago as *Un Chien andalou* in 1928.

Spared the political entanglements and restrictions of the war, a new generation was free to express itself in a way the previ-ous generation hadn't been, free to put self before duty, free to use the cinema not to address immediate crises but as a mirror of the peacetime aspirations of society at large. With the return of peace, the balance had firmly shifted everywhere from public necessity to private aspiration.

Against this background, the quest for a more personal cin-ema was not peculiar to France, but merely a natural aspiration of upcoming generations around the world who sought to enjoy the fruits of peace after the destruction of the war years.

The common desire for a more democratic, more personal form of cinema inspired young film enthusiasts in France, Britain and America, as well as many other countries – even if they often took very different routes to achieve this. A brief examination of their different histories allows us to appreciate the spontaneous, independent but often interlinked development of movements alternative to the mainstream that – whether known locally as 'new wave', 'free cinema' or 'independent cinema' – together formed the components of a generational challenge that not even Hollywood could ignore.

In Britain, this path can be traced through the founding of the film magazine *Sequence* and the subsequent launch of the Free Cinema Movement, which in turn helped to foster the 1960s British film renaissance. The single most influential figure was Lindsay Anderson. As the presiding spirit of *Sequence*, he wrote habitually trenchant and controversial pieces for the magazine that mapped out an agenda for a more personal cinema years before *Cahiers* had even been founded.

In the article 'A Possible Solution', which appeared in the spring 1948 issue of *Sequence*, he wrote:

It is today impossible to make films which will appeal to a moronic mass-audience (critics should be compelled to spend their Sunday evenings sitting in front of cinema queues, just looking at them), and at the same time be good. The best films of the commercial cinema, whose excellence is limited enough anyway, are not generally popular. If artists are to be free to make films about what they like, as they like, they must make them cheaply . . . What is required is a cinema in which people can make films with as much freedom as if they were writing poems, painting pictures or composing string quartets.

At about the same time, but independently, Anderson was expressing Alexandre Astruc's notion of the *caméra-stylo*, which was less a theory than an obvious aspiration.[30] The following year, through a personal connection, Anderson was given the opportunity to make his first film – a promotional documentary about a factory in Bradford that manufactured equipment for the mining industry.[31] The forty-minute film served as a practical apprenticeship, which helped him to establish a successful early career as a documentary film-maker.

In February 1956 he found a platform to promote the personal kind of film-making he had consistently campaigned for in *Sequence*, when the first of the Free Cinema programmes was launched at the National Film Theatre. The considerable press attention that the event won reflected the enormous attraction that the enfranchisement of the individual and the championing of the personal over the conformist held for the society of the period, but equally significant was the international scope of the project.

The Free Cinema highlighted the emergence of a non-conformist, independent cinema not only in Britain but in Europe and the United States too. Over the next three years, its programmes would include the work of film-makers who were French (Truffaut's *Les Mistons*, 1957, and Chabrol's *Le Beau Serge*, 1958), Swiss (Alain Tanner and Claude Goretta's *Nice Time*, 1957), Hungarian (Robert Vas's *Refuge England*, 1959), Italian (Lorenza Mazzetti's *Together*, 1956) and American (Lionel Rogosin's *On the Bowery*, 1957).

The most significant landmark for the independent cinema movement in the United States was John Cassavetes's *Shadows*. Made over a two-year period between 1957 and 1958, *Shadows* had its origins in a series of improvisation sessions that Cassavetes ran with an actors' workshop in New York. Financed through private donations, its successful completion was seized upon by the independent cinema movement as an example of a new spirit in the American cinema. According to Jonas Mekas, writing in *Film Culture*, this spirit was 'akin to that which guides the young British film-makers centered around Free Cinema' and was also being felt 'among French film newcomers such as Claude Chabrol, Alexandre Astruc, François Truffaut, Roger Vadim, Georges Franju':[32]

John Cassavetes' *Shadows* proves that a feature film can be made with only $15,000. And a film that doesn't betray life or cinema. What does it prove? It proves that we can make our films *now* and by *ourselves*. A $15,000 film is financially unbeatable. Television cannot kill it. The apathy of the audience cannot kill it. Theatrical distributors cannot kill it. It is free.[33]

Mekas made these comments on the basis of a one-off screening of the film at the Paris Theater in New York in late 1958, but Cassavetes himself drew a different conclusion from the same screening: 'The style employed in the film, of which we were all so proud, stood surrounded by the thinness of the characters, the lack of all-around design in the storytelling and the inconsistencies within the character development.'[34]

His decision to reshoot the film to fill the holes in narrative and character meant that what Mekas had hailed as a $15,000 film soon turned into a $40,000 one. But still no distributor in America was prepared to take *Shadows*. Its commercial life began in Europe after it received distribution deals from British Lion and the Scandinavian Europa Films at the 1960 Venice Film Festival. Opening in London at the Academy Cinema on 14 October 1960, its successful run there, Cassavetes felt, was in large measure due to the same forces that had supported the new wave of British film-makers:

Our timing couldn't have been better . . . There was a tremendous social and film revolution going on in England – the 'Angry Young Man' thing – and *Saturday Night and Sunday Morning* was just about to be made. The people who were part of that revolution saw that if *Shadows* were to be a success, they would have an opportunity to make the films they wanted. So all kinds of people got behind us and *Shadows* got reviews that were way beyond expectations.[35]

But in spite of its European success, it secured only a handful of bookings in the United States, receiving lacklustre reviews from critics who were, in the words of Ray Carney, 'almost completely under the sway of Hollywood production values, so that all most of them focused on were the film's low-budget origins and technical deficiencies'.[36]

The debacle of *Shadows* was as much a lesson for the French cinema as it was for America's independent film movement. It may have been an American subject, made in the English language, but lacking all the basic components of a Hollywood product – box-office stars, spectacle, a strong narrative – it was as foreign a film as any art-house import from France. Naturally, it experienced the same difficulty that French art-house films had in finding a market.[37]

Forced to re-examine the whole basis of its appeal in the United States, the French film industry discovered that there was one area in which it held a natural advantage over Hollywood. In *Shadows* there is a scene in which the innocent but bright young woman Lelia, who longs to mix in the society of writers and artists, disregards her brother's advice to take a taxi home and wanders out into the night-time streets of Manhattan. In Times Square, she stops outside a cinema and gazes in fascination at a near-lifesize cardboard cut-out of Brigitte Bardot in a swimsuit. The scene, which marks the pull of a previously unknown and forbidden adult world, serves as a useful metaphor for the role that the French cinema was beginning to play in the American consciousness during the 1950s.

As far as most serious film-goers were concerned, the contemporary French cinema had yet to produce anything that could compete with the huge impact of the neo-realist films from Italy – John Cassavetes, for example, would single out *La Terra trema* (Visconti, 1948), *I Vitelloni* (Fellini, 1953), *Umberto D* (De Sica, 1952) and *Bellissima* (Visconti, 1951) as important influences for him when he was making *Shadows*.[38]

The 1930s 'Golden Age' still dominated the American idea of the French cinema at its best. During the summer of 1957, when the Museum of Modern Art put on the major retrospective, 'Sixty Years of French Film', it was greeted in the *New York Times* as an exercise in nostalgia whose chief effect was to show up the poor quality of the current crop of French films. Bosley Crowther noted that many more French films were being exhibited in New York than before, but 'with three or four exceptions, they have been a pretty trite and trashy lot of films, far below the standards set by the French in their famous "Golden Age".'[39]

This perceived drop in standards was due less to any serious absence of intelligent French films than to the received wisdom that such films had little appeal in the post-war American market. Summarising the consensus of opinion in 1948, *Variety* reported that 'bookings of critic-approved films with an appeal confined to long-hair patrons can now garner no more than 200–300 play dates'.[40] The success of the Italian neo-realist films were considered to be an exception to the rule: *Rome, Open City*'s box-office take of $1,200,000 was described as 'something of a freak'. According to the 'experts', *Variety* went on, the only realistic hope distributors of foreign films had of gaining similar access to the circuits was to exploit 'the biological lure', although 'how naughty a film can become without going overboard is still an open question'.[41]

The possibility that there might be more latitude than previously thought was raised when United Artists dared to release Otto Preminger's film *The Moon is Blue* (1953), without a Production Code seal of approval. An otherwise innocuous romantic comedy, it was the first time a Hollywood film had openly used such words as 'virgin' or 'mistress'. Its box-office success helped to encourage the slow crumbling of the Code that took place over the next few years.

Perhaps never had conditions been more favourable for distributors to make a successful box-office commodity out of the reputation for social and sexual openness that the French cinema had always enjoyed. Most of the 'trite and trashy' films that Crowther complained about were examples of such calculated targeting. A brief look at three such films, which all happened to open in New York during July 1957, helps to illustrate the point.

Directed by Georges Lacombe in 1954, *La Lumière d'en face* (American title: *The Light Across the Street*) tells the story of ex-truck driver Georges Marceau, who is warned after a brain injury that he must abstain from having sexual relations with his wife. His young and pretty wife Olivia, played by Brigitte Bardot, fires his frustration, which turns into jealous rage when she begins to visit a handsome stranger who runs a nearby gas station. More accomplished than Crowther suggests, the film was really a 'film noir' in the tradition of *Le Dernier Tournant* (1939), Pierre Chenal's version of *The Postman Always Rings Twice*, but its sexual content was perceived as being the key selling point in the American market.

Directed by Charles Brabant, *Les Possédées* (1956) was adapted from a play by Ugo Betti, which had been performed on Broadway under the title *Island of Goats*. It told the story of the impact that the arrival of a handsome stranger has on the lives of three lonely women who live on a farm in a remote region of France. The power of sexual desire was certainly one of its themes, but it was really much more a thoughtful and intelligent exploration of female psychology. A variation on its original French title would have better reflected its content, but the perception of sex as the chief market appeal of French films dictated the choice of the US release title: *The Passionate Summer*.

The US release title for *Paris Canaille* (1956), directed by Pierre Gaspard-Huit, was *Maid in Paris*. If it suggests the extent to which the notion of the 'naughty French' had become a stereotype that distributors were quick to exploit, Bosley Crowther's review of the film for the *New York Times* was a further index of the strength of such preconceived notions.

'More than a gentle reminder of the American film *The Moon is Blue* is got from the French film *Maid in Paris*, which came to the Baronet yesterday. Only this one, being French and frisky, makes *The Moon is Blue* look like an Elsie story. Purple is more its hue.'[42] Crowther then goes on to explain the plot. When a group of Swiss schoolgirls arrive in Paris on a sightseeing tour, one of them, Penny (played by Dany Robin), begins a romance with a Parisian police inspector (Daniel Gélin). 'It's still beseemly when they sit down at a café,' Crowther continues. 'It stays that way when they go for dinner in a gangster-cluttered dive, then vamoose and drift in the direction of Les Halles when the cops raid the hangout. But it starts to get around to unseemly – or simply French, shall we say – when the girl opts to go home with the fellow and presumably embark on an affair.' Crowther's uncritical acceptance of the stereotype – 'simply French' – to an extent reflected the latest trend. French films were enjoying a resurgence in the US market, but not on the basis of the high-quality production that had characterised French imports during the 1930s and 1940s.

A more commercially attuned French industry, with the strategic direction of a New York-based 'French Film Office', no longer took it for granted that American audiences would embrace French culture, but instead actively sought to find a popular idiom that would work in terms of the American market.

The year 1957 marked a breakthrough. According to *Variety*, the French cinema enjoyed 'far and away the best year for their films in the States',[43] and dominated the foreign-language field. It regained its pre-eminence from the Italians, and doubled the number of theatres in New York that ran French films. But this feat was achieved through the pursuit of visceral box-office appeal rather than any increase in quality. 'With French films pacing the field by a wide margin,' commented *Variety*, 'it's reported that they're definitely making progress in getting more playing time in the regular commercial theatres which, in the past, stayed away from imports. Several sections of the country have "opened up" in a small way to the French, particularly if they've been pictures with a "naughty" aspect.'[44]

The recently adopted practice of dubbing the more commercial films helped this progress, since it lifted the barrier that subtitles tended to impose on access to the circuits. But in spite of this considerable advance, no one could have predicted the extraordinary box-office fortunes that *Et Dieu créa la femme* (1956) would enjoy after its opening in New York in late October 1957. Easily the most important film in re-establishing the international post-war presence of the French cinema, it deserves to be discussed in some detail.

But from this point onwards, it is important to call the film by its English title – *And God Created Woman* – which was how the film was invariably known in the United States. Released into US cinemas in a dubbed English version, *And God Created Woman* was notable for a promotion that minimised the difficulties of the film's foreign provenance while maximising its erotic aspects.

The film represented perhaps the most radical challenge yet to previous ideas of what the French cinema was. Back in its 'Golden Age', for example, Jean Lenauer had commented that the French cinema did not place the same emphasis as Hollywood on the young romantic star. But *And God Created Woman* was as single-minded a star vehicle as any produced in Hollywood's history. Its success was due not to any exceptional artistry, but to the combination of Gallic style and frankness grafted on to the Hollywood values of star appeal, market awareness, showmanship and promotion.

Roger Vadim was a young screenwriter and assistant director who had served his apprenticeship with the veteran French director Marc Allégret. In 1952 he married Brigitte Bardot, who was then beginning to establish herself as an up-and-coming star. Soon afterwards he began to work as a journalist on the mass-market illustrated weekly *Paris-Match*, which had drawn inspiration from the photojournalism of the American magazine *Life*. The experience helped to instil a sense of the contemporary and the discipline to develop his ideas within a commercial framework.

When he returned to the film world, hoping to build on his wife's growing bankability as a film star, he was able to display the very American quality of working consciously *with* the market, tailoring a commodity to its needs. But a vital element in his progress was the backing of producer Raoul Lévy, who gave Vadim the opportunity to write and direct a star vehicle closely modelled around Bardot's personality.

Lévy not only shared Vadim's commercial instincts but also had the necessary background and connections to give the Bardot project genuine international scale. A Belgian who had flown with the RAF during the war, Lévy had been a production assistant for RKO and then worked for Edward Small, who was an independent producer for Columbia. Setting up his own Paris-based production company, Lévy managed to win his own distribution deal with the American studio. From the outset, *And God Created Woman* was conceived as an international movie that would tailor its uniquely French assets to the American market. There was not only the sex appeal of Bardot, but also the setting of the Riviera, which had become hugely fashionable in the wake of the Hitchcock film *To Catch a Thief* (1955) and the subsequent marriage in April 1956 of its star, Grace Kelly, to Prince Rainier III of Monaco. While *And God Created Woman* was being made on location in St-Tropez, several other high-profile productions were being filmed at the same time just along the coast, including *The Monte Carlo Story* (1956) with Marlene Dietrich, and Gérard Philipe's first venture as a director, *Les Aventures de Till l'Espiègle* (1956).[45]

To the local box-office ingredients were added the Hollywood production values of colour and Cinemascope. This considerable extra expense signalled Columbia's intention that *And God Created Woman* should be not just another French film of narrow, specialist appeal, but should work in the mainstream market. With this backing, the film was, already before its release in the United States, being tipped by *Variety* as one of the few productions that would achieve 'box-office honors in the foreign film sweepstakes'.[46]

Its opening was supported by the release at about the same time of four other Brigitte Bardot pictures. In a campaign of careful, calculated promotion, Bardot herself came over to the United States for a publicity tour. Together, all five films served to reinforce her sex goddess image.

When *And God Created Woman* opened, many critics ridiculed the film, but they could not so easily dismiss its star. In the *New York Times*, Bosley Crowther described the story as 'tedious little tattle', but went on:

The sultry exponent of its idea is the fabulous Brigitte Bardot, who has become France's undisputed champion in the international sexpot race. This startlingly shaped little actress is as impudent as an April breeze, ready to exercise her catnip to the full extent of the law.[47]

The power of the star meant that whatever the critics said didn't really matter. Indeed, their disapproval aided a campaign that traded on the attractions of the illicit.

On the release poster were two short quotes chosen to suggest sensation rather than praise. From the *New York Times*: 'A phenomenon you have to see to believe!' And from *Life* magazine: 'Much more than American audiences are used to seeing of what 23-year-old girls are made of!' The visual focus was Brigitte Bardot suggestively straddling the words: '"And God created woman" . . . but the devil invented Brigitte Bardot.'

While in the past distributors often worked hard to hide a film's French origin, here it was a positive asset, promising a level of erotic fantasy that Hollywood, still hampered by the Production Code, could not even come close to reaching. In place of the sexual naivety on which the star persona of America's home-grown sex symbol, Marilyn Monroe, had been founded, Brigitte Bardot offered the promise of willing expertise.

The poster not only suggested the lure of French sophistication over American repression, but also connected Bardot's overt sexuality with the larger revolution that was already shaking American society. Bardot was being called the invention of the devil at precisely the time when a young Elvis Presley was singing the 'Devil's music', and when Hollywood's new movie icons were no longer models of conformity, in the mould of Rooney or Garland, but symbols of youth rebellion.

Providing a female counterpart to Brando or Dean, Bardot embodied the new generation breaking away from the stifling convention of its elders. In the film she plays Juliette the orphanage girl, whose impertinent, disrespectful manner presents such a challenge to her adoptive family that she is allowed to stay in St-Tropez only on condition that she gets married. She makes the necessary compromise, but remains as spontaneous and uninhibited as ever, ready to act on her desires and emotions without restraint, with utter frankness about her enjoyment of sexual pleasure. A priest warns her prospective husband not to marry her – 'This girl is like a wild animal' – while the middle-aged tycoon, who knows he can never possess her, recognises, in words that could serve as an anthem for the new generation, that 'she has the courage to do what she likes when she likes'.

The film's explicit nature quickly brought it into conflict with the self-appointed guardians of American innocence, the National Legion of Decency. As it began to play in commercial circuits, there were alarmed reports that it was outgrossing Cecil B. De Mille's *The Ten Commandments* (1956). In late November 1957, the Legion condemned the film, correctly stating that 'the theme and treatment of this film, developed in an atmosphere of sensuality, dwells without relief upon suggestiveness in costuming, dialog and situations'.[48] It went on, much more controversially: 'In the field of motion picture entertainment the extent and intensity of the objectionability of this picture constitute an open violation of Christian and traditional morality.'

In face of the clear public enthusiasm for the film, the Legion risked seeming like the fanatical Miss Gulch in *The Wizard of Oz* (1939), threatening to have Dorothy's harmless little dog Toto destroyed by the sheriff. Although its pronouncements had long proved a serious deterrent to theatres booking films it disapproved of, it seemed increasingly out of kilter with the fast-changing society of the post-war years.

Treating *And God Created Woman* as a significant test case, *Variety* reported the concerns of one distributor that theatres were paying undue attention to the Legion's condemnation of films with sex themes:

It is an unfortunate and carefully nurtured impression that anything with sex in it automatically must be 'obscene'. I am as moral as the next fellow and I wouldn't play an obscene film in my theatres. But the term 'obscene' means different things to different people, and what may appear that way to the Legion could actually constitute pleasant and completely harmless adult entertainment for a lot of people.[49]

The general consensus was that, even if the film did lose some bookings in Catholic areas, it would still be a box-office success in spite of the Legion's 'C' (i.e., condemned) rating. 'Good indication of the Legion's strength will come in Boston, where *God Created Woman* is breaking records at the Gary Theatre in its fourth week. In theory, the "C" classification should cause a sharp dropoff at the Gary.'[50] In the event, it didn't. Indeed, through December 1957 and into January 1958 the film continued to open in circuit theatres across America, its reputation as the film the Legion condemned seeming only to strengthen its appeal. In mid-January *Variety*'s box-office reports were confirming Bardot's victory over the Legion.[51] *And God Created Woman* was 'best newcomer' in Seattle, 'shapely' in Chicago, and registering 'hardly any drop' in Washington, although it was already in its tenth week. The reports for Pittsburgh, where the film was into its fourth week, served as an accurate summing-up for the nation as a whole – 'a genuine phenomenon with unbelievable grosses'.[52] The film would eventually figure high on *Variety*'s list of 'Top Grossers of 1958' with an estimated US rental of $3,000,000.[53] Bardot and Vadim's follow-up film, *The Night Heaven Fell* (1958), was also on the list, with a rental of $1,000,000.

Seeking to draw a moral from the list of successes, *Variety* observed: 'Always the same obvious truism – show business is a business of names, personalities, values generated by the traits and skills and charms of potent (at the box-office) individuals. So, too, in 1958. Brigitte Bardot's pictures sold like French postcards.'[54]

And God Created Woman was as natural a component in Hollywood's system as *Shadows* was alien. A genuine, mass-market commodity, it was an easily understood film that offered entertainment rather than art. Rendered as easily digestible as

French fries, with its English title and dubbing, it achieved the status of 'movie' rather than 'film', which helped it to triumph in the American circuits.

But as far as the French cinema was concerned, in practice it represented a cul-de-sac. The New Wave film-makers who followed in Vadim's footsteps would enjoy considerable kudos among the educated patrons of America's traditional art-house market, but with few exceptions, they did not make the kind of films that could reach the mass audience that *And God Created Woman* had won.

16

Exporting the Revolution

When *Et Dieu créa la femme* opened in France at the end of 1956, to a mostly hostile reception from the critics, François Truffaut offered a passionate defence of a film that he hailed as belonging to the new generation:

I thank Vadim for the way he has directed his young wife in such a way that she repeats before the camera the ordinary gestures of everyday life, like playing with her sandal, or making love in the afternoon, less ordinary, maybe, but just as real. Instead of imitating other films, Vadim wanted to forget the cinema to copy life, to achieve true intimacy on the screen, and, with the exception of two or three less convincing scenes, he has perfectly achieved his goal.[1]

After the manner of all Truffaut's film writing, the review offered not objective film criticism but a campaign for his own concept of the cinema. *Et Dieu créa la femme* had a primitive plot and mostly two-dimensional characters; it was also deliberately exploitative and titillating, with a deeply chauvinist perspective that portrayed a woman as a wild animal to be subdued. But this mattered less to Truffaut than the fact that it had freshness, energy and style, that it was a made by a young person (Vadim was twenty-eight), and that it could be claimed as personal, not only because Vadim had made a film about his wife, but also because Bardot's portrayal of the character Juliette was in many ways a portrayal of herself, with no clear division between actor and role.

Bardot's performance fitted in perfectly with the preference of Truffaut and his New Wave colleagues for greater realism and spontaneity. Only shortly before, in an article to mark the death of James Dean, Truffaut had lauded him as 'an actor who brings a visceral, physical quality to his performances rather than filtering everything through the intellect'.[2] The same words might have been applied to Bardot, as indeed to Truffaut's own writing, which sacrificed any semblance of balance or objectivity to the personal. Albeit often arbitrary and unfair, the committed, passionate tone chimed in well with the aspirations of a young generation determined to take advantage of its new-found prosperity and freedom.

In France, the origin of the label *nouvelle vague* was attributed – even by the New Wave itself – to a series of articles published in *L'Express* magazine between 3 October and 12 December 1957. Drawing on a research survey on the attitudes of young French people, the series was accompanied by the slogan 'The New Wave Has Arrived!' With *And God Created Woman* in the spring of 1958 standing fourth in the US box-office ratings, it was not surprising that US newspapers should have picked up on the phenomenon. In a feature called 'France's Fabulous Young Five', the *New York Times* profiled Bardot and Vadim, along with Françoise Sagan, the twenty-two-year-old author of *Bonjour tristesse*, the twenty-nine-year-old painter Bernard Buffet and the twenty-two-year-old *haute couture* designer Yves Saint-Laurent.[3] Seeking to find a common essence, the writer of the piece identified a 'depoliticised' generation that exhibited an 'almost fanatical refusal of adulthood'.

Although the remark was a journalist's loose impression, it does serve to highlight the particular character that the New Wave took in France. In Britain 'new wave' meant expressing social and political change, giving a voice to a class that had previously been excluded from the cinema. In the United States, where the dominant ideology of Hollywood had always assimilated rather than yielded to change, it meant creating an entirely alternative system – a counter-culture, which, fiercely oppositional to the dominant ideology, clustered together under such banners as 'independent', 'underground', 'experimental' or 'avant garde'. But in France, the driving force was a cinephilia that made such divorce from Hollywood impossible.

The French 'New Wave' emerged out of a sustained dialogue with the cinema that reached a critical mass at this time. There were notable previous instances of the kind of cinema with which the New Wave would be identified, but they occurred too much in isolation to seem credible contributions to a phenomenon that was as much about momentum and scale as any fixed set of values. The cinephilia and commitment to a personal style could already be found in the work of Jean-Pierre Melville, but if he was happy to be considered an influential godfather, he was finally separate from a movement of younger individuals heading in the same direction and about to achieve prominence at roughly the same time.

An equally important precursor was Agnès Varda. 'Truly the first film of the New Wave,' Georges Sadoul wrote of her first feature La Pointe Courte,[4] which she made in 1954 on a tiny budget borrowed from family and friends. The film tells the story of a young Parisian couple who dwell upon their troubled marriage during a visit to the fishing village of Pointe Courte, near the Mediterranean town of Sète. The lives of the fishing community where they have taken up temporary residence provide a counterpoint to their drama. In its subject-matter, but also its contrast of urban complexity with rural simplicity, and the blend of fiction with documentary observation, the film recalls Roberto Rossellini's Stromboli (1950), about a woman who, in the aftermath of the Second World War, marries an Italian fisherman to escape an internment camp for refugees.

But whether or not Rossellini was a conscious influence, Varda's own recollection of the period stresses her absence of any deep knowledge of the cinema. She found a teacher in Alain Resnais, who was the film's editor. 'Resnais told me about Renoir, Murnau and Mankiewicz, none of whom I knew. And he explained to me that there was such a thing as a Cinémathèque in Paris, suggesting that I should commence my viewing with Dreyer's Vampyr.' One evening she met several of the Cahiers writers in Resnais's flat.

As I didn't know any of these young men, it's only on the basis of a vague recollection of faces that I would get to know later that I can identify them as Chabrol, Truffaut, Rohmer (who had another name), Brialy, Doniol-Valcroze and Godard. I had trouble keeping up with the conversation. They mentioned hundreds of films I had never heard of, all speaking very fast and chatting with great animation. I was the oddity there. I felt small and ignorant, the only girl among the *Cahiers* boys.[5]

In her mid-twenties, Varda had a photographer's training, but no previous experience of making films. Yet she was in the process of doing what 'the boys' still only dreamt of doing in 1954. They had made a handful of short films by this stage, but none of them had yet written and directed a full-length feature. The near-total exclusion of women from a profession that had hitherto been a male preserve makes her achievement all the more extraordinary. As Varda commented herself of *La Pointe Courte*, it had to be made with ten times less money than was usual for a feature of the period, but it required 'ten times more nerve'. If her example offered encouragement to the *Cahiers* writers that they too could make their own films without having to serve a traditional apprenticeship in the industry, her vastly more important role was to serve as a model of inspiration for the 50 per cent of the population who had hitherto been denied any significant voice at all as film-makers. It was Varda who opened the door to Marguerite Duras, Claire Denis and Catherine Breillat, as well as countless other women film-makers beyond France.

La Pointe Courte was given a two-week run in a Paris cinema in early 1956, but received no wider distribution. It went largely unnoticed precisely because it *hadn't* been part of a larger wave that could win it the necessary attention. The *Cahiers* writers, who arrived on the scene a crucial few years later, were able to benefit from the support of the Centre National du Cinéma (CNC), which had by this time been able to develop a coherent policy of encouragement for an approach so at odds with the prevailing structure of the industry. The New Wave was the product of a uniquely opportune moment, in which institutional support and intense media promotion converged on a group of young individuals who, through *Cahiers*, already enjoyed privileged connections with the industry, even if they were not yet of that industry.

By the beginning of 1959 they were ready to take full ownership of the 'New Wave' label, infusing it with their own cinephile tastes. The release of Claude Chabrol's *Le Beau Serge*, on 11 February 1959, heralded a kind of film-making that would be personal, but also deeply indebted to mainstream Hollywood cinema.

The very opening credits seem almost proudly to boast membership of the New Wave project, announcing a film that had not only been 'produced, written and directed by Claude Chabrol', but also entirely shot in the Creuse, a region where Chabrol had spent much of his childhood. The film was also partly autobiographical, the character of the Parisian François standing in for Chabrol himself,[6] and the title character, Serge, drawing on Chabrol's friend Paul Gégauff.

Yet if *Le Beau Serge* is unquestionably a work of personal expression drawing on personal roots, equally notable is its attempt to assume a Hollywood style. As the troubled young drunkard of the title, Gérard Blain, brooding in his leather jacket, evokes those Hollywood icons of youth rebellion, Marlon Brando or James Dean.

His inability to come to terms with the birth of his Down's Syndrome child has driven him to drink, instilling within him a sense of 'bad blood'. As he reflects on the failure he has become, he blames his ruin on the deceased child. His self-pitying lament that, had it not been for the child, he would have passed his exams and become an architect, recalls the famous 'I could have been a contender' scene in *On the Waterfront* (1954), in which Terry (Marlon Brando) reproaches his brother Charlie (Rod Steiger) for causing him to become a 'bum' instead of a successful fighter. Serge too believes that he has been let down by his family.

The intensity of Blain's acting puts one in mind of Truffaut's description of the 'visceral, physical quality' of James Dean, but the too obvious attempt to capture the Actor's Studio style finally makes this performance more mannered than natural, too conscious an attempt to borrow spontaneity to be spontaneous itself.

Le Beau Serge was the work of a gifted novice, who clearly had a deep familiarity with Hollywood cinema, yet struggled to integrate the dramatic pacing of Hollywood drama into the French story and setting. But at least a new system of state aid made it possible for the director to continue to make films with a frequency that would allow him to gain assurance and fluency.

The *prime à la qualité* was at the heart of the New Wave, facilitating what the French film historian Michel Marie has called 'the small budget revolution'.[7] The then director of the CNC, Jacques Flaud, had denounced the effect of the previous automatic aid system, which encouraged producers to play safe, making 'films that always return to the tried and tested talents of established actors with an international box-office reputation'.[8] With the *prime à la qualité* in place, he urged producers instead to attempt films of more artistic ambition, films that would give new directors and new actors an opportunity to make their mark. As Michel Marie has argued, the programme Flaud announced in early 1957 amounted to an institutional version of Truffaut's arguments for a cinema of personal expression.[9]

The CNC did not just dole out money, but worked as an active ally of the new generation to nurture a prestige cinema. In practical terms, this meant that during the production of a suitably qualified film, the CNC might use its discretion to relax union rules. So, for example, Chabrol, Truffaut and Godard were all allowed to make their first films with reduced crews. Ten years previously, Jean-Pierre Melville had been fined by the CNC for such presumption; but now films marginal to the industry – in a sense, 'accursed films', to use Cocteau's label – were receiving the legitimisation of the establishment. Indeed, the support continued long after the film had been made, with the CNC's satellite agency Unifrance, which had been set up under the film legislation of 1948, providing systematic promotion of French films abroad.

In 1959, the agency harnessed the publicity generated by the invention of the 'New Wave' label, staging a conference of young directors at the Cannes Film Festival, where a large number of foreign journalists were present. Those who attended included Truffaut, Chabrol, Godard and Vadim. Published in the journal *Arts*, the proceedings of the conference helped to generate massive media attention, not just in France but in America too.

Suitably primed, the *New York Times* ran a piece that attempted to capture some of the excitement: 'The state of health of motion pictures in Paris this spring has been crackling with fresh vigor and invention that is positively New World in its heavy accent on youth . . . The "New Wave" (La "Nouvelle Vague"), as they are termed, is getting a tremendous play in the French press.'[10] A few weeks later, in publicity orchestrated by the American office of Unifrance, the *New York Times* ran the headline, 'US to see Films Hailed in France':

American audiences soon will have a chance to judge the so called "new wave" of French film-makers that have caused such a sensation in Europe. These are the young directors who have been heralded in their own country as the successors to established artists such as Marcel Carné, Julien Duvivier and René Clément.[11]

The year 1959 was a turning point in the French cinema, not only because of the emergence of the New Wave, but also because the French state reaffirmed its commitment to back the *prime à la qualité* in that year's transfer of the Centre National du Cinéma from the Ministry of Industry and Commerce to the Ministry of Culture. Henceforth, the commission that chose films eligible for the *prime à la qualité* would be made up not of figures from the film industry but of appointees of the minister of culture, André Malraux.

At about the same time Raoul Lévy was dismissing the New Wave as 'one big joke',[12] but although it was certainly as much a publicity campaign as a genuine movement, and although the description lumped together often very different personalities, like the best publicity campaigns it contained a kernel of truth. A new generation of film-makers had arrived, although one very different from what American film-goers might have imagined in the aftermath of *And God Created Woman*.

Aspiring film-makers no longer had to face the struggle of finding a place in mainstream French production, with all the compromises that this entailed, but could take advantage of generous state encouragement to make films that were artistically ambitious rather than commercial. With their subtitles and unorthodox production methods, such films might earn only the most negligible revenues abroad, but they soon proved that they could win huge cultural prestige.

When the first films of Chabrol and Truffaut arrived in America in the autumn of 1959, after months of publicity, their enthusiastic reception caused a swift and radical change in the American perception of the French cinema. Of Truffaut's film, Bosley Crowther wrote in the *New York Times*: 'Let it be noted without contention that the crest of the flow of recent films from the "new wave" of young French directors hit these shores yesterday with the arrival at the Fine Arts Theatre of *The 400 Blows*.'[13] He went on to describe the film as 'a small masterpiece', concluding, 'Here is a picture that encourages an exciting refreshment of faith in films.'

A week later, the film's American distributor, Zenith International, took out a full-page advertisement in *Variety*.[14] Boasting 'the most fabulous press raves New York has seen in a decade', the advertisement reprinted the entire review that had appeared in the *New York Times*. It also reminded readers of its other notable French success, Louis Malle's *Les Amants* (1958), which was breaking box-office records at the Paris Theatre.

At the end of 1959, under the headline, '"Art" back to US Art

Houses', *Variety* summed up the situation. After recent years in which the French cinema had tended to be most readily identified with sex, it was now beginning to win back the kind of acclaim it had enjoyed before the war,[15] although at the same time, the magazine pointed out, the natural audience for these films was limited to the art houses. The foreign film that was able to break out to win bookings in the circuits was as much an exception to the rule as it always had been.

Acclaiming the 'Renaissance of the French Movies', the *New York Times* sought to explain the nature of an 'offbeat, low-cost, high-grade' kind of cinema that, like the neo-realist films after the war, seemed refreshingly different in style from anything that had been made before. The specific characteristics the newspaper identified were 'an original, non-formula story; no name stars, but a cast of young unknown actors and friends; shooting almost exclusively outside movie studios in offices, apartments and streets; good photography, using available light whenever possible'. It also remarked upon the fact that a 'general aura of mutual aid and comfort, such as has rarely been seen in the tough, cut-throat cinema world, exists today among these young French movie men'.[16]

In effect, it was describing an artistic school which, thanks to the support of the French Ministry of Culture, was able to observe primarily cultural rather than commercial rules of operation. In some fundamental sense that would henceforth mark an important dividing-line between the new French cinema and Hollywood, these film-makers didn't live 'in the tough, cut-throat cinema world' at all, but rather in an unusually comfortable artist's garret that subsidised cinema made possible.

A break with the conventional industry and the cinema of the past was part of the appeal of the brand – no 'New Wave' can afford to appear backward-looking – but in practice the young film-makers leant heavily on the cinema they denigrated. *Les 400 Coups* provides an example. When Jean-Luc Godard wrote a jubilant article in celebration of the choice of the film to represent France at the 1959 Cannes Film Festival,[17] he described the occasion as a great victory in 'the battle for the auteur', citing Julien Duvivier in a rather hysterical Stalinist tone of denunciation among the French directors who were guilty of 'false technique'.

But shortly afterwards Julien Duvivier sat on the Cannes jury that awarded *Les 400 Coups* the prize for best direction. The award offered Duvivier an opportunity to express his genuine admiration for Truffaut's achievement, but he would also have been aware – in a way that most of the world's critics were not – how much *Les 400 Coups* owed to his own favourite film, *Poil de Carotte*, of thirty years previously. In the sense that imitation is the sincerest form of flattery, it came closest to offering the acknowledgement that the New Wave never publicly gave him.

The story of a neglected child with an indifferent father and a harsh, unloving mother had autobiographical significance not only for Truffaut but also Duvivier. It was in essence as much an outline of *Poil de Carotte* as *Les 400 Coups*. Like Truffaut's first alter ego, Antoine Doinel, in *Les 400 Coups*, Poil de Carotte longs for the rare occasions when his family will show him some affection, but has come to appreciate that such moments are the exceptions that prove the rule. Antoine enjoys a fleeting moment of family togetherness when his parents take him out to the cinema, while Poil de Carotte longs to go on hunting expeditions with his father, finding some respite in this way from his mother's cruelty. Both boys have to endure a round of endless errands – Antoine setting and clearing away the table, taking out the rubbish, Poil de Carotte closing the hen-house, fetching the firewood, feeding the animals. One errand they even have in common. Antoine is told off angrily by his mother for forgetting to buy some flour and sent to the shops to complete the chore. The same task sparks off Poil de Carotte's rebellion against his mother, as he refuses to go out to the flour mill. Here, too, the dynamic of the two films is the same. The lack of parental love causes both boys to misbehave, which leads to even harsher treatment, and the vicious circle tightens to the point where both children decide that they must leave home. While the famous final freeze-frame of *Les 400 Coups* delivers Antoine up to an uncertain future, Duvivier allows Poil de Carotte to enjoy a more conventional happy ending. But the emotional kernel of the two stories is the same.

The only mention of *Poil de Carotte* I can find in Truffaut's writings is a comment, in 1975, that on a visit to Japan film critics questioned him about a film that was still very popular there. But he did not elaborate any further on why this old film had been drawn to his attention. We may speculate, however, that the Japanese critics recognised the debt that he owed to Duvivier.

Truffaut's own silence about *Poil de Carotte* was echoed by the critics and scholars who later wrote about his films. They often compare *Les 400 Coups* to the work of auteurs that Truffaut admired, but not to the film it most resembles. Annette Insdorf's study of Truffaut's films offers an example:

[Truffaut's] praise of Jean Vigo – the only other director to have rendered childhood with such poetic realism – can now be applied to his own efforts: 'In one sense, *Zéro de Conduite* represents something more rare than *L'Atalante* because the masterpieces consecrated to childhood in literature or cinema can be counted on the fingers of one hand. They move us doubly since the aesthetic emotion is compounded by a biographical, personal and intimate emotion . . . They bring us back to our short pants, to school, to the blackboard, to vacations, to our beginnings in life.'[18]

Was *Poil de Carotte* one of the films that Truffaut counted on the fingers of one hand? *Les 400 Coups* suggests that it must have been. But to acknowledge its influence would have been to identify with a tendency in the French cinema that he had made his career by attacking. And it would have been to undermine the revolution that *Les 400 Coups* launched – the *cinéma de papa* not so dead at all. Resolved to ride the New Wave rather than to compromise on the break with the past, he chose instead to keep a distance.

There are many sequences in *Poil de Carotte* that suggest how much Truffaut owed to Duvivier, but the famous ending to Truffaut's film suffices to make the point. In one of the most written-about sequences in film history, Antoine escapes from reform school during a soccer game, running through the countryside until he reaches the sea, when he turns back to face us in what becomes a last freeze-frame image of the film. Terence Rafferty wrote about it in a 2007 article for the *New York Times*:[19]

That freeze-frame stuck in people's minds, as if it were a sharp, nagging memory of their own. What looks most remarkable now, though, isn't the blank still face that closes the film, but the daringly long run that brings us to it, that allows our emotions to gather and build with each short, stiff step until, without quite understanding why, we end up overwhelmed. It's the movie in miniature, really.

Les 400 Coups (1959)

Rafferty called his piece 'The Trouble-maker Who Led a Revolution', but that 'daringly long run' is already there in *Poil de Carotte*, which Duvivier made more than a quarter of a century earlier. Duvivier's child runs away in despair from a party at which he has suffered one final adult rejection. He leaves the village, passes through a field of sheep and then out on to a country road. The camera keeps pace with him as he runs and runs and runs in a distraught, headlong flight – not towards the sea, but to a pond where he intends to drown himself. An inner voice, which Duviver represents in the form of a ghostly, barely visible twin running behind, tells him, 'Poil de Carotte, you will always be alone. Always! So run!'

Antoine Doinel, Poil de Carotte – two boys who have reached

Poil de Carotte (1932)

the end of the road. Truffaut's borrowing from Duvivier does not diminish the beauty or truth of his own ending, but it does stand as an example of the interconnected nature of artistic creation, which the crude categorisation of directors into auteurs and *metteurs-en-scène* tended to obscure. Indeed, Truffaut captures the dynamic of such homage in *Les 400 Coups*, when he has his alter ego Antoine Doinel describe the death of his grandfather with words that he draws unconsciously from Balzac. But while Antoine builds a shrine to his hero, nearly burning down the house in the process, a much more careful and shrewd Truffaut did not see any purpose in remembering Duvivier.

A school of mostly young directors, it was perhaps to be expected that the New Wave would find its greatest appreciation and understanding among the young, who were unable to make any possibly compromising comparisons with the old. And the profound way in which the cinema had changed since the war needs to be underlined. It was of course a change not just in the film-makers, but the audience. Overall, attendance figures had dropped. Increasingly, in the new age of television, families were staying at home, resulting in a marked shift in the cinema-going audience towards young adults. The existence of this new niche soon made it clear that it was time for a changing of the guard among the critics too, not just in France but everywhere.

Reviewing *A bout de souffle* (1960) at the beginning of 1961,

Bosley Crowther observed: 'As sordid as is the French film, *Breathless* . . . – and sordid is really a mild word for its pile-up of gross indecencies – it is withal a fascinating communication of the savage ways and moods of some of the rootless young people of Europe (and America) today.'[20] The words in parenthesis were significant, suggesting Crowther's own personal bewilderment with the new post-war generation that was beginning to find its own distinctive voice. Yet although he clearly regarded *A bout de souffle* with distaste, he knew it was important; it was just that he lacked the affinity of shared experience to appreciate how. 'Say this, in sum, for *Breathless*: it is certainly no cliché, in any area or sense of the word. It is more a chunk of drama, graphically and artfully torn with appropriately ragged edges out of the tough underbelly of modern metropolitan life.' It was the conclusion of a middle-aged critic floundering to understand a younger generation's language.

France's cinema revolution had been successfully exported to the English-speaking world, but the initiative in making sense of this new cinema passed from the mouthpieces of the establishment like the *New York Times* to a group of younger writers who found a voice in such newly established periodicals as *Movie* and *Oxford Opinion* in Britain or *Film Culture* and the *Village Voice* in the United States. It may have been much less heralded, but even in the land of Hollywood film criticism was beginning to develop a New Wave of its own.

Observing that the contributors to *Film Culture* 'represented a new breed of critic', Andrew Sarris would sum up the difference of attitude as follows: 'The cultural rationale for our worthier predecessors . . . was they were too good to be reviewing movies.'[21] Sarris's comment that the launch of *Film Culture* reminded him of 'microbes under glass' was an index of how revolutionary the very existence of such a magazine was in America, but also suggests the organic growth of a new film culture in America that would be as receptive to outside influences as Hollywood tended to be impervious.

Sarris claimed not to have heard of *Cahiers du cinéma* or André Bazin when *Film Culture* was launched in 1955,[22] but the impact of the French New Wave soon provided the incentive to find out. His friend Eugene Archer, who wrote for *Film Culture*, and would later join the *New York Times*, went to Europe in 1960 on a Fulbright Scholarship and sent back enthusiastic letters about the Cinémathèque, *Cahiers du cinéma* and the ideas that were being developed in the magazine. The following year Sarris himself travelled to France, attending the Cannes Film Festival and then spending nearly a year in Paris. According to his own account, it was this experience that convinced him that 'film not only demanded but deserved as much faith as did any other cultural discipline'.[23]

The account of his conversion is striking for the emphasis it places between two different, conflicting modes of existence. During his 'fateful' stay in Paris he found an environment where 'culture' was not frowned upon but regarded as a natural and organic part of everyday life. 'I have never really recovered from the Parisian heresy (in New York eyes) concerning the sacred importance of the cinema. Hence I returned to New York not merely a cultist but a subversive cultist with a foreign ideology.'[24]

The comments reflect the power of established convention in 1950s America where, in the absence of a strong subsisting culture, any kind of art that didn't offer an obvious commercial justification was considered a challenge to mainstream society. This oppositional mindset meant that, rather than Hollywood, it was the 'subversive cultists' in New York who were the first to learn the lessons of the New Wave.

In 1962, Sarris published an article in *Film Culture* entitled 'Notes on the Auteur Theory',[25] applying Truffaut's phrase *politique des auteurs* to the American cinema. As Sarris himself has observed, since the article had been published in a small, specialist magazine, it might have been completely forgotten had Pauline Kael not launched a ferocious attack on Sarris in her piece for the *Film Quarterly*, 'Circles and Squares'.[26] Dismissing the auteur theory as a 'formula', Kael argued that critics should be relying on their intelligence and intuition rather than rules. She then went on to ridicule Sarris's assertion that the 'distinguishable personality' of the director should be considered a criterion of value: 'The smell of a skunk is more distinguishable than the perfume of a rose; does that make it better?' Sarris was invited to write an article in response to Kael's criticisms in the next issue of the *Film Quarterly*,[27] and the furious debate that followed not only helped to establish Sarris as a film critic at the *Village Voice*, with a large and committed new readership, but also marked the extent to which a flourishing film culture was developing in the United States.

One of the two co-writers of *Bonnie and Clyde* (1967), David Newman, who in the early 1960s worked for *Esquire* magazine, recalled the atmosphere:

There was something going on about cinema . . . that was almost like a religion. Not just for me but all my friends, everyone I knew. I grew up going to the movies every Saturday like a kid, you know . . . double-feature, six cartoons, newsreel. Suddenly, there was the New Wave. One week there would be a Truffaut. The next week there would be a Godard or a Rivette or a Rohmer, or Agnès Varda . . . whatever, that group . . . And then, at the same time, thanks partly to *Cahiérs du cinéma* and the *politique des auteurs* that came out of France, and a few very important American critics, we began to rediscover our own movies.[28]

What the French helped this new American film culture to discover was how much style their films had. They taught Americans at last to appreciate their own cinema, to realise that there was value to be found not only in the intellectual insight or social comment but in *le look*. To possess such a powerful popular idiom was a strength, not a weakness, and a commercial industry could still provide a framework in which great artists could operate – even if Hollywood's single-minded devotion to showmanship and the dollar meant that it would never love the French cinema back.

Such a blossoming in the serious appreciation of the cinema inevitably brings to mind the various film movements in France from Louis Delluc and the ciné-clubs onwards, but in the United States such spontaneous activity was completely new. It was like the opening up of the wilderness to the railroad. It was pursued with such characteristic energy and purpose that it made 'film culture' seem like a big new business.

In France, Truffaut's article 'A Certain Tendency of the French Cinema',[29] which introduced the phrase *politique des auteurs*, had been a polemical piece of deliberate provocation. Its specific purpose was to combat a kind of film-making perceived as too literary in order to pave the way for a more personal approach for a group of young cinephiles who wanted to become film-makers themselves. But across the Atlantic, this diatribe became the basis for a much larger, more methodical enterprise.

Translating *Cahiers du cinéma* into English, Sarris facilitated the implantation of its ideas about the cinema in the United States. He not only turned the *politique des auteurs* into a theory, but also used it, in his columns for the *Village Voice* – and with the publication in 1968 of his landmark book, *The American Cinema* – to build a systematic canon.

Just as Louis Lumière famously observed that the Cinématographe was 'an invention without a future', it is unlikely that François Truffaut entertained much of a future for his *politique des auteurs*; it was much more an idea for immediate use. It required Andrew Sarris to develop its long-term potential. If the title of his first collection of film criticism, *Confessions of a Cultist*,[30] implied a measure of guilt or apology for the 'art for art's sake' approach that he had embraced as a young American in Paris, his subsequent life would more than make up for it, as he built the framework for an industry of film appreciation, providing a career not only for himself but countless scholars to come. As James Schamus put it, Sarris 'helped to make the academic study of cinema a legitimate discipline . . . Suddenly, out of the wasteland of Hollywood, a canon of great works arose, discerned using criteria easily recognisable by humanities scholars in all disciplines.'[31]

The CNC and Unifrance made the most of this more receptive and sophisticated audience, supporting the New Wave in the United States with a highly organised marketing and publicity campaign, so that what had begun as an artistic movement took on many of the characteristics of a brand. But the true significance of this brand lay less in increased box-office revenues for French-speaking films, which remained minimal, than in its provision of a rejuvenated model for a kind of film-making that helped to save Hollywood itself from ossification, albeit one that remained highly policed and controlled. If Hollywood once again looked to the French cinema for renewal, nonetheless it was determined that such renewal should take place on its own terms.

Based on an original script that the *Esquire* writers Robert Benton and David Newman had written on their own initiative, the film *Bonnie and Clyde* (1967) represented a major turning point. It was inspired by a French New Wave that, in the words of Benton, 'allowed us to write with a more complex morality, more ambiguous characters, more sophisticated relationships'.[32] But although the two writers had persuaded François Truffaut to attach his name to the project, it would require the commitment of a Hollywood insider, the film star Warren Beatty, and the choice of an American director to win Warner Brothers' backing.

With Hollywood's decisive switch to the upcoming generation and the simultaneous final dismantlement of a long out-of-touch Production Code, the French cinema had played perhaps its most significant role in the United States. Its commercial impact had always been negligible, but its intellectual influence in the late 1950s and early 1960s was huge, helping to foster in the United States a sophisticated and broad film culture, which displayed itself not only in the birth of more serious film magazines – such as *Cineaste* in 1967 and *Film Comment* in 1970 – but also in the founding of such institutions as the American Film Institute in 1968 and the Film Society of Lincoln Center in 1969. In the academic sphere, this influence continues to the present day. As David Kehr has observed, '*Cahiers*-influenced film studies programs became the means by which French postmodernist philosophy – Foucault, Derrida, Kristeva – entered the American university, where, far more than in its native land, it has prospered and persisted.'[33]

Yet now that Hollywood was free in the aftermath of the Code to make its own more sophisticated cinema, the creative initiative shifted from Europe to Hollywood itself, which with its usual market efficiency was able to apply the necessary lessons to the box-office. As Andrew Sarris observed, 'At a time when the Hollywood censors imposed twin-bed strictures on American movies, foreign films were daringly adult. Once the censors began to depart, in the late 60s, Hollywood was free to supply the ooh-la-la factor.'[34]

The director-oriented, 'new' Hollywood of the 1970s was a response to the more sophisticated film culture that the French cinema had played a pre-eminent role in fostering, but at the same time, its existence helped to pen the French cinema, once and for all, into its subordinate and economically marginal position in America's art-house ghetto. 'Fans of foreign flicks,' wrote Vincent Canby in 1974. 'Where are they now?' In a market that had virtually collapsed, he observed that Eric Rohmer's *Claire's Knee* was considered to be a hit in the US with revenues of $410,000. By comparison the latest Hollywood hit, *The Poseidon Adventure*, had taken $40,000,000.[35]

If Hollywood went to lengths to assimilate new influences during the 1960s, at the same time its fundamental disregard of the French cinema was as much a reality as it ever had been. A new generation of directors might be making more challenging films, but few displayed any great awareness of French cinema.

This absence of an outward gaze stands in striking contrast to the readiness with which the French New Wave embraced Hollywood. While Truffaut or Chabrol integrated such influence into a strong French framework, Jean-Pierre Melville or Jacques Demy displayed an almost deliberate dependency, with films constantly alluding to – and inviting the audience to make comparison with – their original American models.

But of all the French New Wave directors, it was Jean-Luc Godard who most consistently pushed beyond the level of mere homage, allusion or borrowed style, to provide an analytical examination of the relationship between the two cinemas. *A bout de souffle* and *Le Mépris* (1963), in particular, embody the dynamic in their very conception and structure.

Although *A bout de souffle* was Godard's first feature, he went to great lengths to secure the presence of the Hollywood star Jean Seberg, whom *Cahiers du cinéma* had declared to be 'the new Divinity of the cinema'.[36] Setting out the New Wave agenda, Michel Marie would describe an aesthetic that preferred, in place of the conventional reliance of the mainstream industry on box-office stars, to use 'non-professional actors to act the characters', or at least 'young actors'[37] – yet here was Godard willing to spend a quarter of the film's budget on signing Seberg.

An essential quality of the film lies in the contradictions and tensions between the two different kinds of cinema. It featured a Hollywood star, yet – even by the standards of the French film industry – was an extremely low-budget production. Dedicating itself to the Hollywood B-movie studio, Monogram Pictures, it borrowed that most dependable of all Hollywood genres, the gangster film, endlessly referenced American culture – whether cars, film stars or writers – yet, in both narrative and *mise-en-scène*, broke every Hollywood rule.

In this combination of antagonism and fondness, it perfectly expressed the ambivalence of the French cinema's attitude towards Hollywood. Indeed, Michel and Patricia offer a metaphorical representation of the two different cinemas: Michel, the former assistant at Cinécitta, spontaneous, living life on the run, displaying a taste for American culture, but finally always going his own way; Patricia, prudent and career-minded, working within the framework of other people's rules.

At one point Michel declares of their friendship, 'It's a true Franco-American rapprochement', but the rapprochement is doomed to be short-lived. Patricia's dilemma is how to fit into her life someone who is so unpredictable and contrary to all her values. Her realisation that she can't drives her to commit the final act of betrayal.

How to deal with a sponging, unreliable boyfriend – the challenge was pretty much the same for the Hollywood film business in France. Its films were popular, they paid their way, but for the privilege of staying in France it was expected to pay a tax to help prop up the French film industry – which otherwise would have just as much trouble getting by as Michel Poiccard.

It requires only a brief acquaintance with the history of Franco-American trade negotiations to appreciate the French cinema's perennial readiness to feel betrayed by Hollywood, but Michel Poiccard of course also provides an effective alter ego for Godard himself – the great gangster of the cinema, who loves Hollywood, but is fated always to be disappointed and let down by it.

In *Le Mépris* the identification is even more overt, Godard changing Battista, the Italian film producer of Alberto Moravia's source novel, *Il Dispresso* (English title: *A Ghost at Noon*), into the Hollywood producer Prokosch. Not only is the subject openly about the cinema, but Godard does everything possible to rub at the boundary between fact and fiction, having the director Fritz Lang play himself and, as the true director, even directing the film in the same hat that he has the male lead, Michel Piccoli, wear before the camera.

It is hard to specify exactly where the film stops and real life begins. To this extent the American producer Joe Levine – with whom at one point in the film the fictional American producer Prokosch has a telephone conversation – was an invaluable part of the enterprise, in spite of – or, rather, because of – the 'exceptionally violent' rows that, according to Colin MacCabe, occurred after the film's completion.[38] Levine, who considered *Le Mépris* to be primarily a Brigitte Bardot vehicle, insisted that Bardot should be shown nude. According to MacCabe, Godard at first wanted to take his name off the film, but finally agreed to shoot three extra scenes. MacCabe writes, 'The re-shoots demonstrate clearly the difficulty of any aesthetic which would simply oppose creativity and money, for there can be little doubt that *Le Mépris* would be a much less beautiful and moving film without the long opening scene of Bardot naked on a bed.'[39]

Yet surely a key part of the aesthetic of *Le Mépris* lay precisely in Godard's readiness to gamble his creative freedom, to encourage the interaction between fiction and reality. Just as in the film the director Fritz Lang must field the crass demands of the producer Prokosch, so Godard himself must deal with Levine. To the extent that the film echoes or predicts the situation of its making, Godard would surely have welcomed it as a wonderful gift of happenstance.

As Godard has himself observed, 'All the great fiction films incline towards documentary, just as all the great documentaries incline towards fiction.' Douglas Morrey explains Godard's connection of the two forms in these terms: 'Even in the most artificially contrived narrative, the real world, caught on film, will nonetheless make its presence felt; even the most rigorously factual documentary, by virtue of being organised through montage, partakes of fictional construction.'[40] But Godard was imagining much more than simply the formal property of a camera to record what is set before it; he prized as much a link between fiction and reality that was metaphorical, philosophical and romantic.

A fitting companion piece to *Le Mépris* is the Maysles Brothers' *cinéma vérité* documentary, *Showman* (1963), which offers a portrait of the crude, fast-talking producer Joe Levine, filming him as he handles the promotion of Vittorio de Sica's *Two Women* (1960) – drawn from a Moravia story, like *Le Mépris* – and travels to Cannes to present Sophia Loren with the 'Best Actress' Oscar she won for her appearance in the film.

In *Le Mépris*, Prokosch evokes Levine's flamboyant, dictatorial manner, and also embodies many of the details of his life. Levine's breakthrough in the movie business occurred when he bought the US rights to an Italian 'Sword and Sandal' epic, *Hercules* (1958), starring Steve Reeves. Although he later recalled that his first impression was of a film with terrible colour and a botched soundtrack, it also had the box-office attractions of 'musclemen, broads and a shipwreck and a dragon for the kids'.[41] Opening simultaneously in six hundred theatres across America, the film grossed $5 million, a success that accounted for Levine's career axiom, 'You can fool all the people if the advertising is right.'

Le Mépris represented a collision of two different attitudes, two different systems. Co-produced by Carlo Ponti and Joe Levine, Ponti held the distribution rights for Europe, Levine for the United States. In Europe, it was a 'Jean-Luc Godard' film called *Le Mépris*, but in America, it was promoted as a Brigitte Bardot movie called *Contempt*.

The relevant precedent was not Godard's *A bout de souffle*, but Bardot in *And God Created Woman* (1956). Indeed, the famous opening sequence of *Le Mépris*, in which Bardot lies naked on her front, asking her husband if he likes the different parts of her body – the sequence which Levine reportedly demanded that Godard add to the film – reprises the opening scene of *And God Created Woman*. As Bardot sunbathes naked, with just a sheet on a line to protect her modesty, she attracts the admiring gaze of the elderly master of the household in which she lives. 'With your face,' he comments, 'you can have whatever you wish.'

Although in Europe *Le Mépris* was promoted as 'un film de Jean-Luc Godard', the US publicity – in accordance with the traditional Hollywood scale of values – made his role secondary to that of the producer Levine, adopting the formula, 'Jean-Luc Godard, director of Joseph E. Levine's *Contempt* . . .'

But the overwhelming focus of the publicity was Brigitte Bardot. 'More bold! More brazen! And much, much more Bardot!' promised a movie poster slogan. The exhibitors' manual, pointing out that 'BB means Big Business', offered every conceivable suggestion for exploiting her image.[42] Tips for merchandising opportunities included in-store promotions for bath towels: 'A great crowd-stopper would be to have a "live" model in the store window, garbed in a towel as Brigitte is in *Contempt*.' Then there was the red open-top sports car, in which Bardot is seen being driven by Jack Palance. 'Don't neglect those promotion-minded car rental agencies,' the manual urged, seemingly oblivious to the fact that the film ends with the two characters being killed in the car in a fatal traffic accident.

The American campaign, which seemed calculated to suppress the true nature of the film, transformed the work of a leading New Wave auteur into *And God Created Woman II*. Yet at the same time it perfectly exemplified the themes that Godard was seeking to explore. 'Whenever I hear the word "culture", I bring out my cheque book,' Prokosch tells Lang as he hires Paul Jarval, the French screenwriter, to fix the script.

Godard was enacting a template that, in movie mythology, was as enduring as the *Odyssey* that Prokosch was seeking to bring to the screen. It contained distant echoes of Jacques Feyder – the director of Garbo in MGM's *The Kiss* (1929) – sadly observing how Hollywood effaces the very individuality it pays huge sums to acquire;[43] of Jean Renoir having to surrender *Swamp Water* (1941) to Darryl Zanuck in the Twentieth Century-Fox cutting-rooms. Prokosch's cheque lay at the root of Hollywood's intellectual conservatism.

In the film, Paul Jarval finally walks out on the project, a gesture that anticipates Godard's own subsequent rejection of Hollywood in real life – although one can't help feeling that it is as much a case of Hollywood rejecting him. For it is easy to find a story of unrequited love in Godard's film career. Rarely can anyone have been so disregarded by the object of his passion.

The extent to which the symbiotic, but deeply oppositional relationship between Hollywood and European cinema has remained a continuing preoccupation of Godard was borne out not only in his series of video essays, *Histoire(s) du Cinéma* (1988–98), but also in his 2006 exhibition at the Centre Pompidou in Paris, *Voyage(s) en Utopie, JLG 1946–2006: A la recherche d'un théorème perdu*. It opened with a series of scale models for display rooms that would have been constructed full-scale had the necessary funding been available.

The first mock-up exhibition space that greeted the visitor presented a wall bearing the slogan: 'What one presents as a failure of communication in love is in fact the positive element in love. This absence of the other is actually its presence as the other.' Nearby, above twin reels of movie film on an editing-bench, was a still of Robert Mitchum in the *Night of the Hunter* (1955); then fixed to the wooden floor by a nail was a paperback copy of Raymond Chandler's *The Long Goodbye*. One didn't have to remember the words on Mitchum's knuckles to find in this first model the visual representation of a love–hate relationship that ran through the six decades of Godard's creative life. Two subsequent mock-ups, which juxtaposed 'Hollywood – the Cinema's Mecca' and 'Fortress Europe', seemed to make its focus explicit.

17

The Children of Tri-X

One of the disparaging terms that is often attributed to Truffaut, but which he never actually used, is *cinéma de Papa*. His chief argument was for a cinema of personal expression. Many of the film-makers he most admired – whether Jean Cocteau, Jean Renoir or Robert Bresson – belonged to Papa's generation. Neither he nor his colleagues on *Cahiers du cinéma* anywhere argued explicitly for a young person's cinema. But nonetheless that term, *cinéma de Papa*, Dad's cinema, is a useful concept to retain, because it captures so well the alienation between the generations that had an inevitable impact on the way the films of so many established directors were received.

If the films that Marcel Carné or Julien Duvivier made in the 1950s are little remembered today, it is because they had ceased to make films that mattered to an increasingly young audience. They had not so much lost their touch as grown out of touch.

The grey hair and tired eyes of Jean Gabin, who, returning to France after the war, seemed to have aged thirty years in ten, epitomised the problem. In Marcel Carné's *Marie du Port*, he plays a middle-aged businessman who becomes attracted to an eighteen-year-old girl. It is a disturbing, ambiguous romance that, to remain on the right side of the vulgar, must proceed with much hesitation, uncertainty and world-weary reflection on the disparity in ages. Carné plays on the complexity of the situation with considerable sophistication, keeping the audience guessing as to which way the romance will go, but it is at the expense of the more visceral quality that Gabin once brought to the cinema. It is hard not to regret the straightforward romantic lead he once was, able in *Quai des brumes* to embrace the seventeen-year-old Michèle Morgan without such agonising.

By the end of the decade he had reached a position beyond ambiguity again when he made the first of three outings as Inspector Maigret in *Maigret tend un piège*, but this was a conventional film, albeit excellently directed by Jean Delannoy, that appealed more to the parents than their children who were dictating the agenda.

To be relevant in this post-war age required the ability to engage with the idealism and individualism that inspired the young. The few directors of the older generation to whom they accorded respect tended to be those who challenged the status quo rather than reinforced it. Jean Renoir, for example, who through most of his career had struggled to make the films he wished to make, was a far more appealing role model for a young person than an industry insider like Jean Delannoy or Julien Duvivier.

That jewel of 'accursed films', *La Règle du jeu*, serves as an interesting benchmark of how the times had changed. So badly misunderstood when it was released in 1939, it became a standard-bearer for the post-war generation of cinephiles. They watched the truncated version in the ciné-clubs, recognising it as a misunderstood masterpiece in a way that their parents had not been able to appreciate. It seemed no accident that the screening of the restored version, which took place at the Venice Film Festival in 1959, coincided with the arrival of the New Wave, for the film seemed to belong much more to the new generation than the old one that had not known how to appreciate it.

'For all of us, my generation of French film-makers,' observed Louis Malle, '*La Règle du jeu* was the absolute masterpiece.'[1] His third film, *Les Amants* – made in 1958 when he was only twenty-six – seems to offer a conscious reworking for his generation. Jeanne Moreau plays the young upper-class wife of a provincial newspaper proprietor, Henri Tournier (Alain Cuny). To escape the tedium of her unhappy marriage, she often goes to Paris to visit her polo-playing lover, Raoul, or friend, Maggy.

Suspecting the situation, her husband invites Raoul and Maggy to join them for a weekend at their country estate. On her way home, Jeanne's car breaks down. A young motorist, Bernard Dubois-Lambert (Jean-Marc Bory), gives her a lift. He turns out to come from a similarly privileged background, but he confides to her that he 'avoids all those awful people' – the simple 2CV he drives is a measure of his rejection. When they arrive at the estate, Jeanne's husband invites Bernard to spend the weekend with the rest of the party.

Albeit on a smaller scale, the situation echoes *La Règle du jeu*, in which the Marquis de la Cheyniest invites into his home a stranger who has romantic intentions towards his wife. Waiting at table with the faultless deference of a trusted retainer is Gaston Modot, as if Schumacher – dismissed in Renoir's film for killing a guest – has been able successfully to resume his life for a different master.

In *La Règle du jeu*, the characters are trapped in confusion, scarcely knowing what they want, let alone how to obtain it. In their pre-war malaise, they seem incapable of breaking away from an ossified society on the point of collapse. But a generation later, Malle depicts a world in which a new capacity for individual action makes such escape possible. Over the weekend Jeanne turns her back on her 'hateful husband and almost ridiculous lover' to begin an affair with Bernard. After a night of lovemaking and fulfilled sexual desire, the two drive off together in Bernard's car, Jeanne abandoning not only her husband and lover, but also her sleeping daughter. In making their decisive, brutal break with the past, they anticipate a new more egalitarian era, in which individual freedom and self-realisation would increasingly override old ideas of duty, class or conventional morality.

Les Amants may not have attempted any of the revolutionary formal experiments of *A bout de souffle*, but it indicated the more open, hedonistic and sexually explicit direction in which the cinema as a whole was heading. Malle was not a member of the *Cahiers du cinéma* group that formed the core of New Wave film-makers, but it was impossible not to acknowledge his significance. '*Les Amants* is a very important film,' wrote Eric Rohmer. 'It marks . . . the coming to power of a new generation in a French cinema that since the war seemed to be in the grip of men in their forties and then their fifties.'[2] François Truffaut called the film 'the first night of love in the cinema'.[3]

Malle was one of those people who regarded the 'New Wave' as much more an exercise in publicity than a label with any great meaning. In an interview with *Le Monde* in 1959, he commented: 'A new school is characterised by aesthetic rules being turned upside down. Up until now, the only film that has changed the substance of the cinema is *Hiroshima mon amour*.'[4] Godard had yet to make *A bout de souffle*, but Malle's point still held. Godard was Godard, not typical of a coherent school. 'It would be ridiculous to attempt to classify the new *auteurs*. They come from everywhere, and go in many different directions.'[5]

Renoir spoke of the Spirit of '36, when the idealism of the Popular Front unleashed a new energy. Perhaps, in the same way, one could speak of a Spirit of '59, which found a common meaning in the ideas of youth and innovation, but actually comprised many very different camps. This spirit existed less in a shared sensibility than in shared circumstances and age. A new sense of ease, spontaneity and freedom, in its contrast with the necessarily more rigid practices of the past, emphasised the gulf between the generations. As Malle observed,

In a way, we were children of this new Kodak film, the Tri-X, because suddenly it was possible to shoot in the streets, to shoot in real interiors, with very little light, which means a small crew, much smaller budgets, and it gave us the freedom to work infinitely closer to reality than the older generation. The New Wave was a return to what has always been dominant in the French cinema: realism.[6]

In the same year that Truffaut won the Best Director prize at Cannes for *Les 400 Coups*, Alain Resnais's *Hiroshima mon amour* was shown out of competition. It was hailed as one of the great triumphs of the New Wave, but what is most striking is its singularity. Like Jean-Pierre Melville, Resnais had been given a home-movie camera when he was a child. His first film was made when he was only ten, from a script by the actor Gaston Modot that he had found in a magazine. In 1943, he was among the first generation of students to study at the film school IDHEC.

Resnais's intense passion for film-making was evident, but the significant stepping-stones on his road to prominence were not personal projects that he initiated himself but commissions. They seem not so much representative of the auteur cinema associated with the New Wave as examples of the immense value of close collaboration.

In 1946, Resnais was asked by Gaston Diehl, the founder of an art appreciation society called Les Amis de l'Art, to make a short film about Van Gogh. The film was shot with a 16mm camera in Resnais's Paris flat. Based on a script by Diehl, it was in essence an editor's film that reconstructed Van Gogh's life through a montage of his drawings and paintings. The twenty-minute short was shown to producer Pierre Braunberger, who asked Resnais to make it again in 35mm. Yet again, Braunberger proved himself to be the French cinema's major breaker of new talent. The new version won a prize at the Venice Film Festival in 1948 and an Oscar for Best Short Subject in 1950.

Resnais went on to make more art documentaries, the most notable of which was a collaboration with Chris Marker in 1953. Commissioned by a pan-African magazine, *Présence afri-caine*, their film, *Les Statues meurent aussi* (Even Statues Die), featured a commentary, written by Marker, that criticised the way that Western exploitation divorced African art from its true context and meaning. 'When men die, they enter history. When statues die, they enter art. This botany of death is what we call culture.' The film won the Prix Jean Vigo, which was established in 1951 by the writer and publisher Claude Aveline, who had known Vigo, to celebrate 'independence of spirit and originality of style'. As if it were a concomitant of the award, the film was also banned in France for eight years.

In 1954, Resnais edited Agnès Varda's first film, *La Pointe Courte*, but played as crucial a role, according to Varda's own account, in providing her with the film education that she did not have at that time. Resnais's approach was marked by an absence of preconceptions and an openness to the ideas of his collaborators. He considered his chief contribution to be creating the structure that could give those ideas their best expression. 'I am a waffle-iron,' he commented. 'You put in the dough, and it spreads itself freely.'[7] But he was also an inspired catalyst, able to develop concepts that might not otherwise have come fully into existence. In 1955, producer Anatole Dauman, of Argos Films, invited Resnais to make a documentary about the Nazi concentration camps. Wanting to work with someone who had first-hand experience of the camps, Resnais collaborated with the writer Jean Cayrol, whose *Poèmes de la nuit et brouillard* chronicled his experiences as a survivor of the Mauthausen concentration camp. The resulting film, *Nuit et brouillard*, won the Prix Jean Vigo in 1956.

Argos Films then invited Resnais to make a documentary on the atomic bomb. It was a project that once again took decisive shape out of an interaction. Wishing to find an angle on a subject whose very immensity defied a direct approach, he began to think of writers he might work with. Françoise Sagan was suggested, but he thought of Marguerite Duras, because he had greatly admired her novel *Moderato cantabile*. Their discussion of the idea suggested a new framework which would intermingle fact and fiction. Resnais reconstructed their conversation:

Here we are drinking beer or tea and the day is carrying on as usual. So the film we ought to be making is not at all the one that was planned, that is, with the atomic bomb in the foreground. In fact, it should be what you might call a traditional love story, in which the atomic bomb would be in the background.[8]

The fact that the project was a joint venture with a Japanese production company played a significant part in dictating the form that love story would take.

Because Resnais was committed to filming in Japan in August 1958, Duras had only nine weeks to write a script. But in an article that she wrote immediately after the script was finished,[9] she expressed the view that shortage of time contributed valuable immediacy. It was an immediacy that may have been due to the force of circumstance, but was nonetheless an important ingredient in whatever it was that set the 'Spirit of '59' apart from the conventional film industry. Considering the speed with which the script had taken shape, she mused:

One can even wonder whether certain subjects that wait two years to be made don't rot through excessive time . . . And whether the stale tone of some big international films doesn't result from this costly dragging-out of adaptors, screenwriters and directors, who feel obliged to wear themselves out, if not exhaust a subject, before tackling it with a camera.

Resnais encouraged Duras to give free rein to her poetic conception of the story without worrying about the needs of the cinema. 'We're lucky,' he told her, 'because we're not making an expensive film. We can say more or less what we like. So write exactly what you wish.' And on another occasion: 'If our film is shown in just one cinema, that will be a triumph. So follow your instincts.'

In what seems to have been a remarkably harmonious meeting of minds, Duras was struck by the absence of film-industry jargon: 'Not once in nine weeks of working together, did Resnais say the sort of things you hear film people say endlessly: "In the cinema, you see, the perspective is different. In the cinema, you see, that doesn't work. In the cinema, you see, plausibility is vital . . ."'

Arriving in Japan, Resnais maintained a regular correspondence with Duras, sending her photographs of the locations. To help him determine the correct length of the shots, he listened repeatedly to a recording of her reading the screenplay. Yet as evident as the unity of purpose between the creators was a dislocation that mirrored that of the two characters in the story, with their respective pasts briefly crossing to take on new meaning. *Hiroshima mon amour* took form out of Duras's fragments of memory and emotion, but also Renais's integrating eye, marshalling the pieces into a mosaic of refracted meaning.

It was a film that clearly had two authors rather than one, but whose essence lay not in the authorship of one or the other, but in the blend of contrasting, though complementary sensibilities. As the writer Molly Haskell argued: 'The tension was between Resnais's impersonal, montage-oriented approach and the sensuously autobiographical . . . sensibility of Duras.'[10] But the influence of Agnès Varda's *La Pointe Courte*, with its interplay between the relationship of a couple and a strange place, also seems significant. 'I wanted the couple to be something perfectly abstract,' Varda commented of her film, 'a man and a woman who had no names, no jobs.'[11] In *Hiroshima mon amour*, Renoir resumed the same dreamlike distance that had characterised the Varda film, choosing philosophical and symbolic engagement with the characters over any close identification with them as individuals.

The magazine *Cahiers du cinéma* considered the film to be of such importance that, under the title *Hiroshima, notre amour*, it published a round-table discussion to mark its release.[12] Contributors to the conversation included Jacques Doniol-Valcroze, Jean-Luc Godard, Jacques Rivette and Eric Rohmer.

Calling Resnais 'a cubist . . . the first modern film-maker of the sound film', Rohmer suggested that *Hiroshima mon amour* marked a turning point in which the cinema was leaving behind its classical period.

I think that in a few years, in ten, twenty or thirty years, we shall know whether *Hiroshima* was the most important film since the war, the first modern film of sound cinema, or whether it was possibly less important than we thought. In any case, it is an extremely important film, but it could be that it will even gain stature with the years.

Expressing the general sense of awe at Resnais's achievement, Jacques Doniol-Valcroze commented, 'We all feel quite weak when we are confronted with him.' Rohmer joked, 'It's lucky he stays on the Left Bank of the Seine, and we keep to the Right Bank.' Comparing him to Stravinsky and Picasso, Godard expressed his admiration for a film that, being 'without cinematic references', constantly surprised him. Elaborating, he explained that 'seeing *Hiroshima* gave one the impression of watching a film that would have been quite inconceivable in terms of what one was already familiar with in the cinema'.

It was significant timing, because that summer Godard was just about to start making his own first feature film. Shot over four weeks in August and September 1959, *A bout de souffle* was filmed in the same on-the-run manner that Marguerite Duras had found so inspiring. It was a conscious decision to take the modernist path that *Hiroshima mon amour* had opened. 'All was permitted,' commented Godard. 'I said to myself, "There has already been Bresson, we just had *Hiroshima*, a certain kind of cinema has just ended – well, then, let's put the final period to it: let's show that anything goes."'[13]

The strategy led to spectacular dividends. Even before it had opened, *A bout de souffle* quickly became the most talked-about film of the time. Brash and loud, it stole the limelight from *Hiroshima mon amour*, so that by the time it opened in the United States in early 1961, Godard, not Resnais, was hailed as the revolutionary new figure taking the cinema into its modernist future. *Time* celebrated a 'cubistic thriller' of 'eye-opening originality'.[14] It praised the way the film 'distorts, rearranges, relativises time – much as Picasso manipulated space in *Les demoiselles d'Avignon*' – as though this were startlingly new, when really, alluding back to Resnais, it was much more an example of that penchant for quotation that later audiences would come to recognise in Godard.

In France, it was easier to perceive the connection. Writing in *Cahiers du cinéma* soon after the film's French release in the spring of 1960, Luc Moullet observed:

If *A bout de souffle* is better than *Hiroshima*, that is because Godard had seen and written about *Hiroshima* before he started his own film; not because Godard is better than Resnais . . . The young French cinema is the work of very different personalities, but is also partly a collective work.

What seems most striking today is the unpredictable way in which the work of that collective unfolded. For all the great appetite that the New Wave itself showed for theory, subsequent attempts to detect a coherent philosophy seem to be codifying things that happened through chance or necessity rather than in conscious pursuit of any fixed style. Perhaps the most important rule was that there were no rules. Thanks to the *prime de qualité* – and Kodak Tri-X – individuals were free to pursue their own creative paths, to an extent that had not been possible before.

The creative energy of the time, carefully harnessed and supported by the CNC, meant that there was an explosion of distinctive new talent in the French cinema of the 1960s. This is the period in which not only Godard, Rivette, Truffaut and Chabrol established themselves, but also many other film-makers who had no particular connection to *Cahiers*. The cinema of personal expression that the *Cahiers* critics had fought for during the 1950s had unquestionably arrived.

But it was far from being an unalloyed triumph. Resnais may have been content to see *Hiroshima mon amour* play in only one cinema, but the *Cahiers* critics had wanted to change the audience's tastes. The true breakthrough would occur only once they had proved that they could win the mainstream audience that belonged to the older generation of directors they so derided.

A bout de souffle seemed to herald the moment. Luc Moullet wrote upon its release:

It is the first film to be released in cinemas whose audience is essentially made up of 'the public at large', the 'average public' which is untouched by snobbishness. This is the fulfilment of what for ten years has been the new generation's most cherished desire: to make films not just for the art-house audience, but films which will be successful on the magic screens of the Gaumont-Palace, the Midi-Minuit, the Normandie, Radio City Music Hall.[15]

A bout de souffle went on to sell 380,000 tickets on its first French run.[16] It was a solid success that eclipsed *Hiroshima mon amour* (255,000),[17] and compared well with that of *Les 400 Coups* (450,000).[18] But it did not represent the direction in which Godard was heading. Nailing his colours to modernism, he pursued an iconoclastic path that increasingly defied popular comprehension. He sank to a spectacular low point – in box-office terms – when his 1963 film *Les Carabiniers* sold only three thousand tickets. Of his fellow directors in the New Wave, Truffaut and Chabrol turned out to be the most commercially attuned. But even their films failed to reach much beyond their core art-house constituency. In terms of sales, perhaps the most successful director of the New Wave generation was Louis Malle, whose *Au revoir les enfants* sold 3.4 million tickets in 1987.

It only requires one to look at a list of the top-grossing films at the French box-office, to appreciate that the mainstay of the French film industry remained a conservative cinema that depended upon the traditional attractions of star and genre.

In the year of *Les 400 Coups* the top-grossing film at the French box office was *La Vache et le prisonnier*, which sold 8.8 million tickets.[19] It starred the comedian Fernandel, who was a huge box-office star in France. Based on a successful novel, with a script by Henri Jeanson, it told the story of a French prisoner-of-war, who works on a farm in Germany. He makes his escape by walking off with a cow and leading it through the German countryside back to France. The narrative follows the rather touching relationship that develops between the prisoner and the cow, called Marguerite, as they encounter various adventures on the road, It is a well-made, touching, unapologetically sentimental but intelligent film, with a gentle humour and much scenic beauty. Boasting the considerable warmth and charm of Fernandel as its chief asset, it was made not for urban sophisticates but the large family audience that still existed at the time. Intended to be uplifting rather than thought-provoking, it represented no particular landmark in film art, but nonetheless possessed the broad popular appeal that sustains a mainstream film industry. It brings to my mind – and perhaps even inspired – the 1969 Hollywood-financed film *Hannibal Brooks*. In that film, Oliver Reed is a British prisoner-of-war who works in a German zoo as an elephant-keeper. When the zoo is bombed, he is ordered to take the elephant to the safety of a zoo in Austria, but eventually leads the animal to freedom in Switzerland. The process by which Marguerite the cow became Hannibal the elephant reflects the Hollywood instinct for spectacle on the greatest possible scale, but, within the necessarily reduced budgets at their disposal, this was something to which producers in the mainstream French film industry also aspired.

For thirty years, until it was overtaken by the Hollywood film *Titanic* (1997), the most successful box-office film of all time in France was *La Grande Vadrouille* (1965), which sold 17.2 million tickets. A comedy about two Parisians who help an RAF air crew to escape from occupied France, it paired together the two comedians Bourvil and Louis de Funès. Comedy was the single most successful genre at the French box-office. Few such films ever successfully made the journey to Britain or the United States, even if they traded on the same universal ingredients. When Louis de Funès appeared as the bumbling police officer Ludovic Cruchot in *Le Gendarme de Saint-Tropez* (1964), the character clearly took its inspiration from Peter Sellers' Inspector Clouseau, who had made his debut in *The Pink Panther* the previous year. Selling 7.8 million tickets, *Le Gendarme de Saint-Tropez* was the first in a hugely popular series that ended only with *Le Gendarme et les gendarmettes* in 1982.

It was understandable if the directors who made these films often expressed mild contempt for a new generation who won huge press coverage among intellectuals both in France and abroad but not an audience. 'I'm afraid too many of today's film-makers make movies that cause people of sound mind to prefer books to the cinema,' commented Henri Verneuil. 'I refuse to include myself among those directors who, rather than make films that the ordinary spectator can see and enjoy, are concerned only to show and talk about themselves.'[20] For the director of *La Grande Vadrouille*, Gérard Oury, who specialised in comedy, the criterion of success was very simple: whether he made an audience laugh or not. 'I do not make films for small groups of aesthetes. I think that entertainment as a whole – theatre, cinema, television, radio – needs to address itself to the mainstream. Films that are not made for the public do not interest me.'[21]

These directors invariably showed a huge admiration for Hollywood. It provided the ultimate model for their conception of the cinema: a business that existed to provide popular entertainment (rather than art) that appealed to everyone, no matter what their background. Key formative influences for Jean Girault, the director of the *Gendarme* films, were the great American comedies. 'How I loved to see Capra's *You Can't Take It With You*, *Mr Smith Goes to Town*, *It Happened One Night*, or *Good Sam* by Leo McCarey, that wonderful film-maker who had been Tod Browning's assistant and started out as a director making Laurel and Hardy films. I'd skip school to see these films.'[22] Like Girault, a director who specialised in comedy, Gérard Oury also admitted a debt to the great Hollywood comedy directors. Regarding them as touchstones for his own film-making, he believed that an important aspect of their appeal lay in their universality. 'Humour is not only a defining feature of mankind, but also a mark of international brotherhood much more appealing than tears. Laughter is a collective response that has no frontier, a cultural phenomenon as important as any other.'[23]

In 1969, Oury tried to put this theory into practice with his comedy caper film *Le Cerveau* (*The Brain*), about a multi-million-dollar train robbery. Recorded in French and English, it boasted an international cast that included David Niven, Jean-Paul Belmondo and Eli Wallach. Released in the United States by the major Hollywood distributor Paramount, it opened in the 'showplace of America', Radio City Music Hall. The *New York Times* thought it 'one of the freshest, fastest, nimblest and funniest comedies to hit town', [24] even although it was from 'France, of all places'. But although it sold 5.5 million tickets in France, the box-office in both America and Britain was disappointing. Derek Malcolm, who reviewed the film for the *Guardian*, found he laughed only twice in a hundred minutes. 'The chief reason, I suspect, is that international comedies, designed to appeal to everybody, usually end up appealing to fewer than national comedies designed primarily for home consumption.'[25]

Henri Verneuil, who shared Oury's love of American cinema, made a similar bid for success on the Hollywood scale. In 1968 he directed a Western in Mexico, *La Bataille de San Sebastian* (*Guns for San Sebastian*), which starred Anthony Quinn and Charles Bronson. Rather than pursue a distinct European style, after the spaghetti westerns that were so fashionable at the time, his wish was 'to capture the spirit and style of the great American films of the genre'.[26] Keeping alive 'the idea of true international cinema', he hoped to find the universal language that Hollywood seemed able to command so effortlessly. But he too proved unable to convert mainstream popularity at home into success abroad.

Dubbed into English, *Guns for San Sebastian* was distributed by Metro-Goldwyn-Mayer in the United States, where it made little impression at the box-office. Describing the film as 'numbingly bland', the critic Vincent Canby speculated that maybe one reason why was 'because the film, another example of one of those international co-production projects, is so completely de-nationalised. It was produced and directed by Frenchmen, written by Americans, scored by an Italian and played by Americans and Mexicans. No one wins.'[27] The *Observer* dismissed it as 'of familiar convention and not much originality'.[28] There was very little that singled out *La Bataille de San Sebastian* as a film that had been made in 1968 – it might as easily have been 1958. It was as well made as *La Vache et le prisonnier*, but good construction was a quality that Hollywood had no trouble in providing itself. For a French film to do no more than that was merely to provide unwanted competition.

Verneuil's very attachment to the conventional mainstream values of film-making was the reason why he had a large audience within France but was disregarded outside. Indeed, the mumblings of discontent were evident even before the New Wave appeared on the scene. *The Village Feud*, a film that Verneuil had made in 1951, arrived in Britain to a luke-warm reception four years later. 'There is nothing wrong with the French film *The Village Feud*,' wrote the *Guardian*, 'except that many films like it have come from France before.'[29] As the reviewer went on to enumerate all the film's sterling, but very familiar qualities, the ennui residing only just beneath the surface was patent.

The universality of Hollywood, which these more commercial French directors so admired, explained why their own attempts at universality failed to make any lasting impression. What need did an international audience have for the pratfalls of Louis de Funès when it already enjoyed the pratfalls of Peter Sellers?

The value of the French cinema outside France lay in the extent to which it was different. It had to be new. This was true in the 1920s when Jacques Feyder experienced for himself the hunger for 'grist from outside' with which Hollywood sought to restore its edge.[30] It was true in the 1930s when British and US critics marvelled at the way directors such as Carné, Duvivier and Renoir were able to make films with an adult maturity and realism that eluded Hollywood. And it was perhaps especially true in the 1960s when, in the weakening grip of the Code, Hollywood had never seemed so badly in need of reinvention.

Perceived as more laboratory than factory, the point of the French cinema in the Anglophone world had always been to lead the way. It was why the directors of the New Wave, although

they were of only minority appeal in their own country, dominated the attention of American and British critics, while the big
commercial film-makers, such as Oury, Girault or Verneuil, were
scarcely even heard of. But the true identity of the French cinema, so often expressing itself through internal conflict, lies in
the uneasy relationship between these two poles of experiment
and convention.

The psychological thrillers that Claude Chabrol made through
the 1960s capture the dynamic perfectly. The characters in these
films live in a world of wealth, privilege and safety, but the very
predictability of their paradise generates a dullness and fear of
bourgeois complacency that seems to compel them to challenge
the limits. In *La Femme infidèle* (1969), the couple Charles
and Hélène only understand why they love each other after the
affair that leads to their separation, not before. Transgression is
presented as a road that leads towards destruction, but also to
understanding.

Chabrol's films themselves were, in their style and intelligence, the perfect products with which to amuse the gilded class
who featured in them. By the end of the decade he had fashioned a formula that challenged his mentor Alfred Hitchcock
in the certainty of expectation that his films created. But the
very routine, discipline and order that he showed in his fidelity to the genre evoked a sense of icy precision and bourgeois
security that mirrored the world of his characters. While their
stifling circumstances led them into crime, he sought a refuge
from complacency in pushing the boundaries of his chosen
genre. An interesting alter ego for him is the advertising executive Charles Masson in *Juste avant la nuit* (1971). Not content
with the materialistic creativity of his profession, he is writing a
novel and displays a taste in music, art and decor that challenges
established conventions. At a dinner party one evening his architect friend, François, explains the look of the modernist house
he has designed for him. 'It was Charles's idea,' he says. 'He
wanted everything to be modern. He pushed me much further

than I would otherwise have dared go.' Reminding Charles of his underlying motivation, Francois explains, 'It's to do with your fear of becoming bourgeois. You said, quite rightly, that a little taste of the avant-garde avoids sclerosis.' The reasoning seems to shed some light not only on the paradoxically bourgeois but progressive Chabrol, but also on the role of the New Wave within French cinema – and perhaps also, on another level, that of French cinema within world cinema.

Running through the French cinema lay a polarity between chaos and order; flair and convention; art and commerce. The reconciling principle was Cocteau's 'spirit of contradiction'.

Towards the end of the 1960s that spirit produced yet another of the periodic revolts of which Cocteau spoke. This time the rebel to slip between the gears of the machine was Henri Langlois, founder of the Cinémathèque française. On Friday 9 February 1968 he was dismissed from his post as its director. The day afterwards, several prominent New Wave directors, who had famously passed their formative years at the Cinematheque devouring the films that Langlois had tracked down for them, expressed their outrage at the decision. The protests quickly snowballed. Not only did the older generation of French directors – Bresson, Renoir, Clair – join in expressing their solidarity for Langlois, but so did just about every icon of world cinema – from Charlie Chaplin to Luis Buñuel – who was still alive to make their feelings felt. Most agreed to withdraw permission to have their films shown at the Cinémathèque unless Langlois were reinstated. In the early evening of Wednesday 14 February, three thousand people turned up outside the Cinémathèque's theatre in the Palais du Chaillot in response to François Truffaut's call in *Combat* newspaper, but found their way barred. The police charged in an attempt to clear the crowd, knocking some people to the ground. But the stand-off ended only when Jean-Luc Godard gave the order to disperse. Two days later, a 'Committee for the Defence of the Cinémathèque' was formed, with Jean Renoir as its honorary president. There was even the extraordinary spectacle of Marcel Carné marching in public with his previously sworn enemies, François Truffaut and Jean-Luc Godard.

Described by Cocteau as the 'dragon who jealously guards our treasures', Langlois was a living legend. In 1935, when he was only twenty-one, he began an active campaign to save films from the silent era that in the new age of sound were being cast on to the scrap heap. He scoured flea markets and fairs to put together the beginnings of an archive, at first storing the rusty old cans of film in the bathtub of his parents' flat. With his friend Georges Franju, he established Le Cercle du Cinéma, a ciné-club that dedicated itself to showing silent films. Under his direction the Cinémathèque française was established in September 1936 as a non-profit association. Its founding members included Louis Lumière, Ferdinand Zecca and Georges Méliès. Over the next thirty years, Langlois used his energy, enthusiasm and personal charm to build for the Cinémathèque one of the largest film archives in the world. It was of such unquestionable importance that it began to receive financial support from the state – a process that, involving forms of accountability entirely contrary to Langlois's nature, had led to the present conflict.

Writing in Langlois's support the day after his dismissal, the film-maker Alexandre Astruc explained the peculiarly personal nature of his achievement:

The second Henri Langlois leaves the Cinémathèque française, the Cinémathèque ceases to exist. It's not a question, as one might think, of an institution in which one official is being replaced by another for reasons that can be discussed; it's about a private, personal, individual and unique achievement – the blood and flesh, the daughters, wife and children, the sole property of Henri Langlois himself, a private individual who, for reasons entirely understandable, one day felt the need to shelter behind an official administration.[31]

Comparing Langlois to an auteur film-maker, Astruc explained that the Cinémathèque was so imbued with his spirit that it could not function without him.

It was too irresistible a comparison for Godard not to steal when he took part in a press conference a week later:

The director is not just a poet; he is a technician of poetry, or the poet of the technical. The two are totally inseparable. And Henri Langlois, for me, is one of France's greatest directors. In fact, you could say that Henri Langlois was the director and writer of a film called *La Cinémathèque française*, with the CNC as his production manager and the French state as his overall producer.[32]

Putting in a word for that state, the Minister of Culture, André Malraux, had the difficult task of explaining the other side. 'It is indispensable to assure that the management of the Cinémathèque be carried out in a less personal and more controllable manner,' he declared in a statement issued two weeks after Langlois's dismissal. 'What M. Langlois likes, he did well; he did less well what he did not like.' In return for its financial support the state expected 'a minimum of order and clarity' in accounting for expenditure, but Langlois had consistently refused to cooperate with government officials.[33]

It was possible to construct an even more powerful case against Langlois than Malraux dared in the incendiary climate. Capricious, autocratic and tribal, Langlois could be as offhand and rude to people he did not like as he was warm to those he did. He worked brilliantly to secure both acquisition of, and access to, the Cinémathèque's treasures, about which he could talk with unparalleled knowledge, eloquence and perception, but he was less conscientious about the more mundane tasks of cataloguing, preservation and storage. Rusty film cans were piled up higgledy-piggledy in the courtyard of the Cinémathèque's offices at the Rue de Courcelles, until one day in 1959 they caught fire, destroying hundreds of films.[34] Guarding prints that were often of dubious provenance, as well as frequently screening them without legal entitlement, Langlois was so secretive that no one knew exactly what the Cinémathèque contained, except himself and his devoted but sometimes equally difficult colleague

Mary Meerson.* Relying habitually on informal understandings and word-of-mouth agreements, he ran the place in a way that encouraged uncertainty and confusion.

Langlois loved films and film-makers, but disliked rules and bureaucrats. His fiefdom had been run with a passion that involved often maddening arbitrariness, but it took an extraordinary myopia on the part of the state not to appreciate that his inspiration, charisma and influence, as well as the loyalty he commanded, more than made up for his failings. The long-term planning, prudent management and cost-effective but soulless efficiency that the government's chosen successor, Pierre Barbin, might have been able to offer in his place inspired no one.

During his first day in his new job, Barbin bumped into one of the many walking legends whom Langlois had taken under his wing.[35] Sister of the director Jean Epstein and a close collaborator of Jean Benoit-Levy, Marie Epstein had been a leading figure in the pre-war French cinema. Rather than showing any recognition of who she was, Barbin seemed more concerned to impress his authority. 'I am the new director of the Cinémathèque,' he declared. 'The age of the bathtub is over, you understand; it is now the age of the Palais du Chaillot.'

'And who led the Cinémathèque from the bathtub to Chaillot?' asked Epstein.

With some embarrassment, Barbin had to concede that it was Langlois.

'So what are you doing here in his place?'

The encounter epitomised the nature of a struggle that was finally about the respective values of sentiment and reason. A more imaginative, less arrogant government might have found a better way to deal with the situation. Instead, its high-handedness served only to unite against itself the various factions of the French film community, who were more used to squabbling amongst themselves. Realising that it had undertaken a battle

* The widow of the famous art director Lazare Meerson.

that it could not win, the government finally backed down. On 22 April, Langlois was reinstated. The government ended its subsidy of the Cinématheque, but agreed to pay off its debts, allowing Langlois to take up the reins again with a clean slate.

As Truffaut observed,[36] the battle of the Cinémathèque turned out to be just a trailer to the main feature. A few weeks later, on Friday 10 May, the 21st Cannes Film Festival opened, with a screening of a new stereophonic 70mm print of *Gone with the Wind*. 'It looks as if this is going to be a nice festival, interesting, calm and not terribly exciting,' observed Richard Roud, who was covering the event for the *Guardian*.[37] But while the delegates admired the Technicolor flames of Atlanta, France was in the midst of its own civil war, with students confronting police across barricades on the streets of Paris. Over the weekend there were protests against the de Gaulle government in other big cities across the country, and the trade unions called a one-day general strike and demonstration for the Monday. In response to this situation, the festival organisers decided to postpone two films in competition that were scheduled to be shown on that day – *Peppermint Frappé* and *Trilogy*. But the disturbances in the country only worsened as the week progressed.

On Saturday 18 May an event had been organised in which Godard, Truffaut and Resnais were expected to discuss Langlois and the Cinémathèque affair. But instead they used the occasion to invite film-makers to withdraw their films from the festival, in sympathy with the students and the workers. Less than an hour later, Godard led a group into the festival auditorium, where they tried to prevent the screening of the scheduled film – or, rather, rescheduled film, as it was *Peppermint Frappé*, which had been put back from earlier in the week. A fight broke out on the stage and Godard was knocked down in the scuffle, but his supporters succeeded in taking over the projection booth, and the screening was cancelled. Later that day the jury disbanded when four of its members – Monica Vitti, Terence Young, Roman

Polanski and Louis Malle – resigned in sympathy with the strikers. The festival was over.

From the outside the closure looked like a spontaneous outburst of solidarity, but in his report on what had happened, the director of the festival, Robert Favre le Bret, claimed that it was a premeditated plot by a small group of militant students and film technicians, who were looking for 'some grand gesture to mark their desire to "renew" the French cinema'.[38] They found a willing accomplice in Jean-Luc Godard, 'who, as ever self-serving, proved that a Swiss anarchist can sometimes be more intolerant and fanatical than a defrocked priest. With the help of some French directors, who in the past had benefited enormously from this very festival, he obtained the resignations of four members of the jury.'[39]

Saturday 18 May 1968 marked the high point of the hubris of Godard and Truffaut. These often arbitrary dictators of taste had once famously taken on the old guard, but now, in their determination to command the agenda, they seemed as ready to prejudice the careers of young directors. 'One of the attractions of this competition', Favre le Bret wrote in his report, 'lay in the fact that out of the twenty-nine films that were to have been shown, about twenty were the work of young directors, seven of whom were presenting their films for the first time.'[40]

The individualism of the New Wave film-makers struck a chord with the spirit of 1968, but at the same time meant that they continued to be at odds with the mainstream film industry. The re-election of de Gaulle in June 1968 with a landslide victory gave some indication of the deeply conservative core of the society that they were challenging. The choice open to them was either to head into a cul-de-sac, or to attempt a modus vivendi that would bring them into the mainstream. Constitutionally wayward, Godard chose the former, making a series of didactic, polemical films that expressed his militant politics but, eschewing conventional narrative, held no appeal for an ordinary audience. If *A bout de souffle* was an attempt to reinvent the cinema, he seemed more intent in the 1970s – perceiving the medium itself to be intrinsically bourgeois – on pioneering a form of anti-cinema.

The accompaniment of his love for the cinema by a corresponding contempt had already been expressed in *Le Mépris* of 1963. But ten years later, this contempt had developed into partial self-loathing. *Tout va bien* offered a critical assault on the film industry, but also a satire on Godard's own previous concessions to that industry.

'To make a film you need money,' a voice comments at the beginning. Perhaps still mindful of the cheque-book that Prokosch brings out in *Le Mépris*, whenever he hears the word 'culture', Godard shows a close-up of an unseen hand signing the many cheques that make up the costs of a film – cast, script and so on – eventually arriving at the biggest cheque of all, which is for the stars. 'And what do you need to attract the stars?' the voice asks. 'Usually a love story.'

The cheques make way for Yves Montand and Jane Fonda walking along a river, but in defiance of the conventional expectations of a glamorous presentation, they are filmed in long shot so we can scarcely see who they are. Godard continues the deliberate mockery by having Fonda, whom Roger Vadim had once famously dubbed the 'American Brigitte Bardot', reprise Bardot's celebrated opening scene from *Contempt*. 'Do you love me?' she asks. 'Yes. I love your eyes,' Montand replies. 'I love your mouth . . .' The familiar catalogue of assets follows. Eyes, mouth, knees, butt, hair, hands. 'So you love me completely?' In *Le Mépris*, Bardot's body is bathed in a resplendent, colour-changing light, as Godard's camera lingers over her limbs, but in *Tout va bien* Fonda's body is concealed beneath black trousers, cardigan and baggy sweater. Godard subverts the star's image, as he goes on to call into question the point of film-making itself.

As much an alter ego for Godard as Piccoli had been in *Le Mépris*, Yves Montand plays a film director who makes commercials. During a brief break from shooting, he makes an impromptu address to the camera, in which he explains the nature of his creative compromise. He had started out as a screenwriter during the New Wave. 'Already a long time ago, all that. A very long time ago.' Even before May 1968, he had grown tired of making 'art films', but the troubles served to stir a political commitment, albeit ambivalent: 'Active in May? Yes, and no. Like everybody else. It was both serious and not serious at the same time.' Once everything had returned to normal, he got an opportunity to make a thriller based on a David Goodis novel, but it seemed to him more honest to make commercials than to dress up a sell-out as art. 'Excuse me, I must get back to the coalface,' he comments as he returns to filming his latest commercial.

As the ironic title suggests, *Tout va bien* depicts a society in which the stand-off of competing forces – whether workers, bosses, trade unionists or politicians – has resulted in a new status quo. The conclusion contains a Godardian cynicism, but the film still gives the impression that May 1968 is a significant turning point in its awakening of a political commitment, albeit one that has little effect.

Tout va bien marked Godard's pointed abandonment of a medium that he now dismissed as a tool of bourgeois complacency. In the year of its release, he left Paris for Grenoble, a city with a tradition of provincial revolution, where he established with Anne-Marie Melville the alternative production and distribution company, Sonimage. Here, in his self-chosen exile, he made a series of video essays for television that analysed the relationship between the media and society.

Godard's renunciation implied that the cinema was too ensnared in the compromises of the entertainment industry to provide an effective medium for political engagement. But the spirit of 1968 encouraged other French film-makers to take an opposite stand. Marcel Ophüls' long documentary, *Le Chagrin et la pitié* (1971), examined the inglorious reality of the French Occupation, a subject that had previously been either treated as a romantic myth of French resistance or passed over in silence. With a dispassionate, unflinching eye, Ophüls set out the whole spectrum of actual behaviour from resistance to collaboration. When the government-controlled French television station, ORTF, refused to broadcast the documentary, on the grounds that it 'destroyed myths that the French people still needed',[41] the film was shown in a small cinema in the Latin Quarter, where it ran uninterrupted for nearly two years. Ophüls' documentary found a fictional counterpart in Louis Malle's *Lacombe Lucien* (1974), which told the story of a teenage boy in rural France who collaborates with the Nazis after he is turned down by the Resistance. But the new climate that followed in the wake of 1968 encouraged film-makers to address the uncomfortable truths of contemporary society as much as those of the past.

With *Z*, Costa-Gavras pioneered what was a new genre in the cinema – the anti-establishment political thriller. Its story about a right-wing government conspiracy to assassinate an opposition leader had the authoritarian politics of 1960s Greece as its background, but its depiction of the dynamics of power and protest had a wider relevance. ''68 was very present in our minds,' observed Costa-Gavras, 'in the use of police and justice in French society too.'[42]

Z connected with audiences in a way that Godard had long ceased to because it addressed a contemporary issue, but also respected the public's wish to be entertained. It had a political message, yet at the same time contained all the conventional elements of star appeal, action and spectacle. 'An immensely entertaining movie,' wrote Vincent Canby in the *New York Times*, 'a topical melodrama that manipulates our emotional responses and appeals to our best prejudices in such satisfying ways that it is likely to be mistaken as a work of fine – rather than popular – movie art.'[43] The remark betrayed the elitism of a critic still steeped in the cinephilia of the New Wave. But it was precisely the ability of *Z* to engage a mass audience that made it important in America. The first French film to be nominated for a Best

Film Oscar since Jean Renoir's *La Grande Illusion* in 1938, *Z* went on to demonstrate its influence in the Hollywood thrillers that would soon be made following its example, such as *The Parallax View* (1974), *Three Days of the Condor* (1975) and *All the President's Men* (1976). Its success in America lay in expanding the boundaries of what seemed possible. This was the traditional role that the French cinema had to play in its relationship with Hollywood. Films that offered a different way of seeing had a place. Films that did not were redundant in a country that had – or was served by – the biggest film industry in the world.

To this extent, our perception of the French cinema in the English-speaking world has been distorted by what might be called the 'Halliday effect'. The 'French Elvis' is a giant of rock'n'roll in his own country, but hardly known outside.

The film *La Piscine* (1969) was made in the same year as *Z*. It is a memorable and impressive psychological thriller, starring Alain Delon, Romy Schneider, Maurice Ronet and Jane Birkin. Delon plays the writer Jean-Paul, who is staying in a luxury villa near St-Tropez with his lover Marianne (Schneider). Their idyllic time together is disturbed by the arrival of Marianne's former boyfriend Harry (Ronet) and his teenage daughter Penelope (Birkin). In a film that recalls the *huis-clos* atmosphere of Pinter and Losey's *Accident*, Jacques Deray directs with great style, flair and feel for the intrinsic tension of the story, while exploiting to the maximum the movie staples of glamour, spectacle and star mythology. The intertextual background that would have helped to enhance the French audience's appreciation of the film included the facts that Delon and Schneider had been offscreen lovers, and that the film was bringing together for the first time in nine years Delon and Ronet, who had played similar roles as rivals in *Plein soleil* (1960), René Clément's excellent (but little-known outside France) adaptation of the Patricia Highsmith novel, *The Talented Mr Ripley*.

Although *La Piscine* was a huge hit in France, it did not receive a cinema release in the United States, despite possessing so many of the visceral pleasures of a Hollywood-style, star-led, narrative cinema. When it finally did make it across the Atlantic, forty years later, in a DVD box-set of Alain Delon movies, it was dismissed by David Kehr in the *New York Times* as 'a sort of middlebrow, commercial correlative to the bourgeois-bashing films that flourished during this period of political upheaval in France', while its director Jacques Deray was 'not a penetrating enough film-maker to go beyond the burnished images'.[44] Such comments reflect a criterion of appreciation that requires French film-makers to operate within a narrow framework of *cinéma d'auteur*, rather than trespassing on Hollywood territory.

In 1972, Deray trespassed to the point of working in Los Angeles itself. *Un homme est mort* was filmed on location in the city. It stars Jean-Louis Trintignant as a French contract killer who carries out his job, only to find that his employers have hired local hitman Roy Scheider to kill him.

With the chase across the city that ensued, Deray created a marvellous urban thriller, as well as providing an extraordinary outsider's view of a city in which Hollywood itself rarely took any sustained interest. But it was too much a case of 'coals to Newcastle' to win the recognition it deserved outside France. A few years previously, British director John Boorman had also come to America to make a film about a hitman in Los Angeles, but the huge success of *Point Blank* (1967) was possible only because the film was fully part of the Hollywood system.

The English-language title of *Un Homme est mort* was *The Outside Man*, which aptly summed up the reality for French directors who chose to work in a mainstream, popular cinema that Hollywood dominated. Through the 1970s and 1980s Jacques Deray made a series of excellent, star-led crime thrillers, but they never achieved any reputation outside France because they were too similar to what Hollywood already produced itself. The same was true of such other mainstream directors as José Giovanni or Georges Lautner.

A means of achieving differentiation from the Hollywood product, the New Wave was a powerful brand that established the *cinéma d'auteur* as the standard for the way in which French cinema was perceived outside France. But built as it was around an elitist film-making that was of minority appeal even within France, the movement served to encourage the French cinema's marginalisation.

While Godard turned his back on the cinema altogether, his former *Cahiers* colleagues were able in the 1970s to fit comfortably within the bourgeois framework, building for themselves solid careers of consistent achievement by refining themes for which they had become known. Chabrol's thrillers and Rohmer's character studies were accomplished, enjoyable and challenging, but they were familiar commodoties. Truffaut showed greater taste for diversity, but his films, which often contained an obvious alter ego, had in common an autobiographical tendency, as well as a distinctive humanist sensibility that seemed unrepentantly to evoke the influence of Jean Renoir. Settling into their middle age, these directors offered the equivalent of the *tradition de qualité* cinema that they had attacked twenty years previously, only now the basis for this tradition was the auteur film. This was the kind of film-making that Godard's alter ego in *Tout va bien* would surely have dismissed as 'a sell-out dressed up as art'.

Around them in the 1970s had sprung up a new generation, who followed the same auteur model. Maurice Pialat's first feature, *L'Enfance nue* (1968), in its relation of the troubled life of a delinquent boy who is fostered by an elderly couple, recalled *Les 400 coups* of François Truffaut, who was one of the film's producers. Much more raw and hard-edged than Truffaut's film, it was a commercial failure when it opened in France, but the new international art cinema, in which film critics and film festivals drove the agenda, assured it a second life. The positive reception, along with the support of the CNC, provided a platform for the series of films that Pialat would go on to make through the 1970s, which chronicled the transitions and turning points, often bleak, that make up ordinary people's lives. *Nous ne vieil-lerons pas ensemble* (1972) charted the slow breakdown of an abusive relationship. *Passe ton bac d'abord* (1978) was about a group of working-class teenagers in their final year at school, for whom the supposed opportunity of the education system seems to offer little meaning or direction. *La Gueule ouverte* (1974) followed the last days of a woman dying from cancer. Pialat's perspective was that of the wise old fly whose wall had seen everything. In each case the view he offered was unsparing, as true to the longueurs and banalities of life as the epiphanies. If these films could be called 'drama', they were of a kind that seemed wilfully to flout the conventional desire of an audience for a tidy resolution.

But this hardly mattered in an art-house cinema whose pur-pose was to deliver edification rather than entertainment. A review of another French film-maker who came to the fore dur-ing the 1970s captured the attitude. It didn't matter that the picaresque, unsympathetic protagonists of Bertrand Blier's film *Les Valseuses* (1974) defied easy audience identification. For, as Peter Schjeldahl observed in the *New York Times*, it 'was not an agreeable movie, but it might be a great one. In any case, it is an important one, both artistically and as a view of modern society that ought to be attended by anyone interested in the way our century is going.'[45] People who went to art houses *were* inter-ested in the way the century was going.

People who went to art houses expected the cinema to attempt a serious engagement with the society in which they lived. In this respect the French cinema did not disappoint, providing a ready forum in which serious artists could address the political and social upheavals of the time.

Dissatisfied with the film adaptations of her novels, Marguerite Duras decided that she would become a film-maker herself. In 1969, she filmed her novel *Détruire, dit-elle*. 'I wanted to get to know it better,' she explained in an interview, 'that's why I filmed it.'[46] Implied in the comment was the refreshing notion that the cinema could develop rather than compromise its literary source.

The ease with which Duras was able to make the transition to the screen was important encouragement for a new wave of women film-makers attempting to articulate feminist concerns of the time. The directors to achieve prominence during the 1970s included Chantal Ackerman, Nina Companeez, Lilian Dreyfus and Diane Kurys. Yet although their films were warmly received at film festivals, they rarely received substantial distribution outside France. Writing on the occasion of the Second International Festival of Women's Films, held in New York in 1976, Molly Haskell articulated the obstacle that faced women film-makers, but would also increasingly stand in the way of French films in general:

The American film industry is geared almost entirely to large-scale star productions, movies with some form of zap or hype or other salable factor. There is no market for the middle-range film, the genuinely subtle or reticent or rarefied . . . There is no market for those movies that are more experimental but less than blockbusters. There is no market for the kinds of films in which French women film-makers are finding their directorial footing, utilising personal insights and experiences within a loosely defined narrative framework, developing an aesthetic that may or may not be feminist – or even (for want of an acceptable definition) distinctly feminine – but that is consciously anti-masculine.[47]

In the decade of *Jaws* and *Star Wars* France was entrenching its reputation as the safe haven for the intelligent film, even if little protection was to be expected outside. One of the more notable arrivals on the scene during the 1970s was Bertrand Tavernier. Rather than write an original script, he chose to film an adaptation of the Georges Simenon novel *L'Horloger de Saint Paul* (1974), inviting the veteran pairing of Jean Aurenche and Pierre Bost to write the screenplay. Since they remained the principal symbols of the *tradition de qualité* that *Cahiers du Cinéma* had attacked, the choice reasserted the idea of the cinema as a collaborative medium. The film's dedication to Jacques Prévert only served to emphasise Tavernier's appreciation of screenwriters, but in the years of the New Wave the culture of film-making had changed too much for the decisive shift towards the director not to be evident in the film itself. Philippe Noiret plays Michel Descombes, a Lyon clockmaker who learns that his son has been arrested for murder. But from the outset Tavernier puts the story to one side. The events that take place seem of less interest to him than the responses they evoke in the characters. An act of murder is a dull thing compared to what leads to it; eventual guilt or innocence less significant than the underlying state of a person's soul. His desire is to delve deep into character and the environments that shape those characters.

But it is a project that involves a disregard for the conventional expectations of narrative. *L'Horloger de Saint-Paul* is often described as a 'thriller', but in truth, sidestepping the usual sources of suspense, it is really much more an anti-thriller. A Bertrand Tavernier film consists of separate still pools of narrative, rather than a continuous flow. The viewer is required to make the appropriate connections himself. The pace is that of a traveller who enjoys the journey as much if not more than the arrival, and will make the most of the opportunities to linger upon the views along the way. After the police inspector has told Descombes about the arrest of his son, he drives him back to Lyon. Dropping him off, he warns him not to leave the city. Tavernier's camera shows Descombes walking along the pavement as the inspector's car drives off. The viewer now expects the next scene, but the camera drifts away from Descombes to offer a panoramic view of the city in which he lives. The cut that eventually takes place is to Descombes' journey home on a tram: still struggling to recover from the shock of the news, he asks a passenger if he may sit down. Tavernier's focus is consistently on the state of mind of the character in his or her environment, rather than the narrative progression.

Tavernier's *Le Juge et l'assassin* (1976), which he made two years later, is the story of the capture, interrogation and conviction of a nineteenth-century serial killer. But once again Tavernier challenges our conventional expectations of the material. He deliberately deflates the intrinsic suspense of such a story in order to focus on the relationship between judge and murderer, which he turns into an ambitious metaphor for the ills of a deeply divided turn-of-the-century France.

Audiences who have been conditioned by the tight, three-act structure of the Hollywood cinema risk finding Tavernier's films half an hour longer than they really need to be. Their enjoyment requires an effort to curb the instinctive desire to know what happens next, appreciating instead the gradual revelation of complex character. It was the necessity for such active intellectual engagement that made the French cinema seem an increasingly esoteric ordeal during the 1970s.

Woody Allen's *Annie Hall* (1976) captured well the reputation it had come to have, as his character Alvy Singer drags a reluctant Annie off to see all four and a half hours of *Le Chagrin et la pitié* (1971). In their now waning numbers, English-speaking audiences went to see a French film because they thought it would be important, not because they expected to enjoy it.

18

From Bresson to Besson

The French cinema during the 1970s was able to boast an impressive variety of film-making talent. But although the films they made garnered much respectful praise, absent was the visceral excitement that films like *Hiroshima mon amour*, *Jules et Jim* or *A bout de souffle* had caused. The French cinema continued to impress the world with its sensitivity and intelligence, but it no longer changed the way the world thought about cinema.

Hollywood had won back the initiative, assimilating the lessons of the New Wave into its own cinema. To its traditional sense of narrative drive and spectacle was added the personal sensibility of a new generation of college-educated film-makers, who were given licence by the studios to chronicle contemporary America with unprecedented realism. The French cinema ceased to seem so appealing once Hollywood had usurped its traditional role to be innovative and was able to produce films like *Easy Rider* (1969), *Midnight Cowboy* (1969), *Dog Day Afternoon* (1975) or *Taxi Driver* (1976).

In 1983, under the headline, 'Into the Trough', the film critic Richard Roud asked who the successors to the New Wave were. 'The short answer is that there are none, or at least none that have been able to impose themselves internationally.'[1]

The Cannes Film Festival that year offered some insight into the nature of the problem the French cinema was facing. Arriving in the second week of the festival, the editor of *Sight and Sound* 'found only one thing on everybody's mind: the new Palais, its vagaries and eccentricities'.[2] A modernist structure of glass and concrete, the building won few friends. The *Cahiers* critic, Serge Toubiana, compared it to 'an ugly ocean liner'.[3] But at least it provided a distraction from the ennui of many of the films that were being screened inside. Richard Roud singled out Yilmaz Guney's *The Wall*, which had been funded by the French Ministry of Culture: 'after fifteen minutes we all got the picture: Turkish jails are terrible places and the prisoners are atrociously treated. Then the film goes remorselessly on, saying the same thing over and over again for another hour and three-quarters.'[4] But an even more profound index of a new impatience was the reception reserved for the last film of that great icon of the French art cinema, Robert Bresson.

A strong favourite to win the Palme d'Or, *L'Argent* received near-unanimous praise from the critics. But the jury chose instead to award the festival's top prize to the Japanese film *The Ballad of Narayama*, directed by Shohei Imamura. The eighty-one-year-old Bresson might easily have found a hidden message in this story of a healthy old woman who insists that her son observe the village tradition of abandoning her on the summit of Mount Narayama when she reaches the age of seventy, but the festival jury had the grace to award him a special new prize for the 'Cinéma du Création', even if he had to share it with Andrei Tarkovsky.

The award ceremony served to underline the ambivalence about his commanding place in the canon of world cinema. As he walked up to received his award from Orson Welles, catcalls could be heard from the audience. 'Bresson has managed to start a civil war among the festival-goers,' commented the newspaper *Le Matin*.[5] While the critics mostly welcomed the film as 'perhaps Bresson's most perfect and accomplished' masterpiece, the ordinary public regarded it as unwatchable.

In a piece for *Cahiers*, 'Bresson, *L'Argent* et son spectateur', the writer Alain Bergala singled out Bresson's refusal to make concessions to the audience as an important essence of his cinema.

He has always shown an instinctive horror for all the give-and-take that is part of the usual tacit understanding between film-maker and spectator: I give you a little bit of psychology, a few clues; you accept my embellishments of style and meaning. But with every shot, every line and every nuance of Bresson, the audience must either take it or leave it. *L'Argent* is a film that allows no negotiation with its audience.[6]

While more conventional film-makers regarded their job as turning money into spectacle on the screen, Bergala had the impression that Bresson used his larger-than-usual budget of 12.7 million francs to the opposite effect. It was there to distil away the confusion of colours, over-performance and gratuitous style that usually encumbered the cinema, leaving behind a sublime purity for those of the audience who had been able to stay the course.

The trouble was that few people did stay the course. *L'Argent* was 'not an easy film to enjoy', wrote Andrew Sarris in an article for *Village Voice* that captured the dilemma with the faintest praise.

Bressonian blankness has become an acting style all its own, and even non-professionals can master it. Consequently, *L'Argent*, like most Bresson works, plays more like a reading of the film than the film itself. And, really, when you think about it, what could be more 'French' than the idea of the sacredness of the text. Certainly, I wouldn't want the rest of the cinema to be infected by the feverish 'purity' of Bressonianism, and yet Bresson achieves overpowering effects with his method . . . *L'Argent* itself has many such epiphanies. It is getting to them that is the problem. And is it worth getting to them? I suppose that is the big question with Bresson. To the average, general, casual moviegoer, I would say no. One must take the cinema very seriously and the soul very seriously to take even the first step with Bresson.[7]

The response was typical of a wider disenchantment. Writing a journal on his visits to the cinema in Paris for *Film Comment*, David Overbey recalled how some years previously he had set off 'reluctantly' to a press screening with his colleague Jonathan Rosenbaum.

Reluctantly, because as Jonathan then put it, 'every new French film is guilty until it's proved innocent.' He was right then and alas he is still right . . . The usual run of French films is so much boring sludge, very 'guilty' indeed, with even 'big' names like Eric Rohmer managing to be no more than 'charming'.[8]

The boos that echoed around the new Palais du Cinéma suggested that the French themselves were now beginning to question the status quo. If *L'Argent* represented a past tradition of French film-making that was losing its way, another of the official French entries for that year provided plenty of evidence for a countervailing drift. *L'Eté meutrier* was one of the most successful films of 1983, attracting an audience of four and a half million at the French box-office. Although it received no awards at Cannes, it went on to be nominated for nine Césars. Directed by Jean Becker, who had spent the previous two decades mostly making commercials, the film's stylish exploitation of those staple ingredients of glamour, narrative and spectacle was a return to old-fashioned qualities that chimed in well with the hedonistic complexion of the new decade.

As the sexy, provocative but beguiling Eliane, who effortlessly commands the male gaze while secretly plotting revenge, Isabelle Adjani – 'too free, too animal-like', as one character puts it – gave a star performance that had all the allure of a 1980s Brigitte Bardot.

L'Eté meutrier (1983)

'Vachement Marilyn!' Eliane exclaims as she revels in the gift of a new dress. In contrast to the numbing austerity of Bresson, this was a film that understood the pleasure of seeing and entered into a knowing complicity with its audience, indulging their expectations of the cinema every bit as much as Bresson seemed deliberately to starve them.

Perhaps an important lesson of Cannes 1983 was that it was the audience, not the director, who most mattered. One of the most eagerly anticipated films of the festival had been Jean-Jacques' Beineix's *La Lune dans le caniveau*. Inauspiciously screened on Friday the thirteenth, it received such a hostile reception that a journalist who interviewed Beineix for French television the next day spoke of a possible 'plot'.[9] Beineix commented that the film had passed over the critics' heads and that what really counted was how the public would respond.

But this was a difficult truth to sustain in a system that had been so completely re-engineered to laud the vision of the director. Beineix's own career provided an example of the dangers. In 1981, after having worked many years as an assistant, he made a difficult but ultimately triumphant debut with *Diva*. When the film first opened in Paris in March 1981, it received a lukewarm critical response and few people went to see it. But slowly word-of-mouth began to spread, rescuing a film that defied conventional expectations. It was neither thriller nor comedy nor love story, but a little bit of all these things. Going on to win a César for 'Best First Film', it was still playing in Paris a year after its release and went on to become a cult hit in the United States.

With hindsight it can be seen how the film anticipated the mood of a new decade that would celebrate the return of guilt-free consumption and glamour. Its thrillerish plot about a hunt for a pirate recording of an opera singer who is willing to perform only in public was one of deliberate simplicity, for the quest that mattered most was the characters' pursuit of style. It's what the young post-boy hero, Jules, worships in the diva, Cynthia Hawkins. It's what the cool oriental girl on roller-skates looks for in her boyfriends. It is to be found in the extraordinary den that Jules makes for himself in a garage for wrecked automobiles. 'Très chic,' observes the roller-skating arbiter of taste. The quest unites both heroes and villains. When one of the vicious hoods kills his victims, it is always with a small black stiletto dagger carefully chosen to match his punk haircut and dark glasses. It is as much a designer accessory as a weapon to kill. It is the image that counts. Beineix reflects back a fashion-conscious age that is looking for surface rather than depth. But the even greater novelty seemed to be that a French film-maker had finally made a film that a large number of people around the world would enjoy. 'Beineix has a fabulous camera technique and understands the pleasure to be had from a picture that doesn't take itself too seriously,' wrote Pauline Kael in the *New Yorker*.[10] 'Every shot seems designed to delight the audience.'

After his unpleasant Friday the thirteenth in Cannes, Beineix must have hoped that once again he would triumph over an initially frosty reception, but this time around the public showed no more enthusiasm than the critics. Slow, lush, beautifully composed, *La Lune dans le caniveau* was a revenge story whose slight plot is easily lost in its excess of images. Overlong and three times more expensive to make than *Diva*, it was a hugely ambitious film. Beineix was the obvious target for its failings, but perhaps the system itself deserved to take some of the blame, its love affair with the auteur once again luring a director into indulging his own vision at the audience's expense.

Away from Cannes, the twenty-four-year-old Luc Besson was making his debut with *Le Dernier Combat*. The fact that it was shot in black and white with virtually no dialogue might have suggested the austerity of Bresson, but this science-fiction film, with its vision of a post-apocalyptic future, had a showman's boldness. Besson used Cinemascope to transform a small budget film with just a handful of characters into an epic spectacle that owed much more to Hollywood than any French models.

Planning his escape from a wasted city, the hero without a

name builds an improvised aeroplane in a downtown office he has turned into his refuge. When a murderous gang discovers the hideout, he races to make a quick escape. Besson switches back and forth between the gang attempting to force its way in and the hero smashing a hole in the plate-glass windows. With an exhilarating if implausible take-off, at last he soars into the sky in just the nick of time. Irresistibly thrilling, this was the cinema of D. W. Griffith, executed with a confidence that mocked the cerebral smallness of the French cinema. With the sort of ingenuity his hero had shown in building an aeroplane out of scrap, Besson had made a blockbuster movie in France.

But as pleasing was the film's Gallic style. It had nail-biting escapes, thrilling fights and chases, spectacular landscape, but the most charming scene of all was no more than a simple demonstration of the French '*art de vivre*'. With a caveman's drawing of bison on the wall behind them, two survivors sit down amid the ruins to enjoy a well-prepared dinner and a bottle of wine.

Besson's second film, *Subway* (1985), confirmed the arrival of a director who was as keen to embrace a cinema of action and spectacle as he was to disown his membership of traditional French film culture. 'I hate the atmosphere of the Cinémathèque,' he declared, 'and when *Cahiers du cinéma* give me bad reviews, I feel I'm in good company.'[11] If Besson's films none the less displayed a cinema-conscious style, the 'quotes' were heavily in favour of Hollywood films. *Subway* opens with a car chase that recalls *The French Connection* (1972). The single-minded way in which it sets out to grab and hold the attention was new in a cinema that had for so long taken its audience for granted. 'The thing is to be popular – movies for emotion. Intellectuals have to be part of it – a 20 per cent minority on the side. But in France, we take this 20 per cent and pretend all the rest is shit.'[12]

A new rebellion was under way. The French cinema of the 1970s, which had rarely offered the kind of visual pleasure that Beineix and Besson had achieved, seemed irrelevant to them. Explaining the conception of *Diva*, Beineix commented:

I felt it was important to get away from autobiography; to marry one's own ideas with a vision that wasn't simply personal . . . I don't like the cinema as a vehicle for talk and exposition, the kind of thing which has been at the heart of so much French cinema. Unless it's done with great skill, say by Resnais or Bergman, it's unbearable.[13]

Although there was no identifiable band of adherents to argue its principles in magazines, this new school embraced an agenda that put romance before realism and spectacle before narrative, anticipating a fantasy-oriented cinema that would include Carax's *Les Amants du Pont Neuf* (1991) as well as Jeunet and Caro's *Delicatessen* (1991). Over the next decade Luc Besson, in particular, would take this quest for the popular spectacularly forward. *The Big Blue* (1988), *Nikita* (1990) and *Léon* (1994) were all energetic, visual and fiercely commercial. They displayed an American feel for narrative drive and spectacle, yet a distinctive Gallic sensibility in the way they wove through plots of often extreme violence a thread of elegance, sentiment and tenderness.

To the extent that it anticipated Hollywood's embrace of the kind of comic-strip, aestheticised cinema that brought Quentin Tarantino to the fore in the 1990s, the films of Beineix and Besson provided the latest example of the French cinema as avant-garde innovator. But they were scarcely representative. The very fact that Besson was as likely to make his films in English as in French suggested a strategy that the French film industry as a whole would hardly care to follow, but his success did at least help to revive the old-fashioned ambition of pleasing an audience.

'The difference between cinema and television', observed Jean-Luc Godard, 'is that you raise your eyes for cinema and lower your eyes for television.'[14] The comment captured the derision with which so many French film-makers had regarded the medium, but during the 1980s it was television that became the cinema's future.

The cinema had previously been distinct from its most obvious competitor, but the repeal of the state's monopoly over television

in 1981 dramatically changed the landscape. As alternative ave-
nues of exhibition proliferated with the arrival of several new
TV channels, feature films made a mass migration from the cinema to the small screen. In 1984, when Canal+, the first of those
new channels, was launched, 540 feature films were broadcast
on French television. Just five years later, this figure had more
than doubled to 1,289.[15] A drop in cinema admissions was the
other side of the coin: from 200 million in 1980 to only 118 million in 1989.[16] The idea of 'cinema' remained appealing, but it
had become in effect a *cinéma à domicile*.

By the end of the decade, television had become the French
cinema's principal paymaster. In the year 1986–7 alone, its
investment leapt from 206.4 million to 419.6 million francs
to account for more than a fifth of the French film industry's
entire production financing. The competition between the new
channels for programming greatly increased the capital available
to the film industry, but in using that capital producers had to
consider the specific needs of their financiers. Since the channels
favoured features that would hold up in prime time for an older
and more conservative audience, there was a tendency to move
away from the experimental to the more mainstream.

A renewed sense of Hollywood's encroachment must surely
have encouraged the drift. Its relentless advance seemed unstop-
pable during the 1980s. An important psychological turning
point was the year 1986, when for the first time the number
of French people who watched American films overtook that of
those who watched French ones. As the market share of French
films continued to swing the wrong way through the remainder of the decade (from 43 per cent in 1986 to 34 per cent in
1989), it was natural to turn to the tried and tested attractions
of strong narrative, star power and spectacle to turn the tide.
'Producers are beginning to see that people want commercial films,' observed Guillaume de Verges, the head of the film
department at the television station TF1. 'The auteur world will
not last because of television.'[17]

The whole edifice of the French cinema seemed to be collapsing, but the outward manifestation was the kind of retrenchment that occurs in times of uncertainty when people cling to the familiar. The director and producer Claude Berri provided an example of the sort of journey that the 1980s seemed to demand. Starting out as an actor, he became a director after making a fifteen-minute film, *Le Poulet*, which won an Oscar in 1965. His first feature, *Le Vieil Homme et l'enfant*, was a semi-autobiographical film in black-and-white about a Jewish boy who, during the Occupation, finds refuge in the countryside with a retired old man, who is a supporter of Pétain. The relationship challenges the old man's anti-Semitic prejudices. The path that Berri had set out on resembled that of Truffaut as he went on to write, direct and appear in several more films that, drawing on his own experience, featured time after time an alter ego called 'Claude Langmann'.

But in 1986, he commanded the most expensive budget in French cinema history (much of it from the TV station Antenne 2) when he directed *Jean de Florette* and its sequel *Manon des Sources*. An adaptation of Pagnol's *L'Eau des collines*, together they gave the impression of a conscious return to the *cinéma de Papa*, which for all its lack of modernistic flourishes, had at least enjoyed a large audience in France and a significant art-house one beyond. As the *New York Times* reviewer observed, *Jean de Florette* was 'like no other film you've seen in recent years, perhaps not since you last visited your favourite re-run house and saw one of Pagnol's old masterpieces'.[18] It marked a renewed determination to connect with the international audience for French cinema that had bled away through the 1970s.

More of 'Pagnol's old masterpieces' would follow, as the French cinema sought to turn its literary heritage into a trump card. But as its market share continued to decline (to only 27 per cent in 1994), the projection of prestige and pride depended more than ever upon a war-chest of government subsidies and quotas, so that with hindsight films like *La Gloire de mon père*

(1990), *Cyrano de Bergerac* (1990) and *Germinal* (1993) seem to be the first salvoes in France's battle for the 'cultural exception'. This became an increasingly familiar phrase in the first half of the 1990s as GATT negotiators gathered to hammer out an agreement for world trade. The Americans considered the two words to be a smoke-screen for commercial failure. 'Make films as good as your cheeses and you will sell them!' declared America's chief GATT negotiator, Carla Hills.[19] But for the French, they represented a strongly held belief that culture and commerce were distinct entities.

The 1980s was the decade in which the old kind of cinema that people went to see in darkened halls finally crumbled as a major form of entertainment. The cinemas that remained became showcases for a product that would henceforth be overwhelmingly consumed through video and television. If it is hard to be categorical about exactly when the old order was swept away, the death of François Truffaut on 21 October 1984 offers a symbolic milestone. The France he left behind still had only three TV channels, which showed just a handful of films a week. But only two weeks later the launch of Canal+ marked the beginning of the audio-visual revolution. A certain tendency of the French cinema had died.

19

Up Till Now

When journalist and press agent Georges Cravenne founded the Académie des Arts et Techniques du Cinéma in 1974, he hoped to emulate Hollywood's Academy of Motion Picture Arts and Sciences, which provided an obvious model for what would quickly become the French cinema's principal award ceremony. Claiming to have been fascinated by the Oscars since the age of thirteen, Cravenne chose to name their French equivalent after the sculptor who was responsible for the design of the award, César Baldaccini: 'Oscar, César: five letters so close that the birth of the second became a foregone conclusion.'[1] Conceived in a spirit of admiration for a powerful rival, the Césars would over the coming years offer a useful barometer of the French cinema's progress as it sought to hold its own against an ever more dominant Hollywood.

The year 1993 was one of unusual turbulence. In the GATT trade talks negotiators were battling over a proposed 'cultural exception' for France's audio-visual industries. A sign of the increasingly militant stance was the French Academy's announcement in January that only French-language films would be eligible for César awards. But the decision backfired, because several French film-makers were heavily involved in English-language films. Claude Berri and Jean-Jacques Annaud, producer and director of an English-language adaptation of Marguerite Duras's novel *The Lover*, threatened to terminate their membership, while Louis Malle and Roman Polanski protested at a measure that would deny recognition to many French actors and technicians. A compromise was eventually reached. While the award of 'best film' would be reserved for a French-language production, the other categories of the Césars would remain open to all.

It may often have been difficult to reach a consensus on appropriate action, but everyone agreed that something had to be done to protect a French cinema that was becoming an increasingly endangered species. Having successfully resolved his differences with the Academy over English-language films, Claude Berri emerged as the industry's most prominent champion. During the award ceremony for the Césars that year, he projected a trailer for his latest film, which was now close to completion. An adaptation of Emile Zola's famous novel, *Germinal* was Berri's attempt to make a Gallic blockbuster. Costing 172 million francs ($30 million), it was France's most expensive film up to that time. After the brief preview was over, one of the two presenters for the evening, actress Arielle Dombasle, declared, 'Zola est arrivé!'

An allusion to the slogan, 'Beajolais nouveau est arrivé!', it was typical of the showbusiness levity that marked such occasions, but this reference to an advertising jingle for an immature *vin ordinaire* that went on sale only six weeks after the harvest considerably downplayed the cultural ambition of the film. It was left to the second host, Frédéric Mitterrand, to make the necessary adjustment. 'Yes, indeed, Claude Berri, if the French cinema is still alive today, it's in large measure thanks to your support.'

In a career notable for a combination of enterprise, optimism and flexibility, Berri exemplified all the tacks and turns that the French cinema had made since the New Wave in its quest to remain vital and important. He started out as an actor, in the 1960s directing small semi-autobiographical films in which he played the leading role. None achieved any great commercial success. So he began to produce the films of his contemporaries, including Maurice Pialat, Jacques Rivette, Bertrand Blier and Claude Sautet. Then in 1973 he became a partner in the distribution company, AMLF, whose releases ranged from the hugely popular French comedy *Les Ripoux* (1984) to such Hollywood films as *Apocalypse Now* (1979) and *Amadeus* (1984). This varied activity represented the pragmatic attitude of a survivor. As Berri put it himself: 'Out of my failure as an actor was born my desire to direct. Then my relative failure as a director forced me to become a producer. In order to get my films shown, I became a distributor. One had to eat, that's all.'² The journey reflected a French cinema that by the 1990s had become far too diverse to be associated with any single movement or direction, so that the most successful rallying point – especially given the industry's increasing sense of embattlement – was the promotion of Frenchness itself.

With his two adaptations of Marcel Pagnol, *Jean de Florette* and *Manon des sources* (both 1986), Berri had already demonstrated the success with which he could pick up an icon of national culture and lob it at the international box-office. Now he was trying to do the same with Zola, at precisely the time when French officials were busy negotiating a cultural exception at the GATT talks. It meant that *Germinal* was not just another film; it was carrying the flag for the entire industry.

The Césars ceremony that year offered a good example of the French cinema's new diversity. While Berri offered a preview of his latest international blockbuster, the award for 'best film' went to *Les Nuits fauves* (1992). It was the only feature of a young novelist and musician Cyril Collard, who had died of AIDS just three days before the ceremony. The film, in which Collard himself played the central role, told the autobiographical story of a young cameraman who discovers that he is HIV-positive. Collard captured the emotional turmoil of a man raging against the reality of a tragically curtailed life. But he made no concessions to his audience. They were required to engage with a difficult, uncomfortable subject without any of the professional sweetening of the pill that a few months later enabled the Hollywood film *Philadelphia* to introduce a previously taboo subject to the mainstream. Such rejection of artistic compromise was a familiar tendency in the French cinema, which placed a high value on social and cultural significance. For a film like *Les Nuits fauves* to receive the top national award would be unthinkable in Britain or America, but the fact perhaps helps us to understand the sense of conflict that French film-makers felt in the GATT year of 1993.

Not only were France and America at loggerheads in the trade talks, they were heading for a showdown in the multiplexes too. *Germinal* went on general release on 29 September, just three weeks before the arrival in France of Hollywood's latest blockbuster. '*Germinal* is battling with *Jurassic Park*,' reported the *Daily Telegraph*, 'but must attract five million viewers to break even and to help to stop French films from becoming cultural dinosaurs.'[3] The comment echoed the widespread perception of the French cinema's essential weakness.

The peculiar circumstances of the time served only to encourage the sense of a historic battle. The Iron Curtain had just fallen, and the Soviet Union no longer existed, but to many in France it was easy for a free Europe without barriers to seem like a mixed blessing. For what was there now to protect previously diverse and distinctive cultures against the unfettered forces of globalisation? In the first shots of an ideological struggle that would see France emerge as a prominent focus for an anti-globalisation agenda, *Germinal* offered a timely opportunity for a crusade.

Its story of coal miners who are forced by intolerable poverty to go on strike made it a natural symbol of resistance. Whether the perspective was that of workers fearing for their jobs in a country that had one of the highest unemployment rates in Europe, or of an indigenous film industry determined to oppose the relentless encroachment of Hollywood, *Germinal* – the name of a new month created by the leaders of the French Revolution – provided an irresistible sense of cause.

Among the government organisations that put public money into the project were the Ministry of Culture, the Ministry of Education and the Nord–Pas de Calais region, where the film was made. In a heavily publicised campaign, the President of the Republic, François Mitterrand, and the Minister of Culture, Jacques Lang, travelled to a special opening at the Palais de Congrès in Lille aboard a chartered TGV. Safe enough to serve as a tool of national propaganda, *Germinal* was a middle-of-the-road adaptation that, in its need to appeal to a broad constituency, transformed Zola's critique of French society into yet another example of the heritage cinema that had become increasingly popular fare at the French box-office during the 1980s and 1990s. In the wake of Communism's collapse, when statues of Marx and Lenin were being removed from public squares all over eastern Europe, it seemed less an expression of outrage at the exploitation of the proletariat than a nostalgia for a past in which such a class existed.

If *Germinal* was at odds with the way the world seemed to be turning in the 1990s, the scale of the national fanfare was enough for the film to sell the five million tickets necessary to recoup its heavy investment, although *Jurassic Park* still edged into a narrow lead at the box-office. But France's biggest hit of the year by far was a slapstick time-travel comedy, *Les Visiteurs*, which sold fourteen million tickets. If the success of such an unapologetically idiotic film suggested that the pursuit of high culture was a minority interest even in France, at least it offered the solace that it was still possible to stand up to Hollywood, if you made films that French people actually wanted to see.

Not that many people were likely to see *Germinal* outside France. It was a familiar irony that the popular mainstream hits of France's home market rarely reached beyond a narrow, upmarket audience abroad. In Britain, the Communist newspaper, the *Morning Star*, thought it was a 'fine film', but – noting that it was being premiered in 'darkest Mayfair' – pointed out that it was 'unlikely to see the light of day outside the posh art-house circuit'.[4] The British critics ladled out mostly respectful reviews to a film that had the 'feel of a BBC classic serial shown at one

sitting',[5] but were not enraptured enough to resist the opportunity to poke some fun at the only French actor that English-
speaking audiences could be guaranteed to recognise. Gérard
Depardieu's physique was 'one of the wonders of the modern
world', commented the *Sunday Telegraph*. '[H]is chest alone is
so vast you could squeeze six fully grown Chippendales inside
it like sardines.'[6] But perhaps even worse than the laughter was
the common view that the French cinema had no other star. 'It is
now impossible to imagine a French film, and probably impossible to finance one, without the presence of this human whale,'
observed the *Financial Times*. In the United States, *Germinal*
grossed just $378,854.[7]

At the Césars the following year, *Germinal* carried off only
two awards, for cinematography and costume design. The biggest success of the evening was Alain Resnais's *Smoking / No
Smoking*, whose four awards included best film and best direction. Drawn from the play *Intimate Exchanges* by the British
dramatist Alan Ayckbourn, Resnais's film was much more a lesson in the creative possibilities of being open to other cultures
rather than aggressively defending one's own. Indeed, Resnais's
next film, *On connaît la chanson* (1997), was an explicit *homm-
age* to British television writer Dennis Potter, who had inspired
the film's key device of having its characters lip-synch to the
sound of old recordings of popular French songs.

As the title ('We know the song') suggested, one of the chief
attractions of the film lay in its satisfaction of a collective nostalgia. The songs of Piaf, Aznavour or Gainsbourg provided the
reassurance of the familiar. But the value of recognisable cultural
landmarks lay in their appeal not only to audiences, but also to
the new generation of TV executives upon whom the French cinema was now reliant. It perhaps helped to account for the huge
popularity of 'heritage' cinema in the 1990s, which was able to
exploit strong narratives of tested appeal. With the success of
Jean de Florette and *Manon des Sources*, Berri had opened up
a path down which many other French directors would follow.

The genre had obvious sub-categories. There were the adaptations of classic novels or plays. Rolling off the production-line in 1990 alone were the Pagnol stories *Le Château de ma mère* and *La Gloire de mon père*, the Claude Chabrol version of Flaubert's *Madame Bovary* and Jean-Paul Rappeneau's adaptation of Edmond Rostand's *Cyrano de Bergerac*. Then there were the films that, with or without a pre-existing literary model, exploited France's unusually rich and dramatic history. Alain Corneau's *Tous les matins du monde* (1991) told the story of seventeenth-century court musician, Marin Marais; Bertrand Tavernier's *La Fille de d'Artagnan* (1994) imagined the adventures of the famous musketeer's daughter; Patrice Leconte's *Ridicule* told the story of an idealistic young noble who discovers that he must master the art of wit and repartee if he is to make any progress at the court of Louis XVI (1996).

After *Germinal*, Claude Berri went on to produce Patrice Chéreau's adaptation of Alexandre Dumas's novel *La Reine Margot* (1994), about France's religious wars in the sixteenth century. In interviews about the film, Chéreau pointed to parallels with the civil war in Bosnia, but it was not necessary to look abroad to find a contemporary relevance. *La Reine Margot*'s tale of civil war would have struck a chord with a French psyche that, as Jean Renoir observed, was peculiarly attuned to 'endless division'.[8] Whether it was the religious wars of the sixteenth century, the Fronde of the seventeenth, the Revolution of the eighteenth, or the Paris Commune of the nineteenth, simmering conflict and dissension had long been a notable feature of French life. It was perhaps this tension that lay behind its continuing capacity for cultural renewal.

When the GATT agreement was finally signed in 1994, France's negotiators were able to congratulate themselves on having successfully defended the principle of the 'cultural exception'. But if the desire to continue to maintain tariffs and quotas to protect the film industry reflected French pride in its identity, the nation's tendency for self-criticism meant that there was seldom any danger of complacency. The Césars of 1996 provided an example of a country that seemed as ready to display its *angoisse* as its *gloire*. The top prize was awarded to Mathieu Kassovitz's *La Haine* (1995). An indictment of France's failure to integrate its minority communities, the film reflected a deeply divided society in which culture seemed to be the preserve of a privileged, excluding elite.

The central figures are three youths from different ethnic backgrounds who live on a housing project in the *banlieue* of Paris – the Jewish Vinz, the Arab Saïd and the black Hubert. Their daily experience is one of routine confrontation with the police. The film follows the frustrations of existence in their concrete ghetto. A trip into Paris is like travelling into an alien city, where their presence is scarely tolerated. French society offers them nothing. They are members of an underclass that can look for support neither to the traditional solidarity of the workers, as featured in *Germinal*, nor to the liberal intelligentsia.

When they crash a party in a Paris art gallery, they stare with incomprehension at the avant-garde art exhibits. They are warned not to lean on the paintings. An argument breaks out after they make a gauche attempt to chat up a couple of the female party-goers. Hurling obscenities, they take their leave. As one of the sophisticated guests closes the door on them, he makes the comment, 'Trouble from the *banlieue*.'

All their experience encourages the youths in their complete rejection of French values. When they encounter a TV crew reporting on the latest riots to plague the housing projects, they respond to the intrusion with rage, throwing stones at the journalists' car. In issues of style, whether it's haircuts, music or movies, they look not to Paris but to what's going on in New York. In his instinct for revolt, Vinz finds a model in *Taxi Driver*'s Travis Bickle, imitating the 'You lookin' at me?' scene in front of the bathroom mirror.

What effect could 'cultural exception' possibly have in face of such a visceral pull? The award of the 'best film' to *La Haine* captured the contradiction of a French cinema that would always love Hollywood as much as it hated it.

But at the same time it was impossible to pass over such an obvious scapegoat for the French cinema's troubles. With his usual flair for the provocative statement, Jean-Luc Godard – a master of the soundbite long before the term had been invented – summed up the peculiar role that American films were now playing in France's millennial angst. In a 1999 interview with the film magazine *Positif*, he commented, 'Their only goal is to invade! They want to invade, because they have no history of their own. So they have to invade those countries that do have a history. And now they are everywhere!'[9] A book written at about the same time as Godard made these remarks even adopted the notion for its title: Philippe d'Hugues's *The American Invader: Hollywood versus Billancourt* chronicled the 'insidious decline' of the French cinema that Hollywood's aggressive dominance of world markets had occasioned.

If a refusal to address the French cinema's own failings tended to accompany such attacks, then the 1996 film *Irma Vep* offered a welcome response to the crisis. What made it all the more surprising was the pedigree of its director. Olivier Assayas made his debut in features in 1986 after having worked for several years as a critic for that bastion of the New Wave, *Cahiers du cinéma*.

Irma Vep was a perceptive, personal yet nonetheless objective view of the state of French cinema by a young director who was an obvious heir to the legacy of Chabrol, Godard, Rohmer and Truffaut. But if he was following in their footsteps, he did not hesitate to count the cost of the journey. A film about a film about a film, *Irma Vep* follows the attempts of a revered but troubled and ageing auteur, René Vidal, to make a modern version of Louis Feuillade's 1915 film serial *Les Vampires*. To play the part of the catsuit-clad villainess Irma Vep, he turns to Hong Kong action movie star Maggie Cheung.

The presence of François Truffaut's one-time alter ego Jean-Pierre Léaud in the role of the director encourages us to regard the film as a revisionist version of Truffaut's *La Nuit américaine* (1973). In that film Truffaut played the director in front of the camera as well as behind. As the director Ferrand, who guides the production with a steady calm, extracting order out of the chaos around him, he presented an image of wise, benevolent authority. Devoted to his calling, Ferrand embraces the cinema as an answer to the uncertainties of human existence. 'Films are more harmonious than life,' he advises the young actor Alphonse (played by Léaud). 'There are no bottlenecks in films, no dead-time. Films keep rolling forward, like trains, you understand, like trains in the night. People like you and me, you know, are only happy in our work, our work in the cinema.'

But a quarter of a century later, the cinema is less than harmonious. Long past his prime now, the director Vidal is a man in despair who struggles to come to terms with his failing powers. The cinema no longer offers a refuge from the uncertainties of human existence, but is the ultimate example of it. The movie star Maggie Cheung arrives in the production office to find a bad-tempered, bickering crew who seem almost indifferent to her presence. Although they sense that the art cinema in which they work is on the edge of breakdown, they remain unquestioning in their devotion to it, exhibiting the usual prejudice towards the commercial alternative. Taking Cheung out to lunch in a cafeteria, Zoe, the wardrobe mistress for the production, discusses the latest movies with the star. Dismissing an American blockbuster as 'completely crap . . . a movie for the crowds', she is insensitive to the fact that 'movies for the crowd' are exactly the kind of films that her guest has been making. She asks Cheung if she likes the films of René Vidal, but seems blind to the full implications of the reply: 'They don't show them in Hong Kong.'

It remains for an outsider to challenge the film crew's insular assumptions. A young journalist arrives on the set to conduct an interview with the star. Laughing at the attempts of Cheung to be polite about Vidal's work, he launches into a withering attack on its shortcomings. 'It's a boring cinema. It's typical of French cinema. It's cinema about your navel. Only to please yourself. Not for the public. It's only for the intellectuals, you know.' Cheung retorts that there are different audiences who like different films, but the journalist is insistent. 'René Vidal. It's the past. The old cinema. The public doesn't want this film. No success. It's state money. France giving money to France for making a film nobody sees. Only for the intellectuals. But now it's over. It's finished, I hope.'

Irma Vep was an exercise in affectionate self-loathing that was itself an example of France's navel-gazing cinema. Yet the very spontaneity with which it was made, springing out of enthusiasm and a clever idea rather than careful commercial calculation, paradoxically demonstrated France's capacity for regeneration.

Assayas's description of the circumstances of the film's making suggests much of the unruliness and indiscipline of the French cinema that the film itself charts.

Irma Vep was never a sensible idea. The project was not devised in terms of logic. Working conditions were tough, facilities minimal. The budget – with hindsight – seems laughable. We shot on Super-16, in four weeks. The cast and crew were largely paid on profit-share deals. All this meant finding ways of working fast, very fast, knowing there was no safety-net. No going over schedule. No re-shoots. No contingency whatsoever . . . To save money, the rushes weren't printed.[10]

But out of the muddle emerged a witty, engaging film that, for all its withering criticism, caught the heartbeat that will continue to ensure the French cinema's survival – it was the same rhythm that Jean Cocteau had identified years previously, through which the individual in France tended to defy any attempt at system or organisation. However fractious, foolhardy or misguided the film-makers in *Irma Vep* may seem, however confused they may be about what is the correct approach to reward their efforts with success, they possess a bedrock commitment to the cinema that sustains them.

René Vidal's dissatisfaction with the progress of his movie pushes him towards a nervous breakdown. Discussing her role with him, his star Maggie Cheung attempts to restore a sense of proportion: 'It's just a part . . . It's like a game.' 'No, it's not a game,' retorts Vidal. 'It's very important.' His uncompromising attitude may on this occasion push him so much over the edge that another director has to step into his shoes to complete the film, but we can speculate that it is the same passion for his craft that will bring him back at some future time.

When *Irma Vep* opened in New York, J. Hoberman commented in the *Village Voice*, 'I wouldn't want to jinx the miraculous revival of a low-budget, free-wheeling, film-smart French cinema but – *zut alors!* – if it's not already here. *Irma Vep* isn't only about making movies – it demonstrates that making real ones is still actually possible.'[11] The film may have had to content itself with a small art-house release for the 'navel-gazing intellectuals', but at least it was chipping away at the perception, too long entrenched, that French movies were boring. 'You can take most of your preconceptions about the French cinema and throw them out the window,' wrote the reviewer for *Time Out New York*.[12] 'Assayas's film is a rush, a mad romp through cinema's past and present; it's funny, it's kinetic, and it's got Maggie Cheung. This may be the first French film of its generation to be embraced the way the old folks embraced Godard.'

The achievement of *Irma Vep* was to demonstrate that Godard and the other New Wave directors were now themselves 'old folks', who belonged as much to the cinema of France's past as the Feuillade movie that René Vidal was foolishly attempting to remake. The destruction of the myth made space for a release of new energy, but also a return to the universal qualities of spectacle, story and star appeal.

Godard still managed to make it to the 1997 Cannes Film Festival for the screening of parts 3 and 4 of his extended film essay, *Histoire(s) du cinéma*. But although a small, devoted following of intellectuals turned out in Cannes to applaud his typically encyclopaedic and enigmatic tour of cinema history, the poorly attended press conference had the feel of a fringe event.

The main attraction that year was the blockbuster science-fiction movie, *The Fifth Element*, which opened the Festival. Bristling with special effects and starring Bruce Willis, the $80 million movie was an example of the kind of Hollywood excess that Zoe the wardrobe mistress had criticised in *Irma Vep* – 'everything's too much decoration, too much money.' The irony that it was actually a French film served only to highlight the continuing discomfort and doubts that existed over French cinema's identity. For here was a French director, filming in the English language, who seemed to be rejecting his own heritage for the comic-book style of Hollywood. If some European inspiration for what Besson was attempting could possibly be found in Méliès and *Metropolis*, only a few old folks of Godard's generation could have been expected to notice.

Yet for all the efforts of denial, the French character of the project asserts itself in a self-conscious pastiche that privileges *le look* over narrative, whether expressed in overdetermined images that never quite break loose from their storyboard origins or the eye-catching, catwalk costumes of Jean-Paul Gaultier. Of all French directors, Besson may have been the most single-minded in his quest for the universal idiom of popular movie-making, but even he could not ultimately disown his native sense of style, which denied him the childlike simplicity with which Hollywood had always been able to believe its fairy tales.

In a year that saw James Cameron's *Titanic* become the most successful film of all time at the French box-office, there was an obvious commercial logic in the French production company Gaumont backing Besson to make a mainstream movie in English with Hollywood stars. 'I only speak two languages,' comments Bruce Willis in *The Fifth Element*, 'English and Bad English.' But these were the only two languages in the cinema that offered you the chance of making a fortune. It made it possible for the film to win distribution from the Hollywood major, Columbia. In the United States, *The Fifth Element* topped the US box office in its opening weekend with ticket sales of $17 million,[13] going on to sell 13.5 million tickets. Its total tally of 35 million admissions around the world made it easily the most seen 'French' film in history.[14]

To date, the closest rival to *The Fifth Element* has been the hostage thriller *Taken* (2008), another Luc Besson production. But if he provided a model that the French cinema as a whole was unable to emulate, other film-makers were beginning to enjoy commercial success without having to speak bad English. The key was to be audience-aware in a way that had rarely seemed to be a concern of the New Wave.

'The Nouvelle Vague was – ugh! – terrible, really terrible for French cinema,' commented Jean-Pierre Jeunet. 'I got so bored with all these sad stories, films about couples fighting in their kitchen for two hours. Please give us a break!'[15] The occasion of the comment was an interview with the *New York Times* to mark the autumn release in the United States of Jeunet's latest film, *Le Fabuleux Destin d'Amélie Poulain*. Released in France in April 2001, the film had grossed $40 million, winning for itself a wide distribution around the world. In the US, it would become the highest-grossing French language film with box-office receipts of $33 million.[16] This was a French film at last that had the potential to delight a large mainstream audience, if not the intellectuals who had hitherto made up the core of the small constituency of film-goers prepared to see French films outside France. It was a French film that could venture out of the ghetto of the art houses, to be screened in the multiplexes. In Britain, I can recall catching up with it in my local Odeon, where the notice in the lobby – 'You should be aware that this is a foreign film, with subtitles' – marked the rarity of such a visit.

Its success was in large measure due to the more upbeat and aggressive attitude towards the marketing of foreign films that had coincided with the growth of the independent film movement in the 1990s. The distributor of *Amélie*, Miramax, had led the way in breaking through the glass ceiling of expectation.

With films like *Pelle the Conqueror* (1987), *Cinema Paradiso* (1988) or *Life is Beautiful* (1997), it had shown that, as long as they were promoted with sufficient energy and resources, subtitled films could win large audiences beyond the traditional market of the art-house theatres. The only limit was the intrinsic commercial appeal of the film.

But *Amélie* had no trouble in surpassing this particular barrier. An ecstatic review in *Variety* acknowledged the nature of the breakthrough.[17] Here was a film that, in Audrey Tautou, introduced a young actress who was a real star, recalling for many her namesake Audrey Hepburn: she was 'a delight to watch and root for'. Here was a French film at last that matched Hollywood for spectacle: 'Jeunet and co-scripter Guillaume Laurant set the bar for visual and situational imaginativeness at Olympian heights but clear it with ease over and over again.' And here was a French film that understood the appeal of a strong narrative: 'The beauty of the film's mechanism – an accretion of rapid but perfectly observed wacky ingredients – is that every poignant or silly little detail contributes to the story.' This 'wildly entertaining' movie suggested that the French cinema could become an international force again without having to sacrifice its own language.

But France had too exacting and self-critical a culture to welcome the popular success of *Amélie* without question. The Cannes Film Festival declined to select the film for the official competition. The newspaper *Libération* published a letter,[18] entitled 'Amélie pas jolie', in which the film critic Serge Kanganski attacked the film for a sanitised, retrograde view that denied the ethnically diverse nature of the Paris in which it was set. If the National Front leader Jean-Marie Le Pen 'wanted a clip to promote his vision of the people and his idea of France, *Amélie* would be the ideal candidate'. It was perhaps not surprising that a furious debate followed, but the curmudgeonly reluctance of France to applaud success was itself the vital grist for future creation.

For all its rose-tinted nostalgia, *Amélie* was nonetheless innovative in its style. Miramax's distribution of *Les Choristes* in 2005 suggested the extent to which such originality remained an important role for the French cinema. The highest-grossing film in France during 2004, it was the story of a failed musician who gets a job at a boarding school for disturbed children. His kindness and humanity succeed in bringing out the children, whereas the harsh regime of the school's director had only entrenched their defiance. Told with old-fashioned craft and conviction, it was another example of French nostalgia for a cinema of another time – indeed, it was a remake of a 1945 film, *La Cage aux rossignols*, directed by Jean Dréville. In its reliance on traditional narrative, it offered as much of a nod to mainstream English-language cinema as to French models, recalling such films as *Goodbye, Mr Chips*, *To Sir With Love* and *Dead Poets Society*, but its conservatism was at odds with the perception among foreign audiences and critics that the role of the French cinema was to be challenging. 'This feels more like a Hollywood wannabe than a French film,' commented Roger Ebert in the *Chicago Sun-Times*.[19] 'Where's the quirkiness, the nuance, the deeper levels?' Although the US box-office returns of $3,500,000 were colossal compared to the average French export, they came nowhere close to *Amélie*. The French cinema may have learned how to be entertaining once again, but breaking new ground was still an important key to its future prospects.

Today the two tendencies no longer seem so incompatible. The French cinema has come to terms with the disruptive legacy of the New Wave. The undeclared civil war between France's commercial film industry and the *cinéma d'auteur* is over. The career of the director Jacques Audiard exemplifies the reconciliation between the two traditions. In May 2009, he won the Grand Prix at the Cannes Film Festival for the prison drama *Un Prophète*. It is the story of a young Muslim prisoner, who must resort to a life of careful negotiation and murderous violence to survive the internecine strife between the ethnic gangs that inhabit the cell blocks. Perhaps the most remarkable aspect of the accolades the film has received is the way in which it has been able to appeal to different constituencies. Serious audiences can appreciate a film that seems not only to address the contemporary issue of France's overcrowded prisons, but also, in its depiction of the jostling ethnic groups, to offer a representation of a divided France that has struggled to assimilate its minorities. The hyper-real manner in which the minutiae of prison brutality are depicted recalls the familiar naturalism of the French arthouse movie. There is a documentary feel of authenticity that provides the usual Gallic opposition to the comic-book style of Hollywood.

But behind this illusion of truth lies an old-fashioned concept of the movies as a medium that works best as a tool of spectacle and emotion, rather than of intellect. 'There's nothing like that violence in French prisons,' commented a prison guard of the film. 'That comes from American TV shows and films.'[20] And perhaps the true feat of *Un Prophète*, in a model of integration that the French state itself might wish to emulate, is to assimilate those TV shows and films without any loss of its own identity and sense of self.

The French love for Hollywood has been a recurring theme of its history ever since there was a Hollywood. Previously this passion has tended to express itself through self-conscious homage and pastiche, but while a love of American cinema is just as evident in the work of Audiard, he nurtures his hybrid with a sufficient sense of its specific locale that it can take and flourish in French soil.

Behind *Un Prophète*'s dissection of a prison code that offers a dark mirror of wider society lies the ghost of Joseph Losey's 1960 movie, *The Criminal*, but it is far enough buried not to be noticed. The borrowing provides an index of an organic, natural relationship that is profound but unstrained. Audiard seems able to respect, engage with and take inspiration from the American cinema without compromise or self-consciousness.

Audiard's previous film, *De battre, mon coeur s'est arrêté* (2005), was a remake of the 1977 American film *Fingers*, directed by James Toback. 'Incroyable! The French Remake a US Film,' ran a *New York Times* headline.[21] But if it was true that the French cinema could not offer any obvious equivalent of Hollywood's frequent remakes of French films, behind Audiard's apparently unprecedented gesture lay a commitment that stemmed from an older, forgotten tradition that was necessarily personal for him.

Thomas Seyr is the son of a thuggish father and a concert pianist mother who died when he was young. Working as a real-estate agent, he has followed in his father's footsteps, pursuing his business with a routine, sickening aggression. But some sense of another self inspires him to take piano lessons in the hope that, drawing on the inspiration of his mother, he might break away from his brutish, mean existence. In a newspaper interview, Audiard commented that what drew him to the story was the 'theme of affiliation in the relationship of the father and the son, of transfer from one generation to the next: and I started thinking about the idea of inheritance, specifically the heritage of film – what we inherit from the films we love, and what territory we can integrate into our own films today.'[22]

The fact that Audiard's own father, Michel Audiard, was one of the most successful screenwriters of the post-war French cinema makes it irresistible to interpret *De battre, mon coeur s'est arrêté* in terms of not only Audiard's relationship with his father but with French cinema as a whole. For Audiard *père* belonged to the mainstream French cinema that the New Wave had detested. Audiard *père* had written box-office hits for such successful but scorned directors of the French popular cinema as Henri Verneuil, Georges Lautner and Jacques Deray.

While the hero in the film struggles to resolve the starkly conflicting inheritances of his mother and father, Audiard *fils* enjoys a happier outcome, able to integrate into one both the *cinéma d'auteur* and the popular French cinema that had previously been so antagonistic. The passing of the generations had made possible the healing of a deep trauma. While the New Wave auteurs seemed to win critical acclaim and fame from abroad in inverse proportion to the small size of the audiences that went to see their films at home, the commercial school of French film-makers, to whom Audiard's father belonged, enjoyed box-office success at home but had to accept a critical disregard abroad in spite of their admiration for, and efforts to emulate, the international appeal of Hollywood.

But perhaps it is a change in the nature of the American cinema that has helped the generation of Audiard *fils* to narrow the gulf. Hollywood is no longer the monolith whose inverse image helped the European cinema to define itself. The growth of an increasingly varied landscape of independent movie-making over the last quarter of a century has not only made it easier for English-speaking audiences to appreciate and to perceive difference from abroad, but has also offered foreign film-makers a more challenging and sophisticated range of American models to emulate. When Audiard's 2001 thriller *Sur mes lèvres* was released, comparisons were made to Hitchcock. But if its deaf heroine reading the lips of hoodlums from a rooftop with the aid of a pair of binoculars pays an obvious debt to *Rear Window* (1954), her taste for spying seems to owe as much to David Lynch's *Blue Velvet* (1986). When she smuggles herself into the gangsters' apartment, she hides in a wardrobe with wooden slats that might easily have been bought in a yard sale from Dorothy Vallens.

The development of a solid stretch of common ground between French film-makers and the US independent sector made it possible for Sony Picture Classics to open a film like Laurence Cantet's Cannes Palme d'Or winner of 2008, *Entre les murs*, on twenty-five screens across the United States, where it would eventually play on as many as a hundred, grossing $3.8 million.[23] On the surface, it gave the appearance of belonging to a strong French social-realist tradition of cinema. A young

teacher faces the daily battle of dealing with a class of often disruptive teenagers in a Paris school. Cantet's cast of non-professional actors includes François Bégaudeau, the former teacher
on whose autobiographical novel the film was based, and a class
of real Parisian children, acting out situations that were close
to their own daily lives. It is to this extent an inner-city cousin
of Nicolas Philibert's documentary *Etre et avoir* (2000). Winner
of the Prix Louis Delluc, it was another surprise hit among the
English-language art-house audience, chronicling a year in the
class of a rural primary school. But the way in which Cantet's
film pushes realism to an extreme recalls the famous Hitchcock
comment about cinema being 'life with the boring bits left out'.
Bégaudeau's class is not one where the banal or prosaic detail
of the everyday can possibly exist. So full is the film of dysfunc-
tion, conflict and incipient rebellion that it seems a small miracle
that the teacher makes it safely to the school bell at the end of
each day. Certainly it seems no surprise when he is pushed over
the edge into calling one of his pupils a 'slut'. It is the dramatic
incident that provides the narrative drive in the last third of a
film that has the feel for the story arc, crisis and resolution of a
mainstream Hollywood movie.

In spite of the hyper-realism of the settings, in spite of the
fidelity to the texture of contemporary life, Cantet works to
engineer a conflict of deliberately polarised forces. The idealistic teacher recalls Franck, the young graduate in Cantet's earlier film *Ressources humaines* (1999), who arrives from Paris to
take up a trainee management position in the factory where his
father works at a machine on the shop floor. Caught between
two classes, Franck tries in vain to reconcile the opposed attitudes of management and labour. The drama plays itself out
with the determinism of a morality tale, in which the characters
are not so much individuals as allegorical types. The father does
a job of epic, mind-numbing boredom that involves the one endlessly repeated action of slotting a bolt into a hole; the managers with whom Franck works are ruthlessly duplicitous in their

manipulation of the workforce; and the union representative is the epitome of confrontational, hatchet-faced obduracy. Beneath the varnish of naturalism lies a solid three-act structure of exposition, climax and dénouement. From the moment Franck arrives off the train from Paris in the opening scene to his decision – after discovering the impossibility of accommodation – to return there at the film's close, he is on the familiar Hollywood journey through Conflict, Crisis and Reversal.

The pattern is perceptible even in the work of the most austere practioners of social realism. The Dardenne brothers have a reputation for bleak, uncompromising films, but they too offer the narrative comfort of a clear journey. In *Rosetta* (1999), the relentless, obsessive struggle to find a job drives the title character to the point of treachery and almost self-destruction, but it is her very voyage to the depths that makes a return to humanity possible. This is the familiar pattern of the Dardenne brothers' films: a turning point into self-discovery and redemption after a grim spiritual journey. Bruno, the small-time thief in *L'Enfant* (2005), sells his girlfriend's baby, but we know that he is on the road to spiritual recovery from the moment his remorse drives him to recover the child. And in *Le Fils* (2002), the carpenter Olivier embarks on a similar moral journey when he takes on the boy from reform school who is responsible for the death of his son. For all the obvious pain, his ability to offer forgiveness represents a renewal of his own humanity and, as the title suggests, a way of recovering a son. These are all happy endings of a kind. Although the tale may be told with a far greater respect for truth and integrity of character, it nonetheless contains the heartening validation of humanity upon which Hollywood was built.

To make this observation is not in any way to diminish these films, but on the contrary to suggest that the category of 'social realism' to which they are so often consigned is a rather dour, limiting term that fails to do justice to the full range of satisfactions that they provide. The often admiring English-language reviews dwell on the intelligence and complexity of such films, but rarely challenge the expectation that a foreign-language movie will be an improving but dull ordeal.

Abdel Kechiche's *La Graine et le mulet* (2007) is set among Arab immigrants from Tunisia in the port town of Sète on France's Mediterranean coast. It tells the story of sixty-year-old Slimane Beiji, who is made redundant from his job in the town's shipyard. With the support of an extended family that includes his children by his ex-wife as well as his new partner and her daughter, he opens a Tunisian restaurant. In France, it was a deserved winner of the 2008 César for 'best film', repeating Kechiche's success with *L'Esquive* (2003) three years earlier. But in spite of the glowing reviews, the English-language distributors struggled to put across its universal appeal. While Cantet's *Entre les murs* found a resonant English-language title, *The Class*, that at once struck a chord with anyone who had ever been to school, Kechiche's film presented much more of a problem. A literal translation of the French title, 'The Grain and the Mullet', does not so readily offer up its meaning. It loses the double meaning of the word *mulet*, which in French means mule as well as fish, while still requiring a gloss to be comprehensible. 'It's a fish with true character,' Kechiche explained, 'it's hard to catch and has extraordinary energy. It's the only fish that has the capacity to jump over the nets. It's a very strong symbol for me. I consider that it's almost a part of the popular classes, and at the same time it carries that capacity of revolt.' But the British and US distributors called the film respectively *The Secret of the Grain* and *Couscous*, which captured neither Kechiche's own sense of what he had created nor the universal note of a film that, in spite of its focus on one immigrant family, touched a much larger humanity. 'It's what's universal in this family that interested me,' commented Kechiche. 'What I really wanted to describe was a social milieu and a family we can find in all the families of the world: all the secrets, the affections, the heart-wrenchings, the treachery are things we find in every family.'[24]

The film itself successfully fulfils this aspiration. It contains extended set-piece scenes that recreate the daily life of a French-Tunisian family with documentary fidelity, but these scenes are carefully integrated into the larger story and the great warmth with which they're shot wins the sympathy of the audience. The obstacle to its success beyond France seems to have been much more a failing in promotion, and perhaps Kechiche's tendency to challenge rather than accommodate an audience whose expectations have been conditioned by Hollywood cliché.

In the finale of the film, Rim, the daughter of Slimane's partner, Latifa, performs a belly-dance to distract the dinner guests while he sets off on a forlorn hunt to find the missing couscous that should be the showpiece of the restaurant's opening night. If it had been a Hollywood movie, the Seventh Cavalry would have arrived in the nick of time with the couscous. But Kechiche refuses a solution that offends his sense of what life is really like. The uncomfortable belly-dance of uncertainty takes on a touch of Scheherazade: it goes on to put off the fact that there will be no happy ending for Slimane, who is left to battle forlornly against the haphazard cruelty of the world. He chases after some kids who have stolen his moped. They taunt him mercilessly: they wait for him and then, every time he nearly catches up, speed off again. The last time we see him he is collapsed on the ground.

But for all the lack of conventional relief, Kechiche does offer a positive, life-enhancing conclusion. It surely lies in the love of Slimane's family who try so hard to make the restaurant work for him – in the way, for example, that his continuing absence causes his girlfriend, Latifa, to slip off quietly to make the couscous herself, even though it must now be a lost cause. In its warmth, humanity and realism, Kechiche's work recalls Jean Renoir, whose film *Toni* was also about an immigrant community in the south of France. But although *Toni* inspired Italian neo-realism and led some of Renoir's New Wave admirers to think of themselves as 'the Children of *Toni*', it remained little known outside France.

The producer of *La Graine et le mulet* was Claude Berri, of whose 1967 film, *Le Viel Homme et l'enfant*, Truffaut once commented, 'All the children of *Toni* will recognise themselves in it.'[25] But the strength of the French cinema forty years on is that it can no longer easily be divided into such elect groups. Berri was able to appreciate and support an auteur director like Kechiche, yet at the same time produce the mainstream comedy, *Bienvenue chez les Ch'tis* (2007). Starring the comedian Dany Boon, it was the latest in a long line of comedies that may have been little known or appreciated abroad but were hugely popular in France. Its considerable feat, with twenty million admissions, was to shatter the forty-year-old box-office record held, perhaps inevitably, by another comedy, *La Grande Vadrouille*. Berri's achievement was to show that art and commerce did not have to be mutually exclusive. When he died in January 2009, he left behind a French cinema that had, after his example, created a much broader constituency for itself. Its cultural ambition remained as great as ever, yet it had learned again how to connect with an audience both within and beyond France.

A feature of today's French cinema is the knowing fluidity with which it seems able to pass through different styles. The movements of old have made way for a postmodern sophistication, in which the film-maker is able not only to draw on, but also to combine, what might previously have seemed incompatible sources of inspiration. François Ozon has been one of the most prominent and prolific of France's contemporary film-makers, directing a dozen full-length films since his debut with *Sitcom* in 1998. He has made his reputation as an auteur, yet at the same time boasts a record of continuous production that recalls the career of a veteran from Hollywood's Golden Age. His 2004 film *5×2* chronicles the breakdown of a marriage. As the narrative travels back from the couple's divorce to their first meeting during a seaside holiday, each stage is told in a different cinematic style. 'On set my joke was, "We're starting with Bergman, we'll end with Lelouch,"' commented Ozon.[26] But the joke has been the basis for a career that has defied any attempt at tidy categorisation. A student of Eric Rohmer at La Fémis – France's national film school that emerged out of the old IDHEC in 1986 – he can one moment affect the elegant naturalism of the director of *Comédies et proverbes*, the next plunge into Hollywood-style melodrama. His most successful film to date, *8 Femmes* (2002), has the deliberate look of a 1950s Douglas Sirk movie, but as consciously seeks to evoke the full richness of the French film tradition. In the iconic presence that they bring, the stars who play the eight women of the title span as many decades of French cinema history. 'We're starting with Darrieux, we'll end with Ardant,' Ozon might have joked on this particular shoot.

In interviews Ozon has spoken of his wish that each of his films should be as different as possible from the one that preceded it. But the persisting idea through all the change seems to be the attractiveness of a world of make-believe where the protagonists marshal reality or retreat into fantasy according to their need. In *The Swimming Pool* (2003), English thriller writer Sarah Morton finds a sanctuary in her publisher's French country house, where she embarks on her next novel. When her peace is disturbed by the appearance of the publisher's sexually promiscuous daughter, she regains control by using the daughter for literary inspiration. In *Sous le sable* (2000), Marie Drillon refuses to accept the likelihood that her husband has drowned and conjures him back as a continuing, visible presence in her life. The title character of *Angel* (2007) is a successful romantic novelist, who, unwilling to form mature, equal relationships in the real world, relies on the sustenance of a fictional one. Headstrong and petulant, Angel is not a very likeable character, but she wins our grudging admiration with the energy that she pours into her literary ambitions.

Angel's determination to keep reality at bay finds a counterpart in Ozon's construction of fictional worlds out of cinematic allusion. With the use of back projection and a lush orchestral score, he created a pastiche that had touches of Sirk but, with its

English setting, was even more evocative of 1940s Gainsborough melodrama. Filming in English, he was able to venture entirely beyond a French framework of reference to play off another cinema's past, reflecting a French film culture that has always shown a readiness to recognise and celebrate other cinema traditions as well as its own.

If the resulting hybrid was too outlandish to receive either critical approval or box-office success, it is hard to escape the impression that Ozon was a victim of the sophistication that remains both asset and hurdle in the French cinema's progress abroad. It is the spirit of innovation and the auteur's sensibility that English-language audiences continue to look for in the French cinema, but the same qualities also limit the French cinema's commercial potential. The unanimous praise for *Un Prophète* after its success at Cannes suggested that it would turn out to be a breakthrough film, but its box-office performance turned out to be modest.

French efforts to be unapologetically mainstream will always suffer from the Achilles heel of language. In the summer of 2008, the French resistance movie *Female Agents* had a cinema release in the UK. A kind of *Dirty Dozen* with pretty women, it boasted many of the familiar ingredients of popular success – action, nudity, extreme violence. In its promotion, every effort was made to play down the difference, from the suppression of the original title, *Les Femmes de l'ombre*,* to a wordless trailer that highlighted its more spectacular moments. But the minimal effort that was required for comprehension still effectively put it beyond the mainstream audience it was aimed at. The online comments of a viewer who mistakenly rented the movie on its DVD release make the point:

Unfortunately I did not know this was a foreign language film. Because if I had picked that bit of information up first, I would not of hired

---

* Few English-speaking viewers would have been aware of the allusion to the celebrated Jean-Pierre Melville film, *L'Armée des ombres*.

it. I did try to watch it and found myself not watching the film but constantly watching the bottom and so really not enjoying the film, which looked like it was a good film. If I spoke French or German. If reading the words at the bottom of the screen is for you, you will love it. Otherwise give it a wide birth . . . Shame!'[27]

Among English-language audiences, the French cinema will continue to remain an acquired taste. Through its history, the most consistently reliable market beyond its own shores has been that of the connoisseur rather than the consumer. It provides best not the mass entertainment that Hollywood already makes with such efficiency, but a standard of quality and ambition. Its appeal is that of the timeless over the ephemeral.

In the 1970s, when the French cinema was in danger of becoming a byword for boredom, few of its film-makers could escape the association. 'I saw a Rohmer movie once, it was kind of like watching paint dry,' said Gene Hackman in the 1975 movie *Night Moves*. But it is a characteristic of the French cinema to outlast such passing judgements. Eric Rohmer died in January 2010 just a few days after the worldwide release of the latest Hollywood blockbuster, *Avatar*. The *New York Times* invited its readers to give their comments online. The first post was from Russ G. of Urbana, Illinois: 'There was a time when there were movies for grownups. Now we have $200M video games about good and evil with obligatory battle scenes, people hanging by one hand from helicopters and blue aliens who all speak English as a second language. I'd rather watch paint dry.'[28] The French cinema may be unlikely ever to rival the economic might of Hollywood, but long may it continue to enjoy the last laugh.

Bibliography

Books

Abel, Richard, *The Ciné Goes to Town: French Cinema 1896–1914* (Berkeley: University of California Press, 1994)
— *French Film Theory and Criticism: A History/Anthology, vol. 1, 1907–1929* (Princeton: Princeton University Press, 1988)
— *The Red Rooster Scare: Making Cinema American 1900–1910* (Berkeley: University of California Press, 1999)
Anderson, Benedict, *Imagined Communities* (revised edn, London: Verso, 1991)
Anderson, Lindsay, *Never Apologise*, ed. Paul Ryan (London: Plexus, 2004)
Armes, Roy, *French Cinema since 1946* (London: Zwemmer, 1970)
Assayas, Olivier, *Kenneth Anger: Vraie et fausse magie du cinéma* (Paris: Editions de l'Etoile, 1999)
Assouline, Pierre, *Simenon* (Paris: Juillard, 1992)
Aurenche, Jean, *La Suite à l'écran* (Lyon: Institut Lumière/Actes Sud, 1993)
Bachy, Victor, *Alice Guy-Blaché (1873–1968): La Première Femme cinéaste du monde* (Paris: Institut Jean Vigo, 1993)
Baecque, Antoine de, *Les Cahiers du cinéma: Histoire d'une revue* (Paris: Editions Cahiers du cinéma, 1991)
Bardèche, Maurice and Robert Brasillach, *Histoire du cinéma* (Paris: Denoël et Steele, 1935). Translated and edited by Iris Barry as *History of the Film* (London: Allen & Unwin, 1938)
Bergan, Ronald, *Jean Renoir: Projections of Paradise* (London: Bloomsbury, 1994)
Bergé, Pierre, *Album Cocteau* (Paris: Gallimard, 2006)
Bertin-Maghit, Jean-Pierre, *Le Cinéma sous l'Occupation* (Paris: Olivier Orban, 1989)
Bessy, Maurice and Lo Duca, *Georges Méliès, Mage et 'Mes Mémoires' par Méliès* (Paris, 1945)
Bessy, Maurice, *Les Passagers du souvenir* (Paris: Albin Michel, 1977)

Beylie, Claude, *Marcel Pagnol, ou Le Cinéma en liberté* (Paris: Atlas Lherminier, 1985)

Billard, Pierre, *L'Age classique du cinéma français: du cinéma parlant à la Nouvelle Vague* (Paris: Flammarion, 1995)

Biskind, Peter, *Easy Riders, Raging Bulls: How the Sex 'n' Drugs 'n' Rock 'n' Roll Generation Saved Hollywood* (London: Bloomsbury, 1998)

— *Down and Dirty Pictures* (London: Bloomsbury, 2004)

Black, Gregory D., *Hollywood Censored: Morality Codes, Catholics, and the Movies* (Cambridge: Cambridge University Press, 1994)

Blair, Betsy, *The Memory of All That: Love and Politics in New York, Hollywood and Paris* (New York: Alfred A. Knopf, 2003)

Bocquet, José-Louis, *Henri-Georges Clouzot Cinéaste* (Sèvres: La Sirène, 1993)

Bonnefille, Eric, *Julien Duvivier: Le mal aimant du cinéma français* (Paris: L'Harmattan, 2002)

Bordwell, David, Janet Staiger and Kristin Thomson, *The Classical Hollywood Cinema: Film Style and Mode of Production to 1960* (London: Routledge, 1985)

Bouquet, Jean-Louis, *L'Idée et l'écran: Opinions sur le cinéma* (Haberschill and Sergent, 1925)

Braunberger, Pierre, *Cinémamémoire* (Paris: Centre Georges Pompidou, 1987)

Brownlow, Kevin, *The Parade's Gone By* (London: Secker & Warburg, 1968)

Buñuel, Luis, *My Last Breath* (London: Jonathan Cape, 1984)

Carné, Marcel, *Ma vie à belles dents* (Paris: L'Archipel, 1996)

Carney, Ray, *Cassavetes on Cassavetes* (London: Faber, 2001)

Chambrun, René (ed.), *Paris during the German Occupation* (Stanford: Hoover Institution Press, 1986)

Chardère, Bernard (ed.), *Jean Renoir* (Lyon: Premier Plan, 1962)

Charensol, Georges and Roger Régent, *Un Maître du cinéma: René Clair* (Paris: La Table Ronde, 1952). Updated as *50 ans de cinéma avec René Clair* (Paris: La Table Ronde, 1979)

Chateau, René, *Le Cinéma sous l'Occupation 1940–1944* (Paris: Editions René Chateau et La Mémoire du Cinéma français, 1995)

Chirat, Raymond, *Julien Duvivier* (Lyon: Premier Plan, 1968)

Clair, René, *Réflexion faite* (Paris: Gallimard, 1951). Translated by Vera Traill as *Reflections on the Cinema* (London: W. Kimber, 1953)

Coe, Brian, *The History of Movie Photography* (Westfield, NJ:
Eastview Editions, 1981)

Colville-Andersen, Mikael, *New York Conversations: Four American
Screenwriters* (Copenhagen: Danske Filmskole, 1999)

Creton, Laurent, *Histoire économique du cinéma français* (Paris:
CNRS, 2004)

— *Le Cinéma à l'epreuve du système télévisuel* (Paris: CNRS, 2002)

Crisp, Colin, *The Classic French Cinema 1930–1960* (Bloomington:
Indiana University Press, 1993)

Daquin, Louis, *Cinéma, notre métier* (Paris: Les Editeurs Français
Réunis, 1960)

Daria, Sophia, *Abel Gance: hier et demain* (Paris: La Palatine, 1959)

Darrieux, Danielle, *Filmographie commentée par elle-même* (Paris:
Ramsay Cinéma, 1995)

Delannoy, Jean, *Aux Yeux du souvenir* (Paris: Les Belles Lettres,
1998)

Deslandes, Jacques, *Victorin-Hippolyte Jasset 1862–1913* (Paris:
L'Avant-scène, supplément Anthologie No. 85, Nov. 1975)

Desrichard, Yves, *Julien Duvivier* (Paris: BiFi/Durante, 2001)

— *Henri Decoin* (Paris: BiFi/Durante, 2003)

D'Hugues, Philippe, *L'Envahisseur américain: Hollywood contre
Billancourt* (Lausanne: Favre, 1999)

— *Les Ecrans de la guerre: Le Cinéma français de 1940 à 1944* (Paris:
Editions de Fallois, 2005)

Diamant-Berger, Henri, *Il était une fois le cinéma* (Paris: Editions
Jean-Claude Simoën, 1977)

Drazin, Charles, *Korda: Britain's Only Movie Mogul* (London:
Sidgwick & Jackson, 2002)

Ehrlich, Evelyn, *Cinema of Paradox: French Film-making under
the German Occupation* (New York: Columbia University Press,
1985)

Ezra, Elizabeth, *Georges Méliès* (Manchester: Manchester University
Press, 2000)

— and Sue Harris, *France in Focus: Film and Nationality* (Oxford:
Berg, 2000)

Feyder, Jacques and Françoise Rosay, *Le Cinéma: Notre métier*
(Geneva: Pierre Cailler, 1946)

French, Philip (ed.), *Malle on Malle* (London: Faber, 1993)

Fresnay, Pierre and François Possot, *Pierre Fresnay* (Paris: Editions de
la Table Ronde, 1975)

Frey, Hugo, *Louis Malle* (Manchester: Manchester University Press, 2004)

Gauteur, Claude and Ginette Vincendeau, *Jean Gabin: Anatomie d'un mythe* (Paris: Editions Nathan, 1993)

Gauthier, Christophe, *La Passion du cinéma: Cinéphiles, ciné-clubs et salles spécialisées à Paris de 1920 à 1929* (Paris: Ecole Nationale des Chartes, 1999)

Gleick, James, *Chaos* (London: Heinemann, 1988)

Guitry, Sacha, *Le Cinéma et moi* (Paris: Ramsay, 1984)

Guy, Alice, *Autobiographie d'une pionnière du cinéma 1873–1968* (Paris: Denöel, Association Musidora, 1976)

Harding, James, *Sacha Guitry: The Last Boulevardier* (London: Methuen, 1968)

Harmetz, Aljean, *Round Up the Usual Suspects* (New York: Hyperion, 1992)

Hayward, Susan, *French National Cinema* (London: Routledge, 1993)

Hecht, Ben, *A Child of the Century* (New York: Simon & Schuster, 1954)

Hofstadter, Richard, *Anti-Intellectualism in American Life* (London: Jonathan Cape, 1964)

Icart, Roger, *Abel Gance ou le Prométhée foudroyé* (Lausanne: L'Age d'Homme, 1983)

Insdorf, Annette, *François Truffaut* (revised edn, Cambridge: Cambridge University Press, 1994)

Jackson, Julian, *France: The Dark Years 1940–1944* (Oxford: Oxford University Press, 2001)

James, David E. (ed.), *Jonas Mekas and the New York Underground* (Princeton: Princeton University Press, 1992)

Jeanson, Henri, *Jeanson par Jeanson* (Paris: René Chateau, 2000)

Kermabon, Jacques, *Pathé: Premier empire du cinéma* (Paris: Centre Georges Pompidou, 1994)

Knight, Arthur, *The Liveliest Art* (New York: Mentor Books, 1957)

Lamarr, Hedy, *Ecstasy and Me: My Life as a Woman* (London: Mayflower, 1966)

Langlois, Georges Patrick and Glenn Myrent, *Henri Langlois* (Paris: Denoël, 1986)

Lasky, Jesse, *I Blow My Own Horn* (London: Victor Gollancz, 1957)

Lebo, Harlan, *Casablanca: Behind the Scenes* (New York: Simon & Schuster, 1992)

Leff, Leonard J. and Jerold L. Simmons, *The Dame in the Kimono* (London: Weidenfeld and Nicolson, 1990)

Leguèbe, Eric, *Confessions: Un Siècle de cinéma français par ceux qui l'ont fait* (Paris: Ifrane Editions, 1995)

Lévy, Emanuel (ed.), *Citizen Sarris, American Film Critic: Essays in Honor of Andrew Sarris* (Lanham, MD: Scarecrow Press, 2001)

L'Herbier, Marcel, *La Tête qui tourne* (Paris: Belfond, 1979)

Lherminier, Pierre, *Jean Vigo* (Lherminier, 1984)

Lumière, Auguste, *Mes Travaux et mes jours* (Paris, 1953)

MacCabe, Colin, *Godard: A Portrait of the Artist at 70* (London: Bloomsbury, 2003)

Manvell, Roger and R. K. Neilson Baxter, *The Cinema 1952* (Harmondsworth: Penguin, 1952)

Malthête-Méliès, Madeleine, *Méliès L'Enchanteur* (Paris: Hachette, 1973)

Marais, Jean, *Mes Quatre Verités* (Paris: Editions de Paris, 1957)

Marie, Michel, *La Nouvelle Vague: une école artistique* (Paris: Nathan, 2000)

Mazdon, Lucy, *Encore Hollywood: Remaking French Cinema* (London: BFI Publishing, 2000)

McMahan, Alison, *Alice Guy Blaché: Lost Visionary of the Cinema* (London: Continuum, 2002)

Mesguich, Félix, *Tours de Manivelle* (Paris, 1933)

Milne, Tom (ed.), *Godard on Godard* (London: Secker & Warburg, 1972)

Mitry, Jean, *Max Linder* (Paris: Bernard Grassett: *Anthologie du cinéma*, vol. 2, 1967)

Morrey, Douglas, *Jean-Luc Godard* (Manchester: Manchester University Press, 2005)

Moussinac, Léon, *L'âge ingrat du cinéma* (Paris: Editeurs français réunis, 1967)

Musser, Charles, *Before the Nickelodeon: Edwin S. Porter and the Edison Manufacturing Company* (Berkeley: University of California Press, 1991)

Nogueira, Rui, *Melville on Melville*, transl. Tom Milne (London: Secker & Warburg, 1971)

O'Brien, Charles, *Cinema's Conversion to Sound* (Bloomington, IN: Indiana University Press, 2005)

Pagnol, Marcel, *Cinématurgie de Paris* (Paris: Editions Pastorelly, 1980)
— *Confidences: Mémoires* (Paris: Julliard, 1981)

Pathé, Charles, *De Pathé frères à Pathé cinéma* (Lyon: Premier-Plan, 1970)

— *Ecrits autobiographiques*, ed. Pierre Lherminier (Paris: L'Harmattan, 2006)

[Political and Economic Planning], *The British Film Industry* (London: Political and Economic Planning, 1952)

Prédal, René, *Cinquante ans de cinéma français* (Paris: Nathan, 1996)

Ramsaye, Terry, *A Million and One Nights* (New York: Simon & Schuster, 1926)

Régent, Roger, *Cinéma de France* (Paris: Editions Bellefaye, 1946)

Renaitour, Jean-Michel, *Où va le cinéma français?* (Paris: Baudinière, 1937)

Renoir, Jean, *Ma Vie est mes films* (Paris: Flammarion, 1974). Translated by Norman Denny as *My Life and My Films* (London: Collins, 1974)

— *Ecrits 1926–1971* (Paris: Ramsay, 1989)

— *Letters*, ed. David Thompson and Lorraine LoBianco (London: Faber, 1994)

— *La Règle du jeu*, ed. Olivier Curchod (Paris: Livre de Poche, 1998)

Richebé, Roger, *Au-delà de l'écran* (Monte Carlo: Pastorelly, 1977)

Rossell, Deac, *Living Pictures: The Origins of the Movies* (New York: State University of New York Press, 1998)

Sadoul, Georges, *Histoire générale du cinéma* (6 vols., Paris: Denöel, 1948)

— *French Film* (London: Falcon Press, 1953)

— *Lumière et Méliès* (Paris: Lherminier, 1985)

— *Dictionnaire des films*, ed. Emil Breton (Paris: Editions de Seuil, 1990)

Sarris, Andrew, *Confessions of a Cultist* (New York: Simon & Schuster, 1970)

Schatz, Thomas, *The Genius of the System: Hollywood Filmmaking in the Studio Era* (New York: Simon & Schuster, 1988)

Schickel, Richard, *D. W. Griffith: An American Life* (London: Pavilion Books, 1984)

Seldes, Gilbert, *The Seven Lively Arts* (New York: Harper & Brothers, 1924)

Sesonske, Alexander, *Jean Renoir: The French Films, 1924–39* (Cambridge, MA: Harvard University Press, 1980)

Shirer, William, *The Collapse of the Third Republic: An Inquiry into the Fall of France 1940* (New York: Simon & Schuster, 1969)

Bibliography

Siclier, Jacques, *La France de Pétain et son cinéma* (Paris: Henri Veyrier, 1981)

Sitney, P. Adams (ed.), *Film Culture* (London: Secker & Warburg, 1971)

Smoodin, Eric and Ann Martin (eds.), *Hollywood Quarterly: Film Culture in Postwar America, 1948–1957* (Berkeley: University of California Press, 2002)

Sowerwine, Charles, *France Since 1870: Culture, Politics and Society* (London: Palgrave, 2000)

Steegmuller, Francis, *Cocteau: A Biography* (London: Constable, 1986)

Temple, Michael and Michael Witt (eds.), *The French Cinema Book* (London: BFI Publishing, 2004)

Théry, Jean-François, *Pour en finir une bonne fois pour toutes avec la censure* (Paris: Editions du Cerf, 1990)

Thomson, David, *Biographical Dictionary of the Cinema* (London: André Deutsch, 1994)

Truffaut, François, *Les Films de ma vie* (Paris: Flammarion, 1975). Translated by Leonard Mayhew as *The Films in My Life* (London: Allen Lane, 1980)

Ulff-Møeller, Jens, *Hollywood's Film Wars with France: Film Trade Diplomacy and the Emergence of the French Film Quota Policy* (Rochester, NY: University of Rochester Press, 2001)

Varda, Agnès, *Varda par Agnès* (Paris: Editions Cahiers du Cinéma, 1994)

Vincendeau, Ginette, *Pépé le Moko* (London: BFI Publishing, 1998)

Waldman, Harry, *Paramount in Paris* (Lanham, MD: Scarecrow Press, 1998)

Wallis, Hal B. and Charles Higham, *Starmaker: The Autobiography of Hal Wallis* (New York: Macmillan, 1980)

Willemen, Paul, *Ophüls* (London: BFI Publishing, 1978)

Williams, Raymond, *Problems in Materialism and Culture* (London: Verso, 1980)

— *Resources of Hope: Culture, Democracy, Socialism* (London: Verso, 1989)

Zukor, Adolph, *The Public is Never Wrong* (London: Cassell, 1954)

Articles

Alpert, Hollis, 'Movies', *Saturday Review*, April 1960

Anderson, Lindsay, 'Angles of Approach', *Sequence* 2, Winter 1947

Bazin, André, 'Le Journal d'un curé de campagne et la stylistique de Robert Bresson', *Cahiers du cinéma*, no. 3, June 1954

Bernstein, Matthew, 'A Tale of Three Cities: The Banning of Scarlet Street', *Cinema Journal*, vol. 35, no. 1, Autumn 1995

Guzman, Tony, 'The Little Theatre Movement: The Institutionalisation of the European Art Film in America', *Film History*, vol. 17, no. 2/3, 2005

Jeancolas, Jean-Pierre, 'De 1944 à 1948', in Michel Ciment and Jacques Zimmer (eds.), *La Critique de cinéma en France* (Paris: Ramsay Cinéma, 1997)

— 'From the Blum–Byrnes Agreement to the GATT Affair', in Geoffrey Nowell-Smith and Steven Ricci (eds.), *Hollywood and Europe: Economics, Culture, National Identity 1945–1995* (London: BFI Publishing, 1998)

Kael, Pauline, 'Circles and Squares', *Film Quarterly*, vol. 16, no. 3, Spring 1963

Maltby, Richard, 'More Sinned Against than Sinning: The Fabrications of Pre-Code Cinema', *Senses of Cinema*, November 2003

Mannoni, Laurent, 'Henri Langlois and the Musée du Cinéma', *Film History: An International Journal*, vol. 18, no. 3, 2006

O'Brien, Charles, 'Film Noir in France: Before the Liberation', *Iris*, no. 21, Spring 1996

Sarris, Andrew, 'The Auteur Theory and the Perils of Pauline', *Film Quarterly*, vol. 16, no. 4, Summer 1963

Temple, Michael and Michael Witt, 'Classicism and Conflict', in Michael Temple and Michael Witt (eds.), *The French Cinema Book* (London: BFI Publishing, 2004)

Truffaut, François, 'Une certaine tendance du cinéma français', *Cahiers du cinéma*, no. 31, January 1954

Venhard, Gilles, 'La Marguerite au dessus des vagues 1925–45', in Philippe d'Hugues and Dominique Muller (eds.), *Gaumont: 90 ans de cinéma* (Paris: Editions Ramsay, 1986)

Vincendeau, Ginette, 'Noir is Also a French Word', in Ian Cameron (ed.), *The Movie Book of Film Noir* (London: Studio Vista, 1992)

Newspapers and Periodicals

Arts, 12 December 1956

Atlantic, January 1915

Boston Herald, 18 March 1941

Bibliography

Cahiers du cinéma, no. 1, April 1951; no. 3, June 1951; no. 5,
    September 1951; no. 12, May 1952; no. 31, January 1954; no. 70,
    April 1957; no. 80, February 1958; no. 97, July 1959; no. 138
    (undated); no. 106, April 1960; no. 348/349 June/July 1983
Candide, 21 November 1930
Chicago Sun-Times, 28 January 2005
Cinema Quarterly, vol. 3, no. 2, Winter 1935
Cinématographie française, 19 March 1937; 5 August 1938; 23
    December 1938; 14–24 October 1939; 27 January 1940; 8 May
    1948; 4 December 1948
Cinémonde, 31 December 1939
Ciné-mondial, 8 August 1941
Daily Express, 8 May 1994
Daily Telegraph, 28 September 1993
Dial, 11 April 1918
The Economist, 25 September 1993
Ecran français, L', March 1944; 24 October 1945; 14 August 1946;
    21 August 1946; 28 August 1946; 13 January 1948; 10 February
    1948; 30 March 1948; 26 December 1951
Esprit, March 1936; August 1950
Le Figaro, 13 October 1928; 25 January 1929; 31 March 1929; 7
    July 1929; 24 November 1929; 22 December 1929; 27 April 1930;
    9 November 1930; 16 November 1930; 22 February 1935; 22
    September 1935; 29 January 1937; 1 October 1938; 3 December
    1938; 8 July 1939
Film Comment, vol. 17, no. 6, November–December 1981;
    September–October 2001
Film Culture, no. 27, Winter 1962/3
France-Observateur, 31 July 1958
Guardian, 23 July 1955; 26 February 1968; 14 May 1968; 19
    December 1969; 2 September 1982; 6 January 1983; 5 September
    1985; 2 February 1995; 14 January 2009; 4 April 2009
Hollywood Citizen, 9 April 1941
Hollywood Reporter, 14 February 1938; 16 April 1938; 25 May
    1938; 27 May 1938; 24 June 1938; 28 June 1938; 29 June 1938; 7
    July 1938; 14 July 1938; 20 July 1938; 27 July 1938; 28 July 1938;
    21 August 1938; 31 October 1938; 20 November 1938; 14 January
    1939; 14 February 1939; 13 March 1939; 1 April 1939
Humanité, 10 April 1936; 18 July 1936
Les Lettres français, 31 August 1950

Liberation, 31 May 2001

Los Angeles Times, 8 April 1941; 12 April 1941; 28 April 1941; 6 August 1944

Le Matin, 17 May 1983

Le Monde, 11 January 2009

Morning Star, 9 May 1994

Music and Letters, vol. 3, no. 2 (April 1922)

Nation, 10 October 1936; 16 February 1946; 13 April 1946; 12 April 1947; 13 September 1947; 19 November 1949; 28 June 1952

National Board of Review Magazine, January 1939; April 1939; January 1942

New York Times, 23 May 1920; 10 October 1921; 1 January 1922; 21 May 1931; 19 November 1934; 23 September 1936; 4 November 1936; 14 February 1937; 11 September 1937; 24 December 1937; 17 July 1938; 21 August 1938; 13 September 1938; 27 September 1938; 5 February 1939; 18 February 1939; 19 March 1939; 1 January 1941; 4 March 1941; 9 March 1941; 26 February 1946; 20 February 1947; 26 December 1947; 29 February 1948; 21 March 1948; 29 April 1948; 16 May 1948; 17 January 1950; 6 April 1954; 2 May 1954; 12 August 1956; 13 July 1957; 4 August 1957; 22 October 1957; 30 March 1958; 7 June 1959; 26 August 1959; 17 November 1959; 20 March 1960; 8 February 1961; 23 April 1967; 3 September 1967; 17 September 1967; 21 March 1968; 1 May 1968; 19 September 1968; 14 November 1969; 9 December 1969; 17 February 1974; 2 June 1974; 21 June 1987; 1 August 1987; 8 January 1996; 2 May 1999; 28 October 2001; 5 July 2005; 23 September 2007; 1 April 2008; 24 December 2008; 7 October 2009

New Yorker, 24 September 1938; 15 February 1947; 19 April 1982

News Chronicle, 14 July 1937; 19 March 1944

Newsweek, 21 July 1952

Observer, 13 April 1968

Paris-Cinéma, 2 April 1946

Positif, no. 1, May 1952; no. 11, September–October 1954

La Semaine, 9 April 1942

Sequence, no. 3, Spring 1948; no. 13, 1951

Sight and Sound, Summer 1955; Summer 1957; no. 210, Summer 1983

Sunday Telegraph, 8 May 1994

Le Temps, 18 November 1908; 5 December 1930

Time, 7 December 1936; 18 February 1940; 19 August 1940; 8
December 1947; 17 February 1961
Time Out New York, 1 May 1997
The Times, 25 May 1919; 28 January 1939
Unifrance, 2 March 2009
Variety, 10 June 1930; 31 May 1931; 15 May 1934; 9 March 1938;
14 April 1948; 5 May 1948; 9 June 1948; 18 May 1949; 9 October
1957; 27 November 1957; 4 December 1957; 15 January 1958; 7
January 1959; 25 November 1959; 30 December 1959; 30 April
2001
Vedettes, 16 November 1940
Village Voice, 12 January 1961; 13 January 1961; 16 November
1961; 24 March 1975; 11 October 1976; 10 April 1984; 6 May
1997

Exhibitors' Manuals

Carnival in Flanders (American Tobis Corporation, 1937); *Contempt*
(Donald L. Velde Enterprises, 1963); *Lydia* (United Artists
Corporation, 1941); *Mayerling* (Pax Films International, 1937)

Unpublished Manuscripts and Theses

Borradaille, Osmond, 'Life through a Lens: Journals of a
Cinematographer', manuscript, Kevin Brownlow Collection,
London
Cavalcanti, Alberto, 'One Man and the Cinema', unfinished manu-
script, Cavalcanti Papers, BFI Library Special Collection
Vincendeau, Ginette, 'French Cinema in the 1930s: Social Text and
Context of a Popular Entertainment Medium', thesis, University of
East Anglia, 1985

Notes

Preface

1 *New York Times*, 30 July 1967

1 Light and Magic

1 See Brian Coe, *The History of Movie Photography* (Westfield, NJ: Eastview Editions, 1981), p. 54

2 Deac Rossell, *Living Pictures: The Origins of the Movies* (New York: State University of New York Press, 1998), p. 128

3 Auguste Lumière, *Mes Travaux et mes jours* (Paris, 1953), p. 32

4 Terry Ramsaye, *A Million and One Nights* (New York: Simon & Schuster, 1926), pp. 242–3

5 Charles Musser, *Before the Nickelodeon: Edwin S. Porter and the Edison Manufacturing Company* (Berkeley: University of California Press, 1991), p. 50

6 Produced by Georges Gaudu for Radio-Télévision Scolaire and broadcast in the series 'Aller au cinéma'

7 *La Magie Méliès*, documentary by Jacques Mény, 1997

8 For a detailed description of the Praxinoscope, see Georges Sadoul, *Histoire générale du cinéma* (6 vols., Paris: Denöel, 1948), vol. 1, pp. 113–15

9 Ibid., vol. 1, pp. 121–7

10 Ibid., vol. 1, pp. 238–40

11 Quoted in Madeleine Malthête-Méliès, *Méliès L'Enchanteur* (Paris: Hachette, 1973), p. 135

12 Ibid., p. 136

13 Ibid., p. 142

14 Sadoul, *Histoire générale du cinéma*, vol. 1, pp. 279–80

15 Maurice Bessy and Lo Duca, *Georges Méliès, Mage et 'Mes Mémoires' par Méliès* (Paris, 1945), p. 171

16 Georges Sadoul, *Lumière et Méliès* (Paris: Lherminier, 1985), p. 154

17 Quoted in Madeleine Malthête-Méliès, *Méliès L'Enchanteur*, p. 174
18 Ibid., p. 203
19 Ibid., p. 209
20 Charles Pathé, *De Pathé Frères à Pathé Cinéma* (Lyon: Premier-Plan, 1970), p. 44

2 Birth of the Movie Moguls

1 Charles Pathé, *De Pathé frères à Pathé cinéma*, p. 56
2 Ibid., p. 18
3 Ibid., pp. 18–19
4 Ibid., p. 36
5 Victor Bachy, *Alice Guy-Blaché (1873–1968): La Première Femme cinéaste du monde* (Paris: Institut Jean Vigo, 1993), p. 32
6 Ibid., p. 184
7 Richard Abel, *The Ciné Goes to Town: French Cinema, 1896–1914* (Berkeley: University of California Press, 1994), p. 299
8 *Le Temps*, 18 November 1908
9 *Dial*, 11 April 1918
10 Richard Abel, *The Red Rooster Scare: Making Cinema American, 1900–1910* (Berkeley: University of California Press, 1999), p. 150
11 Adolph Zukor, *The Public is Never Wrong* (London: Cassell, 1954), p. 46
12 Jean Mitry, *Max Linder* (Paris: *Anthologie du cinéma*, vol. 2, 1967), p. 303
13 Georges Sadoul, *French Film* (London: Falcon Press, 1953), p. 15
14 Philippe D'Hugues, *L'Envahisseur américain: Hollywood contre Billancourt* (Lausanne: Favre, 1999), p. 17

3 The Changing of the Guard

1 Richard Abel, *French Film Theory and Criticism: A History/Anthology, vol. 1, 1907–1929* (Princeton: Princeton University Press, 1988), pp. 127–8
2 Jean-Louis Bouquet, *L'Idée et l'écran: Opinions sur le cinéma* (Haberschill and Sergent, 1925), vol. 1, p. 374
3 Léon Moussinac, *L'âge ingrat du cinéma* (Paris: Editeurs français réunis, 1967), p. 83
4 Maurice Bardèche and Robert Brasillach, *Histoire du cinéma* (Paris: Denoël et Steele, 1935), p. 120
5 Pierre Braunberger, *Cinémamémoire* (Paris: Centre Georges

Pompidou, 1987), p. 20

6 Henri Diamant-Berger, *Il était une fois le cinéma* (Paris: Editions Jean-Claude Simoën, 1977), p. 30

7 Quoted in Richard Abel, *French Film Theory and Criticism*, p. 110

8 Carnet IV, January–May 1917, BnF, Arts du Spectacle

9 Kevin Brownlow, *The Parade's Gone By* (London: Secker & Warburg, 1968) p. 528

10 Ibid.

11 Quoted in Roger Icart, *Abel Gance ou le Prométhée foudroyé* (Lausanne: L'Age d'Homme, 1983), p. 75

12 *Le Temps*, 10 March 1917. Quoted in Icart, *Abel Gance*, p. 77

13 Quoted in Sophia Daria, *Abel Gance: hier et demain* (Paris: La Palatine, 1959), p. 56

14 Ibid., p. 56

15 Ibid., p. 58

16 Quoted in Roger Icart, *Abel Gance*, p. 105

17 Brownlow, *The Parade's Gone By*, p. 533

18 Quoted in *New York Times*, 23 May 1920

19 *The Times*, 25 May 1919

20 Roger Icart, *Abel Gance*, p. 125

21 *New York Times*, 10 October 1921

22 *New York Times*, 1 January 1922

23 *Cinémagazine*, 17 March 1922. Quoted in Roger Icart, *Abel Gance*, p. 127

24 Pathé, *De Pathé frères à Pathé cinema*, pp. 92–4

25 Quoted in *Dictionnaire du cinéma français des années vingt* (Paris: AFRHC, 2001), p. 212

26 Ibid., p. 299

4 The Avant Garde

1 See Christophe Gauthier, *La Passion du cinéma: Cinéphiles, ciné-clubs et salles spécialisées à Paris de 1920 à 1929* (Paris: Ecole Nationale des Chartes, 1999), pp. 14–15, 42–5

2 See www.studiodesursulines.com/histoire

3 Jean Renoir, *My Life and My Films*, transl. Norman Denny (London: Collins, 1974), p. 80

4 Delluc, 'Beauty in the Cinema', *Le Film*, no. 73, 6 August 1917, translated in Richard Abel, *French Film Theory and Criticism*, pp. 138–9

5 François Truffaut, *The Films in My Life*, transl. Leonard Mayhew (London: Allen Lane, 1980), p. 297

6 Georges Charensol and Roger Régent, *50 ans de cinéma avec René Clair* (Paris: La Table Ronde, 1979), p. 36

7 René Clair, *Reflections on the Cinema*, transl. Vera Traill (London: W. Kimber, 1953), p. 60

8 Georges Auric, Louis Durey, Arthur Honegger, Darius Milhaud, Francis Poulenc and Germaine Tailleferre

9 Clair, *Reflections on the Cinema*, p. 16

10 Marcel L'Herbier, *La Tête qui tourne* (Paris: Belfond, 1979), pp. 96–7

11 Ibid., p. 97

12 Ibid., p. 102

13 Alberto Cavalcanti, unpublished memoir, 'One Man and the Cinema', 'The So-Called Avant-Garde', p. 6, Calvalcanti Papers, British Film Institute Special Collection

14 Luis Buñuel, *My Last Breath* (London: Jonathan Cape, 1984), p. 103

15 Ibid., p. 104

16 Ibid., p. 104

17 Ibid., p. 105

18 *Le Figaro*, 9 November 1930

19 *Le Temps*, 5 December 1930

5 Sound

1 Alison McMahan, *Alice Guy Blaché: Lost Visionary of the Cinema* (London: Continuum, 2002), p. 46

2 Colin Crisp, *The Classic French Cinema 1930–1960* (Bloomington: Indiana University Press, 1993), p. 99

3 Ibid., p. 101

4 Quoted in Jacques Kermabon, *Pathé: Premier empire du cinéma* (Centre Georges Pompidou, 1994), p. 227

5 *Le Figaro*, 25 January 1929

6 *Le Figaro*, 31 March 1929

7 *Le Figaro*, 7 July 1929

8 *Le Figaro*, 22 December 1929

9 Charles Pathé, *Ecrits autobiographiques*, ed. Pierre Lherminier (Paris: L'Harmattan, 2006), p. 211

10 Kermabon, *Pathé: Premier empire du cinema*, p. 228

11 Information taken from Gilles Willems, 'Rapid Film et ses branches production, un groupe cinématographique performant au cours des années vingt', in Kermabon, *Pathé: Premier empire du cinéma*, pp. 269–73

12 L'Herbier, *La Tête qui tourne*, p. 191

13 Ibid., pp. 191–2

14 *Le Figaro*, 27 April 1930

15 Pathé, *Ecrits autobiographiques*, p. 241

16 *Le Figaro*, 13 October 1928

17 Quoted in Gilles Venhard, 'La Marguerite au dessus des vagues 1925–45', *Gaumont: 90 ans de cinéma*, eds. Philippe d'Hugues and Dominique Muller (Editions Ramsay, 1986), p. 80

18 Clair, *Reflections on the Cinema*, p. 59

19 Ibid., p. 92

20 Ibid., p. 98

21 *Le Figaro*, 24 November 1929

22 *Le Figaro*, 16 November 1930

23 *Candide*, 21 November 1930

24 Alexandre Arnoux, *Pour Vous*, 15 January 1931. Quoted in Charles O'Brien, *Cinema's Conversion to Sound* (Bloomington, IN: Indiana University Press, 2005), p. 74

25 O'Brien, *Cinema's Conversion to Sound*, p. 74

26 *New York Times*, 21 May 1931

27 Maurice Bardèche and Robert Brasillach, *History of the Film*, transl. Iris Barry (London: Allen & Unwin, 1938), p. 334

28 Crisp, *The Classic French Cinema*, p. 23

29 Jesse Lasky, *I Blow My Own Horn* (London: Victor Gollancz, 1957), p. 224

30 Harry Waldman, *Paramount in Paris* (Lanham, MD: Scarecrow Press, 1998), pp. viii–x

31 Ginette Vincendeau, 'French Cinema in the 1930s: Social Text and Context of a Popular Entertainment Medium', unpublished thesis (University of East Anglia, 1985), p. 32

32 Alberto Cavalcanti, 'One Man and the Cinema', unpublished manuscript (Cavalcanti Papers, BFI Special Collection), chapter 14, p. 7

33 Ibid.

34 Ibid.

35 *Ciné-Magazine*, November 1930

36 The American model was called *Devil's Holiday* (1930). Starring

Nancy Carroll, it was written and directed by Edmund Goulding.

37 Cavalcanti, 'One Man and the Cinema', chapter 14, p. 8

38 Osmond Borradaille, 'Life through a Lens: Journals of a Cinematographer', unpublished manuscript, Kevin Brownlow Collection

39 For Marcel Pagnol's account of working with Paramount see *Confidences: Mémoires* (Paris: Julliard, 1981), pp. 200–32

40 Pierre Fresnay and François Possot, *Pierre Fresnay* (Paris: Editions de la Table Ronde, 1975), p. 42

41 Clair, *Reflections on the Cinema*, p. 106

42 It was not until April 1933 that *Marius* would be released in the United States. The *Variety* review described the film as so typically and completely French as to be 'hopeless for general United States consumption', while the *New York Times*, reviewing a US release version that had already been cut from 131 minutes to 108 minutes, observed that the story 'could be considerably abbreviated with advantage to the action'. See Waldman, *Paramount in Paris*, pp. 23–4

43 First introduced in the Paramount film *Applause* (1930), directed by Rouben Mamoulian

44 Claude Beylie, *Marcel Pagnol, ou Le Cinema en liberté* (Paris: Atlas Lherminier, Paris), p. 85

45 *Le Journal*, 17 May 1930. Reproduced in Marcel Pagnol, *Cinématurgie de Paris* (Paris: Editions Pastorelly, 1980), pp. 21–5

46 *Pour Vous*, July 1930. Quoted in René Clair, *Reflections on the Cinema*, pp. 102–3

6 A Personal Voice

1 Quoted in Pierre Lherminier, *Jean Vigo* (Paris: Lherminier, 1984), p. 93

2 Ibid., p. 93

3 Ibid., p. 94

4 Ibid., p. 172

5 François Truffaut, *The Films in My Life*, p. 28

6 Lherminier, *Jean Vigo*, p. 176

7 *Cinema Quarterly*, vol. 3, no. 2, Winter 1935

8 Lindsay Anderson, *Never Apologise*, ed. Paul Ryan (London: Plexus, 2004), p. 530

9 'Angles of Approach', *Sequence* 2, Winter 1947

10 Truffaut, *The Films in My Life*, p. 28

11 *Le Figaro*, 22 February 1935

12 Foreword to Sacha Guitry, *Le Cinéma et moi* (Paris: Ramsay, 1984), p. 12

13 James Harding, *Sacha Guitry: The Last Boulevardier* (London: Methuen, 1968), p. 77

14 *Le Figaro*, 22 September 1935

15 Quoted in Pierre Billard, *L'Age classique du cinéma français: du cinéma parlant à la Nouvelle Vague* (Paris: Flammarion, 1995), p. 93

16 Guitry, *Le Cinéma et moi*, p. 58

17 Ibid., p. 57

18 *Time*, 7 December 1936

19 Roger Manvell and R. K. Neilson Baxter, *The Cinema 1952* (Harmondsworth: Penguin, 1952), pp. 52–3

20 *New York Times*, 27 September 1938

7 The Professional

1 *Le Figaro littéraire*, 7 November 1967

2 Graham Greene, *Mornings in the Dark* (Harmondsworth: Penguin, 1995), p. 256

3 Maurice Bessy, *Les Passagers du souvenir* (Paris: Albin Michel, 1977), p. 48

4 Ibid., p. 46

5 Ibid., p. 48

6 *Hebdo Film*, 22 October 1921 and 12 November 1921. Quoted in Eric Bonnefille, *Julien Duvivier: Le mal aimant du cinéma français* (Paris: L'Harmattan, 2002), vol. 1, p. 22

7 Bonnefille, *Julien Duvivier: Le mal aimant du cinéma français*, vol. 1, p. 55

8 Bessy, *Les Passagers du souvenir*, pp. 48–9

9 Ibid., p. 50

10 *Cinémonde*, 13 February 1930. Quoted in Bonnefille, *Julien Duvivier: Le mal aimant du cinéma français*, vol. 1, p. 58

11 Raymond Chirat, *Julién Duvivier* (Lyon, 1968), p. 53

12 *Opéra*, 20 December 1950. Quoted in Claude Gauteur and Ginette Vincendeau, *Jean Gabin: Anatomie d'un mythe* (Paris: Editions Nathan, 1993), p. 19

13 *Cinémonde*, 1 December 1937. Quoted in Gauteur and

Vincendeau, *Jean Gabin: Anatomie d'un mythe*, p. 19

14 Graham Greene, *Mornings in the Dark*, p. 243

15 *News Chronicle*, 19 March 1944

16 *Le Figaro*, 29 January 1937

17 *Cinémonde*, 31 December 1939

18 See for example the discussion of *Algiers* in Ginette Vincendeau's monograph on *Pépé le Moko* (London: BFI Publishing, 1998), pp. 66–7. Cromwell is mentioned twice, but Wanger, who formulated the very strict brief that the director implemented, not at all

19 Hedy Lamarr, *Ecstasy and Me: My Life as a Woman* (London: Mayflower, 1966), p. 57

20 Quoted in Hollis Alpert, 'Movies', *Saturday Review*, April 1960

21 *New York Times*, 17 July 1938

22 *Hollywood Reporter*, 20 July 1938

23 *New York Times*, 4 March 1941

24 18 March 1941

25 9 April 1941

26 Interview for documentary *You Must Remember This*, on *Casablanca* DVD, Warner Home Video, 2000

27 Hal B. Wallis and Charles Higham, *Starmaker: The Autobiography of Hal Wallis* (New York: Macmillan, 1980), p. 84

28 Ibid., p. 85

29 Aljean Harmetz, *Round Up the Usual Suspects* (New York: Hyperion, 1992), p. 89

30 Ibid., p. 92

31 Harlan Lebo, *Casablanca: Behind the Scenes* (New York: Simon & Schuster, 1992), p. 77

32 Ibid., pp. 142–3

33 *Los Angeles Times*, 12 April 1941

34 *Los Angeles Times*, 28 April 1941

35 Yves Desrichard, *Julien Duvivier* (Paris: BiFi/Durante, 2001), p. 49

36 *Waltzes from Vienna* (1933), *The Man Who Knew Too Much* (1934), *The 39 Steps* (1935), *Secret Agent* (1936), *Sabotage* (1936), *Young and Innocent* (1937), *The Lady Vanishes* (1938)

8 The Art House

1 Quoted in *Nation*, 10 October 1936

2 *Ibid.*

3 *New York Times*, 23 September 1936

4 *New York Times*, 14 February 1937

5 Exhibitors' guide for *Carnival in Flanders* (American Tobis Corporation, 1937), Pacific Film Archive Library

6 *New York Times*, 24 December 1937

7 *Variety*, 9 March 1938

8 Exhibitors' guide for *Mayerling* (Pax Films International, 1937), Pacific Film Archive Library

9 *Hollywood Reporter*, 25 May 1938

10 Ibid.

11 *Hollywood Reporter*, 27 May 1938

12 *Hollywood Reporter*, 7 July 1938

13 *Hollywood Reporter*, 28 July 1938

14 *Hollywood Reporter*, 14 January 1939

15 *New York Times*, 21 August 1938

16 *Hollywood Reporter*, 13 March 1939

17 *Hollywood Reporter*, 24 June 1938

18 *Hollywood Reporter*, 31 October 1938

19 Maurice Bardèche and Robert Brasillach, *The History of the Film* (London: Allen and Unwin, 1938), p. xi

20 *National Board of Review Magazine*, January 1939

21 *New Yorker*, 24 September 1938

22 *New York Times*, 13 September 1938

23 A summary of the broadcast was printed in the *National Board of Review Magazine*, January 1939.

24 Indeed, not long after the broadcast, *La Grande Illusion* itself would make a hat-trick.

25 Jens Ulff-Møeller, *Hollywood's Film Wars with France: Film Trade Diplomacy and the Emergence of the French Film Quota Policy* (Rochester, NY: University of Rochester Press, 2001), p. 117

26 The figure stated by Will Hays, president of the MPPDA, quoted in *Cinématographie française*, 5 August 1938

27 *Hollywood Reporter*, 16 April 1938

9 The Golden Age

1 *The Times*, 14 July 1937

2 Jacques Feyder and Françoise Rosay, *Le Cinéma: Notre métier* (Geneva: Pierre Cailler, 1946), pp. 17–18

3 Ibid., p. 22

4 *Jacques Feyder ou le cinéma concret* (Comité National Jacques

Feyder, Palais des Beaux-Arts, Bruxelles, 1949), p. 76

5 Feyder and Rosay, *Le Cinéma: Notre métier*, p. 35

6 *Jacques Feyder ou le cinéma concret*, p. 33

7 Eric Leguèbe, *Confessions: Un Siècle de cinéma français par ceux qui l'ont fait* (Paris: Ifrane Editions, 1995), p. 68

8 Ibid., p. 70

9 Ibid., p. 63

10 *Cinémonde*, 14 February 1940. Quoted in Yves Desrichard, *Henri Decoin* (BIFI/Durante, 2003), p. 140

11 Quoted in Desrichard, *Henri Decoin*, p. 130

12 Alberto Cavalcanti, 'One Man and the Cinema', unfinished manuscript, Cavalcanti Papers, BFI Library Special Collection, chapter 14

13 Jean Delannoy, *Aux Yeux du souvenir* (Paris: Les Belles Lettres, 1998), p. 63

14 Leguèbe, *Confessions*, p. 101

15 In France, the Prix-Louis Delluc and the Grand Prix national du cinéma; in Italy, the Golden Lion at the Venice Film Festival; in the United States, National Review Board award for Best Foreign Film. 16 Marcel Carné, *Ma vie à belles dents* (Paris: L'Archipel, 1996), pp. 31–2

17 Ibid., p. 70

18 Ibid., p. 71

19 Ibid., p. 107

10 The Spirit of '36

1 Renaitour Commission, *Où va le cinéma français?* (Paris: Baudinière, 1937), p. 44

2 Ibid., p. 52

3 Ibid., p. 52

4 Ibid., p. 117

5 Charles Sowerwine, *France Since 1870: Culture, Politics and Society* (London: Palgrave, 2000), p. 149

6 William Shirer, *The Collapse of the Third Republic: An Inquiry into the Fall of France 1940* (New York: Simon & Schuster, 1969), p. 305

7 Carné, *Ma vie à belles dents*, p. 67

8 Renoir, *My Life and My Films*, p. 125

9 Quoted in Ronald Bergan, *Jean Renoir: Projections of Paradise* (London: Bloomsbury, 1994), p. 148

10 *Espirit*, March 1936

11 Sowerwine, *France Since 1870*, p. 149

12 *Humanité*, 18 July 1936

13 *Humanité*, 10 April 1936

14 *Cinématographie française*, 19 March 1937

15 William Shirer, *The Collapse of the Third Republic*, 1969, p. 302

11 Breaking the Rules

1 *New York Times*, 19 November 1934

2 *New York Times*, 4 November 1936

3 *New York Times*, 11 September 1937

4 *New York Times*, 26 February 1939

5 Jean Renoir, *Letters*, ed. David Thompson and Lorraine LoBianco (London: Faber, 1994), p. 59

6 *The Times*, 28 January 1939

7 *Le Figaro*, 3 December 1938

8 Renoir, *My Life and My Films*, p. 171

9 Interview in Jacques Rivette, *La Règle et l'exception* (1966)

10 *Music and Letters*, vol. 3, no. 2 (April 1922), pp. 117–21

11 Interview in Jacques Rivette, *La Règle et l'exception* (1966)

12 *Ce Soir*, 25 March 1937. Reproduced in Jean Renoir, *Ecrits 1926–1971* (Paris: Ramsay, 1989), p. 139

13 *Ce Soir*, 7 October 1938. Reproduced in Renoir, *Ecrits 1926–1971*, p. 244

14 *Le Figaro*, 1 October 1938

15 Jean Renoir, *La Règle du jeu*, ed. Olivier Curchod (Paris: Livre de Poche, 1998), pp. 37–8

16 Billard, *L'Age classique du cinéma français*, p. 340

17 Answers: 5 Across: Nora Grégor; 5 Down: Jean Renoir

18 *Le Figaro*, 8 July 1939

19 Alexander Sesonske, *Jean Renoir: The French Films, 1924–39* (Cambridge, MA: Harvard University Press, 1980), p. 384

20 Renoir, *My Life and My Films*, p. 172

21 *Le Figaro*, 4 July 1939

22 *Le Figaro*, 8 July 1939

23 *Le Figaro*, 12 July 1939

24 The French selection was: *Enfer des anges* (Christian-Jaque), *La Loi du Nord* (Jacques Feyder), *La Charrette fantôme* (Julien Duvivier), *L'Homme du Niger* (Jacques de Baroncelli)

25 *New York Times*, 8 May 1939

26 *Cinématographie française*, 14–24 October 1939

27 Renoir, *My Life and My Films*, p. 173

28 *Ce Soir*, August 1939

29 *Cinéastes de notres temps: Jean Renoir, le patron* (Jacques Rivette, 1967)

30 Renoir, *Letters*, p. 65

31 Ibid., p. 72

32 Renoir applied for American citizenship as early as 1942.

12 The Occupation

1 *New York Times*, 9 March 1941

2 Philippe d'Hugues, *L'Envahisseur américain: Hollywood contre Billancourt* (Lausanne: Favre, 1999), pp. 43–4

3 Louis Daquin, *Cinéma, notre métier* (Paris: Les Editeurs Français Réunis, 1960), p. 115

4 Quoted in Billard, *L'Age classique du cinéma français*, p. 387

5 Ibid., p. 399

6 See Evelyn Ehrlich, *Cinema of Paradox: French Film-making under the German Occupation* (New York: Columbia University Press, 1985)

7 L'Herbier, *La Tête qui tourne*, p. 280

8 *Cinématographie française*, 27 January 1940

9 Quoted in Jacques Siclier, *La France de Pétain et son cinéma* (Paris: Henri Veyrier, 1981), pp. 45–6

10 *Paris-Cinéma*, 2 April 1946

11 Quoted in Crisp, *The Classic French Cinema*, p. 49

12 Ehrlich, *Cinema of Paradox*, pp. 150–53

13 Jean-Pierre Bertin-Maghit, *Le Cinéma sous l'Occupation* (Paris: Olivier Orban, 1989), p. 23

14 Ibid., p. 27

15 Quoted in José-Louis Bocquet, *Henri-Georges Clouzot Cinéaste* (Sèvres: La Sirène, 1993), p. 15

16 For details of the presence in the German production industry see René Chateau, *Le Cinéma sous l'Occupation 1940–1944* (Editions René Chateau et la Mémoire du Cinéma français, Paris, 1995), p. 20.

17 Danielle Darrieux, *Filmographie commentée par elle-même* (Paris: Ramsay Cinéma, 1995), p. 55

18 Siclier, *La France de Pétain et son cinema*, p. 41

19 Ibid., pp. 35–6

20 Bertin-Maghit, *Le Cinéma sous l'Occupation*, p. 27

21 Footnote in Jean Aurenche, *La suite à l'écran* (Institut Lumière/ Actes Sud, Lyon, 1993), p. 115

22 Darrieux, *Filmographie commentée par elle-même*, p. 56

23 Roger Richebé, *Au-delà de l'écran* (Monte Carlo: Pastorelly, 1977), p. 123

24 Aurenche, *La Suite à l'écran*, pp. 114–15

25 Siclier, *La France de Pétain et son cinema*, p. 48

26 Quoted in Gregory D. Black, *Hollywood Censored: Morality Codes, Catholics, and the Movies* (Cambridge: Cambridge University Press, 1994), pp. 245–6

27 Ibid., p. 246

28 Quoted in Philippe d'Hugues, *Les Ecrans de la guerre: Le cinema français de 1940 à 1944* (Paris: Editions de Fallois, Paris, 2005), p. 119

29 Ibid., p. 119

30 Ibid., pp. 169–70

31 Bocquet, *Henri-Georges Clouzot Cinéaste*, p. 23

32 Pierre Assouline, *Simenon* (Paris: Juillard, 1992), p. 314

33 Quoted in Bocquet, *Henri-Georges Clouzot Cinéaste*, p. 28

34 *L'Ecran français*, March 1944, no. 1

35 Bocquet, *Henri-Georges Clouzot Cinéaste*, p. 34

36 Ibid., p. 33

37 Ibid., p. 37

38 Quoted in ibid., pp. 34–5

39 Darrieux, *Filmographie commentée par elle-même*, p. 47

40 Siclier, *La France de Pétain et son cinema*, p. 49

41 *La Semaine*, 9 April 1942

42 Darrieux, *Filmographie commentée par elle-même*, p. 56

43 *Ciné-Mondial*, 8 August 1941

44 The full text of the Production Code is reproduced in Leonard J. Leff and Jerold L. Simmons, *The Dame in the Kimono* (London: Weidenfeld and Nicolson, 1990), pp. 285–300.

45 Bertin-Maghit, *Le Cinéma sous l'Occupation*, p. 60

46 Ibid., p. 74

47 Crisp, *The Classic French Cinema*, p. 53

48 Quoted in Chateau, *Le Cinéma sous l'Occupation 1940–1944*, p. 227

49 Richard Maltby, 'More Sinned Agianst than Sinning: The Fabrications of Pre-Code Cinema', *Senses of Cinema*, November 2003

50 Julian Jackson, *France: The Dark Years 1940–1944* (Oxford: Oxford University Press, 2001), p. 149

51 Ibid., p. 149

52 Richard Hofstadter, *Anti-Intellectualism in American Life* (London: Jonathan Cape, 1964), p. 123

53 Siclier, *La France de Pétain et son cinema*, p. 99

13 Irreconcilable Differences

1 Billard, *L'Age classique du cinéma français*, p. 428

2 Quoted in Billard, *L'Age classique du cinéma français*, p. 515

3 D'Hugues, *L'Envahisseur américain: Hollywood contre Billancourt*, p. 57

4 i.e., the presidents of the Syndicat des producteurs; the Fédération des distributeurs; and the Fédération des directeurs de cinémas

5 *L'Ecran français*, 13 January 1948

6 *L'Ecran français*, 10 February 1948

7 Quoted in Billard, *L'Age classique du cinéma français*, p. 518

8 *New York Times*, 26 February 1946

9 *Nation*, 13 April 1946

10 *Nation*, 16 February 1946

11 *New York Times*, 20 February 1947

12 Yet the American release version was forty minutes shorter than the original three-hour-long film.

13 *New Yorker*, 15 February 1947

14 *Nation*, 12 April 1947

15 Roger Régent, *Cinéma de France* (Paris: Editions Bellefaye, 1946), pp. 279, 286

16 *Nation*, 13 September 1947

17 *Variety*, 9 June 1948

18 *Variety*, 14 April 1948

19 *Cinématographie française*, 8 May 1948

20 See *The British Film Industry* (a report published by Political & Economic Planning, London, 1952), pp. 159–61

21 *The Lovers of Zero* (1927), *Johann the Coffin-maker* (1927), *A Hollywood Extra* (1928), *Skyscraper Symphony* (1929)

22 *Cinématographie française*, 4 December 1948

23 Georges Charensol and Roger Régent, *Un Maître du cinéma: René Clair* (La Table Ronde, Paris, 1952), p. 220

24 Charensol and Régent, *Un Maître du cinéma: René Clair*, pp. 220–1

25 *Cinématographie française*, 4 December 1948

26 Interview with Francis Korval, *Sight and Sound*, Summer 1955

27 Paul Willemen, *Ophüls* (London: BFI Publishing, 1978), p. 8

28 *New York Times*, 26 December 1947

29 *Time*, 8 December 1947

30 *New York Times*, 29 April 1948

31 Interview with Francis Korval, *Sight and Sound*, Summer 1955

32 Quoted in Raymond Chirat, *Julien Duvivier* (Lyon: Premier Plan, 1968), p. 15

33 Ibid., p. 17

34 Ibid., p. 15

35 Thomas Schatz, *The Genius of the System: Hollywood Filmmaking in the Studio Era* (New York: Simon & Schuster, 1988), p. 340

36 *National Board of Review Magazine*, January 1942

37 *Los Angeles Times*, 6 August 1944

38 Renoir's version would not be shown in the United States until 1975.

39 See Matthew Bernstein, 'A Tale of Three Cities: The Banning of Scarlet Street', *Cinema Journal*, vol. 35, no. 1, Autumn 1995, pp. 27–52

40 Schatz, *The Genius of the System: Hollywood Filmmaking in the Studio Era*, p. 357

41 *L'Ecran français*, 14 August 1946

42 See Charles O'Brien, 'Film Noir in France: Before the Liberation', *Iris*, no. 21, Spring 1996

43 Nino Frank, 'Un nouveau genre 'policier': l'aventure criminelle', *L'Ecran français*, 28 August 1946

44 *Variety*, 9 June 1948

45 *New York Times*, 29 February 1948

46 *New York Times*, 21 March 1948

47 *New York Times*, 17 January 1950

48 Truffaut's notorious piece, 'Une certaine tendance du cinéma français', appeared in the January 1954 issue of *Cahiers du cinéma*, but, as we shall consider in the following chapter, André Bazin had already made the auteurist argument for Bresson long before that,

in his essay 'Le Journal d'un curé de campagne et la stylistique de Robert Bresson', which appeared in the third issue of Cahiers du cinéma (June 1951).

49 New York Times, 6 April 1954
50 New York Times, 2 May 1954
51 Ibid.
52 New York Times, 20 February 1947
53 Variety, 5 May 1948
54 Ibid.

14 Accursed Films

1 Francis Steegmuller, Cocteau: A Biography (London: Constable, 1986), pp. 460–1

2 Rui Nogueira, Melville on Melville, transl. Tom Milne (London: Secker & Warburg, 1971), p. 13

3 Interview with Gideon Bachmann for the WBAI radio programme Film Art, 1961, on Criterion DVD of Bob, le flambeur, released 2002, Criterion Collection, no. 150

4 New York Times, 16 May 1948

5 Noguiera, Melville on Melville, p. 34

6 See, for example, Jean Marais, Mes Quatre Vérités (Paris: Editions de Paris, 1957), pp. 172–3

7 Jean Cocteau, Entretiens sur the cinématographe (Paris: Editions du Rocher, 2003), p. 55

8 Nogueira, Melville on Melville, p. 38

9 Interview on Criterion DVD of Les Enfants terribles, Criterion Collection, no. 398

10 Nogueira, Melville on Melville, p. 42

11 Nogueira, Melville on Melville, pp. 39–40

12 Quoted in Pierre Bergé, Album Cocteau (Paris: Gallimard, 2006), p. 296

13 Cocteau's notes for The Strange Ones (US title), distributor materials, Arthur Mayer-Edward Kingsley Inc., 1952

14 Jean Cocteau, Entretiens sur the cinématographe, p. 104

15 Ibid., p. 76

16 Note in programme to the festival

17 Variety, 18 May 1949

18 Newsweek, 21 July 1952

19 Village Voice, 24 March 1975

15 A Changing Culture

1 *Cahiers du cinéma*, no. 31, January 1954

2 Billard, *L'Age classique du cinéma français*, p. 566

3 For example, in *Les Cahiers du cinéma: histoire d'une revue*, vol. 1 (Editions Cahiers du cinéma, Paris, 1991), p. 13, Antoine de Baecque writes of 'les riches heures de la cinéphilie', while Pierre Billard (*L'Age classique du cinéma français*, p. 566) considered the new film magazines of the period to be 'tous animés par le feu sacré de la cinéphilie'.

4 René Prédal, *Cinquante ans de cinéma français* (Paris: Nathan, 1996), p. 71

5 *Cahiers du cinéma*, no. 1, April 1951

6 Prédal, *Cinquante ans de cinéma français*, p. 70

7 *Les Lettres français*, 31 August 1950

8 Jean-Pierre Jeancolas, 'De 1944 à 1948', in Michel Ciment and Jacques Zimmer (eds.), *La critique de cinéma en France* (Paris: Ramsay, 1997), p. 75

9 Quoted in Jeancolas, 'De 1944 à 1948', p. 76

10 Ibid., p. 75

11 In 2005 the Milan Film Festival would rerun the programme in honour of what it called the first 'festival du film d'auteur'. The films exhibited included *Zéro de conduite* (1933), *L'Atalante* (Jean Vigo, 1934), *Ossessione* (Luchino Visconti, 1942), *Les Dames du Bois de Boulogne* (Robert Bresson, 1944), *The Southerner* (Jean Renoir, 1945), *They Live by Night* (Nicholas Ray, 1949).

12 *Cahiers du cinéma*, no. 1, April 1951

13 *L'Ecran français*, 30 March 1948

14 *L'Ecran français*, 21 August 1946

15 *Cahiers du cinéma*, no. 1, April 1951

16 Jean Douchet, *Sequence*, no. 13, 1951

17 Roland Monod, *Sight and Sound*, Summer 1957

18 *Cahiers du cinéma*, no. 31, January 1954

19 *Cahiers du cinéma*, no. 12, May 1952

20 'De la politique des auteurs', *Cahiers du cinéma*, no. 70, April 1957

21 *Positif*, no. 1, May 1952

22 *Positif*, no. 11, September–October 1954

23 *L'Ecran français*, 26 December 1951. After a long lay-off, Carné directed a French–Italian production of *Thérèse Raquin* (1953). The *Reine Margot* venture would finally be realised in 1954, but

with another director, Jean Dréville, hired in Carné's place.
24 *Cahiers du cinéma*, no. 5, September 1951
25 See Olivier Assayas, *Kenneth Anger: Vraie et fausse magie du cinéma* (Paris: Editions de l'Etoile, 1999), p. 33
26 Betsy Blair, *The Memory of All That: Love and Politics in New York, Hollywood and Paris* (New York: Alfred A. Knopf, 2003), pp. 159–60
27 P. Adams Sitney (ed.), *Film Culture* (London: Secker & Warburg, 1971), p. viii
28 Quoted in Michel Marie, *La Nouvelle Vague: Une école artistique* (Paris: Editions Nathan, 2000), p. 49
29 *Van Gogh* (1947), *Guernica* (1950) and *Gauguin* (1950)
30 Alexandre Astruc's essay coining the term, 'Naissance d'une nouvelle avant-garde', was published in *L'Ecran français*, 30 March 1948
31 *Meet the Pioneers*
32 Quoted in Sitney, p. 74
33 Ibid., p. 75
34 Ray Carney, *Cassavetes on Cassavetes* (London: Faber, 2001), p. 80
35 Ibid., p. 96
36 Ibid., p. 98
37 The example of *Shadows* perhaps also serves to show how France's defence of the cultural exception has been less a battle against *American* culture than against a closed-system corporate culture.
38 Carney, *Cassavetes on Cassavetes*, p. 61
39 *New York Times*, 4 August 1957
40 *Variety*, 9 June 1948
41 Ibid.
42 *New York Times*, 13 July 1957
43 *Variety*, 27 November 1957
44 Ibid.
45 *New York Times*, 12 August 1956
46 *Variety*, 9 October 1957
47 *New York Times*, 22 October 1957
48 Quoted in *Variety*, 4 December 1957
49 *Variety*, 4 December 1957
50 Ibid.
51 *Variety*, 15 January 1958
52 Ibid.
53 *Variety*, 7 January 1959
54 Ibid.

16 Exporting the Revolution

1 *Arts*, 12 December 1956
2 Quoted in François Truffaut, *Les Films de ma vie* (Paris: Flammarion, 1975), p. 315
3 *New York Times*, 30 March 1958
4 Georges Sadoul, *Dictionnaire des films*, ed. Emil Breton (Paris: Editions du Seuil, 1990), p. 263
5 Agnès Varda, *Varda par Agnès* (Paris: Editions Cahiers du Cinéma, 1994), p. 13
6 Marie, *La Nouvelle Vague: Une école artistique*, p. 53
7 Prédal, *Cinquante ans de cinéma français*, p. 151
8 Quoted in Marie, *La Nouvelle Vague: Une école artistique*, p. 49
9 Ibid., p. 49
10 *New York Times*, 7 June 1959
11 *New York Times*, 26 August 1959
12 Quoted in Marie, *La Nouvelle Vague: Une école artistique*, p. 12
13 *New York Times*, 17 November 1959
14 *Variety*, 25 November 1959
15 *Variety*, 30 December 1959
16 *New York Times*, 20 March 1960
17 *Arts*, 22 April 1959. Quoted in Tom Milne (ed.), *Godard on Godard* (London: Secker & Warburg, 1972), p. 146
18 Annette Insdorf, *François Truffaut* (Cambridge: Cambridge University Press, revised edn, 1994), p. 145
19 *New York Times*, 23 September 2007
20 *New York Times*, 8 February 1961
21 Emanuel Lévy (ed.), *Citizen Sarris, American Film Critic: Essays in Honor of Andrew Sarris* (Lanham, MD: Scarecrow Press, 2001), p. 6
22 David E. James (ed.), *Jonas Mekas and the New York Underground* (Princeton: Princeton University Press, 1992), p. 65
23 Lévy, *Citizen Sarris*, p. 7
24 Ibid., p. 7
25 *Film Culture*, no. 27, Winter 1962/3
26 Pauline Kael, 'Circles and Squares', *Film Quarterly*, vol. 16, no. 3, Spring 1963
27 Andrew Sarris, 'The Auteur Theory and the Perils of Pauline', *Film Quarterly*, vol. 16, no. 4, Summer 1963
28 Mikael Colville-Andersen, *New York Conversations: Four*

American Screenwriters (Copenhagen: Danske Filmskole, 1999), pp. 145–6

29 *Cahiers du cinéma*, no. 31, January 1954

30 Andrew Sarris, *Confessions of a Cultist* (New York: Simon and Schuster, 1970)

31 Lévy, *Citizen Sarris*, p. 151

32 Quoted in Peter Biskind, *Easy Riders, Raging Bulls: How the Sex 'n' Drugs 'n' Rock 'n' Roll Generation Saved Hollywood* (London: Bloomsbury, 1998), p. 27

33 *Film Comment*, September–October, 2001

34 *New York Times*, 2 May 1999

35 *New York Times*, 17 February 1974

36 *Cahiers du cinéma*, no. 80, February 1958

37 Marie, *The French New Wave: An Artistic School*, p. 63

38 Colin MacCabe, *Godard: A Portrait of the Artist at 70* (London: Bloomsbury, 2003), p. 153

39 Ibid., p. 154

40 Douglas Morrey, *Jean-Luc Godard* (Manchester: Manchester University Press, 2005), p. 4

41 *New York Times*, 1 August 1987

42 Exhibitor's manual for *Contempt* (Donald L. Velde Enterprises, 1963), Pacific Film Archive Library

43 See my discussion of the Hollywood fortunes of Feyder on pp. 144–5

17 The Children of Tri-X

1 Philip French (ed.), *Malle on Malle* (London: Faber, 1993), p. 24

2 Rohmer, *Arts*, 1958; quoted in Jean Douchet, *Nouvelle Vague* (Paris: Hazan, 1998), p. 110

3 Quoted in Hugo Frey, *Louis Malle* (Manchester: Manchester University Press, 2004), p. 5

4 Quoted in ibid., p. 7

5 Ibid., p. 8

6 French (ed.), *Malle on Malle*, p. 32

7 Quoted by Richard Roud in the National Film Theatre programme, October–December 1968

8 Interview on Criterion DVD of *Hiroshima, mon amour*, Criterion Collection, no. 196

9 *France-Observateur*, 31 July 1958

10 Quoted in Cinémathèque Ontario Film Programme Guide, Autumn 1994

11 Quoted in Roy Armes, *French Cinema since 1946* (London: Zwemmer, 1970), p. 100

12 *Cahiers du cinéma*, no. 97, July 1959

13 *Cahiers du cinéma*, no. 138, December 1962

14 *Time*, 17 February 1961

15 *Cahiers du cinéma*, April 1960, no. 106

16 Michel Marie, *La Nouvelle Vague: une école artistique*, p. 65.

17 Prédal, *Cinquante ans de cinéma français*, p. 155

18 Marie, *The French New Wave: An Artistic School*, p. 61

19 Prédal, *Cinquante ans de cinéma français*, p. 186

20 Leguèbe, *Confessions*, p. 192

21 Ibid., p.179

22 Ibid., p. 246

23 Ibid., p. 179

24 *New York Times*, 14 November 1969

25 *Guardian*, 19 December 1969

26 Leguèbe, *Confessions*, p. 192

27 *New York Times*, 21 March 1968

28 *Observer*, 13 April 1968

29 *Guardian*, 23 July 1955

30 Feyder and Rosay, *Le Cinéma, notre metier*, p. 35

31 *Cahiers du cinéma*, no. 199, March 1968

32 Quoted in Georges Patrick Langlois and Glenn Myrent, *Henri Langlois* (Paris: Denoël, 1986), p. 332

33 *Guardian*, 26 February 1968

34 See Laurent Mannoni, 'Henri Langlois and the Musée du Cinéma', *Film History: An International Journal*, vol. 18, no. 3, 2006, pp. 274–87

35 Quoted in Langlois and Myrent, *Henri Langlois*, p. 322

36 See Truffaut's foreword to Richard Roud, *A Passion for Films: Henri Langlois and the Cinémathèque Française* (John Hopkins University Press, 1999), p. viii

37 *Guardian*, 14 May 1968

38 Archives, Cannes Film Festival

39 'Rapport moral du festival 1968', archive of the Cannes International Film Festival

40 Archives, Cannes Film Festival

41 Arthur Conte, president of ORTF, quotation taken

from www.ina.fr/fresques/jalons/notice/InaEdu04001/
le-chagrin-et-la-pitie-de-marcel-ophüls

42 *Guardian*, 4 April 2009
43 *New York Times*, 9 December 1969
44 *New York Times*, 1 April 2008
45 *New York Times*, 2 June 1974
46 Banc d'essai, RTF, 30 November 1969
47 *Village Voice*, 11 October 1976

18 From Bresson to Besson

1 *Guardian*, 6 January 1983
2 *Sight and Sound*, no. 210, Summer 1983
3 *Cahiers du cinéma*, no. 348/349, June/July 1983
4 *Sight and Sound*, no. 210, Summer 1983
5 *Le Matin*, 17 May 1983
6 *Cahiers du cinéma*, no. 348/349, June/July 1983
7 *Village Voice*, 10 April 1984
8 *Film Comment*, vol. 17, no. 6, November–December 1981
9 'Festival de Cannes', FR3, 14 May 1983, INA
10 *New Yorker*, 19 April 1982
11 *Guardian*, 5 September 1985
12 *Guardian*, 2 February 1995
13 *Guardian*, 2 September 1982
14 Quoted by Alan Riding, *New York Times*, 8 January 1996
15 Laurent Creton, *Le Cinéma à l'epreuve du système télévisuel* (CNRS, Paris, 2002), p. 11
16 Prédal, *Cinquante ans de cinéma français*, p. 448
17 Quoted in *New York Times*, 8 January 1996
18 *New York Times*, 21 June 1987
19 Quoted in *The Economist*, 25 September 1993

19 Up Till Now

1 Quoted in *Le Monde*, 11 January 2009
2 *Guardian*, 14 January 2009
3 *Daily Telegraph*, 28 September 1993
4 *Morning Star*, 9 May 1994
5 Sheridan Morley, *Daily Express*, 8 May 1994
6 *Sunday Telegraph*, 8 May 1994
7 Internet Movie Database

8 Interview, *Gros Plan*, ORTF TV

9 *Positif*, 1999

10 Zeitgeist Films, Distributor Materials, Cinefiles, Pacific Film Archive

11 *Village Voice*, 6 May 1997

12 *Time Out New York*, 1 May 1997

13 Unifrance, 2 March 2009

14 Unifrance, 2 March 2009

15 *New York Times*, 28 October 2001

16 Peter Biskind, *Down and Dirty Pictures* (London: Bloomsbury, 2004), p. 445

17 *Variety*, 30 April 2001

18 *Liberation*, 31 May 2001

19 *Chicago Sun-Times*, 28 January 2005

20 *New York Times*, 7 October 2009

21 *New York Times*, 3 July 2005

22 Ibid.

23 Source: Internet Movie Database

24 *New York Times*, 24 December 2008

25 *New York Times*, 19 September 1968

26 'Interviews about 5×2', official François Ozon website (www. francois-ozon.com)

27 Found on the website lovefilm.com

28 ArtsBeat Blog, *New York Times Online*, 11 January 2010

Index

Page numbers in **bold** refer to illustrations

A bout de souffle (*Breathless*): Hollywood relationship, 321–2; influence, 324; influences on, 269–70, 330, 335–7; reception, 315, 337, 359; style, 329, 349
A Nous la liberté, 71, 72
A propos de Nice, 80, 81–2, 86–7
Abel, Richard, 28
Abus de confiance, 148
Académie des Arts et Techniques du Cinéma, 370
Academy Cinema, London, 128, 291
Accident, 352
Achard, Marcel, 77
Ackerman, Chantal, 356
Acme Theatre, New York, 170
Adjani, Isabelle, 362
L'Age d'or, 56, 57
Agee, James, 226, 227, 229, 235
Albatros Film, 44, 53, 69, 77
Alexandre, Robert, 135
Algiers, 112–15, 116–17, 118–21, 141
Alison, Joan, 117
All the President's Men, 352
Allégret, Marc, 296
Allemand, M., 11
Allen, Woody, 358
L'Alliance Cinématographique Européenne (ACE), 193, 196
Amadeus, 372
Les Amants, 309, 328–30
Les Amants du Pont Neuf, 366
Ambigu theatre, Paris, 21
Amélie, see Le Fabuleux Destin d'Amélie Poulain
American Film Institute, 320
Les Amis de l'Art, 331
Les Amis du Cinéma, 81
AMLF, 371
And God Created Woman, see Et Dieu créa la femme
Anderson, Lindsay, 85–6, 289–90
Angel, 394–5
Anger, Kenneth, 285–6
Les Anges du péché, 190, 245, 277–8
Anna Christie, 144
Anna Karenina, 238

Annabella, 156
Annaud, Jean-Jacques, 370
Annie Hall, 358
Antenne 2, 368
Antoine, André, 45, 104
Apocalypse Now, 372
Aragon, Louis, 179, 186–7
Archer, Eugene, xv
Ardant, Fanny, 394
L'Argent, 360–2
Argos Films, 332
Argosy Pictures, 241
Arletty, 157, 196
L'Armée des ombres, 395n
Arnoux, Alexandre, 71
Arzner, Dorothy, 73
L'Assassin habite au 21, 205–6, 207
L'Assassinat du duc de Guise, 27, 29
L'Assassinat du Père Noël, 147, 199–202, 204
Assayas, Olivier, 378, 380
Astaix, Maurice, 15
Astruc, Alexandre, 275, 289, 290, 344–5
L'Atalante, 82–3, 84, 85, 86, 266, 312
L'Atlantide, 144, 145
Au revoir les enfants, 337
Aubert, Louis, 44
Aubert-Palace, Paris, 61, 62, 165
Audiard, Jacques, 385–8
Audiard, Michel, 387–8
Aumont, Jean-Pierre, 156
Aurenche, Jean, 147, 156, 199, 280, 356
Auriol, Jean-Georges, 203, 272, 281
Autant-Lara, Claude, 52, 147–8, 221
Avatar, 396
Aveline, Claude, 331
Les Aventures de Till l'Espiègle, 297
Ayckbourne, Alan, 375

Bachelet, Jean, 173
Baine d'une mondaine, 24
Balcon, Michael, 99
Baldaccini, César, 370
Balin, Mireille, 108, 117
The Ballad of Narayama, 360
Ballets suédois, 50, 52
Balzac, Honoré de, 237, 314
La Bandera, 107, 108, 109, 112, 155

Barbershop Scene, 3
Barbier-Krauss, Charlotte, 106
Barbin, Pierre, 346
Bardèche, Maurice, 32, 71, 135
Bardot, Brigitte: *Et Dieu créa la femme*, 296–300, 302–3, 324; image, 292, 298, 303, 325, 362; *La Lumière d'en face*, 293; *Le Mépris*, 323, 324–5, 349
Barrault, Jean-Louis, 157–9
Barry, Iris, 135
Les Bas-fonds, 168, 170
Bataille, Henri, 66
La Bataille de San Sebastian (Guns for San Sebastian), 340–1
La Bataille du rail, 264
Battement de coeur, 148, 149, 210
Baur, Harry, 200
Bazin, André: on Bresson, 279–81; influence, 280–1, 283, 316; work for *Cahiers*, 272, 274, 276–7, 279–80; work for *L'Ecran français*, 372–3; work for *Esprit*, 272
Beatty, Warren, 319
Le Beau Serge, 287, 290, 306–7
Becker, Jacques, 164, 197, 227
Becker, Jean, 362
Bégaudeau, François, 389
Beineix, Jean-Jacques, xi, 363–4, 365–6
La Belle Equipe, 107, 168–9
La Belle et la bête, 59, 94–5, **94**, 230, 261, 262, 264
Bellissima, 292
Belmondo, Jean-Paul, 270, 340
Bennett, Joan, 241
Benoit, Pierre, 144
Benoit-Levy, Jean, 346
Benton, Robert, 319
Bergala, Alain, 360–1
Bergman, Ingrid, 119
Berlioz, Hector, 158–9, 194
Bernanos, Georges, 245, 277
Bernard, Raymond, 33
Bernard, Tristan, 143
Bernhardt, Sarah, 28, 34, 90
Berri, Claude, 368, 370–2, 375–6, 392–3
Bertin-Maghit, Pierre, 195–6, 213
Besson, Luc, 364–6, 382–3
Bessy, Maurice, 103, 106, 149
The Best Years of Our Lives, 276
La Bête humaine, 108, 178, 180
Betti, Ugo, 294
Bicycle Thieves, 229
Le Bidon d'or, 147
Bienvenue chez les Ch'tis, 393
The Big Blue, 366
The Big Sleep, 221
Billard, Pierre, 191, 221, 271
Biographical Dictionary of the Cinema (Thomson), xiii

Birkin, Jane, 352
Birth of a Nation, 30
Blaché, Herbert, 26
Black, Gregory, 202
Blain, Gérard, 306–7
Blair, Betsy, 286
Blanchar, Pierre, 196, 197, 206
Blavette, Charles, 164
Blier, Bertrand, 355, 371
The Blue Veil, 219
Blue Velvet, 388
Blum, Léon, 163, 165–6, 168–9, 220–1, 224
Blum-Byrnes agreement (1946), 220–1, 222–3, 224, 232, 239
Bob le flambeur, **268**, 269–70
Bocquet, José-Louis, 205
Bogart, Humphrey, 119
Un Bon Bock, 9, 10
Bonjour tristesse, 303
Bonne chance, 91
Bonnes à tuer, 149
Bonnie and Clyde, 317, 319
Boon, Dany, 393
Boorman, John, 353
Borchard, Adolphe, 95
Borlin, Jean, 52
Borradaille, Osmond, 75
Bory, Jean-Marc, 329
Bost, Pierre, 147, 280, 356
Boston Herald, 117
La Boulangère de Monceau, xiv
Boult, Sir Adrian, 177
Bouquet, Jean-Louis, 32
Bourvil, 338
Boyer, Charles, 112, 113, 117, 119, 133, 139
Brabant, Charles, 294
The Brain, see Le Cerveau
Brando, Marlon, 298, 306
Brasillach, Robert, 32, 71, 135
Braunberger, Pierre, 32, 256, 285, 288, 331
Breathless, see A bout de souffle
Breen, Joseph, 202
Breillat, Catherine, 305
Bresson, Robert: *Les Anges du péché*, 245, 277–8; *L'Argent*, 360–2; Bazin on, 280–1; career, 277, 327; Cinémathèque affair, 343; *Un condamné à mort s'est échappé*, 278–9; *Les Dames du Bois de Boulogne*, 278; *Journal d'un curé de campagne*, 245–6, 277, 278; style, 279–80, 335, 362–3, 364; US treatment of films, 245–6
Brialy, Jean-Claude, 305
Brief Encounter, 93
Brighton Rock, 110
British International Pictures, 53
British Lion, 291
Broadway Melody, 78
Bronson, Charles, 340

Index

Brooks, Van Wyck, 27
Browning, Tod, 339
Bruller, Jean, *see* Vercors
Brunius, Jacques, 164
Buffet, Bernard, 303
Buñuel, Luis, 46, 54–5, 57, 343
Burnett, Murray, 117

La Cage aux rossignols, 385
Cahiers du Cinéma: on *A bout de souffle*, 335–6; Bazin's work, 272, 274, 276–7, 279–80; Besson's career, 365; on Bresson, 360–1; circulation, 274; first issues, 274–6; foundation, 79, 101, 272, 273; generation of critics, 142, 148; *Hiroshima* discussion, 334; New Wave film-makers, 305–6, 329–30, 354; readership, 272, 274, 316; role, 272, 281–2; on Seberg, 321; on *tradition de qualité*, 356; translation, 318; Truffaut's work, 101–2, 245, 271; writers, xiv, 272, 283–7, 304–6, 316, 378
Les Cahiers du Silence, 253
Cain, James M., 112–13, 115, 240
California Theater, 40
Cameron, James, 382
Canal+, 367, 369
Canby, Vincent, 320, 340, 351
Candide, 70
Cannes Film Festival: first (1939), 150, 185; (1959), 308, 311; (1961), 316; (1968), 347–8; (1983), 359, 362–3; (1997), 381–2; (2001), 384; (2008), 388; (2009), 385, 395
Cantet, Laurence, 388–9
Canudo, Ricciotto, 271
Capitaine Benoit, 185
Capitol Cinema, Berlin, 196
Capra, Frank, 148, 241, 339
Caprices, 198, 211
Les Carabiniers, 337
Carax, Leos, 366
Carné, Marcel: career, 88, 150–2, 163–4, 283–4, 308, 341; Cinémathèque affair, 344; *Drôle de drame*, 155, 158; *Eldorado ou Dimanche*, 151–2; *Les Enfants du paradis*, 157–9, 227–8; *Hôtel du Nord*, 156; *Jenny*, 152–3, 154, 155; *Le Jour se lève*, 99, 108, 156–7, 186; *La Marie du port*, 283, 327; *Les Portes de la nuit*, 225; Prévert relationship, 150, 154–7; *Quai des brumes*, 99, 108, 155–6, 181, 186, 327; *Sous les toits de Paris*, 152; style, 109; *Les Visiteurs du soir*, 158, 191, 229
Carnet de bal, 103, 109–10, 120, 123, 124
Carney, Ray, 291
Carnival in Flanders, *see La Kermesse héroïque*
Caro, Marc, 366
La Carrière de Suzanne, xiv
Carter, Lincoln, 18
Cartier-Bresson, Henri, 164

Casablanca, 112, 117–23, 216, 221
Cassavetes, John, 290–2
Castanier, Jean, 164–5
Caught, 236
Cavalcanti, Alberto: career, 53, 73–4, 84, 99; on Delannoy, 149; *Feu Mathias Pascal*, 53; *French Communiqué*, 99; Independent Cinema Congress (1930), 81; *L'Inhumaine*, 52; *Rien que les heures*, 53–4; *Sarah and Son*, 73; *Toute sa vie*, 75; *Le Train sans yeux*, 53; *Les Vacances du diable*, 75; on Vigo, 84; work with Paramount, 73–4, 75, 149
Les Caves du Majestic, 208
Cayrol, Jean, 332
Ce Soir, 179, 186, 188
Cécile est morte, 208
Centre National de la Cinématographie (CNC), 225, 250, 255–6, 287
Centre National du Cinéma (CNC), 305, 307–8, 319, 336, 354
Le Cercle du Cinéma, 344
Le Cercle rouge, 270
Le Cerveau (The Brain), 339–40
Césars, 362, 363, 370–2, 375, 377, 391
Ceux de chez nous, 90
Chabrier, Jacques, 244–5
Chabrol, Claude: *Le Beau Serge*, 287, 290, 306–7; *Cahiers* group, 283, 287, 305; Cannes conference (1959), 308; career, 287, 307, 336, 337, 354; *Les Cousins*, 287; *La Femme infidèle*, 342; Hollywood relationship, 321; *Juste avant la nuit*, 342–3; *Madame Bovary*, 376; *L'Oeil de Vichy*, 217n; style, 342, 354; US reception of films, 309
Chacun sa chance, 196
La Chagrin et la pitié, 350–1, 358
Chandler, Raymond, 326
Un Chapeau de paille d'Italie, 69
Chaplin, Charlie: career, 29; Cinémathèque affair, 343; Cocteau on, 56; Florey relationship, 232; influence, 30; *Monsieur Verdoux*, 222–3; United Artists, 171
Chardère, Bernard, 283
Charensol, Georges, 190–1, 233
Le Château de ma mère, 376
The Cheat, 30–2, 31, 34, 35–6, 47
Le Chemin du paradis, 70–1
Chenal, Pierre, 294
Chéreau, Patrice, 376
Cheung, Maggie, 378–81
Chevalier, Maurice, 73
Chicago Sun-Times, 385
Un Chien andalou, 54–5, 54, 58, 288
La Chienne, 153, 240
Chiqué, 65
Les Choristes, 385
Chrétien, Henri, 67
Christian-Jaque, 88, 146–7, 200

435

Chronophone process, 26
Ciboulette, 147
Ciné-Alliance, 155
Ciné-Journal, 18
Ciné-Liberté, 166, 167, 168, 171
Ciné-Mondial, 211–12, 218
Cinéa, 33
Cineaste, 320
Cinegraphic, 51
Cinema: A Critical Dictionary (Haskell), xiii
Cinéma du look, 270
Cinéma et cie, 33
Cinema Quarterly, 84
Cinemascope, 67, 297, 364
Cinémathèque, Paris, 7
Cinémathèque française, 5, 343–7, 365
Cinématographe: development, 3, 6–7;
  exhibitions, 6; filming, 5–6, 13; first public
  showing, 1, 8, 10–11, 24, 25; Lumière's
  opinion of, 318; Pathé agreement, 24–5;
  versatility and portability, 3–4, 5, 6
La Cinématographie française, 168, 192, 230,
  232
Cinémonde, 106
Cinéromans, 43, 65, 73
Cinex, 205n
5X2, 393–4
Citizen Kane, 221, 239–40, 242, 275, 276
Clair, René: *A Nous la liberté*, 71, 72; Bresson
  relationship, 277; career, 44, 50–1, 79;
  Carné relationship, 152; *Un Chapeau de
  paille d'Italie*, 69; on cinema, 49–50, 78–9,
  80; Cinémathèque affair, 343; debate with
  Pagnol, 78–9, 80; *Entr'acte*, 54; on Feyder,
  144; in Hollywood, 233–4, 237, 239, 282;
  on *Jean de la lune*, 77; *Le Million*, 71, 72;
  Paris qui dort, 48–50, **48**, **49**, 69; *La Proie
  du vent*, 69; *Quatorze juillet*, 71; reputation,
  71, 88, 131, 233–4; *Le Silence est d'or*,
  233–4; *Sous les toits de Paris*, 69–70, 70, 72,
  152; use of sound, 69–70, 71–2; work with
  Tobis, 72, 74, 131, 196
Claire's Knee, 320
The Class, see Entre les murs, 391
Clément, René, 264, 308, 352
Cloistered, 135–6
Close-up, 285
Clouston, Storer, 155
Clouzot, Henri-Georges, 149, 196, 204–7
Le Clown et ses chiens, 9
Cluny, Raymond, 95
Cocinor, 288
Cocteau, Jean: *La Belle et la bête*, 59, 94–5, **94**,
  261, 262; on cinema, 51; cinema of personal
  expression, 96, 265, 277; on *Le Corbeau*,
  207; *Les Dames du Bois de Boulogne*, 278;
  on élites, 251, 380; *Les Enfants terribles*,
  263–6, 267; *L'Eternel Retour*, 150, 262;

Festival du Film Maudit, 266–7, 274, 307;
  influence, 285, 327; on Langlois, 344;
  Les Mariés de la tour Eiffel, 50; Melville
  relationship, 263–5, 268; *Orphée*, 58, 262;
  reputation, 271; *Le Sang d'un poète*, 56–9,
  142, 263; 'spirit of contradiction', 343
Cohl, Emile, 26
Colette, 31–2
Colisée cinema, Paris, 83, 91, 181
Collard, Cyril, 372
La Collectionneuse, xiv
Columbia, 297, 382
Combat, 257, 343
Comédies et proverbes, 394
Comité de Défense du Cinéma, 222, 223–4
Comité de l'Organisation de l'Industrie
  Cinématographique (COIC), 193, 194, 211,
  213–15, 225
Companeez, Nina, 356
Un condamné à mort s'est échappé, 278–9
Confessions of a Nazi Spy, 183–4
Connolly, Cyril, 253
Contempt, 324–5, 349
Continental Films, 193–200, 204, 206–9
Le Corbeau, 190, 206–7, 244
Corneau, Alain, 376
Corniglion-Molinier, Edouard, 155
Costa-Gavras, 351
Le Coup du berger, 288
Le Coupable, 104
Couscous, see La Graine et le mulet
Les Cousins, 287
Coward, Noël, 93, 98
Cravenne, Georges, 370
Creelman, Eileen, 131
Le Crime de Monsieur Lange, 139, 152, 153,
  164–5, 250
The Criminal, 386
Cromwell, John, 113, 114, 115
Crowther, Bosley: on *And God Created
  Woman*, 297–8; on *Breathless*, 315; on *Les
  Enfants du paradis*, 227–8; on Golden Age of
  French films, 244, 292–3; on Truffaut, 309;
  US perspective on French films, 243–7, 294–5
Cuny, Alain, 328
Curzon Cinema, London, 128
Cyrano de Bergerac, 368, 376

Dabit, Eugène, 156
Daily Telegraph, 38, 373
Daladier, Edouard, 162, 163, 180
d'Alcy, Jehanne, 14
Dalí, Salvador, 54–5, 57
Dalio, Marcel, 173, 175–6, 196
Les Dames du Bois de Boulogne, 190, 278
Daquin, Louis, 190, 196–7, 205n
Dardenne brothers, 390

436

Darmetal, Jacques, 66
Darrieux, Danielle: *Caprices*, 198, 211; career, 148–9, 197, 198, 208, 210–11, 217; Decoin relationship, 148–9, 208; *Le Domino vert*, 148, 194; *La Fausse Maîtresse*, 198, 211; *8 Femmes*, 394; *Mayerling*, 133; *Premier rendez–vous*, 208–11
Dasté, Jean, 164
Dauman, Anatole, 332
Day, Josette, 185
Daybreak, 144
de Baroncelli, Jacques, 33
De battre, mon coeur s'est arrêté, 386–7
de Bretagne, Joseph, 173
de Carmoy, Guy, 160n, 192–3
de Croisset, François, 147
de Flers, Robert, 147
de Funès, Louis, 338, 341
de Gaulle, Charles, 347, 348
de Limour, Jean, 65
de Maré, Rolf, 50
De Mille, Cecil, 30–2, 35
De Mille, Cecil B., 299
De Sarajevo à Mayerling, 234
De Sica, Vittorio, 229, 292, 324
de Verges, Guillaume, 367
Dean, James, 47–8, 298, 302, 306, 307
Deburau, Baptiste, 158
Decoin, Henri, 88, 148–9, 208–9, 210
Degas, Edgar, 90
Delair, Suzy, 206, 210
Delannoy, Jean, xi, 88, 149–50, 328, 328
Delicatessen, 366
Delluc, Louis: *Cinéa*, 33; death, 48; *La Femme de nulle part*, 45; *Le Film*, 33; on *Les Frères corses*, 104; on Hayakawa, 47; influence, 45, 47, 271, 318; *Le Journal du Ciné–Club*, 45; *Le Train sans yeux*, 53
Delon, Alain, 352–3
Delubac, Jacqueline, 89–90, 91, 95
Demy, Jacques, 321
Denis, Claire, 305
Depardieu, Gérard, 375
Deray, Jacques, 353, 387
Dernier atout, 250
Le Dernier Combat, 364–5
Le Dernier des six, 204, 205, 207
Le Dernier Tournant, 294
Desrichard, Yves, 123
Détruire, dit-elle, 355–6
Deuxième bureau, 185
The Devil's Envoys, see Les Visiteurs du soir
d'Hugues, Philippe, 190, 203–4, 221, 378
Le Diable au corps, 280
Diamant-Berger, Henri, 33, 50
Diana Productions, 241
Die klugen Frauen, 196
Diehl, Gaston, 331

Dietrich, Marlene, 225, 297
Les Disparus de Saint-Agil, 147, 200
Il Dispresso, 322
Diva, xi, 363–4, 365–6
Dmytryk, Edward, 275
Dog Day Afternoon, 359
Dombasle, Arielle, 371
Le Domino vert, 148, 194
Doniol-Valcroze, Jacques, 275, 305, 334–5
Dostoyevsky, Fyodor, 197
Double crime sur la ligne Maginot, 185–6
Double Indemnity, 221, 240–1, 242
Douce, 147
Douchet, Jean, 278
Le Doulos, **269**, 270
Dozier, William, 236
Drazin, Charles, 203n
Die Drei von der Tankstelle, 70
Dréville, Jean, 385
Dreyer, Carl Theodor, 304
Dreyfus, Lilian, 356
Le Droit à vie, 35, 36
Drôle de drame, 155, 158
Duchamp, Marcel, 46
La Duchesse de Langeais, 237
Dulac, Germaine, 45, 81
Dumas, Alexandre, 283
Duras, Marguerite, 305, 332–4, 355–6, 370
Durbin, Deanna, 197
Duryea, Dan, 241
Duverger, Paul, 95
Duvivier, Julien: *Anna Karenina*, 238; art-house cinemas, 128; background, 103–4, 105–6; *La Bandera*, 107, 109, 112; *La Belle Equipe*, 107, 168–9; career, 88, 104–5, 111–12, 142; *Carnet de bal*, 103, 109–10, 120, 124; Christian–Jaque's work, 146–7; on cinema, 102–3; *La Fin du jour*, 238; Gabin relationship, 107–9, 112; *The Great Waltz*, 237–8; *Halcedama*, 104–5; in Hollywood, 106–7, 124–7, 233, 237–8, 239, 282; influence, 101, 103, 110–14, 118–19, 123; influence on Truffaut, 311–14; *Lydia*, 124–6; *Maria Chapdelaine*, 107; *Pépé le Moko*, 103, 107, 109, 111, 112–18, 120–1, 123; *Poil de Carotte*, 103, 105–6, 109, 311–14, 313; reputation, 102–3, 109, 125–6, 140, 172, 308, 327, 328, 341

Ealing Studios, 99
Eastman, George, 2, 11
Easy Rider, 359
L'Eau des collines, 368
L'Eau du Nil, 68
Ebert, Roger, 385
Eclair, 17, 18, 44
L'Ecole des facteurs, 248, 249
L'Ecran français, 206, 222, 272–5, 277, 283

Edeson, Arthur, 120
Edison, Thomas, 2–4, 6, 9, 10, 11, 15, 22, 23, 24
Edison Company, 17
Editions du Minuit, 252
Education de prince, 64
Eisenstein, Sergei, 41, 81
The Elusive Pimpernel, 231
L'Enfance nue, 354
L'Enfant, 390
L'Enfant d'amour, 65, 66
Les Enfants du paradis: cut for US release, 247; making of, 190, 216, 228–9, 248; origins, 157–9; reception, 227–9; storyline, 159
Les Enfants terribles (The Strange Ones), 263–8
Entr'acte, 54
Entre les murs (The Class), 388–9, 391
Entre onze heures et minuit, 149
Epinay Studios, 70, 72
Epstein, Jean, 44, 45, 346
Epstein, Julius, 119
Epstein, Marie, 346
Epstein, Philip, 119
Ermolieff, Joseph, 44
Ernst, Max, 57
L'Escamotage d'une dame chez Robert–Houdin, 14, 15
Esnault, Philippe, 198
Espoir, 187
Esprit, 272
L'Esprit de 1936, 163, 330
Esquire, 317, 319
Esquire Theatre, Los Angeles, 120
L'Esquive, 391
Essanay, 29
Et Dieu créa la femme (And God Created Woman), 295–301, 302, 309, 324
L'Eté meurtier, 361, 362–3
L'Eternel Retour, 150, 262
Etre et avoir, 389
Europa Films, 291
Everybody Comes to Rick's, 117, 118
Everyman Cinema, London, 128
The Exile, 235
Exposition Internationale des Arts Décoratifs et Industriels Modernes, 52
L'Express, 303

Le Fabuleux Destin d'Amélie Poulain, 383–5
Fahrendes Volk, 196
Fairbanks, Douglas Jr., 235
Falbalas, 250
The Fallen Idol, 109
Famous Players, 28
Fanny, 77
Farrebique, 230, 244
La Fausse Maîtresse, 198, 211
Favre le Bret, Robert, 348

Fayard, Jean, 70
Fellini, Federico, 292
Female Agents, 395–6
La Fémis, 394
La Femme de nulle part, 45
La Femme infidèle, 342
Les Femmes de l'ombre, 395
Fernandel, 337–8
Fescourt, Henri, 32
Festival du Film Maudit, 266–7, 274, 285
Feu Mathias Pascal, 53
Feuillade, Louis: career, 26, 42, 143, 232, 273; death, 42; techniques, 276; *Les Vampires*, 378, 381
Feuillère, Edwige, 119, 185
Feyder, Jacques: Albatros Film, 44; *L'Atlantide*, 144, 145; career, 88, 142, 143–5; Carné relationship, 151–2; Ciné–Liberté, 166; *Le Film*, 33; *Les Gens du voyage*, 196; *Le Grand jeu*, 145–6, 152; in Hollywood, 144–5, 151, 325; *La Kermesse héroïque*, 142–3, 152; *The Kiss*, 144, 325; *Les Nouveaux Messieurs*, 151; *Pension Mimosas*, 145, 152; Tobis, 74, 196
Fifth Avenue Playhouse, 245, 247
The Fifth Element, 382–3
Le Figaro, 184; on *L'Age d'or*, 57; cinema page, 62, 183; on *The Jazz Singer*, 61; on Munich agreement, 180; on *Pasteur*, 91; society column, 174; on Tobis, 70
'Figaro Film', 66
La Fille de d'Artagnan, 376
La Fille de l'eau, 46, 54
La Fille du puisatier, 227
Le Film, 32–3
Film Comment, 320, 362
Film Culture, 286, 290, 315–16
Film d'Art, 27, 34, 43
Film français, 272
Film Quarterly, 317
Film Society of Lincoln Center, 320
Filmarte, New York: *La Fin du jour*, 238; *La Grande Illusion*, 136, 171; *La Kermesse héroïque*, 128–9, 138; manager, 285; *Mayerling*, 132; opening, 128; owner, 128, 129–30, 138
Filmgoer's Companion, Halliwell's, xii–xiii
Films de Losange, xiv
Les Films Sonores Tobis, *see* Tobis
Le Fils, 390
La Fin du jour, 238
Financial Times, 375
Fine Arts Theatre, New York, 309
Fingers, 387
Fireworks, 285–6
Flaherty, Robert, 172, 189
Flaubert, Gustave, 170, 376
Flaud, Jacques, 307

Florey, Robert, 40, 232, 234, 236, 282
Fonda, Jane, 349
Fontaine, Joan, 236–7
Ford, John, 129, 147, 241
Fort Apache, 137
The Four Feathers, 126
The 400 Blows, see Les Quatre cents coups
France, Anatole, 90
Francen, Victor, 185–6
Franju, Georges, 290, 344
Frank, Nino, 242
Free Cinema, 86–7, 289, 290
Fréhel, 121
Freire, Dido, 172, 187, 188–9
French Communiqué, 99
The French Connection, 365
Les Frères corses, 104
Fresnay, Pierre, 76, 172, 206, 208
Frogerais, Pierre, 156

Gabin, Jean: *La Bandera*, 107, 109, 112, 155;
    La Belle Equipe, 107; *La Bête humaine*, 108;
    career, 108–9, 134, 196, 225, 327–8; *Chacun
    sa chance*, 196; Duvivier relationship,
    107–8, 112; *La Grande Illusion*, 154, 172;
    Gueule d'amour, 108; *Le Jour se lève*, 108,
    156–7; *Maigret tend un piège*, 328; *Marie
    du port*, 327; *Moontide*, 120; *Pépé le Moko*,
    107, 109, 112, 117, 120; *Quai des brumes*,
    108, 155–6, 327; quoted, 169; wartime
    experiences, 190
The Gambler, 197
Gance, Abel: career, 34–5, 45, 87, 96, 273;
    Le Droit à vie, 35–6; *Le Film*, 33; *J'accuse*,
    37–40, 247; *Mater Dolorosa*, 36; wartime
    experiences, 36–7
Garbo, Greta, 140, 144, 326
Gary Theatre, Boston, 300
Gaspard-Huit, Pierre, 294
GATT talks and agreement, 369, 370, 372–3,
    376
Gaultier, Jean-Paul, 382
Gaumont: Chronophone process, 26;
    distribution, 42; Feyder's career, 143; *The
    Fifth Element*, 382; film production, 42, 68,
    143–4; history, 25–6, 60, 67–8, 153, 160;
    MGM relationship, 42; organisation, 17; *La
    Règle du jeu*, 181
Gaumont, Léon: career, 16, 25–6, 42, 61, 63;
    retirement, 68; sound system, 67–8
Gaumont-British, 126–7
Gaumont-Franco-Film-Aubert (GFFA), 68,
    81–2, 85, 148, 153, 160
Gaumont Palace, 68
Gégauff, Paul, 306
Gélin, Daniel, 294
Le Gendarme de Saint Tropez, 338
Le Gendarme et les gendarmettes, 338

Les Gens du voyage, 196
Germinal, 368, 371, 372–6
The Ghost Goes West, 123, 234
Gide, André, 150
Giovanni, José, 354
Giraudoux, Jean, 245, 277
Girault, Jean, 339, 342
The Girl from Arizona, 27
La Gloire de mon père, 368, 376
Godard, Jean-Luc: *A bout de souffle*, 269,
    321–2, 335–7, 349; on American cinema,
    378; *Cahiers* group, 283, 305, 334;
    Cannes (1968), 347–8; Cannes (1997),
    381–2; Cannes conference (1959), 308; *Les
    Carabiniers*, 337; career, 307, 326, 330, 348–
    9, 350, 351; on cinema and television, 366;
    Cinémathèque affair, 343–4, 347; *Histoire(s)
    du cinéma*, 381; *Le Mépris*, 95–6, 96, 321,
    322–5, 349; New Wave, 317, 321, 330; on
    Les Quatre cents coups, 310–11; style, 148,
    321; *Tout va bien*, 349–50
Goebbels, Joseph, 194–5, 196, 210
Goebbels, Magda, 210
Golden, Nathan, 135
Goldwyn, Sam, 130, 138, 171
Gone with the Wind, 347
Good Luck, see Bonne chance
Good Sam, 339
Goodis, David, 350
Goretta, Claude, 290
Gorky, Maxim, 168, 17–
Goupi mains rouges, 227
GPO Film Unit, 84, 99
La Graine et le mulet, 391–2
Le Grand Jeu, 145, 146, 152
Grand Prix (Cannes Festival), 150, 385
Grand Prix du cinéma français, 129
Grand Prix national du cinéma, 181
La Grande Illusion: awards, 180, 184, 352;
    making of, 153–4; reception, 136–7, 139,
    170–1, 172, 178; story, 174–5
La Grande Vadrouille, 338, 339, 393
The Great Waltz, 123, 237–8
Greco, Juliette, 268
Greene, Graham, 103, 107, 109–11, 128
Grégor, Nora, 173–4, 175, 176, 178
Grémillon, Jean, 88, 108, 221
Greven, Alfred: career, 193–4, 250; Clouzot's
    work, 204–7; Continental Films, 194–5, 197,
    198–9, 210; policies, 194–5, 198–9, 208,
    210–11
Griffith, D. W., 30, 38, 39, 171, 273, 365
Grivolas, Claude, 16–17, 25
Gros Plan (ORTF TV), 167
Groupe Octobre, 164, 165
Guardian, 340, 341, 347
Gueule d'amour, 108
La Gueule ouverte, 355

Guinée, Jean, 82
Guinness, Alec, 100
Guitry, Lucien, 89, 90
Guitry, Sacha: American audiences, 229; *Bonne chance*, 91; career, 88, 89–92, 140; *Ceux de chez nous*, 90; on cinema, 51, 92–3; influence, 87, 98–100; *Pasteur*, 89, 91; *Le Roman d'un tricheur*, 88–9, 93–8, 94, 95, 97
Guney, Yilmaz, 360
Guns for San Sebastian, see La Bataille de San Sebastian
Gurie, Sigrid, 117
Guy, Alice, 26

Hackman, Gene, 396
La Haine, 377–8
Hakim, Robert and Raymond, 112
Halcedama ou Le Prix du sang, 104–5
Halley des Fontaines, André, 164, 250
Halliday, Johnny, 352
Hamer, Robert, 99, 100
Hannibal Brooks, 338
Harvey, Lilian, 70
Haskell, Molly, xiii, 334, 356
Hawks, Howard, 115–16
Hayakawa, Sessue, 30, 47
Hays Code, *see* Production Code
Hébertot, Jacques, 50
Hecht, Ben, 125
Hercules, 324
L'Héritier de Mondésir, 197
Hessling, Catherine, 46, 172
Heuzé, André, 106
Highsmith, Patricia, 352
Hills, Carla, 369
Hiroshima mon amour, 330–7, 359
His First Offence, 155
Histoire du cinéma (History of the Film), 32, 71, 135
Histoire d'un crime, 20–2, 20
Histoire(s) du cinéma, 326, 381
Hitchcock, Alfred: as *auteur*, 281; career, 126–7, 273; on cinema, 389; influence, 342, 388; *To Catch a Thief*, 297
Hitler, Adolf, 174, 179, 196, 261
Hoberman, J., 381
Hofstadter, Richard, 217
Hollywood Citizen, 117
Hollywood Reporter, 114, 133, 134
Homme à abattre, 185
L'Homme d'orchestre, 7–8
Un Homme est mort (The Outside Man), 353
L'Honorable Catherine, 203
Hopper, Hedda, 120
L'Horloger de Saint Paul, 356–7
Hôtel du Nord, 156
Houllé, Marguerite (Renoir), 172, 181, 187
Houseman, John, 236

How Green was My Valley, 242
Howe, James Wong, 113, 120
Hughes, Howard, 235
Hugon, André, 63n, 65
8 Femmes, 394
L'Humanité, 166, 167, 188
Huston, John, 240
Hypergonar process, 67

L'Idiot, 230
If . . ., 85
Illusions, 120
Imamura, Shohei, 360
Imperial-Film, 156
Les Inconnus dans la maison, 149, 204–5, 207
Ingram, Rex, 80
L'Inhumaine, 52
Insdorf, Annette, 312
Institut Lumière, 2
Institut des hautes études cinématographiques (IDHEC), 221, 394
Intimate Exchanges, 375
Irma Vep, 378–82
It Always Rains on Sunday, 99
It Happened One Night, 339

J'accuse, 36–41, 247
Jackson, Julian, 217
Jacob, Gilles, 281, 282–3
Jacques le fataliste, 278
Jasset, Victorin–Hippolyte, 18, 26, 143
Jaubert, Maurice, 83, 157
The Jazz Singer, 61–2
Jean de Florette, 368, 372, 375
Jean de la lune, 77
Jeancolas, Jean–Pierre, 273
Jeanson, Henri, 102, 115, 156, 166, 167, 237
Jedem seine Chance, 196
Jenny, 152–3
Jeunet, Jean–Pierre, 366, 383, 384
Jeux interdits, 280
Jolson, Al, 62
Joly, Joseph, 23–4
Jones, Jennifer, 150
Jour de fête, 248–9, 251
Le Jour se lève, 99, 108, 110, 156, 186
Le Joueur, 197
Jourdan, Louis, 209
Le Journal du Ciné–Club, 45
Journal d'un curé de campagne, 245–6, 250, 277–8
Journal d'un scélérat, 284
Jouvet, Louis, 166, 221
Joyce, James, 52
Joyless Street, 46
Le Juge et l'assassin, 357–8
Jules et Jim, 359
Jurassic Park, 373, 374

Index

Juste avant la nuit, 342–3

Kael, Pauline, 316–17, 364
Kamenka, Alexandre, 44, 53, 69
Kane, Robert, 76, 77
Kanganski, Serge, 384
Kassovitz, Mathieu, 377
Kaufman, Boris, 80
Kazan, Elia, 48
Keaton, Buster, 56, 147
Kechiche, Abdel, 391–3
Kehr, David, 353
Kelly, Gene, 286
Kelly, Grace, 297
La Kermesse héroïque (Carnival in Flanders):
    awards, 129, 137; distribution, 131–2;
    reception, 129–32, 136, 138–9, 142–3;
    screenplay, 145; star, 130, 140, 152, 196
Kichi, Toyou, 4
Kind Hearts and Coronets, 99–100
Kinetograph, 2, 3
Kinetoscope, 2–4, 10, 11, 15, 23–4
The Kiss, 144, 325
Knife Thrower, 285
Kodak, 2, 63; Tri-X, 330, 336
Korda, Alexander: *Anna Karenina*, 238; career,
    76, 109, 111, 123–6, 231; *The Fallen Idol*,
    109; *Illusions*, 120; *Lady Hamilton*, 202–3;
    Marius, 76
Kosma, Joseph, 173
Krauss, Henri, 106
Kurys, Diane, 356

La Barthe, Henri, 112
La Fouchardière, Georges de, 240
Lacombe, Georges, 204, 293
Lacombe Lucien, 351
Lady from Shanghai, 242
Lady Hamilton, 202–3
Lalique, René, 52
Lamarr, Hedy, 113, 117, 119
Lang, Jacques, 374
Lang, Fritz, 103, 240–2, 322, 323, 325
Langlois, Henri, 5, 7, 285, 343–7
Lasky, Jesse, 72–3, 75, 114
Laughton, Charles, 107
Laura, 242
Laurant, Guillaume, 384
Laurel and Hardy, 339
Lautner, Georges, 354, 387
Lavedan, Henri, 27
Lawson, John Howard, 113, 114, 115
Laydu, Claude, 278
Le Chanois, Jean-Paul (Dreyfuss), 199
Le Pen, Jean-Marie, 384
Lean, David, 93
Léaud, Jean-Pierre, 378–9
Leconte, Patrice, 376

Lee, Irene, 117
Leenhardt, Roger, 165, 274
Lefèvre, René, 82
Léger, Fernand, 50, 51, 52
Lemarchand, Leopold, 65
Lenauer, Jean, 128, 129–30, 137–41, 296
Léon, 366
Letter from an Unknown Woman, 236
Lettres d'amour, 147
Levine, Joseph E., 323, 324–5
Lévy, Raoul, 296–7, 309
L'Herbier, Marcel: Autant-Lara's work, 147;
    career, 44, 45; Cinegraphic, 51–2; *L'Enfant
    d'amour*, 65, 66; *Feu Mathias Pascal*,
    53; *L'Honorable Catherine*, 203; IDHEC
    presidency, 221n; *L'Inhumaine*, 52; memoirs,
    192
Libération, 257, 384
Liberty Films, 241
Liberty Magazine, 131
Liebelei, 235
Life is Beautiful, 384
Life magazine, 253, 296, 298
*The Light Across the Street, see La Lumière
    d'en face*
Lindbergh, Charles, 180
Linder, Max, 28–9
Little Carnegie Theatre, New York, 234
The Little Foxes, 221, 242, 276
Litvak, Anatole, 132, 133
London Film Institute Society, 172
The Long Goodbye, 326
Loren, Sophia, 324
Los Angeles Times, 120, 240
Losey, Joseph, 352, 386
Louis Lumière, 5
Louis-Nounez, Jacques, 82
Les Loups entre eux, 185
Lourié, Eugène, 173
Love, Bessie, 78
The Lover, 370
Lubitsch, Ernst, 147, 148
Lucachevitch, Joseph, 156
Luciano Serra Pilota, 184–5
Lucien, Marcel, 95
Lumière, Antoine, 3, 6, 10–11, 17
Lumière, Auguste, 1–2, 3
Lumière, Louis, 2, 3, 5, 7, 318, 344
*La Lumière d'en face (The Light Across the
    Street)*, 293–4
Lumière d'été, 190
Lumière family, 1–7, 12, 14, 24, 49, 276
La Lune dans le caniveau, 363, 364
La Lune des lapins, 285
Lydia, 120, 123–6
Lynch, David, 388
Lysès, Charlotte, 91

Ma nuit chez Maude, xiv–xv
Mac Orlan, Pierre, 107, 108, 155
MacCabe, Colin, 323
Madame Bovary, 136, 170, 376
Mademoiselle ma mère, 148
Magnani, Anna, 230
The Magnificent Ambersons, 242
Maid in Paris, see Paris Canaille
Maigret tend un piège, 328
Malcolm, Derek, 340
Malle, Louis: *Les Amants*, 309, 328–30; *Au revoir les enfants*, 337; Cannes (1968), 348; César protest, 370; *Lacombe Lucien*, 351
Mallet-Stevens, Robert, 52
Malraux, André, 187, 308, 345
Maltby, Richard, 216
The Maltese Falcon, 221, 240, 242–3
Malthête–Meliès, Madeleine, 10
Man Ray, 46, 52, 57, 151
Manet, Edouard, 90
Mankiewicz, Joseph, 304
Le Manoir du diable, 14–15
Manon des Sources, 368, 372, 375
Marais, Jean, 222, 262
Marais, Marin, 376
Maria Chapdelaine, 107
Mariage de Chiffon, 147
Le mariage de Figaro, 182–3
Marie, Michel, 307, 321
La Marie du port, 283, 327
Les Mariés de la tour Eiffel, 50
Marius, 76–7
Marker, Chris, 331
La Marseillaise, 136, 167–8
Marthe Richard: Espionne au service de la France, 185
Martin, Marie-Geneviève (Marie Recio), 158–9
Martin Roumagnac, 156
Masson, Charles, 342
Mater Dolorosa, 36, 45
La Maternelle, 82
Le Matin, 43, 360
Mauclaire, Jean–Placide, 46
Maurice, Clément, 10, 17
Mayer, Louis B., 113, 134
Mayerling, 132–3, 135, 136, 137, 139
Maysles Brothers, 323–4
Mazetti, Lorenza, 86, 290
McCarey, Leo, 339
McCarten, John, 228
Meerson, Lazare, 44, 346n
Meerson, Mary, 346
Mekas, Jonas, 286, 290–1
Meliès, Gaston, 17–18
Meliès, Georges: career, 8–11, 15–19, 22; Cinémathèque française, 344; *L'Escamotage d'une dame chez Robert–Houdin*, 14, 15; first films, 11–13; *L'Homme d'orchestre*, 7–8;

influence, 382; *Le Manoir du diable*, 14–15; studio, 15–16; style, 16–17, 20, 21; trick photography, 13–14, 22; *Le Voyage dans la lune*, 17
Melville, Anne-Marie, 350
Melville, Jean-Pierre (Grumbach): *L'Armée des ombres*, 395n; *Bob le flambeur*, 268, 269–70; career, 251–2, 268–9, 271, 307, 321, 331; cinephilia, 268, 304; Cocteau relationship, 262–5; *Les Enfants terribles*, 263–5, 266, 268; Festival du Film Maudit, 266–7; making of *Le Silence de la mer*, 251–6; *Quand tu liras cette lettre*, 268; showing of *Le Silence de la mer*, 256, 261, 266; *Le Silence de la mer*, 256–62, 257, 258, 259, 270
Menjou, Adolphe, 65
Le Mépris, 96, 321, 322–5, 349
Mercanton, Louis, 28
La Merveilleuse Vie de Jeanne d'Arc, 64
Metro-Goldwyn-Mayer (MGM): *Algiers*, 112, 119; Autant-Lara's work, 147; Borehamwood studio, 231; Duvivier's career, 237; Feyder's work, 144, 325; Gabin offer, 134; Gaumont relationship, 42; *The Great Waltz*, 123, 237; *Guns for San Sebastian*, 340; management, 199; *Test Pilot*, 141
Metropolis, 382
Meyer, Arthur, 9
Midnight Cowboy, 359
A Midsummer Night's Dream, 285
Milhaud, Darius, 52
Le Million, 71, 72
A Million and One Nights (Ramsaye), 4
Miracle in Milan, 229
Miramax, 383, 385
Mirbeau, Octave, 90
Miró, Joan, 57
Les Mistons, 290
Mitchum, Robert, 326
Mitterrand, François, 374
Mitterrand, Frédéric, 371
Modot, Gaston, 116, 164, 166, 329, 331
Moi, un noir, 288
Moisson, Charles, 3
Momma Don't Allow, 86
Mon Gosse de père, 65
Le Monde, 330
Monet, Claude, 5
Monod, Roland, 278–9
Monogram Pictures, 321
Monroe, Marilyn, 298
Monsieur Verdoux, 222–3
Monsieur Vincent, 250
Montand, Yves, 225, 270, 349–50
The Monte Carlo Story, 297
The Moon is Blue, 293, 294
Moontide, 120
The Moral Tales, xiii–xv

Moravia, Alberto, 322
Moreau, Jeanne, 328
Moreno, Marguerite, 95
Morgan, Michèle, 119, 327
Morgenstern, Ignace, 288
Morlay, Gaby, 218–19
Morning Star, 374
Morrey, Douglas, 323
Mosher, John, 137
Motion Picture Producers and Distributors
  Association, 213
Moullet, Luc, 335–6
Moussinac, Léon, 32
Movie, 315
Mr Smith Goes to Town, 339
Murat, Jean, 185
Murder, My Sweet, 242–3
Murnau, F. W., 304
Musée Grevin, 9–10
Mussolini, Benito, 179, 184–5, 186
Mussolini, Vittorio, 185, 186
Myrga, Laurence, 46
Le Mystère du château du Dé, 151

Nadejdine, Serge, 44
La Naissance du Cinéma, 32
Nalpas, Louis, 34, 35, 36, 43
Nana, 30
Natan, Bernard, 63–7
Nation, 128, 226, 227
National Board of Review Magazine, 239, 241
National Film School, 86
National Film Theatre, London, 86, 87, 290
National Legion of Decency, 299–300
Nattier, Nathalie, 225
Navarre, René, 43
Neue Babelsberg studios, 148, 194, 196
New Wave (Nouvelle Vague): 'accursed films',
  267; agenda, 321; arrival, 328; attacks
  on Delannoy, 150; auteur cinema, 150,
  310–11, 316–17, 318, 354, 385, 387; Berri's
  career, 371; birth of, 102; British response
  to, 341–2; *Cahiers* group, 329–30, 336;
  Cannes conference (1959), 308; cinema of
  personal expression, 157, 306, 307, 336;
  cinephilia, 303–4, 351; comparison with
  Delluc group, 47; criticisms of Carné, 155;
  elitism, 351, 354; filming practices, 270;
  Hollywood influences, 321; institutional
  backing, 308–9; mainstream cinema and,
  387–8; Malle's position, 330, 337; origins,
  303–6; passing of, 381, 383, 385; philosophy,
  336; *prime à la qualité*, 307, 308, 336;
  realism and spontaneity, 302; sales, 337; shift
  towards director, 357; spirit of 1968, 348;
  US response, 301, 309–10, 316–18, 319–21,
  325, 341–2; Vigo's views, 87
New York Film Critics' prize, 137, 180, 239

New York Times: on *Algiers*, 115, 117; *Avatar*
  comments; on Bardot and Vadim, 303; on
  Les Bas-fonds, 170; on Beineix, 364; on
  Le Cerveau, 340; Crowther's reviews, *see*
  Crowther; on *Double crime sur la ligne
  Maginot*, 186; on *Les Enfants du paradis*,
  227–8; on *The Exile*, 235; on *Fingers*
  remake, 387; on Golden Age of French
  cinema, 244, 292; on *La Grande Illusion*,
  137; on Guitry, 100; on *J'accuse*, 39, 40; on
  Jean de Florette, 368; Jeunet interview, 383;
  on *Journal d'un curé de campagne*, 245–6;
  on *La Kermesse héroïque*, 129–31; on *Letter
  from an Unknown Woman*, 236–7; on *Le
  Million*, 71; on New Wave, 308, 309, 310,
  315; on *Pépé le Moko*, 117; on *La Piscine*,
  353; on *Les 400 coups*, 313; on Renoir, 171;
  on *Rome, Open City*, 226; on *Silence of the
  Sea*, 254–5; on *La Symphonie pastorale*, 150;
  on *Les Valseuses*, 355; on *Z*, 351
New Yorker, 137, 228
Newman, David, 317, 319
News Chronicle, 110
Newsweek, 267
Nice Time, 290
The Night Heaven Fell, 300
Night Moves, 396
Night of the Hunter, 326
Nijinsky, Vaclav, 52
Nikisch, Arthur, 176–7
Nikisch, Mitja, 176, 178
Nikita, 366
Nissotti, Arys, 169
Niven, David, 340
Noailles, Vicomte and Vicomtesse de, 55–7,
  59, 265
Nobody's Kid, 107
Nogent, Eldorado ou Dimanche, 151–2
Noiret, Philippe, 357
Nono, 89
Noro, Line, 112, 117
The Notebooks of Captain X, 153
Nous ne vieillerons pas ensemble, 355
Les Nouveaux Messieurs, 151
Nouvelles Editions Françaises (NEF), 171, 172
Novarro, Ramón, 144
Nugent, Frank, 100, 129, 131, 137, 139
La Nuit américaine, 378–9
Nuit et brouillard, 332
Les Nuits fauves, 372–3

O Dreamland, 86–7
Oberon, Merle, 124, 125
Objectif 49, 273–4
Observer, 340
Odd Man Out, 111
Odéon Theatre, Paris, 103, 104
L'Oeil de Vichy, 217n

Olympia, 184
On connaît la chanson, 375
On the Bowery, 290
On the Waterfront, 306
Ophüls, Marcel, 350–1
Ophüls, Max, 233, 234–7, 238, 239
Orain, Fred, 248, 250
Orphée, 58, 262
ORTF, 167, 351
Oscars, 219, 324, 331, 352, 368, 370
Ossessione, 266
Oury, Gérard, 339–40, 342
The Outside Man, see Un Homme est mort
Overbey, David, 362
Oxford Opinion, 315
Ozon, François, 393–5

Pabst, Georg Wilhelm, 46, 210
Pagnol, Marcel: *Cahiers du Film*, 79; *La Château de ma mère*, 376; conception of cinema, 78–9; Duvivier's view of, 102; *L'Eau des collines*, 368; *Fanny*, 77; *La Fille du puisatier*, 227; on film sound, 78, 80; *La Gloire de mon père*, 376; influence, 87; *Marius*, 76–7; Marseilles studio, 192; *Toni*, 170; US audiences, 229, 368
Painlevé, Jean, 151
Paisà, 229
Palais des Variétés, 91
Palais du Cinéma, 362
Palais Rochechouart, 83
Palance, Jack, 325
Palme d'Or, 360, 388
Panthéon cinema, Paris, 166
Paracelsus, 210
The Parallax View, 352
Paramount, 72–7, 114, 149, 232, 240, 340
Paramount-France, 196
Paramount Theatre, Paris, 72
Paris: Universal Exhibition (1878), 8–9; Universal Exhibition (1900), 21, 60
Paris Canaille (Maid in Paris), 294
Paris Cinema, New York, 245
Paris-Deauville, 149
Paris et le monde, 61
Paris Film, 112
Paris-Match, 296
Paris-Midi, 33
Paris qui dort, 48–50, **48**, **49**, 69
Paris Soir, 160
The Parisian, 65
Passe ton bac a'abord, 355
Passion, 28
The Passionate Summer, see Les Possédées
Passionnelle, 244
Pasteur, 89, 91
Pasteur, Louis, 89
Pathé, Charles: career, 16, 21–5, 63, 67; on 'French Hollywood', 61, 62, 251; Méliès relationship, 18; memoirs, 18, 21–2, 41–2; Pathé Baby equipment, 251; resignation, 67; sale of Pathé name, 43; sale of Pathé subsidiaries, 63; support for Gance, 40–1
Pathé, Emile, 24
Pathé Baby projector, 251–2
Pathé: collapse, 153; distribution, 34, 41; end of film production, 41–2, 60, 144; *Les Enfants du paradis*, 225; expansion, 25–6; finances, 25; French film production, 28–9, 41–2; Gance's work, 35, 40–1; *Histoire d'un crime*, 20–1, 20; Méliès relationship, 16–17, 18; name, 25, 29, 43; *Passion*, 28; production formula, 35; *Le Silence est d'or*, 233; US studio, 27–8; Zecca's career, 21–2, 35
Pathé Cinéma, 63–4, 244
Pathé-Consortium, 43, 63, 65
Pathé-Kodak, 63
Pathé-Natan, 63–7, 85
Paul, Robert, 11
Paulin, Gaston, 9
Pauvre Pierrot, 9
Pax International, 132
Pension Mimosas, 145, 152
Pépé le Moko: ending, 111; Gabin's role, 112; influence, 103, 109, 110–11, 115, 118, 120–1, 123, 141; influences on, 115–16; reception, 117, 120–1, 218; theme, 107
Pépinière cinema, Paris, 45
Peppermint Frappé, 347
Perret, Leonce, 80
Pétain, Marshal, 191, 215, 216–17, 368
Philadelphia, 372
Philibert, Nicolas, 389
Philipe, Gérard, 297
Pialat, Maurice, 354–5, 371
Picabia, Francis, 50
Picasso, Pablo, 50, 52, 335
Piccoli, Michel, 322
Picpus, 208
Pierre-Bodin, Richard, 56, 57
The Pink Panther, 338
Pinkevich, Albert, 152, 153–4
Pinoteau, Claude, 264
Pinter, Harold, 352
Pirandello, Luigi, 53
La Piscine, 352–3
Pius XI, Pope, 135
Plein soleil, 352
Ploquin, Raoul, 155, 193, 194, 211–12, 213, 218
Plunkett, Joseph, 40
Poil de Carotte, 103, 105–6, 107, 109, 311–14, 313
Point Blank, 353
La Pointe Courte, 304, 305, 332, 334
Polanski, Roman, 348, 370

Ponti, Carlo, 324
Porter, Edwin S., 28
Les Portes de la nuit, 225, 226–7
The Poseidon Adventure, 320
Positif, 272, 281, 282–3, 378
Les Possédées (*The Passionate Summer*), 294
The Postman Always Rings Twice, 294
Potter, Dennis, 375
Le Poulet, 368
Pound, Ezra, 52
Pour Vous, 71, 78
Powell, Michael, 154
Praxinoscope, 9
Prédal, René, 271–2
Préjean, Albert, 208, 210, 211
Premier rendez–vous, 148, 208–11
Preminger, Otto, 293
Présence africaine, 331
Présentation ou Charlotte et son steak, 284
Presley, Elvis, 298, 352
Pressburger, Emeric, 154
Prévert, Jacques: Carné relationship, 150, 154–7; *Ciboulette*, 147; *Le Crime de Monsieur Lange*, 152, 165; *Drôle de drame*, 155, 158; Duvivier's influence, 109; influence, 357; *Les Enfants du paradis*, 157–9; *Jenny*, 152–3, 154, 155; *Le jour se lève*, 99, 186; *Quai des brumes*, 99, 155–6, 186; *Les Visiteurs du soir*, 158, 191; wartime politics, 198–9
La Princesse de Clèves, xi
Prison de velours, 152
The Prisoner of Zenda, 28, 113
The Private Life of Henry VIII, 123
Prix Louis Delluc, 389
Prix Jean Vigo, 331, 332
Production Code (Hays Code): administration, 202, 215; approval, 241; audience sizes, 141; end, 319, 320; influence, 122, 125, 213, 216, 217, 293, 298, 341; requirements, 113, 116; self–regulation, 162; text, 212–13
La Proie du Vent, 69
Un Prophète, 385–6, 395
The Public Enemy, 270
Purviance, Edna, 64
Put Out the Light, 253

Quai des brumes: awards, 151, 181; censorship, 186, 217; Gabin's role, 108, 155–6, 327; influence, 99; reception, 110, 139, 151; revival, 110; screenplay, 155–6
Quand tu liras cette lettre, 268–9
Quatorze juillet, 71
Les Quatre cents coups (*The 400 Blows*), 312; awards, 330; *L'Enfance nue* comparison, 354; financing, 288; *Poil de Carotte* comparison, 311–14; reception, 309, 310–11; sales, 337
Queen Elizabeth, 28

Quinn, Anthony, 340
Quinze Rounds, 148

Rabinovitch, Gregor, 155–6
Raccords, 281, 283
Radio City Music Hall, New York, 115, 130, 340
Rafferty, Terence, 313–14
Raft, George, 115, 119
Ramsaye, Terry, 4
Rapid Film, 64
Rappeneau, Jean–Paul, 376
Ravel, Gaston, 62, 143
Ray, Nicholas, 48, 266
RCA, 60, 65
Rear Window, 388
The Reckless Moment, 236, 237
Reed, Carol, 109, 110, 111
Reed, Oliver, 338
Reeves, Steve, 324
Refuge England, 290
Régent, Roger, 228–9, 233
Reggiani, Serge, 205n, 222
La Règle du jeu: cast and characters, 173–8; costs, 180–1; influence, 328–9; political background, 178–80, 185; production team, 172–3; reception, 139, 181–3, 186–8, 217–18, 328
Der Reigen, 237
La Reine Margot, 283, 376
Reinhardt, Max, 285
Reisz, Karel, 86, 87
Renard, Jules, 105
Renaud, Madeleine, 196
Renoir, Alain, 172
Renoir, Claude, 172
Renoir, Marguerite (Houllé), 172, 181, 187
Renoir, Pierre–Auguste, 90, 175
Renoir, Jean: Autant-Lara's work, 147; *Les Bas–fonds*, 168, 170; *La Bête humaine*, 108, 180; career, 87, 127; *La Chienne*, 153, 240; childhood, 90; Cinémathèque affair, 343; *Le Crime de Monsieur Lange*, 152, 153, 164–5; on Duvivier, 101, 102; *La Fille d'eau*, 46, 54; on French schisms, 376; *La Grande Illusion*, 153–4, 170–1, 172, 180, 352; influence, 327, 328, 354, 392; influences on, 30; on Lumière films, 5; *Madame Bovary*, 170; *La Marseillaise*, 167, 168; move to Hollywood, 189, 237, 238–9, 325; *Nana*, 30; Nouvelles Editions Françaises (NEF), 171–2; personal life, 172, 187, 188–9; *La Règle du jeu*, 172–88, 328; reputation, 170–1, 304, 341; return to France, 233; on the Spirit of 1936, 330; status, 140; *Swamp Water*, 325; techniques, 276; *Toni*, 77, 153, 170, 392; *La Vie est à nous*, 164, 165–7
Resnais, Alain: *Cahiers* group, 304–5; Cannes

(1968), 347; career, 331; *Hiroshima mon amour*, 330–1, 332–6; influence, 304, 332, 335; *On connaît la chanson*, 375; short films, 274, 288, 331; *Les Statues meurent aussi*, 331–2
Ressources humaines, 389–90
Retour à l'aube, 148
Reulos, Lucien, 12
La Revue du cinéma, 203, 272, 281
Reynaud, Emile, 9–10
Richardson, Tony, 86, 87
Ridicule, 376
Riefenstahl, Leni, 184
Rien que les heures, 53, 54
Riéra, Albert, 82
Rim, Carlos, 199
Les Ripoux, 371
Rivette, Jacques, 175, 288, 317, 334, 336, 371
RKO Pictures, 29, 131, 225, 233–4, 242, 297
Robain, Jean-Marie, 255
Robin, Dany, 294
Robinson, Edward G., 240–1
Rodin, Auguste, 90
Rogers, Jimmy, 53
Rogosin, Lionel, 290
Rohmer, Eric: *Cahiers* group, 283, 305, 354; *Claire's Knee*, 320; death, xi, 396; on Hitchcock, 281; influence, 394; *Journal d'un scélérat*, 284; *Louis Lumière*, 5; *The Moral Tales*, xiii–xv; names, 281, 305; New Wave, 317; *Présentation*, 284; reception of films, 362, 396; on Resnais, 335; review of *Hiroshima mon amour*, 334; review of *Les Amants*, 330; *Le Signe du lion*, xi–xiii
Le Roman d'un tricheur, 88–9, 92–4, **94**, **95**, 96–8, **97**, 100
Romance, Viviane, 197, 210
Rome, Open City, 226, 229, 230, 293
Ronet, Maurice, 352
Rosay, Françoise, 130, 140, 142, 151, 152, 196
Rosenbaum, Jonathan, 362
Rosetta, 390
Rossellini, Roberto, 274, 304
Rostand, Edmond, 90, 376
Rouch, Jean, 288
Roud, Richard, 347, 359, 360
La Roue, 40–1
Roxy cinema, New York, 130
La Rue des vertus, 156–7

Sadoul, Georges, 12, 13, 29, 272, 304
Sagan, Françoise, 303, 332
Saint-Laurent, Yves, 303
Saint-Saëns, Camille, 27
Samuel Goldwyn Company, 231
Sandberg, Serge, 43–4, 95
Le Sang d'un poète, 57–9, 142, 263, 265
Sapène, Jean, 43

Sarah and Son, 73
Sarris, Andrew, 315–17, 318–19, 320, 361
Satie, Erik, 52
Sautet, Claude, 371
Scarface, 115–16, 270
Scarlet Street, 240–1, 242
Schamus, James, 318–19
Scheider, Roy, 353
Scherer, Maurice, 281
Scheuer, Philip, 240
Schjeldahl, Peter, 355
Schneider, Romy, 352
Schroeder, Barbet, xiv
Scott, John L., 120
Scotto, Vincent, 113
The Searchers, 137
Seberg, Jean, 321
Second Congress of Independent Cinema (1930), 81
The Secret of the Grain, see La Graine et le mulet
Sellers, Peter, 338, 341
Selznick, David, 113, 119, 150, 171
Selznick, Myron, 234
Selznick Releasing Organisation, 231
Sequence, 86, 289
Service du Cinéma, 192–3, 214–15
Shadows, 290–2, 300
Shirer, William, 163
Shoeshine, 229
Siclier, Jacques, 197, 199, 210, 219
Sight and Sound, 359
Le Signe du Lion, xi–xiii, xiv
Signoret, Simone, 205n, 222
Le Silence de la mer, 257, **258**, **259**; Cocteau's response to, 261–3, 265; description of film, 256–61; filming, 254–6, 269, 270; novel, 252–3; reception, 256, 266–7
Le Silence est d'or, 233, 234
Simenon, Georges, 149, 204, 205, 207–8, 283, 356
Simon, Michel, 147
The Singing Fool, 62
Siodmak, Robert, 235
Sirk, Douglas, 219, 394, 395
Sitcom, 393
Les Six, 50
Six hommes morts, 204
Skirt Dog Dance, 4
Small, Edward, 297
Smithson, Henriette, 158
Smoking / No Smoking, 375
Société de Gestion et d'Exploitation de Cinéma (SOGEC), 193
Société Industrielle Cinématographique (SIC), 44
Soeurs d'armes, 185
Son of India, 144

Index

Sonimage, 350

Sony Picture Classics, 388

Sortie de l'usine Lumière à Lyon, 1–2, 1

Sous le sable, 394

Sous les toits de Paris, 69–70, 70, 72, 152

Spaak, Charles: on Gabin, 108; on Greven, 194; influence, 152; work with Duvivier, 102, 108; work with Feyder, 145, 146; work with Renoir, 153, 172

Starfilm, 17

Stahremberg, Prince Ernst Rüdiger von, 173–4, 178

Les Statues meurent aussi, 331

Stavisky, Alexandre, 162

Steeman, Stanislas-André, 204

Steiger, Rod, 306

Stelli, Jean, 218

Stéphane, Nicole, 255, 268

Stevens, George, 48, 241

Still Life, 93

Stiller, Mauritz, 176

The Story of a Cheat see *Le Roman d'un tricheur*

The Strange Ones, see *Les Enfants terribles*

Stroheim, Erich von, 30, 147, 180, 185, 273

Stromboli, 304

Studio des Ursulines, Paris, 46, 54, 81, 151

Studio One cinema, London, 142

Studio 28, Paris, 46, 57

Sturges, Preston, 223, 235, 273

Subway, 365

Summersault Dog, 4

Sun, 131

Sunday Telegraph, 375

Sunset Boulevard, 274

Sur la cour, 164

Sur mes lèvres, 388

Swamp Water, 325

Swanson, Gloria, 274

The Swimming Pool, 394

La Symphonie fantastique, 158, 159, 194

La Symphonie pastorale, 150, 280

Taken, 383

The Talented Mr Ripley, 352

Tales of Manhattan, 107

Tanguy, Yves, 57

Tarantino, Quentin, 366

Tarkovsky, Andrei, 360

Tati, Jacques, 248–50, 251, 271

Tauris, Jean, 81

Tauris, roi d'eau, 81n

Tautou, Audrey, 384

Tavernier, Bernard, 356–8, 376

Taxi Driver, 359, 377

Technicolor, 248

Tedesco, Jean, 45–6

Tellier, Armand, 46

Templier, Raymond, 52

Le Temps, 27, 36

The Ten Commandments, 299

La Terra trema, 292

La Terre, 104

TF1, 367

Thalberg, Irving, 199

That Hamilton Woman, 126

Le Théâtre, 50

Théâtre des Champs–Elysées, Paris, 50–1

Théâtre Optique, Paris, 9–10

Théâtre Robert-Houdin, Paris, 8, 11, 12, 14, 15, 18

They Live By Night, 266

The Thief of Bagdad, 126

The Third Man, 109, 110–11, 231

Thomas, Gabriel, 10, 11

Thomson, David, xiii

Thomsoncolor, 248

Thorez, Maurice, 162, 163, 165, 224

Those of Our Land, see *Ceux de chez nous*

Three Days of the Condor, 352

The Three Musketeers, 50

Time magazine, 98, 235

Time Out New York, 381

Times, 38, 142

Titanic, 338, 382

To Catch a Thief, 297

Toback, James, 387

Tobis Corporation, 130, 131, 132

Tobis Klangfilm, 60, 70, 72; Epinay productions, 70, 72, 74, 196

Toboggan, 148

Together, 86, 290

Toland, Gregg, 276

Toluboff, Alexander, 113

Toni, 77, 153, 170, 392–3

La Tosca, 186, 188

Toubiana, Serge, 359

Tourjansky, Viktor, 44

Tourneur, Maurice, 65

Tous les matins du monde, 376

Tout va bien, 349–50

Toute sa vie, 75

Le Train sans yeux, 53–4

Trauner, Alexandre, 157

Les Travailleurs de la mer, 104

Trilogy, 347

Trintignant, Jean–Louis, xv, 353

Les Trois Masques, 63n, 65

Truffaut, François: awards, 330; on Berri's work, 393; *Cahiers* group, 283, 305; Cannes conference, 308; Cannes (1968), 347–8; career, 368; on Carné, 155; 'A Certain Tendency in the French Cinema', 101–2, 271, 280, 284, 318; on cinema history, 87, 327; Cinémathèque affair, 343–4, 347; CNC relationship, 307, 336; on Dean, 47–8,

302–3, 307; death, 369; and Duvivier, 103, 104, 311–14; Hollywood relationship, 321; Les Mistons, 290; New Wave, 317, 319, 321, 337; La Nuit américaine, 378–9; on politique des auteurs, 245, 281, 316, 318; Les Quatre cents coups, 288, 311–14, 312, 330, 354; review of Et Dieu créa la femme, 302; sales, 337; US reception of films, 309; on Vigo, 83
Tschernoff, Professor Ivan, 4
Twentieth Century–Fox, 120, 325
Two Women, 324

UFA: distribution, 207; French–language films, 70, 148, 155, 193, 194, 196; Greven's career, 193–4, 195; 1920s, 136; propaganda department, 155
UGC, 250
Ulff-Møller, Jens, 139
Umberto D, 229, 292
. . . und das ist die Hauptsache!?, 178
Unifrance, 308, 319
United Artists, 39, 40, 112, 125, 171, 293
Universal Studios, 133, 197, 208, 235, 241, 242

Les Vacances du diable, 75
La Vache et le prisonnier, 337–8, 341
Vadim, Roger: Cannes conference, 308; career, 290, 296, 300–1, 303; Et Dieu créa la femme, 296, 300, 302; on Fonda, 349; The Night Heaven Fell, 300
Vaillant–Couturier, Paul, 166
Valentin, Albert, 197
Valéry, Paul, 51
Les Valseuses, 355
Les Vampires, 378
Vampyr, 304
Van Doren, Mark, 128–9
Vanel, Charles, 194, 196
Varda, Agnès, 304–5, 317, 332, 334
Variety: on foreign films, 293, 297; on French films, 247–8, 295, 309–10; on Italian films, 230; on sex themes, 299–300; on Le Silence de la mer, 267
Vas, Robert, 290
Vedettes, 208
Vendetta, 235
Venice Film Festival, 184, 291, 328, 331
Vercors (Jean Bruller), 252–5, 257–60, 262–3
Verneuil, Henri, 339, 340–1, 342, 387
Vernon, Howard, 255
Vertov, Dziga, 80
Véry, Pierre, 147, 200
La Victoire de Samothrace, 34
La Vie est à nous, 164, 165–7
Le Vieil Homme et l'enfant, 368, 393
Le Vieux-Colombier theatre, Paris, 46, 57, 80
Vigo, Jean: A propos de Nice, 80, 81–2, 86–7;

L'Atalante, 82–3, 84, 85, 86, 266, 312; career, 80–3; death, 83; reputation, 83–7, 312, 331; views on cinema, 80–1, 96; Zéro de conduite, 82, 84, 86, 312
The Village Feud, 341
Village Voice, 315, 317, 318, 361, 381
Viot, Jacques, 157
Visconti, Luchino, 266
Visions d'Art, 27
Les Visiteurs, 374
Les Visiteurs du soir (The Devil's Envoys), 158, 190, 191, 229
Vitagraph, 61
I Vitelloni, 292
Vitti, Monica, 348
Vivere in pace, 229
Le Voile bleu, 218–19
Volkoff, Alexandre, 44
Le Voyage dans la lune, 17
Voyage(s) en Utopie, 326
Le Voyageur de la Toussaint, 205, 207
Vuillermoz, Emile, 36

Wald, Jerry, 119
The Wall, 360
Wallach, Eli, 340
Wallis, Hal B., 117, 119–20
Wanger, Walter, 112–14, 171, 237, 241
Warner Brothers, 89, 117, 132, 183, 232, 319
Weinberg, Herman G., 285
Welles, Orson: at Cannes, 360; career, 240, 242; Citizen Kane, 242, 275; influence, 273–4; reputation, 223
Western Electric, 60, 68
Who Killed Santa Claus?, 201
Wilder, Billy, 240
Willis, Bruce, 382
Winnington, Richard, 110
The Wizard of Oz, 299
WNYC, 137
Wolff, Pierre, 160
World Cinema, New York, 120
Wuthering Heights, 124, 125
Wyler, William, 241, 273, 276
Wyman, Jane, 219

You Can't Take It With You, 339
Young, Terence, 348

Z, 351–2
Zampa, Luigi, 229
Zanuck, Darryl, 325
Zay, Jean, 134, 161, 181, 184, 185, 186
Zecca, Ferdinand, 20–2, 26, 35, 276, 344
Zenith International, 309
Zéro de conduite, 82, 84, 86, 312
Zola, Emil, 30, 108, 371, 372, 374
Zukor, Adolphe, 28